CENSORED

"Project Censored is one of the organizations that we should listen to, to be assured that our newspapers and our broadcasting outlets are practicing thorough and ethical journalism."—Walter Cronkite

"[*Censored*] should be affixed to the bulletin boards in every newsroom in America. And, perhaps read aloud to a few publishers and television executives."—Ralph Nader

"[*Censored*] offers devastating evidence of the dumbing-down of mainstream news in America. . . . Required reading for broadcasters, journalists and well-informed citizens."—*Los Angeles Times*

"A distant early warning system for society's problems."
—*American Journalism Review*

"One of the most significant media research projects in the country."
—I. F. Stone

"A terrific resource, especially for its directory of alternative media and organizations. . . . Recommended for media collections."
—*Library Journal*

"Project Censored shines a spotlight on news that an informed public must have . . . a vital contribution to our democratic process."
—Rhoda H. Karpatkin, President, Consumer's Union

"Buy it, read it, act on it. Our future depends on the knowledge this collection of suppressed stories allows us."—*San Diego Review*

"This volume chronicles 25 news stories about events that could affect all of us, but which we most likely did not hear or read about in the popular news media."—*Bloomsbury Review*

"*Censored* serves as a reminder that there is certainly more to the news than is easily available or willingly disclosed. To those of us who work in the newsrooms, it's an inspiration, an indictment, and an admonition to look deeper, ask more questions, then search for the truth in the answers we get."—*Creative Loafings*

"This invaluable resource deserves to be more widely known."
—*Wilson Library Bulletin*

CENSORED2008

The Top 25 Censored Stories

Edited by PETER PHILLIPS, ANDREW ROTH, and PROJECT CENSORED

INTRODUCTION BY DENNIS LOO
CARTOONS BY JOHN JONIK

Seven Stories Press

New York / London / Melbourne / Toronto

A Seven Stories Press First Edition

Seven Stories Press
140 Watts Street
New York, NY 10013
www.sevenstories.com

In Canada: Publishers Group Canada, 559 College Street, Suite 402, Toronto,
ON M6G 1A9

In the U.K.: Turnaround Publisher Services Ltd., Unit 3, Olympia Trading
Estate, Coburg Road, Wood Green, London N22 6TZ

In Australia: Palgrave Macmillan, 15–19 Claremont Street, South Yarra, VIC 3141

College professors may order examination copies of Seven Stories Press titles
for a free six-month trial period. To order, visit www.sevenstories.com/textbook/
or fax on school letterhead to 212.226.1411.

ISSN 1074-5998

9 8 7 6 5 4 3 2 1

Book design by Jon Gilbert

Printed in the U.S.A.

Contents

Dedicated to Molly Ivins,
1944–2007

Reporter, Columnist, and Truth Teller

Two Perspectives on Media Bias and Accountability September 21, 2005

"What we need in this country . . . is a Media Accountability Day. The real scandal in the media . . . is laziness and bad news judgment. Our failure is what we miss, what we fail to cover, what we let slip by . . . Happily, the perfect news peg, as we say in the biz, for Media Accountability Day already exists—it's Project Censored's annual release of the 10 biggest stories ignored or under covered by the mainstream media."

Project Censored now holds an annual Media Accountability Conference at Sonoma State University in October of each year.

Thank you Molly Ivins,
your legacy will live on inspiring us all.

WHEN THE LIGHTS WENT OUT

by Andrew Sloan

"What's called the dominant culture will fade away as soon as the electricity goes off." —Lawrence Ferlinghetti, 11/6/05

When the lights went out
The people got brighter
The trees grew taller

Televisions and household
    appliances filled dumps
Then the amount of waste declined
Cars piled—one on top of the other
The scrap metal was used for
    bicycles

Telephones were abandoned
And families got closer
Clocks stopped
And time went on—but just a bit
    slower

Electric guitars were traded in for
    acoustics and banjos and fiddles
    and flutes
Microphones became obsolete
And so too did rock stars
People sang and talked louder

Ears were opened
And grandma's stories were
    listened to
People began to distinguish
The voices and patterns of bird's
    callings

Relationships were formed
Between producers and consumers
People met the cows and chickens
That gave them milk and eggs

Cash crops died
And the third world grew stronger
Local sustenance determined foreign
    policy
Produce had seasons again

For the first time since their erection
Every window in every skyscraper
    went dark
And the starry sky reigned everywhere
And the moon's expressions could
    be seen

Industrial buildings were remodeled
Into communal housing and green-
    houses
People were given the right to grow
    their own food without owning
    land
People were given the right to sleep
    and to shit

The patent office closed down
Medicine became accessible to anyone
Manuscripts were shared
Passed from hand to hand until its
    pages frayed beyond readability

News was reported by people who
    were affected by it
A labor section in the paper replaced
    the business section
Investigative reporting was encour-
    aged and demanded
Sensationalism was replaced by
    Socratic questioning

Politics and economics were talked
about
Because the GNP started taking into
account
The interdependency of the economy
Not just the things making money

People were forced to deal with each
other
And conversations were waged in
place of wars
Rehabilitation facilities were built
Instead of penitentiaries

The social stigma of prohibiting
alcohol to youths ceased
As the act of being responsible
trumped the ability to be
responsible
Marijuana became legalized
Stalks of the plant used for rope,
canvas and paper
50,000 people walked out of prison

Role models became people you'd
actually want to follow—
The people who knew survival
And Hollywood stars
Were demoted to human beings

Books and board games came out of
closets, attics and basements
Reading became a hobby for kids,
not a punishment
Schools taught to the children
Not to standardized testing

Punch cards were eliminated from
the workplace
And people came early
The dominion of bosses subsided
As co-ops became the primary
structure for business

A parent could actually tell their kid
where their goldfish was going
when it went down the toilet
People knew where their water was
coming from and going to
They knew that trash wasn't going to
be sent to outerspace
Recyclables took the place of plastic
and Styrofoam

People formed movements
Everyone was directly affected
People formed movements
When the lights went out

Preface

by Peter Phillips, Andrew Roth, and Project Censored

Nineteenth-century American abolitionist leader Frederick Douglass once said, "The limits of tyrants are prescribed by the endurance of those whom they oppress." Find out what people will quietly submit to, Douglass said, and you will learn the extent of the injustice and wrong that will be imposed upon them. That injustice and wrong will continue until the oppressed resist.

Douglass's insights challenge us to address uncomfortable contemporary questions. Are we complicit in tyranny—and, if so, how? Are we oppressed? If so, how close are we to the limits of our endurance? Might the people of the United States be both tyrannical and oppressed, simultaneously?

In 2007–2008—when Habeas Corpus is no longer the law of the land in the United States, when our politicians show no sign of abating the ongoing human catastrophe initiated by the US as a "global war on terror"—we must confront Douglass's insight and the questions it entails, no matter how uncomfortable they make us.

More than ever, we need Real News. Real News strengthens democracy by making the wrongdoings of tyrants *and* the accomplishments of freedom's champions known. Real News looks and sounds like the United States's diverse population. You won't find Real News in frozen, prepackaged containers—it's fresh and local.

If you're reading this book, you probably agree with FCC Commissioner Michael J. Copps: The US needs a new media contract. If the American public gives broadcasters free use of the nation's most valuable spectrum, then those broadcasters owe us a lot in return. A similar point can be made for print media, of course. (Copps unveiled his "New America Media Contract" at the 2007 National Conference for Media Reform in Memphis.)

Over the past several years, an increasingly large and diverse segment of the American public has called for media reform. Perhaps "oppression" is too strong a term, but these people have reached the limits of their endurance for news that reflects a narrow, corporate, pre-spun view of what really matters.

Censored 2008 celebrates the accomplishments of independent journalists and organizations who show us what Real News look like. It reminds us that we must continue to expand the movement—its membership and its agenda—in order to realize its ultimate goal of truly democratic media.

Welcome to our thirty-first annual listing of the news not covered by corporate media. Chapter 1, the twenty-five most important censored news stories of the year, is our feature effort that some two hundred faculty and students spent thousands of hours researching. Project Censored's support staff person Tricia Boreta serves as our primary editor for Chapter 1. Chapter 2 follows with updates on censored stories from our 2007 volume as well as key under-covered stories from prior years. Chapter 3, Junk Food News and News Abuse, is our in-depth review of the most frivolous news stories contrasted with important real news from the same time periods. Kate Sims of the Project Censored support staff coordinated the research effort on Chapter 3 again this year.

New this year in Chapter 4 is our collaboration with *Yes! Magazine* edited by Kate Sims. It covers stories of hope and change we didn't hear about in 2006 and 2007. Chapter 5 was written by our media reform team under the supervision of Andrew Roth and features interviews with key activists who attended the Media Reform Conference in Memphis in January of 2007.

Sonoma State University graduate student Jeff Huling completed Chapter 6 on media bias and the case of the Cuban Five. His chapter is a shining example of independent student research on key media issues being undertaken by Project Censored.

In Chapter 7, Peter Phillips examines and updates Noam Chomsky and Ed Herman's propaganda model theory of media censorship and extends the implications of self-censorship to the liberal independent media in the US.

Chapter 8 is an extensive review of front-page photos relative to the Iraq and Afgan wars. Completed by a team of SSU students—Zoe Huffman, Jeff Huling, Kevin Stolle, and Jocelyn Thomas—and supervised by Andrew Roth, the team examined over 6,000 front-page news photos to determine the nature of war in corporate media's coverage of current conflicts.

Censored 2008's chapters 9, 10, and 11 include contributions from Diane Farsetta of the Center for Media and Democracy, Janine

Jackson with FAIR, and Jo Glanville and Natasha Schmitz with the Index on Censorship (London). They provide a comprehensive review of the state of the media in the US and the world.

Jacques Brodeur, from Montréal, Canada, where media advertising to children is illegal, writes Chapter 12 on the promising practice of protecting children from the power of big media.

Ben Frymer, assistant professor of sociology at Sonoma State University in the Hutchins School of Liberal Studies, gives us Chapter 13 on the media spectacle of alienated youth. And Greg Guma, Executive Director of Pacifica Foundation radio network, provides our anchor Chapter 14 on deliberate perception management in corporate media today.

Project Censored's students, faculty, staff, and national judges welcome you to *Censored 2008*.

Acknowledgments

by Peter Phillips

Project Censored is managed through the Department of Sociology in the School of Social Sciences at Sonoma State University. We are an investigative sociology and media analysis project dedicated to journalistic integrity and the freedom of information throughout the United States.

Sociology professor Andrew Roth is our new associate director of Project Censored. He provides a new perspective on thirty-one years of Censored research that is refreshing, provocative, and distinguished. Welcome Dr. Roth as co-editor of *Censored 2008*.

I want to personally thank those close friends and intimates who have counseled and supported me through another year of Project Censored. Most important is my wife Mary Lia, who as my lover, friend, and partner provides daily consultative support to Project Censored. The men in the Green Oaks Breakfast Group, Noel Byrne, Bob Butler, Bob Klose, Derrick West, Colin Godwin, and Bill Simon, are personal advisors and confidants who help with difficult decisions. A special thanks also to Carl Jensen, founder of Project Censored, and director for 20 years. His continued advice and support are critical to the Project. Tricia Boreta and Kate Sims are Project Censored coordinators and associate administrators. Their dedication and enthusiasm are greatly appreciated.

A big thanks goes to the people at Seven Stories Press. They are not just a publishing house, but also have become close friends, who help edit our annual book in record time, and serve as advisors in the annual release process of the "Most Censored Stories." Publisher Dan Simon is dedicated to building democracy in America through knowledge and literature. He deserves full credit for assembling an excellent support crew including: Jon Gilbert, Veronica Liu, Anna Lui, Theresa Noll, Tara Parmiter, Lars Reilly, Amy Scholder, Ruth Weiner, Crystal Yakacki, and Interns: Sophie Goldstein, Liz Guenard, Isabel Wohlstetter, and Karen Fu.

Thanks also to Bill Mokler and the sales staff at Consortium

Books, who will see to it that every independent bookstore, chain store, and wholesaler in the U.S. is aware of *Censored 2008*. Thanks to Publishers Group Canada, our distributors up north, as well as Turnaround Publishers Services Ltd. in Great Britain and Palgrave Macmillan in Australia.

We especially thank and welcome Novi Mondi Media in Italy for translating and distributing the *Censored* yearbooks in Italian and Spanish. Dar El Shorouk is our Arabic publisher in Cairo, Egypt.

Thank you to Dennis Loo who wrote the introduction to the *Censored 2008* edition. Dennis is a Project Censored national judge and co-editor of the book, *Impeach the President: The Case Against Bush and Cheney* (2006) from Seven Stories Press.

Thanks also to the authors of the most censored stories for 2008, for without their often-unsupported efforts as investigative news reporters and writers, the stories presented in *Censored* would not be revealed.

Our guest writers this year include: Jacques Brodeur, Janine Jackson, Greg Guma, Hilary Goldstein, Josh Mitteldorf, Steven E. Jones, Andrew Sloan, Bill Gibbons, Diane Farsetta, Zoe Huffman, Jeff Huling, Kevin Stolle, Jocelyn Thomas, Kat Pat Crespan, Jenni Leys, Regina Marcheschi, Donald Nelson, Jo Glanville, and Ben Frymer. They represent a unique combination of scholars, journalists, and activists dedicated to media freedom through a diversity of news and opinion. Thank you to each and all for your unique contribution to *Censored 2008*.

This year's book features the cartoons of John Jonik. We welcome his brilliant and satirical work to our 2008 edition.

Our national judges, some of whom have been involved with the Project for 31 years, are among the top experts in the country concerned with First Amendment freedoms and media principles. We are honored to have them as the final voice in ranking the top 25 *Censored* stories.

An important thanks goes to our financial supporters including: The Sonoma State University Instructionally Related Activity Fund, the School of Social Sciences at Sonoma State University, The Wallace Fund, Lori Grace, Cornelia Fletcher, Mark Swedlund & Deborah Dobish, Lynn & Leonard Riepenhoff, and especially the thousands of individuals who purchase books and send us financial gifts each year. You are our financial base, who continue to give year after year to this important student-run media research project.

This year we had over 100 faculty/community evaluators assisting with our story assessment process. These expert volunteers read and rated the nominated stories for national importance, accuracy, and credibility. In April, they participated with over 100 students in selecting the final top 25 stories for 2006-07.

Most of all, we need to recognize the Sonoma State University students in the Spring 2007 Media Censorship class and the Fall 2006 Sociology of Media class, who worked thousands of hours nominating and researching some 300 under-published news stories. Students are the principle writers of the Censored news synopses in the book each year. Additionally, over 60 students served as interns for the project, working on various teams including: public relations, web design, news story research, office support, events/fund raising, and broadcast production. Student education is the most important aspect of Project Censored, and we could not do this work without the dedication and effort of our student interns.

An extremely special thank you to Joni Wallent for her work coordinating the spring 2006 PR team—and to her mom, Sheila Wallent, for acting as volunteer coordinator and caterer for our 2006 conference.

Erica Wilcher is the web coordinator for the Project Censored web site www.projectcensored.org. Our website has expanded under her leadership to over 25,000 people a day logging on to Project Censored in 2006-07.

Lastly, I want to thank our readers and supporters from all over the United States and the world. Hundreds of you nominated stories for consideration as the censored news story of the year. Thank you very much!

PROJECT CENSORED STAFF

Peter Phillips, Ph.D.	Director
Andrew Roth, Ph.D.	Associate Director
Carl Jensen, Ph.D.	Director Emeritus and Project Advisor
Tricia Boreta	Coordinator/Editor
Katie Sims	Coordinator/Broadcast Team Leader/Editor
Joni Wallent	PR Team Leader/Student Events Coordinator
Sadie Melgar	Administrative Support

SPRING & FALL 2006 & 2007 INTERNS AND COMMUNITY VOLUNTEERS

David Abbott, Chris Bachelder, Joseph Bellamy, John Bertucci, Lew Brown, Toni Catelani, Christina Carey, Emily Chavez, Kat Pat Crespan, Suzanne Daly, Issac Dolido, Kelly Fadela, Erin Flaherty Camelia Gannon-Patino, Bill Gibbons, Justin Heinrich, Megan Hope, Zoe Huffman, Jeff Huling, Patricia Jenkins, Eric Jilburg, Jonathan Kaufmann, Jenni Leys, Heather Leidner, Regina Marcheschi, Heather Moffett, Donald Nelson, Stephanie Nelson, Kaitlyn Pinson, Janeen Rashmawi, Rainer Raysor Jessica Rodas, Alexandra Rubin, Julia Stein, Kevin Stolle, Destiny Stone, Jocelyn Thomas, Bridget Thornton, Morgan Ulery, Ryan Walker, Bree Watson, Celeste Winders, Joni Wallent

STUDENT RESEARCHERS IN SOCIOLOGY OF MEDIA CLASS, FALL 2006

Lauren Abruzzo, Christy Baird, Julie Bickel, Toni Catelani, Erica Haikara, Jennifer Huss, Michael Januleski, Erik Jilburg, Sandra Karnes, Heather Leidner, Mayra Madrigal, Adrienne Magee, Misty Mariedth, Heather Moffett, Angela Purcaro, Alexandra Rubin, Jesse Stites, Charlene Topliff, Morgan Ulery

STUDENT RESEARCHERS IN SOCIOLOGY OF MEDIA CENSORSHIP CLASS, SPRING 2007

Rebecca Bazell, Fernanda Borras, Bryce Cook, Jenifer German, Erica Haikara, Madeline Hall,Rachel Icaza, Kristen Kebler,William Lemming, Ioana Lupu, Bianca May, Marley Miller, Ann Marie O'Toole, Phillip Parfitt, Amanda Spigut, Jonathan Stoumen, Cedric Therene, Severre Tysl, Celeste Winder

SPECIAL STUDIES RESEARCH TEAM

Bridget Thornton, Lew Brown, Andrew Sloan, Zoe Huffman, Eric Jilburg, Erica Haikara, Jeff Huling, David Abbott, Jenni Lays, Jocelyn Thomas

PROJECT CENSORED 2006–07 BROADCAST SUPPORT

John Bertucci, Megan Hope, Rainer Raysor, Ryan Walker, Destiny Stone, Dora Ruhs, Paul Sarran, Sandy Brown, Michael Litle, Rachel Olea-Lizarraga, Charlotte Goodman-Smith, Meegan Moonan, Angelica Tercero

PROJECT CENSORED 2007 NATIONAL JUDGES

ROBIN ANDERSEN, associate professor and chair, Department of Communication and Media Studies, Fordham University

LIANE CLORFENE-CASTEN, cofounder and president of Chicago Media Watch; award-winning journalist with credits in national periodicals such as *E Magazine, The Nation, Mother Jones, Ms., Environmental Health Perspectives, In These Times,* and *Business Ethics*; she is the author of *Breast Cancer: Poisons, Profits, and Prevention*

LENORE FOERSTEL, Women for Mutual Security, facilitator of the Progressive International Media Exchange (PRIME)

ROBERT HACKETT, professor, School of Communication, Simon Fraser University; co-director of News Watch Canada since 1993. His most recent publications include *Democratizing Global Media: One World, Many Struggles* (co-edited with Yuezhi Zhao, 2005) and *Remaking Media: The Struggle To Democratize Public Communication* (with William K. Carroll, 2006)

CARL JENSEN, professor emeritus communication studies, Sonoma State University; founder and former director of Project Censored; author of *Censored: The News That Didn't Make the News and Why* and *20 Years of Censored News*

SUT JHALLY, professor of communications and executive director of the Media Education Foundation, University of Massachusetts

NICHOLAS JOHNSON,* professor, College of Law, University of Iowa; former FCC Commissioner (1966-1973); author of *How to Talk Back to Your Television Set*

RHODA H. KARPATKIN, president of Consumers Union, non-profit publisher of *Consumer Reports*

CHARLES L. KLOTZER, editor and publisher emeritus, *St. Louis Journalism Review*

NANCY KRANICH, past president of the American Library Association (ALA)

JUDITH KRUG, director of the Office for Intellectual Freedom, American Library Association (ALA); editor of *Newsletter on Intellectual Freedom, Freedom to Read Foundation News,* and *Intellectual Freedom Action News*

MARTIN LEE, investigative journalist, media critic, and author; an original founder of Fairness and Accuracy in Reporting in New York and former editor of *Extra! Magazine*

DENNIS LOO, associate professor of sociology at California State Polytechnic University, Pomona; co-editor of *Impeach the President: The Case Against Bush and Cheney* (Seven Stories Press, 2006)

WILLIAM LUTZ, professor of English, Rutgers University; former editor of *The Quarterly Review of Doublespeak;* author of *The New Doublespeak: Why No One Knows What Anyone's Saying Anymore* (1966)

JULIANNE MALVEAUX, PH.D., economist and columnist for King Features and Pacifica radio talk show host

BRIAN MURPHY, associate professor communications studies, Niagara University, specializing in media programming and management, investigation and reporting, media history and theory, and international communication.

JACK L. NELSON,* professor emeritus, Graduate School of Education, Rutgers University; author of sixteen books, including *Critical Issues in Education,* and author of more than 150 articles

MICHAEL PARENTI, political analyst, lecturer, and author of numerous books, including *The Culture Struggle, Superpatriotism, The Assassination of Julius Caesar, A People's History of Ancient Rome, The Terrorism Trap, September 11 and Beyond,* and *Democracy for the Few*

BARBARA SEAMAN, lecturer; author of *The Greatest Experiment Ever Performed on Women: Exploding the Estrogen Myth, The Doctor's Case Against the Pill, Free and Female: Women and the Crisis in Sex Hormones,* and other books; cofounder of the National Women's Health Network

NANCY SNOW, professor, College of Communications, California State University-Fullerton; Senior Fellow, USC Center on Public Diplomacy; Adjunct Professor, University of Southern California, Annenberg School for Communication; author of *Propaganda, Inc., Information War,* and co-editor with Yahya R. Kamalipour of *War, Media and Propaganda*

SHEILA RABB WEIDENFELD,* president of D.C. Productions, Ltd.; former press secretary to Betty Ford

*Indicates having been a Project Censored judge since our founding in 1976

PROJECT CENSORED 2005 & 2006 FACULTY, STAFF, AND COMMUNITY EVALUATORS

Melinda Barnard, Ph.D. Communications
Philip Beard, Ph.D. Modern Languages
Jim Berkland, Ph.D. Geology
Stephen Bittner, Ph.D. History
Barbara Bloom, Ph.D. Criminal Justice Administration
Andrew Botterell, Ph.D. Philosophy
Maureen Buckley, Ph.D. Counseling
Elizabeth Burch, Ph.D. Communications
Ken Burrow, Ph.D. Journalism, SFSU
Noel Byrne, Ph.D. Sociology
James R. Carr, Ph.D. Geology
Yvonne Clarke, M.A., University Affairs
Liz Close, Ph.D. Nursing (Chair)
G. Dennis Cooke, Ph.D. Zoology
Bill Crowley, Ph.D. Geography
Victor Daniels, Ph.D. Psychology

Laurie Dawson, Ph.D. Labor Education
James Dean, Ph.D. Sociology
Randall Dodgen, Ph.D. History
Stephanie Dyer, Ph.D. Cultural History
Carolyn Epple, Ph.D. Anthropology
Gary Evans, M.D.
Michael Ezra, Ph.D. Chemistry
Tamara Falicov, M.A. Communication Studies
Fred Fletcher, Community Expert Labor
Dorothy (Dolly) Friedel, Ph.D. Geography
Patricia Leigh Gibbs, Ph.D. Sociology
Robert Girling, Ph.D. Business Economics
Mary Gomes, Ph.D. Psychology
Myrna Goodman, Ph.D. Sociology
Scott Gordon, Ph.D. Computer Science
Karen Grady, Ph.D. Education
Diana Grant, Ph.D. Criminal Justice Administration
Bill Griggs, Ph.D. Sociology, Eastern Oregon University
Velma Guillory-Taylor, Ed.D. American Multicultural Studies
Chad Harris, M.A. Communication Studies
Laurel Holmstrom, Academic Programs; M.A. English
Jeffrey Holtzman, Ph.D. Environmental Sciences
Mickey Huff, M.A. History/Media Studies
Kevin Howdy, Ph.D. Communications, DePauw University
Pat Jackson, Ph.D. Criminal Justice Administration
Tom Jacobson, J.D. Environmental Studies & Planning
Sherril Jaffe, Ph.D. English
Paul Jess, Community Expert Environmental Law
Cheri Ketchum, Ph.D. Communications
Patricia Kim-Rajal, Ph.D. American Culture
Mary King, M.D. Health
Paul Kingsley, M.D.
Jeanette Koshar, Nursing
John Kramer, Ph.D. Political Science
Heidi LaMoreaux, Ph.D. Liberal Studies
Virginia Lea, Ph.D. Education
Benet Leigh, M.A. Communications Studies
Wingham Liddell, Ph.D. Business Administration
Jennifer Lillig Whiles, Ph.D. Chemistry

Thom Lough, Ph.D. Sociology
John Lund, Community Expert Business & Political Issues
Rick Luttmann, Ph.D. Math
Robert Manning, Community Expert Peace Issues
Regina Marchi, M.A. Communication Studies
Ken Marcus, Ph.D. Criminal Justice Administration
Perry Marker, Ph.D. Education
Elizabeth Martinez, Ph.D. Modern Languages
David McCuan, Ph.D. Political Science
Eric McGuckin, Ph.D. Liberal Studies
Robert McNamara, Ph.D. Political Science
Andy Merrifield, Ph.D. Political Science
Jack Munsee, Ph.D. Political Science
Ann Neel, Ph.D. Sociology
Catherine Nelson, Ph.D. Political Science
Leilani Nishime, Ph.D. Ethnic Studies Department
Linda Nowak, Ph.D. Business
Tim Ogburn, Community Expert International Business
Tom Ormond, Ph.D. Kinesiology
Wendy Ostroff, Ph.D. Liberal Studies
Ervand M. Peterson, Ph.D. Environmental Sciences
Jorge E. Porras, Ph.D. Modern Languages
Jeffrey T. Reeder, Ph.D. Modern Languages
Rick Robison, Ph.D. Library
R. Thomas Rosin, Ph.D. Anthropology
Richard Senghas, Ph.D. Anthropology/Linguistics
Rashmi Singh, Ph.D. American Multicultural Studies
Cindy Stearns, Ph.D. Sociology
Greg Storino, Community Expert American Airlines Pilot
Meri Storino, Ph.D. Counseling
Elaine Sundberg, M.A. Academic Programs
Scott Suneson, M.A. Sociology/Political Science
Laxmi G. Tewari, Ph.D. Music
Karen Thompson, Ph.D. Business
Suzanne Toczyski, Ph.D. Modern Languages
Carol Tremmel, M.A. Extended Education
Charlene Tung, Ph.D. Women's & Gender Studies
David Van Nuys, Ph.D. Psychology
Francisco H. Vazquez, Ph.D. Liberal Studies

Greta Vollmer, Ph.D. English
Alexandra (Sascha) Von Meier, Ph.D. Environmental Sciences
Albert Wahrhaftig, Ph.D. Anthropology
Tim Wandling, Ph.D. English
Tony White, Ph.D. History
John Wingard, Ph.D. Anthropology
Craig Winston, J.D. Criminal Justice
Richard Zimmer, Ph.D. Liberal Studies

SONOMA STATE UNIVERSITY SUPPORTING STAFF AND OFFICES

Ruben Arminana: President, Sonoma State University and staff
Eduardo Ochoa: Chief Academic Officer and staff
Carol Blackshire-Belay: Vice Provost Academic Affairs
Elaine Leeder: Dean of School of Sciences and staff
Erica Wilcher: Administrative Manager
Katie McCormick: Operations Analyst
Connie Lewsadder: Dean's Assistant
William Babula: Dean of School of Arts and Humanities
Barbara Butler and the SSU Library Staff
Paula Hammett: Social Sciences Library Resources
Jonah Raskin and Faculty in Communications Studies
Susan Kashack, Jean Wasp, and staff in SSU Public Relations Office

Colleagues in the Sociology Department: Noel Byrne, Kathy Charmaz, Teresa Ciabattari, Andy Deseran, Myrna Goodman, Melinda Milligan, James Dean, Andrew Roth, Thom Lough, Elaine Wellin, Madeleine Rose, Cindy Stearns, and department coordinators Lisa Kelley-Roche and Katie Musick

Thanks also to our ongoing supportive friends in the Sonoma State community, Cecilia O'Brian, Peter Flores, Linda Williams, Bruce Berkowitz, Jerry Uhlig, Mo Llanef, Martha Ezell, Henry Amaral, Bill Bayley, Rod Baraz, Angela Hardin, Katie Pierce, Kamen Nikolov, John Wright, John Connole, and Nadir Vissanjy.

The Project Censored crew (SSU faculty, students, and PC staff).

Introduction

by Dennis Loo

The first time I came across a copy of *Censored* was in the early 1990s while browsing in a Santa Cruz bookstore. It was one of those moments one never forgets. I can even remember where I was standing and how the light hit the pages. Here was a group giving attention to explosive accounts of malfeasance, crimes, and government and corporate lying. It was like those X-ray glasses they used to sell in comic book ads, only these glasses really did reveal truth beneath the lies.

Project Censored has done this work every year for more than three decades, exposing a much wider audience to stories that have been overlooked or underplayed by the corporate media.

Censored 2008's mission stands out all the more for its vital importance in these times.

Habeas corpus—your right to challenge your detention, dating from the Magna Carta, almost nine hundred years old and one of the American Revolution's explicit grievances against the British—has been stripped from people, citizens and non-citizens alike, who can now be designated "unlawful enemy combatants" at the President's whim.

The President and Congress have *legalized torture* and it is being practiced as policy.

The 2000 and 2004 presidential elections were stolen in plain sight.

The government is breaking the law by openly spying on hundreds of millions of Americans, peering over our shoulders at our e-mails and our Web surfing, listening in on our phone conversations, checking out what we're reading at our local library, tracking our financial transactions, what we buy, where we buy it, where we go, and with whom we associate.

The White House has been caught lying about the reasons for an invasion of another country that did not threaten us. The US has committed, according to the UN Charter, the highest war crime of all, and yet the killing continues.

Hundreds of thousands—nearly a million—people have died because of these indefensible acts.

A whistleblower's wife, a covert CIA agent, has had her cover blown, an act of treason by the White House, as an act of revenge.

New Orleans, a storied and unique American city and its indigent, were left to drown, ravaged by Hurricane Katrina and by a spectacularly indifferent White House that knew that a Category Five hurricane was coming and still did nothing.

The President has issued hundreds of "signing statements" negating laws passed by Congress and nullifying the Constitution.

Science, evidence, and analysis have been treated by the White House as *unnecessary*.

Congress has passed martial law provisions at the White House's request that make it legal for the president to declare a "public emergency" on his say-so alone, to conduct mass roundups, arrests, and detentions, and to be answerable to no one, and hardly anyone in the US even knows about it.

Scandal after scandal has rocked the White House and its Congressional supporters.

The startlingly long list of outrages goes on and on.

And yet . . . and yet . . . they are still . . . getting away with it all!

Like the hookah-smoking caterpillar in *Alice in Wonderland*, this administration's words mean whatever they want them to mean.

It seems no lie is too tall, no crime too depraved, and no debacle too great for this administration. They've crossed so many lines that the ground they traverse looks like graph paper.

How have things come to this pass? The short answer to this question is that the corporate media and this country's political leadership have cooperated and colluded in the commission of these deeds, thus disorienting and so far demobilizing the mass public. But why has this happened? What is the context for the work of *Censored 2008*, which you hold in your hand?

One part of the answer comes to us courtesy of a former conservative and insider, David Brock. As his indispensable book *The Republican Noise Machine: Right-Wing Media and How It Corrupts Democracy* details, the radical right laid plans in the early 1970s to permanently transform the American political landscape. The key to this strategy was building its own right-wing media empire. To succeed they had to first eliminate the Fairness Doctrine, a New Deal rule requiring that public broadcasters provide equal time to opposing viewpoints. After heavy lobbying by deep-pocketed radical right-wing interests, the

Fairness Doctrine was repealed under Ronald Reagan in 1987. The coast was then clear for them to establish the influence of demagogues like Rush Limbaugh, Bill O'Reilly, Ann Coulter, and other pundits who need not bother with anyone contradicting their made-up facts.

One indicator of how extraordinarily successful this strategy has been is the fact that a sizable percentage of the US population still thinks that Iraq had something to do with 9/11. Another indicator of its success is that Bush and Cheney took office in the first place, and still have not been removed from office despite the obvious fraud of their "election" and the unprecedented list of crimes and offenses they have committed that are on the public record.

The radical right understood that the entire country's political leadership could be made up of Democrats (or Greens for that matter) and if the organs of public opinion-making are controlled by the radical right, then the legislative bodies are going to be more guided by right-wing politics than by the parties actually in office.

Their strategy is based on a two-fold recognition: 1. whoever sets the public debate's parameters also dictates public policy—what is treated as acceptable and what is ruled as unacceptable predetermines the "debate's" outcome; and 2. the information people have access to determines what they will or won't do.

The radical right-wing media could not exercise the clout that they do today—they would not be setting the terms of the overall discussion—were it not for the second factor shaping our polity today: a sea change in the nature of media ownership. Ben Bagdikian warned back in 1997 that media ownership was becoming monopolistic:

> In the last 5 years, a small number of the country's largest industrial corporations has acquired more public communications power—including ownership of the news—than any private businesses have ever before possessed in world history.
>
> Nothing in earlier history matches this corporate group's power to penetrate the social landscape . . .
>
> At issue is the possession of power to surround almost every man, woman, and child in the country with controlled images and words . . . to alter the political agenda of the country. And with that power comes the ability to exert influence that in many ways is greater than that of schools, religion, parents, and even government itself.[1]

The power of this new media is a point not yet fully understood by most people. Most still think that political institutions control and trump the power of economic interests. This conventional wisdom has never really been true; vested economic interests have always been dominant, but the conventional wisdom has never been further from the truth than it is today.

What is in the public and planet's interest is decidedly secondary to the priorities for profit of these colossal conglomerates. And as these corporations become more elephantine through mind-bogglingly large mergers, and as the disparities of wealth more generally in the society become even more one-sided, the relationship between the public interest and profit have and will become ever more disengaged.

Viacom is one of these new media behemoths. Here is what its chairman, Sumner Redstone, said in September 2004:

> Speaking to some of America's and Asia's top executives gathered for *Forbes* magazine's annual Global CEO Conference, Mr. Redstone [a self-described liberal democrat] declared: "I look at the [upcoming November 2004] election from what's good for Viacom. I vote for what's good for Viacom. I vote, today, Viacom. [F]rom a Viacom standpoint, the election of a Republican administration is a better deal. Because the Republican administration has stood for many things we believe in, deregulation and so on . . . [T]he election of a Republican administration is better for our company."[2]

Redstone's personal political preferences thus take a back seat to his company's best interests. A clearer statement of how decisions are made in this new economic order could hardly be imagined.[3] Beyond Redstone as an individual, media and political leaders in general also weigh their actions (especially what stories they will cover and how they will cover them) relative to what is best for their careers' and the companies' interests that they work for or own. There are exceptions to this, but these exceptions are exceedingly few (Jon Stewart, Bill Maher, Stephen Colbert, Keith Olbermann)[4] and many end up paying the price for speaking too much truth by losing their jobs (for example, Phil Donahue, Ashleigh Banfield, Eason Jordan).

Of the one hundred largest economic entities in the world today, more than half of them are transnational corporations, not countries.

The richest 497 individuals in the world have as much wealth as do the bottom 50 percent of the world's population. "Billions [of dollars] versus billions [of people]" would be one way to describe this criminally lopsided situation. Given this, what should we rightly expect to emerge from the pages and broadcast studios of the major media conglomerates? How well would truth fare in the contest between it and wealth beyond the wildest dreams of emperors in previous eras?

Both the GOP and the Democratic Party operate within this universe of mega-corporations, globalization, and the presence of a powerful radical right-wing movement. Is it any wonder that they would be unwilling to buck this trend? How could anything less than a social movement from below that shakes this country to its roots provide any hope of a reversal of these virulent trends?

We have an extraordinary situation today, created by the two factors I've discussed above, in which the White House has blatantly violated both de facto—and critically, *de jure*—long-standing principles crucial to what most people have historically believed distinguished the US from fascist, totalitarian, and banana republic regimes: due process, civil liberties, the right not to be spied upon by your government, the right to resist unreasonable search and seizure, the right to confront your accusers and to see the evidence against you, habeas corpus, prohibitions against torture and against unprovoked aggression upon other countries, government regulators whose primary interest is not deregulation, freedom of speech and assembly, the Freedom of Information Act, fair elections where the votes are all counted and the winner takes office . . . the list goes on and on.

Despite this, and so much more, the corporate media and the "loyal opposition" continue to insist—against all law, morality, and simple common decency—that impeachment is out of the question! The crimes and malfeasances of this administration are so extensive, so egregious, and some of it so obvious, that despite the wall of silence that mass media and the Democratic Party have erected, Bush and Cheney are at historic lows in approval ratings and a majority of Americans have for some time told pollsters that they want impeachment.

But this majority sentiment, this flood, is being held back by the media and the Democratic Party with their collective fingers in the dike.

The problem runs deeper than one of partisan rivalry between the Democrats and the Republicans, for the Republicans don't represent capitalism and the Democrats something else. They both represent capitalism. Where they principally differ is that the GOP is the cutting edge—the most aggressive, ruthless, unapologetic representatives of globalization and of neoliberalism (also known as free market fundamentalism).

The battle to see that justice and truth prevail is a more difficult one for all of the foregoing reasons than ever. The stakes are exceedingly high. If these unprecedented steps by the White House aren't repudiated while Bush and Cheney are still in office, this country will have been irrevocably and fundamentally changed.

The forces arrayed against the people are strategically positioned, exceptionally wealthy, and exceedingly powerful. But they are extremely few in number. Moreover, their policies and program are directly against the interests of the vast majority of the people and the interests of the planet.

Can *Censored 2008* by itself make the difference? Of course not. Not by a long shot. Is *Censored 2008* part of the solution? Absolutely.

The only ray of hope from this bleak picture—and it's a big ray that warms the room and fills the shadows—is that truth is a very powerful thing indeed. Our rulers cannot continue down the path they've sent us down, clanging and jangling, without having to twist, lie, and censor. They have to lie to people to get their way. They are like vampires who must do their dirty deeds in the dark and when exposed to the sunlight, instantly burst into flames and ashes.

Enjoy this book. Share it with others. Spread the light. We have much to do and little time.

Dennis Loo, Ph.D. is associate professor of sociology at Cal Poly Pomona, a former journalist, co-editor of *Impeach the President: the Case Against Bush and Cheney*, and author of "No Paper Trail Left Behind: the Theft of the 2004 Presidential Election." His blog is http://dennisloo.blogspot.com.

Notes

1. *Media Monopoly*, preface to the Fifth Edition.
2. "Guess Who's A GOP Booster? The CEO of CBS's parent company endorses President Bush," *Asian Wall Street Journal*, September 24, 2004, http://www.opinionjournal.com/extra/?id=110005669
3. Redstone made this statement at a time when he and Viacom were under attack for "Rathergate," the CBS story on George Bush's National Guard service during the Vietnam War.
4. Note that three of these are humorists. When the Shah of Iran banned political dissent, political dissent went underground into the mosques. In the US most of the political dissent in broadcasting has gone to cable and into comedy.

The Top Censored Stories of 2006 and 2007

by Tricia Boreta, Peter Phillips, Andrew Roth, Kate Sims, and Project Censored

Chapter I of *Censored 2008* summarizes the twenty-five most important news stories censored in the United States from 2006-2007. The corporate media somehow failed to cover each of these stories in adequate detail. Censorship in the US is seldom direct or overt. Instead, it results from the corporate media's inability to address a range of truly serious events and issues about which every American should be aware

People in the US believe in the First Amendment. Despite our busy lives we want to be informed about serious decisions made by the powerful. We want full inclusion as participants in democratic decision-making, and we want the ability to hold our leaders accountable—especially when they act ostensibly in our name but contrary to core democratic tenets. Without news coverage that extends beyond the narrow range of people, power structures, and politics addressed by the corporate media, we remain blind to the machinations of the powerful and we become further marginalized from the basic democratic tasks of political, economic, and social decision-making.

The systemic erosion of human rights and civil liberties, in both the US and the world, is the common theme of the most censored stories for our 2008 volume. The continuing consolidation of private for-profit bureaucracies with public governmental entities results nothing less than the diminishment of personal freedoms for all persons. Corporate avarice interlocked with governmental police power is fascism in the making. Only democratic resistance by the people can forestall this ongoing process.

Strong, autonomous media are essential to democratic resistance against unchecked power. By supporting independent media, a free internet, transparent government, participatory decision-making, and by upholding our core values of due process and human rights, we can stand with our neighbors, friends, and communities to build a better tomorrow. Please share these stories with others, and keep yourselves informed and active.

1

No Habeas Corpus for "Any Person"

Sources:
Consortium, October 19, 2006
Title: "Who Is 'Any Person' in Tribunal Law?"
Author: Robert Parry

Consortium, February 3, 2007
Title: "Still No Habeas Rights for You"
Author: Robert Parry

Common Dreams, February 2, 2007
Title: "Repeal the Military Commissions Act and Restore the Most American Human Right"
Author: Thom Hartmann

Student Researchers: Bryce Cook and Julie Bickel
Faculty Evaluator: Andrew Roth, Ph.D.

With the approval of Congress and no outcry from corporate media, the Military Commissions Act (MCA) signed by Bush on October 17, 2006, ushered in military commission law for US citizens and non-citizens alike. While media, including a lead editorial in the *New York Times* October 19, have given false comfort that we, as American citizens, will not be the victims of the draconian measures legalized by this Act—such as military roundups and life-long detention with no rights or constitutional protections—Robert Parry points to text in the MCA that allows for the institution of a military alternative to the constitutional justice system for "any person" regardless of American citizenship. The MCA effectively does away with habeas corpus rights for "any person" arbitrarily deemed to be an "enemy of the state." The judgment on who is deemed an "enemy combatant" is solely at the discretion of President Bush.

The oldest human right defined in the history of English-speaking civilization is the right to challenge governmental power of arrest and detention through the use of habeas corpus laws, considered to be the most critical parts of the Magna Carta which was signed by King John in 1215.

Alexander Hamilton wrote in *The Federalist #84* in August of 1788:

> The establishment of the writ of habeas corpus . . . . are perhaps greater securities to liberty and republicanism than any it [the Constitution] contains. . . . The practice of arbitrary imprisonments have been, in all ages, the favorite and most formidable instruments of tyranny. The observations of the judicious [British eighteenth-century legal scholar] Blackstone, in reference to the latter, are well worthy of recital:

> "To bereave a man of life" says he, "or by violence to confiscate his estate, without accusation or trial, would be so gross and notorious an act of despotism, as must at once convey the alarm of tyranny throughout the whole nation; but confinement of the person, by secretly hurrying him to jail, where his sufferings are unknown or forgotten, is a less public, a less striking, and therefore a more dangerous engine of arbitrary government."

While it is true that some parts of the MCA target non-citizens, other sections clearly apply to US citizens as well, putting citizens inside the same tribunal system with non-citizen residents and foreigners.

Section 950q of the MCA states that, "Any person is punishable as a principal under this chapter [of the MCA] who commits an offense punishable by this chapter, or aids, abets, counsels, commands, or procures its commission."[1]

Section 950v. "Crimes Triable by Military Commissions" (26) of the MCA seems to specifically target American citizens by stating that, "Any person subject to this chapter who, in breach of an allegiance or duty to the United States, knowingly and intentionally aids an enemy of the United States, or one of the co-belligerents of the enemy, shall be punished as a military commission under this chapter may direct."[1]

"Who," warns Parry, "has 'an allegiance or duty to the United States' if not an American citizen?"

Besides allowing "any person" to be swallowed up by Bush's system, the law prohibits detainees once inside from appealing to the traditional American courts until after prosecution and sentencing, which could translate into an indefinite imprisonment since there are no timetables for Bush's tribunal process to play out.

Section 950j of the law further states that once a person is detained, ". . . not withstanding any other provision of law (including section 2241 of title 28 or any other habeas corpus provision) no court, justice, or judge shall have jurisdiction to hear or consider any claim or cause of action whatsoever . . . relating to the prosecution, trial, or judgment of a military commission under this chapter, including challenges to the lawfulness of procedures of military commissions."[1]

Other constitutional protections in the Bill of Rights, such as a speedy trial, the right to reasonable bail, and the ban on "cruel and unusual punishment," would seem to be beyond a detainee's reach as well.

Parry warns that, "In effect, what the new law appears to do is to create a parallel 'star chamber' system for the prosecution, imprisonment, and possible execution of enemies of the state, whether those enemies are foreign or domestic.

"Under the cloak of setting up military tribunals to try al-Qaeda suspects and other so-called unlawful enemy combatants, Bush and the Republican-controlled Congress effectively created a parallel legal system for 'any person'—American citizen or otherwise—who crosses some ill-defined line."

In one of the most chilling public statements ever made by a US Attorney General, Alberto Gonzales opined at a Senate Judiciary Committee hearing on Jan. 18, 2007, "The Constitution doesn't say every individual in the United States or citizen is hereby granted or assured the right of habeas corpus. It doesn't say that. It simply says the right shall not be suspended."

More important than its sophomoric nature, Parry warns, is that Gonzales's statement suggests he is still searching for arguments to make habeas corpus optional, subordinate to the President's executive powers that Bush's neoconservative legal advisers claim are virtually unlimited during "time of war."

Citation

1. "Military Commissions Act of 2006" Public Law 109-366, 109th Congress. See http://frwebgate.access.gpo.gov/cgi-bin/getdoc.cgi?dbname=109_cong_public_laws&docid=f :publ366.109.

UPDATE BY ROBERT PARRY

The Consortium series on the Military Commissions Act of 2006 pointed out that the law's broad language seems to apply to both US citizens and non-citizens, contrary to some reassuring comments in the major news media that the law only denies habeas corpus rights to non-citizens. The law's application to "any person" who aids and abets a wide variety of crimes related to terrorism—and the law's provisions stripping away the jurisdiction of civilian courts—could apparently thrust anyone into the legal limbo of the military commissions where their rights are tightly constrained and their cases could languish indefinitely.

Despite the widespread distribution of our articles on the Internet, the major US news media continues to ignore the troubling "any person" language tucked in toward the end of the statute. To my knowledge, for instance, no major news organization has explained why, if the law is supposed to apply only to non-citizens, one section specifically targets "any person [who] in breach of an allegiance or duty to the United States, knowingly and intentionally aids an enemy of the United States." Indeed, the "any person" language in sections dealing with a wide array of crimes, including traditional offenses such as spying, suggests that a parallel legal system has been created outside the parameters of the US Constitution.

Since publication of the articles, the Democrats won control of both the House and Senate—and some prominent Democrats, such as Senate Judiciary Committee chairman Patrick Leahy, have voiced their intent to revise the law with the goal of restoring habeas corpus and other rights. However, other Democrats appear hesitant, fearing that any attempt to change the law would open them to charges that they are "soft on terrorism" and that Republicans would torpedo the reform legislation anyway. Outside of Congress, pro-Constitution groups have made reform of the Military Commissions Act a high priority. For instance, the American Civil Liberties Union organized a national protest rally against the law. But the public's lack of a clear understanding of the law's scope has undercut efforts to build a popular movement for repeal or revision of the law.

To learn more about the movement to rewrite the Military Commissions Act, readers can contact the ACLU at

https://secure.aclu.org/site/SPageServer?pagename=DOA_learn>
https://secure.aclu.org/site/SPageServer?pagename=DOA_learn.

COMMENT

On June 8, 2007 the Senate Judiciary Committee passed the Habeas Corpus Restoration Act on an 11-8 vote. If approved, the bipartisan bill, authored by Senator Patrick Leahy of Vermont and Senator Arlen Specter of Pennsylvania, will restore habeas rights that were taken away last year by the Military Commissions Act. The bill will move to the full Senate for vote late June 2007.

2

Bush Moves Toward Martial Law

Sources:
Uruknet, October 26, 2006
Title: "Bush Moves Toward Martial Law"
Author: Frank Morales

Student Researchers: Phillip Parfitt and Julie Bickel
Faculty Evaluator: Andy Merrifield, Ph.D.

The John Warner Defense Authorization Act of 2007, which was quietly signed by Bush on October 17, 2006, the very same day that he signed the Military Commissions Act, allows the president to station military troops anywhere in the United States and take control of state-based National Guard units without the consent of the governor or local authorities, in order to "suppress public disorder."

By revising the two-century-old Insurrection Act, the law in effect repeals the Posse Comitatus Act, which placed strict prohibitions on military involvement in domestic law enforcement. The 1878 Act reads, "Whoever, except in cases and under circumstances expressly authorized by the Constitution or Act of Congress, willfully uses any part of the Army or Air Force as a posse comitatus or otherwise to execute the laws shall be fined under this title or imprisoned not more than two years, or both." As the only US criminal statute that outlaws military operations directed against the American people, it has been our best protection against tyranny enforced by martial law—the harsh system of rules that takes effect when the military takes control of the normal administration of justice. Historically martial law has been imposed by various governments during times of war or occupation to intensify control of populations in spite of heightened unrest. In modern times it is most commonly used by authoritarian governments to enforce unpopular rule.[1]

Section 333 of the Defense Authorization Act of 2007, entitled "Major public emergencies; interference with State and Federal law," states that "the President may employ the armed forces, including the National Guard in Federal service—to restore public order and enforce the laws of the United States when, as a result of a natural disaster, epidemic, or other serious public health emergency, terrorist attack or incident, or other condition in any State or possession of the United States, the President determines that domestic violence has occurred to such an extent that the constituted authorities of the State or possession are incapable of (or "refuse" or "fail" in) maintaining public order—in order to suppress, in any State, any insurrection, domestic violence, unlawful combination, or conspiracy."

Thus an Act of Congress, superceding the Posse Comitatus Act, has paved the way toward a police state by granting the president unfettered legal authority to order federal troops onto the streets of America, directing military operations against the American people under the cover of "law enforcement."

The massive Defense Authorization Act grants the Pentagon $532.8 billion to include implementation of the new law which furthermore facilitates militarized police round-ups of protesters, so-called illegal aliens, potential terrorists, and other undesirables for detention in facilities already contracted and under construction, (see *Censored 2007*, Story #14) and transferring from the Pentagon to local police units the latest technology and weaponry designed to suppress dissent.

Author Frank Morales notes that despite the unprecedented and shocking nature of this act, there has been no outcry in the American media, and little reaction from our elected officials in Congress. On September 19, a lone Senator Patrick Leahy (D-Vermont) noted that 2007's Defense Authorization Act contained a "widely opposed provision to allow the President more control over the National Guard [adopting] changes to the Insurrection Act, which will make it easier for this or any future President to use the military to restore domestic order without the consent of the nation's governors."

A few weeks later, on September 29, Leahy entered into the Congressional Record that he had "grave reservations about certain provisions of the fiscal Year 2007 Defense Authorization Bill Conference Report," the language of which, he said, "subverts solid, longstanding posse comitatus statutes that limit the military's involvement in law enforcement, thereby making it easier for the President to declare martial law." This had been "slipped in," Leahy said, "as a rider with little study," while "other congressional committees with jurisdiction over these matters had no chance to comment, let alone hold hearings on, these proposals."

Leahy noted "the implications of changing the [Posse Comitatus] Act are enormous." "There is good reason," he said, "for the constructive friction in existing law when it comes to martial law declarations. Using the military for law enforcement goes against one of the founding tenets of our democracy. We fail our Constitution, neglecting the rights of the States, when we make it easier for the President to declare martial law and trample on local and state sovereignty."

Morales further asserts that "with the president's polls at a historic low . . . and Democrats taking back the Congress . . . it is particularly worrisome that President Bush has seen fit, at this juncture to, in effect, declare himself dictator."

Citation

1. See http://en.wikipedia.org/wiki/Martial_law, "Martial Law," May 2007

UPDATE BY FRANK MORALES

On April 24, 2007, Major General Timothy Lowenberg, the Adjutant General, Washington National Guard, and Director of the Washington Military Department, testified before the Senate Judiciary Committee on "The Insurrection Act Rider and State Control of the National Guard." He was speaking in opposition to Section 1076 of the recently passed 2007 National Defense Authorization Act (NDAA), which President Bush quietly signed into law this past October 17. The law clears the way for the President to execute martial law, commandeer National Guard units around the country and unilaterally authorize military operations against the

American people in the event of an executive declaration of a "public emergency."

This move toward martial law, which is intended to facilitate more effective counterinsurgency measures on the home front, took place, according to Lowenberg, "without any hearing or consultation with the governors and without any articulation or justification of need." This, despite the fact that Section 1076 of the new law "changed more than one hundred years of well-established and carefully balanced state-federal and civil-military relationships." In other words, with one swipe of the pen, says the General, "one hundred years of law and policy were changed without any publicly or privately acknowledged author or proponent of the change."

Its "Federal Plans for Implementing Expanded Martial Law Authority" are to be executed via the recently created domestic military command, the Northern Command or NORTHCOM. "One key USNORTHCOM planning assumption," says Lowenberg, "is that the President will invoke the new Martial Law powers if he concludes state and/or local authorities no longer possess either the capability or the will to maintain order." In fact, this "highly subjective assumption," as Lowenberg puts it, has been in the works for some time now. According to the General, the "US Northern Command has been engaged for some time in deliberative planning for implementation of Section 1076 of the 2007 National Defense Authorization. The formal NORTHCOM CONPLAN 2502-05 was approved by Secretary of Defense Gates on March 15, 2007,"

Further, according to the General, the 2007 NDAA provisions "could be used to compel National Guard forces to engage in civil disturbance operations under federal control." In that case, NORTHCOM will effectuate its move to martial law, its "CONPLAN," by way of its very own "civil disturbance plan," Department of Defense Civil Disturbance Plan 55-2, code-named Garden Plot. Major Tom Herthel, of the United States Air Force Judge Advocate General School, recently laid out the Rules of Engagement & Rules for the Use of Force during the implementation of "GARDEN PLOT," which according to Herthel, is "the plan to provide the basis for all preparation, deployment, employment, and redeployment of all designated forces, including National Guard forces called to active federal service, for use in domestic civil disturbance operations as directed by the President." Among other things, the "rules" allow for the use of lethal force during domestic "civil disturbance operations."

That is why many are urging Congress to repeal Section 1076 of the 2007 NDAA through immediate enactment of Senate Bill 513. Introduced in February 2007, and sponsored by Senator Patrick Leahy (D-Vt.), the bill seeks to repeal, or as the Congress puts it, "revive previous authority on the use of the Armed Forces and the militia to address interference with State or Federal law, and for other purposes," through the "Repeal of Amendments made by Public Law 109-364-Section 1076 of the John Warner National Defense Authorization Act for Fiscal Year 2007."

It is critical that Senate Bill 513 becomes law, and that our popular struggle succeeds in beating back the President's attempt to further codify the immoral and criminal seizure of state control via woefully ill-advised and dictatorial moves toward martial law and military rule.

3

AFRICOM: US Military Control of Africa's Resources

Source:
MoonofAlabama.org 2/21/2007
Title: "Understanding AFRICOM"
Author: Bryan Hunt

Student Researcher: Ioana Lupu
Faculty Evaluator: Marco Calavita, Ph.D

In February 2007 the White House announced the formation of the US African Command (AFRICOM), a new unified Pentagon command center in Africa, to be established by September 2008. This military penetration of Africa is being presented as a human-itarian guard in the Global War on Terror. The real objective is, however, the procurement and control of Africa's oil and its global delivery systems.

The most significant and growing challenge to US dominance in Africa is China. An increase in Chinese trade and investment in Africa threatens to substantially reduce US political and economic leverage in that resource-rich continent. The political implication of an economically emerging Africa in close alliance with China is resulting in a new cold war in which AFRICOM will be tasked with achieving full-spectrum military dominance over Africa.

AFRICOM will replace US military command posts in Africa, which were formerly under control of US European Command (EUCOM) and US Central Command (CENTCOM), with a more centralized and intensified US military presence.

A context for the pending strategic role of AFRICOM can be gained from observing CENTCOM in the Middle East. CENTCOM grew out of the Carter Doctrine of 1980 which described the oil flow from the Persian Gulf as a "vital interest" of the US, and affirmed that the US would employ "any means necessary, including military force" to overcome an attempt by hostile interests to block that flow.

It is in Western and Sub-Saharan Africa that the US military force is most rapidly increasing, as this area is projected to become as important a source of energy as the Middle East within the next decade. In this region, challenge to US domination and exploitation is coming from the people of Africa—most specifically in Nigeria, where seventy percent of Africa's oil is contained.

People native to the Niger Delta region have not benefited, but instead suffered, as a result of sitting on top of vast natural oil and natural gas deposits. Nigerian people's movements are demanding self-determination and equitable sharing of oil-receipts. Environmental and human rights activists have, for years, documented atrocities on the part of oil companies and the military in this region. As the tactics of resistance groups have shifted from petition and protest to more proactive measures, attacks on pipelines and oil facilities have curtailed the flow of oil leaving the region. As a Convergent Interests report puts it, "Within the first six months of 2006, there were nineteen attacks on foreign oil operations and over $2.187 billion lost in oil revenues; the Department of Petroleum Resources claims this figure represents 32 percent of 'the revenue the country [Nigeria] generated this year.'"

Oil companies and the Pentagon are attempting to link these resistance groups to international terror networks in order to legitimize the use of the US military to "stabilize" these areas and secure the energy flow. No evidence has been found however to link the Niger Delta resistance groups to international terror networks or jihadists. Instead the situation in the Niger Delta is that of ethnic-nationalist movements fighting, by any means necessary, toward the political objective of self-determination. The volatility surrounding oil installations in Nigeria and elsewhere in the continent is, however, used by the US security establishment to justify military "support" in African oil producing states, under the guise of helping Africans defend themselves against those who would hinder their engagement in "Free Trade."

The December 2006 invasion of Somalia was coordinated using US bases throughout the region. The arrival of AFRICOM will effectively reinforce efforts to replace the popular Islamic Courts Union of Somalia with the oil industry–friendly Transitional Federal Government. Meanwhile, the persistent Western calls for "humanitarian intervention" into the Darfur region of Sudan sets up another possibility for military engagement to deliver regime change in another Islamic state rich in oil reserves.

Hunt warns that this sort of "support" is only bound to increase as rhetoric of stabilizing Africa makes the dailies, copied directly out of official AFRICOM press releases. Readers of the mainstream media can expect to encounter more frequent usage of terms like "genocide" and "misguided." He notes that already corporate media decry China's human rights record and support for Sudan and Zimbabwe while ignoring the ongoing violations of Western corporations engaged in the plunder of natural resources, the pollution other peoples' homelands, and the "shoring up" of repressive regimes.

In FY 2005 the Trans-Sahara Counter Terrorism Initiative received $16 million; in FY 2006, nearly $31 million. A big increase is expected in 2008, with the administration pushing for $100 million each year for five years. With the passage of AFRICOM and continued promotion of the Global War on Terror, Congressional funding is likely to increase significantly.

In the end, regardless of whether it's US or Chinese domination over Africa, the blood spilled will be African. Hunt concludes, "It does not require a crystal ball or great imagination to realize what the increased militarization of the continent through AFRICOM will bring to the peoples of Africa."

UPDATE BY BRYAN HUNT

By spring 2007, US Department of Energy data showed that the United States now imports more oil from the continent of Africa than from the country of Saudi Arabia. While this statistic may be of surprise to the majority, provided such information even crosses their radar, it's certainly not the case for those figures who have been pushing for increased US military engagement on that continent for some time now, as my report documented. These import levels will rise.

In the first few months following the official announcement of AFRICOM, details are still few. It's expected that the combatant command will be operational as a subunit of EUCOM by October 2007, transitioning to a full-fledged stand-alone command some twelve months later. This will most likely entail the re-locating of AFRICOM headquarters from Stuttgart, Germany, where EUCOM is headquartered, to an African host country.

In April, US officials were traversing the continent to present their sales pitch for AFRICOM and to gauge official and public reaction. Initial perceptions are, not surprisingly, negative and highly suspect, given the history of US military involvement throughout the world, and Africa's long and bitter experience with colonizers.

Outside of a select audience, reaction in the United States has barely even registered. First of all, Africa is one of the least-covered continents in US media. And when African nations do draw media attention, coverage typically centers on catastrophe, conflict, or corruption, and generally features some form of benevolent foreign intervention, be it financial and humanitarian aid, or stern official posturing couched as paternal concerns over human rights. But US military activity on the continent largely goes unnoticed. This was recently evidenced by the sparse reporting on military support for the invasion of Somalia to rout the Islamic Courts Union and reinstall the unpopular warlords who had earlier divided up the country. The Pentagon went so far as to declare the operation a blueprint for future engagements.

The DOD states that a primary component of AFRICOM's mission will be to professionalize indigenous militaries to ensure stability, security, and accountable governance throughout Africa's various states and regions. Stability refers to establishing and maintaining order, and accountability, of course, refers to US interests. This year alone, 1,400 African military officers are anticipated to complete International Military Education and Training programs at US military schools.

Combine this tasking of militarization with an increased civilian component in AFRICOM emphasizing imported conceptions of "democracy promotion" and "capacity-building" and African autonomy and sovereignty are quick to suffer. Kenyans, for example, are currently finding themselves in this position.

It is hoped that, by drawing attention to the growing US footprint on Africa now, a contextual awareness of these issues can be useful to, at the very least, help mitigate some of the damages that will surely follow. At the moment, there is little public consciousness of AFRICOM and very few sources of information outside of official narratives. Widening the public dialogue on this topic is the first step toward addressing meaningful responses.

4

Frenzy of Increasingly Destructive Trade Agreements

Sources:
Oxfam International, March 2007
Title: "Singing Away The Future"
IPS coverage of Oxfam Report March 20, 2007
Title: "Free Trade Enslaving Poor Countries"
Author: Sanjay Suri

Student Researcher: Ann Marie O'Toole
Faculty Evaluator: Peter Phillips, Ph.D.

The Oxfam report, "Signing Away the Future," reveals that the US and European Union (EU) are vigorously pursuing increasingly destructive regional and bilateral trade and investment agreements outside the auspices of the WTO. These agreements are requiring enormous irreversible concessions from developing countries, while offering almost nothing in return. Faster and deeper, the US and EU are demanding unprecedented tariff reductions, sometimes to nothing, as the US and EU dump subsidized agricultural goods on undeveloped countries (see story #21), plunging local farmers into desperate poverty. Meanwhile the US and EU provide themselves with high tariffs and stringent import quotas to protect their own producers. Unprecedented loss of livelihood, displacement, slave labor, along with spiraling degradation of human rights and environments are resulting as economic governance is forced from governments of developing countries, and taken over by unaccountable multinational firms.

During 2006, more than one hundred developing countries were involved in FTA or Bilateral Investment Treaty (BIT) negotiations. "An average of two treaties are signed every week," the report says, "Virtually no country, however poor, has been left out."

Much of the recent debate and controversy over trade negotiations has revolved around the increasingly devastating trade-distorting practices of rich countries versus the developing countries' needs for food security and industrial development. The new generation of agreements, however, extends far beyond this traditional area of trade policy—imposing a damaging set of binding rules in intellectual property, services, and investment with much deeper consequences for development and impacts on the poor.

Double standards in the intellectual-property rights chapters of most trade agreements are glaring. As new agreements limit developing countries' access to patented technology and medicines—while failing to protect traditional knowledge—the public-health consequences are staggering. The US-Colombia FTA is expected to reduce access to medicines by 40 percent and the US-Peru FTA is expected to leave 700,000 to 900,000 Peruvians without access to affordable medicines.

US and EU FTAs also require the adoption of plant-breeder rights that remove the right to share seeds among indigenous farmers. The livelihood of the world's poorest farmers is thus made even more vulnerable, while profit margins of the world's largest agribusinesses continue to climb. US FTAs are now pushing for patents on plants, which will not only limit the rights of farmers to exchange or sell seeds, but also forbid them to save and reuse seed they have grown themselves for generations. Under US FTAs including DR-CAFTA, US–Peru and US–Colombia FTAs, developing-country governments will no longer be able to reject a patent application because a firm fails to indicate the origin of a plant or show proof of consent for its use from a local community. As a result, communities could find themselves forced to pay for patented plant varieties based on genetic resources from their own soil.

New rules also pose a threat to essential services as FTAs allow foreign investors to take ownership of healthcare, education, water, and public utilities.

Investment chapters of new FTAs and BITs allow foreign investors to sue for lost profits, including anticipated future profits, if governments change regulations, even when such reforms are in the public interest. These rules undermine the sovereignty of developing nations, transferring power from governments to largely unaccountable multinational firms. A growing number of investment chapters and treaties further tip the scales of justice by preventing governments from screening or regulating foreign investment—banning the use of all 'performance requirements' in all sectors including mining, manufacturing, and services.

More than 170 countries have signed international investment agreements that provide foreign investors with the right to turn immediately to international investor-state arbitration to settle disputes, without first trying to resolve the matter in national courts. Such arbitration fails to consider public interest, basing decisions exclusively on commercial law.

Not only is the legal basis for investment arbitration loaded against public interest, so are the proceedings. Despite the fact that many arbitration panels are hosted at the World Bank and the United Nations, the investment arbitration system is shrouded in secrecy. It is virtually impossible to find out what cases are being heard, let alone the outcome or rationale for decisions. As a result, there is no body of case decisions to inform governments of developing countries when drafting investments agreements.

Oxfam notes that the only group privy to this information is an increasingly powerful select group of commercial lawyers, whose fees often place them out of reach of developing-country governments. These lawyers, according to the Oxfam report, are eager to advise foreign investors regarding opportunities to claim compensation from developing countries under international investment agreements.

Strong opposition is growing to the political asymmetry inherent in these bilateral trade and investment agreements (see stories #8, #19, and #21). As Oxfam notes, "It is in nobody's long-term interest to have a global economy that perpetuates social, economic, and environmental injustice."

UPDATE BY LAURA RUSU OF OXFAM INTERNATIONAL

While real progress toward achieving a development-friendly outcome in the World Trade Organization's Doha Round is still quite elusive, the negotiation of bilateral and regional free trade agreements (FTAs) that would undermine development continues at an unabated pace.

In the United States, the new Democratic leadership in Congress recently negotiated changes in the areas of labor, environment, and intellectual property in regard to access to medicines that are to be incorporated into the completed FTAs awaiting Congressional ratification. If implemented as agreed, these changes would mean important progress in enforcing core International Labor Organization standards and multilateral environmental agreements, and in promoting public health over private profits by reducing onerous protections for pharmaceutical monopolies. Still, more must be done in these areas, and harmful provisions remain in several other areas that will adversely affect developing countries, particularly the poor.

Without further changes, the FTAs create a profoundly unfair situation in which the US provides massive domestic agricultural supports and subsidies that allow products to be exported below their cost of production, while developing country trading partners are left with no means of protection. With large portions of their populations dependent upon agriculture for their livelihoods, the FTAs provide no effective safeguard to protect poor farmers from unfair competition. In addition, investment rules in the FTAs will hinder local and national governments from directing foreign investment so that it contributes to sustainable development. The investment chapter will give foreign companies leeway to challenge investment regulations, such as laws to protect the environment and public health. These and other provisions would deny developing countries the policy space needed to further their own development.

The US Administration hopes to bring FTAs with Peru, Panama, Colombia and Korea to a vote this year, although it remains doubtful whether there would be sufficient Congressional support to move the latter two. Congressional leadership is insisting that Colombia must also address its serious problems of violence and impunity, particularly as suffered by trade unionists, and has raised market-access concerns with regard to South Korea.

In a similar vein, the European Union has proceeded with FTA negotiations with African, Caribbean, and Pacific countries by pushing forward negotiating texts that will undermine the ability of poor countries to effectively govern their economies, protect their poorest people, improve livelihoods, and create new jobs. Going beyond the provisions negotiated at a multilateral level, the EU is making requests that would impose far-reaching, hard-to-reverse rules in the areas of market access, agriculture, services and intellectual property. At the same time, the EU is proceeding to open formal negotiations with Central American countries for an FTA that would impose similar rules that undermine development. A similar agreement with Andean countries is expected to follow, and plans have been announced to open negotiations with ASEAN, India, and South Korea. In all of these negotiations, the EU, like the US, is failing to put development first.

For more information, please see http://www.oxfamamerica.org.

5
Human Traffic Builds US Embassy in Iraq

Source:
CorpWatch, October 17, 2007
Title: "A US Fortress Rises in Baghdad: Asian Workers Trafficked to Build World's Largest Embassy"
Author: David Phinney

Student Researcher: Kristen Kebler and Angela Purcaro
Faculty Evaluator: Andrew Roth, Ph.D.

The enduring monument to US liberation and democracy in Iraq will be the most expensive and heavily fortified embassy in the world—and is being built by a Kuwait contractor repeatedly accused of using forced labor trafficked from South Asia under US contracts. The $592 million, 104-acre fortress equal in size to the Vatican City is scheduled to open in September 2007. With a highly secretive contract awarded by the US State Department, First Kuwaiti Trading & Contracting has joined the ranks of Halliburton/KBR in Iraq by using bait-and-switch recruiting practices. Thousands of citizens from countries that have banned travel or work in Iraq are being tricked, smuggled into brutal and inhumane labor camps, and subjected to months of forced servitude—all in the middle of the US-controlled Green Zone, "right under the nose of the US State Department."

Though Associated Press reports that, "The 5,500 Americans and Iraqis working at the embassy are far more numerous than at any other US mission worldwide,"[1] there is no mention in corporate media of the 3,000 South Asian laborers working for contractors in dangerous and abysmal living and working conditions.

One such contractor is First Kuwaiti Trading and Contracting. FKTC has procured several billion dollars in US construction contracts since the war began in March 2003. Much of its work is performed by cheap labor hired from South Asia. The company currently employs an estimated 7,500 foreign laborers in theaters of war.

American FKTC employees report having witnessed the issuance of false boarding passes to Dubai, and passport seizure from planeloads of South Asian workers, who were instead routed to war-torn Baghdad. Former US Embassy construction manager for FKTC, John Owen, disclosed to author David Phinney that the deception had all the appearance of smuggling workers into Iraq.

On April 4, 2006, the Pentagon issued a contracting directive following an investigation that officially confirmed that contractors in Iraq, many working as subcontractors to Halliburton/KBR, were illegally confiscating worker passports, using deceptive bait-and-switch hiring practices, and charging recruiting fees that indebted low-paid migrant workers for many months or even years to their employers.

Section 1. (U) of the Pentagon directive states, "An inspection of contracting activities supporting DoD in Iraq revealed evidence of illegal confiscation of worker (Third Country National) passports by contractors/subcontractors; deceptive hiring practices and excessive recruiting fees, substandard worker living conditions at some sites, circumvention of Iraqi immigration procedures by contractors/subcontractors and lack of mandatory trafficking in persons awareness training. This FRAGO [fragmentary order] establishes responsibilities within MNF-I for combating trafficking in persons."

An April 19, 2006 memorandum from Joint Contracting Command in Baghdad to All Contractors again states that, "Evidence indicates a widespread practice of withholding employee passports to, among other things, prevent employees 'jumping' to other employers. . . . All contractors engaging in the above mentioned practice are directed to cease and desist in this practice immediately."

The Pentagon has yet to announce, however, any penalty for those found to be in violation of US labor trafficking laws or contract requirements.

In a resignation letter dated June 2006, Owen told FKTC and US State Department officials that his managers at the US Embassy site regularly beat migrant workers, demonstrated little regard for worker safety, and routinely breached security. He also complained of poor sanitation, squalid living conditions and medical malpractice in labor camps where several thousand low-paid migrant workers, recruited from the Philippines, India, and Pakistan lived. Those workers, Owen noted, earned as little as $10 to $30 for a twelve-hour workday.

Rory Mayberry, a medic subcontracted to FKTC to attend construction crews at the Embassy, shares similar complaints about treatment of migrant laborers. In reports made available to the US State Department, the US Army, and FKTC, Mayberry called for the closure of the onsite medical clinic, listing dozens of serious safety hazards, unsanitary conditions, as well as routine negligence and malpractice. He furthermore called for an investigation into deaths that he suspected resulted from medical malpractice. Mayberry is not aware of any follow-up on his allegations.

Owen says that State Department officials supervising the US Embassy project are aware of abuse, but apparently do nothing. He recalls, "Once when seventeen workers climbed the wall of the construction site to escape, a State Department official helped round them up and put them in virtual lockdown."

Phinney says that more FKTC employees are stepping forward to say that Owen's and Mayberry's testimonies "only begin to scratch the surface" of the conditions workers are forced to endure in building this monument to US liberation and democracy in Iraq.

Citation:
1. Associated Press, "New US Embassy in Iraq Cloaked in Mystery," MSNBC, April 14, 2006.

UPDATE BY DAVID PHINNEY

When I first heard that Project Censored would recognize this story on the low-wage migrant laborers from South Asia building the US embassy in Baghdad, I admit I felt the story was a failure. Allegations of forced labor, lousy treatment of workers and beatings struck me as something that should rise to the level of torture at Abu Ghraib. Despite what appears to be a whitewash review of the embassy project by the State Department Inspector General that exonerated the contractor—even though more than a dozen sources on the site say conditions were abysmal—I am now encouraged by a recent effort at the US Justice Department to investigate allegations of labor trafficking and other matters. But the problem of labor abuse has been found to be "widespread" among contractors in the theater of war in Iraq. Unfortunately, not one contractor has been penalized—in fact, many are being rewarded with new US-funded contracts. That is a crime to humanity that may haunt the United States for years to come.

6

Operation FALCON Raids

Sources:

SourceWatch, November 18, 2006
Title: "Operation Falcon"
Author: Artificial Intelligence

Ukernet, February 26, 2007
Title: "Operation Falcon and the Looming Police State"
Author: Mike Whitney

Student Researcher: Erica Haikara and Celest Winders
Faculty Evaluator: Ron Lopez, Ph.D.

Under the code name Operation FALCON (Federal and Local Cops Organized Nationally) three federally coordinated mass arrests occurred between April 2005 and October 2006. In an unprecedented move, more than 30,000 "fugitives" were arrested in the largest dragnets in the nation's history. The operations directly involved over 960 agencies (state, local, and federal) and were the brainchild of Attorney General Alberto Gonzales and US Marshal's Director Ben Reyna. The DoJ supplied television networks government-shot action videotape of Marshals and local cops raiding homes and breaking down doors, "targeting the worst of the worst criminals on the run," emphasizing suspected sex offenders. Yet less than ten percent of the total 30,150 were suspected sex offenders and less than two percent owned firearms. The press has not asked, "Who were the others?" And to date, the US Marshal's office has issued no public statement as to whether the people arrested in Operation Falcon have been processed or released. Author Mike Whitney cautions that Attorney General Gonzales has little interest in the petty offenders who were netted in this extraordinary crackdown. This action is instead, he warns, a practice roundup in the move toward martial law.

Altogether, there were three FALCON Operations, each netting roughly 10,000 criminal suspects. Between April 4–10, 2005, FALCON I swept up 10,340 fugitives in the largest nationwide mass arrest (to that date) in American history. Alberto Gonzalez proudly announced on April 15 through corporate media, "Operation FALCON is an excellent example of President Bush's direction and the Justice Department's dedication to deal both with the terrorist threat and traditional violent crime. This joint effort shows the commitment of our federal, state, and local partners to make our neighborhoods safer, and it has led to the highest number of arrests ever recorded for a single initiative of its kind. We will use all of our Nation's law enforcement resources to serve the people, to pursue justice, and to make our streets and Nation safer."

Operation FALCON II, carried out the week of April 17–23, 2006, arrested another 9,037 individuals from twenty-seven states mostly west of the Mississippi River. Operation FALCON III, conducted during the week of October 22–28, 2006, netted another 10,733 fugitives in twenty-four states east of the Mississippi River.

The US Marshals Service has not yet disclosed the names of the people arrested in these massive sweeps nor of what crimes they were accused. We have no way of knowing whether they were provided with due process of law, where they are now, or whether they have been abused while in custody.

SourceWatch contributors further ask for clarification, "Although Attorney General Gonzales stated on April 15, 2005 that Operation FALCON was 'an excellent example of President Bush's direction and the Justice Department's dedication to deal both with the terrorist threat and traditional violent crime,' where is the connection between the Operation FALCON roundups and catching terrorists?

Why did police wait for federally orchestrated raids to arrest known sex offenders and suspected murders? Why were state and federal agencies integrated with local law enforcement to simply carry out routine police work?"

The media played an essential role in concealing the important details of the Operation. In fact, the non-critical "cookie cutter" articles which appeared in newspapers across the country suggest that the media may have collaborated directly with the Justice Department. (see Chapter 9, Fake News) Whitney notes that nearly identical "news" segments and articles put the best possible spin on a story that most Americans might find deeply disturbing, and perhaps frightening.

While mass militarized police roundups make little sense as a method of apprehending fugitives, the FALCON program does make sense as a means of effectively setting up a chain-of-command structure that radiates from the Justice Department and relocates the levers of control to Washington where they can be manned by members of the administration. Whitney warns that the plan behind the FALCON program appears to have been devised to enhance the powers of the "unitary" executive by putting state and local law enforcement under federal supervision, ready for the institution of martial law (see story #2.)

UPDATE BY MIKE WHITNEY

Operation FALCON presents the first time in US history that all of the domestic police agencies have been put under the direct control of the federal government. The implications for American democracy are quite profound.

Operation FALCON serves no purpose except to centralize power and establish the basic contours of an American police state. It is not an effective way of apprehending criminals.

For the most part, the media completely ignored FALCON. In fact, these extraordinary police-state sweeps did not elicit even one editorial or one column-inch of commentary from any journalist in the country. Following the government's version of events, the story was simply brushed aside as trivial. For those who care to explore the media's true role in undermining the fundamental rights of Americans; FALCON is probably a good place to begin. It illustrates how the media deliberately obscures facts that do not serve the overall interests of the state.

The last FALCON operation was carried out on October 28,

2006. Since then, the project has been put on "hold," presumably until some time in the future when it will be reactivated by presidential decree. The precedents have now been established for law enforcement agencies across the nation to be taken over by the chief executive at a moment's notice. If there is another terrorist attack within the United States, or the outbreak of an epidemic, or a natural disaster on the scale of Hurricane Katrina; we can expect that President Bush will consolidate his power by asserting direct control over all of the various federal, state, and local police agencies. Eventually, we will see that FALCON was organized with that very purpose in mind.

Recent changes to the Insurrection Act of 1807 as well as to the Posse Comitatus Act of 1878 allow President Bush to declare martial law at his own discretion and to take control of the National Guard from the state governors. That means that Bush now has a complete monopoly on all the means of organized violence in the country.

With the aid of the corporate media and an alliance of far-right organizations, Bush has successfully removed all the traditional obstacles to absolute power. The groundwork has been laid for an American dictatorship. FALCON is just one small part of that much larger plan.

UPDATE BY ARTIFICIAL INTELLIGENCE

A more recent and less publicized sweep was made March 7, 2007, in Baltimore, with the arrest of about two hundred fugitives. The rationale for this sweep is more puzzling, perhaps, as it was the only city involved. This sweep received only local media attention.

Numerous questions, as stated in the Operation FALCON article, remain unanswered. The mainstream press does not appear to be interested in exploring beyond the initial sweep events.

Both House and Senate committees on the judiciary and government oversight are digging into DoJ operations due to the US attorney firings and politicization of the Department, with all roads leading to the White House. It is not unreasonable to expect that these sweeps may eventually come under investigation as well.

The mainstream press, to my knowledge, has not responded at all to my *SourceWatch* coverage of this story. The press coverage that Operation FALCON received appears to be limited to DoJ and USMS news releases with the addition of an occasional local interest story.

Information on the fate of the 30,000 plus who were arrested is conspicuous by its absence.

Additional information on this story should be available from both the DoJ and USMS. In reality, it most likely will not be, as neither has provided any updates. The *SourceWatch* article will continue to be updated when or if additional information becomes available.

7

Behind Blackwater Inc.

Source:
Democracy Now! January 26, 2007
Title: "Our Mercenaries in Iraq: Blackwater Inc and Bush's Undeclared Surge"
Author: Jeremy Scahill

Student Researcher: Sverre Tysl
Faculty Evaluator: Noel Byrne, Ph.D.

The company that most embodies the privatization of the military industrial complex—a primary part of the Project for a New American Century and the neoconservative revolution is the private security firm Blackwater. Blackwater is the most powerful mercenary firm in the world, with 20,000 soldiers, the world's largest private military base, a fleet of twenty aircraft, including helicopter gunships, and a private intelligence division. The firm is also manufacturing its own surveillance blimps and target systems.

Blackwater is headed by a very right-wing Christian-supremist and ex-Navy Seal named Erik Prince, whose family has had deep neo-conservative connections. Bush's latest call for voluntary civilian military corps to accommodate the "surge" will add to over half a billion dollars in federal contracts with Blackwater, allowing Prince to create a private army to defend Christendom around the world against Muslims and others.

One of the last things Dick Cheney did before leaving office as Defense Secretary under George H. W. Bush was to commission a Halliburton study on how to privatize the military bureaucracy. That study effectively created the groundwork for a continuing war profiteer bonanza.

During the Clinton years, Erik Prince envisioned a project that would take advantage of anticipated military outsourcing. Blackwater began in 1996 as a private military training facility, with an executive board of former Navy Seals and Elite Special Forces, in the Great Dismal Swamp of North Carolina. A decade later it is the most powerful mercenary firm in the world, embodying what the Bush administration views as "the necessary revolution in military affairs"—the outsourcing of armed forces.

In his 2007 State of the Union address Bush asked Congress to authorize an increase in the size of our active Army and Marine Corps by 92,000 in the next five years. He continued, "A second task we can take on together is to design and establish a volunteer civilian reserve corps. Such a corps would function much like our military reserve. It would ease the burden on the Armed Forces by allowing us to hire civilians with critical skills to serve on missions abroad when America needs them."

This is, however, precisely what the administration has already done—largely, Jeremy Scahill points out, behind the backs of the American people. Private contractors currently constitute the second-largest "force" in Iraq. At last count, there were about 100,000 contractors in Iraq, 48,000 of which work as private soldiers, according to a Government Accountability Office report. These soldiers have operated with almost no oversight or effective legal constraints and are politically expedient, as contractor deaths go uncounted in the official toll. With Prince calling for the creation of a "contractor brigade" before military audiences, the Bush administration has found a back door for engaging in an undeclared expansion of occupation.

Blackwater currently has about 2,300 personnel actively deployed in nine countries and is aggressively expanding its presence inside US borders. They provide the security for US diplomats in Iraq, guarding everyone from Paul Bremer and John Negroponte to the current US ambassador, Zalmay Khalilzad. They're training troops in Afghanistan and have been active in the Caspian Sea, where they set up a Special Forces base miles from the Iranian border. According to reports they are currently negotiating directly with the Southern Sudanese regional government to start training the Christian forces of Sudan.

Blackwater's connections are impressive. Joseph Schmitz, the former Pentagon Inspector General, whose job was to police the war contractor bonanza, has moved on to become the vice chairman of the Prince Group, Blackwater's parent company, and the general counsel for Blackwater.

Bush recently hired Fred Fielding, Blackwater's former lawyer, to replace Harriet Miers as his top lawyer; and Ken Starr, the former Whitewater prosecutor who led the impeachment charge against President Clinton, is now Blackwater's counsel of record and has filed briefs with Supreme Court to fight wrongful death lawsuits brought against Blackwater.

Cofer Black, thirty-year CIA veteran and former head of CIA's counterterrorism center, credited with spearheading the extraordinary rendition program after 9/11, is now senior executive at Blackwater and perhaps its most powerful operative.

Prince and other Blackwater executives have been major bankrollers of the President, of former House Majority Leader, Tom DeLay, and of former Senator, Rick Santorum. Senator John Warner, the former head of the Senate Armed Services Committee, called Blackwater, "our silent partner in the global war on terror."

8

KIA: The US Neoliberal Invasion of India

Sources:

Democracy Now! December 13, 2006
Title: "Vandana Shiva on Farmer Suicides, the US-India Nuclear Deal, Wal-Mart in India"
Author: Vandana Shiva with Amy Goodman

Global Research, October 9, 2006
Title: "Genetically Modified Seeds: Women in India Take on Monsanto"
Author: Arun Shrivastava

SciDev.Net
Title: "Sowing Trouble: India's 'Second Green Revolution'"
Author: Suman Sahai

Student Researchers: Jonathan Stoumen and Michael Januleski
Faculty Evaluator: Phil Beard, Ph.D.

Farmers' cooperatives in India are defending the nation's food security and the future of Indian farmers against the neoliberal invasion of genetically modified (GM) seed. As many as 28,000 Indian farmers have committed suicide over the last decade as a result of debt incurred from failed GM crops and competition with subsidized US crops, yet when India's Prime Minister Singh met with President Bush in March 2006 to finalize nuclear agreements, they also signed the Indo-US Knowledge Initiative on Agriculture (KIA), backed by Monsanto, Archer Daniels Midland (ADM), and Wal-Mart. The KIA allows for the grab of India's seed sector by Monsanto, of its trade sector by giant agribusiness ADM and Cargill, and its retail sector by Wal-Mart.

Though the contours of KIA have been kept so secret that neither senior Indian politicians nor the scientific community know its details, it is clear that Prime Minister Singh has agreed to sacrifice India's agriculture sector to pay for US concessions in the nuclear field.

In one of very few public statements by a US government official regarding KIA, Nicholas Burns, Under Secretary of State for Political Affairs, states, "While the civilian nuclear initiative has garnered the most attention . . . Our first priority is to continue giving governmental support to the huge growth in business between the Indian and American private sectors. Singh has also challenged the United States to help launch a second green revolution in India's vast agricultural heartland by enlisting the help of America's great land-grant institutions."[1]

Vandana Shiva translates, "These are twin programs about a market grab and a security alignment . . . Burns announced that while the nuclear deal is the cutting edge, what the US is really seeking is agricultural markets and real estate markets . . . to take over the land of people, not through a market mechanism, but using the state and an old colonial law of land acquisition to grab the land by force."

Through KIA, Monsanto and the US have asked for unhindered access to India's gene banks, along with a change in India's intellectual property laws to allow patents on seeds and genes, and to dilute provisions that protect farmers' rights. A combination of physical access to India's gene banks and a possible new intellectual property law that allows seed patents will in essence deliver India's genetic wealth into US hands. This would be a severe blow to India's food security and self-sufficiency.

At the same time KIA has paved the way for Wal-Mart's plans to open five hundred stores in India, starting in August 2007, which will compound the outsourcing of India's food supply and threaten 14 million small family venders with loss of livelihood.

"This is not about 'free trade,'" Shiva explains, "Today's trade system, especially in agriculture, is dishonest, and dishonesty has become a war against farmers. It's become a genocide."

Farmers are, however, organizing to protect themselves against this economic invasion by maintaining traditional seed banks and setting up exemplary systems of community agrarian support. In response to the flood of debilitating debt tied to GM/hybrid seeds and the toxic petroleum based fertilizers and pesticides these crops depend on, one woman in the small village of Palarum says, "We do not buy seeds from the market because we suspect they may be contaminated with genetically engineered or terminator seeds." Instead village women save and trade hardy traditional seeds that have evolved over centuries to produce low-maintenance, nutritious "crops of truth."

Each village in this rural area of India has formed its own community-based organization called a *sangham*. Seventy-two sanghams are part of a regional federation. These sanghams form an informal social security network that, through the maintenance of seed banks, will come to the rescue of individuals or entire villages in times of crop failure. Every member of the community has access to food and is assured of some work even if landless. The federation furthermore trains students in skills such as carpentry, computing, pottery, bookbinding, veterinary science, herbal medicine, sewing, farming, waste management, and agro-forestry.

Author Arun Shrivastava comments that, "These seventy-two villages were once horizontally and vertically stratified along caste, class, and religious lines. Food scarcity was endemic, people were malnourished, the majority worked as unskilled day wagers. Today they are cohesive, interdependent. I did not see one malnourished person. Rarely do people go to urban centers to seek work." Shrivastava continues, "The community is the most important entity that can help us ensure food and nutrition security . . . The right of access to natural resources—land, rivers, forests, air, and everything that Nature has given us, including seeds, is the fundamental right of the communities, not of the corporations or the state or the individual. No corporation has the right to expropriate what Nature gave us."

Professor of genetics Suman Sahai concludes, "India must be cautious that it does not become the dumping ground for a technology and its controversial products that have been rejected in many parts of the world and whose safety and usefulness remain questionable . . . Food security is an integral part of national security. All India's efforts in the nuclear arena to shore up its national security goals will be undermined if it allows itself to become insecure in the matter of food."

Citation:

1. Nicholas Burns, "'Heady Times' For India And the US," *Washington Post*, April 29, 2007.

UPDATE BY ARUN SHRIVASTAVA

Nature has given us seeds and 'crops of truth' that do not require any tending but give us nutrition at no or low-cost. This knowledge needs to be rapidly disseminated; soon our lives may depend on it.

With current farming and food distribution systems it takes ten calories of fossil fuel energy to transport one calorie of food from farm to fork. That is unsustainable now; the era of cheap oil is effectively finished. Since we are already past peak oil, we all must learn to ensure food and nutrition security for our family and community. We will have to learn basic skills like conserving seeds, growing nutritious food, and medicinal crops without chemicals and machines. We will need more cohesive and interdependent local communities, like the women of Zaheerabad have shown.

The women of Zaheerabad save seeds in community-held seed banks and grow nutrition-dense food through a system that ensures health and livelihood for all. They have established how self-sufficient, sustainable communities might live in a post-carbon world.

A handful of multi-national corporations are patenting seeds. These genetically modified (GM) seeds neither increase yield nor reduce costs nor enhance nutritive content of foods, nor reduce dependence on oil. The seeds of deception have destroyed farmers in India, the US, and elsewhere.

Patenting ensures monopoly control while subverting farmers' right to save seeds; it is antithetical to natural rights of local communities. The Indo-US Knowledge Initiative in Agriculture covertly seeks to gain access and control over community-held seeds.

Since publication of the article, Deccan Development Society (DDS) has extended the model to twenty-six more villages but the community FM radio station remains silent.

At People's SAARC (South Asia Association for Regional Cooperation) summit in Kathmandu (March 2007) participants voted for a "GM-free South Asia," community control over seeds and protection of South-Asian biodiversity. Over six million farmers requested the Supreme Court of India (April 2007) to ban open field trials of GM seeds because of the dangers of irreversible contamination of community-held seeds and adverse impact on health.

The mainstream media is silent. They don't have space for disseminating information that will save us from disease and starvation. These are unglamorous issues.

For more information on growing crops of truth and the need for a new social order, the following are ideal sources:

1. The Web site of Deccan Development Society (DDS), initiator and facilitator of the sanghams, is http://www.ddsindia.com/www/default.asp. Contact PV Satheesh, Director of Zaheerabad Project.

2. Beej Bachao Andolan (BBA, Save the Seeds Movement) is a well-known movement of farmers who save traditional seeds of the Himalayan region. Contact Biju Negi, negi.biju@gmail.com.

3. For information on growing food for health and personal freedom, go to www.soilandhealth.org.

4. For information on threats posed by multinational seeds firms, go to www.gmwatch.org and www.mindfully.org.

5. *The Seeds of Deception* by Jeffrey Smith discusses how GM foods, introduced in the US in 1993 without proper biosafety assessment, endanger our health. It is available at www.seedsofdeception.com. See also the research of Dr. Irina Ermakova at http://irina-ermakova.by.ru/eng/articles.html/, and of Dr. Arpad Pusztai: http://www.freenetpages.co.uk/hp/a.pusztai/.

6. "*Heartless in the Heartland*" is the ghastly story of how Monsanto blackmailed US farmers not to save their seeds. See www.mindfully.org.

7. For an excellent summary, watch *The Future of Food*, a documentary by Deborah Koons Garcia, downloadable from www.mindfully.org.

8. For discussions on peak oil and food security, see Richard Heinberg's *Fifty Million Farmers*, published on November 17, 2006, available at http://www.energybulletin.net/22584.html. Also visit the Association for the Study of Peak Oil, managed by Dr. Colin Campbell, one of world's leading oil experts, at http://www.peakoil.net.

9. My two recent papers also shed light on the subject: "The attack on our seeds," a related article published by *Farmer's Forum* in India (contact the editor at bksnd@airtelbroadband.in), and "The Silent War on the People of India," which can be found at http://www.thepeoplesvoice.org/cgi-bin/blogs/voices.php/2007/03/22/the_silent _war_on_the_people_of_india.

UPDATE BY VANDANA SHIVA

The Indo-US Knowledge Initiative on Agriculture impacts 650 million farmers of India and 40 million small retailers and it is redefining the relationships between people in the two biggest democracies in the world.

A new movement on retail democracy has begun in India that is bringing together small shopkeepers, street hawkers, trade unions and farmers unions. On August 9, 2007, which is Quit India Day, the movement will be organizing actions across the country telling Wal-Mart to leave India.

For more information, visit our website at www.navdanya.org.

9
Privatization of America's Infrastructure

Sources:

Mother Jones, February 2007
Title; "The Highwaymen"
Author: Daniel Schulman with James Ridgeway

Human Events, June 12, 2006
Title: "Bush Administration Quietly Plans NAFTA Super Highway"
Author: Jerome R. Corsi

Student Researcher: Rachel Icaza and Ioana Lupu
Faculty Evaluator: Marco Calavita, Ph.D.

We will soon be paying Wall Street investors, Australian bankers, and Spanish contractors for the privilege of driving on American roads, as more than twenty states have enacted legislation allowing public-private partnerships to build and run highways. Investment firms including Goldman Sachs, Morgan Stanley, and the Carlyle Group are approaching state politicians with advice to sell off public highway and transportation infrastructure. When advising state officials on the future of this vital public asset, these investment firms fail to mention that their sole purpose is to pick up infrastructure at the lowest price possible in order to maximize returns for their investors. Investors, most often foreign companies, are charging tolls and insisting on "noncompete" clauses that limit governments from expanding or improving nearby roads.

In 1956, President Eisenhower signed the Federal-Aid Highway Act, which called for the federal and state governments to build 41,000 miles of high-quality roads across the nation, over rivers and gorges, swamps and deserts, over and through vast mountain ranges, in what would later be called the "greatest public works project in human history." Eisenhower considered the interstate highway system so vital to the public interest that he authorized the federal government to assume 90 percent of the massive cost.

Fifty years later, states are selling off our nation's enormous, and aging, infrastructure to private investors. Proponents are celebrating these transactions as a no-pain, all-gain way to off-load maintenance expenses and increase highway-building funds without raising taxes. Opponents are lambasting these plans as a major turn toward handing the nation's valuable common asset over to private firms whose fidelity is to stockholders—not to the public transportation system or the people who use it.

On June 29, 2006, Indiana's governor Mitch Daniels announced that Indiana had received $3.8 billion from a foreign consortium made up of the Spanish construction firm Cintra and the Macquarie Infrastructure Group (MIG) of Australia. In exchange the state handed over operation of a 157-mile Indiana toll road for the next seventy-five years. With the consortium collecting the tolls, which will eventually rise far higher, the privatized road should generate $11 billion for MIG-Cintra over the course of the contract.

In September 2005, Daniels solicited bids for the project, with Goldman Sachs serving as the state's financial adviser—a role that would net the bank a $20 million advisory fee. When Goldman Sachs, one of the nation's most active and most profitable investment banks, with deep connections to Washington, began advising Indiana on selling its toll road, it failed to mention the fact that, even as it was advising Indiana on how to get the best return, its Australian subsidiary's mutual funds were ratcheting up their positions in MIG—becoming de facto investors in the deal.

Many are suspicious that governors like Daniels across the nation are taking questionable advice from corporate investment banks—and from Washington.

Despite public concerns, privatization of US transportation infrastructure has the full backing of the Bush administration. Tyler Duvall, the US Department of Transportation's assistant secretary for transportation policy, says the DoT has raised the idea with "almost every state" government and is working on sample legislation that states can use for such projects. Across the nation, there is now talk of privatizing the New York Thruway to the Ohio, Pennsylvania, and New Jersey turnpikes, as well as of inviting the private sector to build and operate highways and bridges from Alabama to Alaska.

In Texas, Governor Rick Perry still refuses to release details of a $1.3 billion contract his administration signed with Cintra for a forty-mile toll road from Austin to Seguin, or of an enormous $184 billion proposal to build a 4,000-mile network of toll roads through Texas.

It is known, however, that the Bush administration is quietly advancing the plan to build a huge ten-lane NAFTA Super Highway through the heart of the US along Interstate 35, from the Mexican border at Laredo, Texas to the Canadian border north of Duluth, Minnesota, financed largely through public-private partnerships. The Texas Department of Transportation will oversee the Trans-Texas Corridor as the first leg of the NAFTA Super Highway, which will be leased to the Cintra consortium as a privately operated toll road. Construction is slated to begin in 2007.

Authors Daniel Schulman and James Ridgeway warn that, just as the creation of a National Highway system promised to "change the face of America," in Eisenhower's words, so too could its demise.

10

Vulture Funds Threaten Poor Nations' Debt Relief

Source:

BBC Newsnight, February 14, 2007
Title: "Vulture Fund Threat to Third World"
Author: Greg Palast with Meirion Jones

Student Researcher: Jenifer German
Faculty Evaluator: Robert Girling, Ph.D.

Vulture funds, otherwise known as "distressed-debt investors," are undermining UN and other global efforts to relieve impoverished Third World nations of the debt that has burdened them for many decades.

Vulture funds are financial organizations that buy up debts that are near default or bankruptcy. The vulture fund will pay the original investor pennies on the dollar for the debt and then approach the debtor to arrange a better repayment on the loan, or will go after the debtor in court.

In the private financial world, these funds, like the birds they are named for, provide a useful function for investors who are unable to follow up on defaulted debts and are themselves facing financial ruin if the debtor reneges entirely.

Under normal circumstances, distressed-debt investing—like day trading—is risky business. It is a gamble and the company knows that going in. The vulture fund may get nothing for its investment if the debtor continues to default and has no assets to attach. However, if there is still meat on the bones (the debtor has considerable assets to liquidate) the vulture fund can make millions.

A problem has arisen in recent years, however, as vulture funds have begun inserting themselves into an increasingly globalized "free market"—where no distinction is made between an irresponsible and defaulted company and a destitute and impoverished nation.

In the case of nations, the actions of vulture funds are corrupting the process begun in 1996 to provide debt relief for Third World nations struggling to emerge from the heavy debt laid upon them by previous corrupt rulers and colonial masters.

In one recent case, the poverty-stricken nation of Zambia was negotiating with Romania to reduce a $40 million debt still owed from a 1979 loan to buy Romanian tractors. In 1999, Romania had agreed to liquidate the entire loan for $3 million. Zambia planned to use the debt cancellation to invest in much-needed nurses, teachers, and basic infrastructure. Just before the deal was finalized however, investors at the England-based vulture fund Donegal International convinced the Romanian government to sell them the loan for just under $4 million—not much more than Zambia had offered. Donegal then turned around and sued Zambia (where the average wage is barely a dollar a day) for the full $40 million.

Throughout the lawsuit, global NGOs have pleaded with the English High Court to void the new contract and allow Zambia to honor the original agreement of $3 million. But on February 15, 2007, an English court ruled that Donegal was entitled to much of what it was seeking—at least $15 million, perhaps more.[1]

In a last desperate plea, global NGOs working to relieve Third World debt (such as Oxfam and the Jubilee Debt Campaign) turned to Donegal directly, asking them to forgive the debt. Donegal knows that, as a national entity, even a cash-poor country like Zambia has access to considerable resources; in this case copper, cobalt, gem stones, coal, uranium, marble, and much more. Public works and other civic improvement projects can also be liquidated.

Also, Donegal has no history of mercy toward impoverished nations. In 1996 it paid $11 million for a discounted Peruvian debt and threatened to bankrupt the country unless they paid $58 million. Donegal got its money. Now they're suing Congo Brazzaville for $400 million for a debt they bought for $10 million. Donegal and other vulture funds have teams of lawyers combing the world for assets that can be seized.

Even worse, many of these vulture funds have influential ties to powerful world leaders like the Bush administration. The risk normally faced by distressed-debt investors is virtually eliminated when they have political influence that is greater than the poor nation they are suing. They raise most of their money through legal actions in US courts, where lobbying and political contributions hold influence. And many vulture fund CEOs have close links to top officials both in the US and England.

President Bush has the power to block collection of debts by vulture funds, either individual ones or all of them, if he considers it to be at odds with US foreign policy—in this case debt relief for poor countries.[2] According to Congressman John Conyers, "It's our position that the Foreign Corrupt Practices Act and the comity doctrine brought from our constitution allows the president to require the courts defer in individual suits against foreign nations. And so, we're conducting a couple of things. First of all, we want to know where these practices are going on at the present time, and, two, how we can get this information to President Bush so that he can, as he indicated to us, stop it immediately."[3]

Chancellor Gordon Brown, now the prime minister of England, calls the vulture funds perverse and immoral. Oxfam and Jubilee have urged the chancellor to use his influence as chair of the International Monetary Fund's key decision-making committee to make sure that new regulations are devised that prevent private companies from bypassing international debt rules and pursuing debts from very poor countries.

Citations

1. Ashley Seager, "Court Lets Vulture Fund Claw Back Zambian Millions," *The Guardian*, February 16, 2007.
2. Ashley Seager, "Bush Could Block Debt Collection by 'Vulture' Funds," *Guardian Unlimited*, February 22, 2007.
3. "Conyers Confronts Bush On Vulture Bonds," an interview with *Democracy Now!*, February 16, 2007.

11

The Scam of "Reconstruction" in Afghanistan

Sources:
Tomdispatch.com, August 27, 2006
Title: "Why It's Not Working in Afghanistan"
Author: Ann Jones

CorpWatch, October 6, 2006
Title: "Afghanistan Inc: a CorpWatch Investigative Report"
Author: Fariba Nawa

Student Researchers: Madeline Hall and Julie Bickel
Faculty Evaluator: James Dean, Ph.D.

A report issued in June 2005 by the non-profit organization Action Aid reveals that much of the US tax money earmarked to rebuild

Afghanistan actually ends up going no further than the pockets of wealthy US corporations. "Phantom aid" that never shows up in the recipient country is a scam in which paychecks for overpriced, and often incompetent, American "experts" under contract to USAID go directly from the Agency to American bank accounts. Additionally, 70 percent of the aid that does make it to a recipient country is carefully "tied" to the donor nation, requiring that the recipient use the donated money to buy products and services from the donor country, often at drastically inflated prices. The US far outstrips other nations in these schemes, as Action Aid calculates that 86 cents of every dollar of American aid is phantom.

Authors Ann Jones and Fariba Nawa suggest that in order to understand the failure and fraud in the reconstruction of Afghanistan, it is important to look at the peculiar system of American aid for international development. International and national agencies—including the World Bank, the International Monetary Fund and USAID, that traditionally distribute aid money to developing countries—have designed a system that is efficient in funneling money back to the wealthy donor countries, while undermining sustainable development in poor states.

A former head of USAID cited foreign aid as "a key foreign policy instrument" designed to help countries "become better markets for US exports." To guarantee that mission, the State Department recently took over the aid agency. USAID and the Army Corps of Engineers now cut in US business and government interests from the start, making sure that money is allocated according to US economic, political, strategic, and military priorities, rather than according to what the recipient nation might consider important.

Though Afghans have petitioned to allocate aid money as they find appropriate, donor countries object, claiming that the Afghan government is too corrupt to be trusted. Increasingly frustrated and angry Afghan communities meanwhile claim that the no-bid, open-ended contracts being awarded to contractors such as Kellogg, Brown, and Root/Halliburton, DynCorp, Blackwater, and the Louis Berger Group are equivalent to licensed bribery, corruption, theft, and money laundering.

The Karzai government, confined to a self-serving American agenda, has delivered little to the average Afghan, most of whom still live in abject poverty. Western notions of progress evident in US-contracted hotels, restaurants, and shopping malls full of new electronic gadgets and appliances are beyond the imaginations or practicalities of 3.5 million war torn Afghan citizens who are without food, shelter, sewage systems, clean water or electricity.

Infrastructure hastily built with shoddy materials and no knowledge or respect for geologic or climatic conditions is culminating in one expensive failure after another. USAID's website, for example, boasts of its only infrastructure accomplishment in Afghanistan—the Kabul-Kandahar Highway—a narrow and already crumbling highway costing Afghanis $1 million a mile. The highway was featured in the *Kabul Weekly* newspaper in March 2005 under the headline, "Millions Wasted on Second-Rate Roads." The article notes that while other bids from more competent construction firms came in at one-third the cost, the contract went to the Louis Berger Group, a firm with tight connections to the Bush administration—as well as a notorious track record of other failed and abandoned construction projects in Afghanistan.

Former Minister of Planning, Ramazan Bashardost, complained that when it came to building roads, the Taliban had done a better job. "And," he also asked, "Where did the money go?" Now, in a move certain to lower President Karzai's approval ratings and further diminish US popularity in the area, the Bush administration has pressured Karzai to turn this "gift from the people of the United States" into a toll road, charging each driver $20 for a road-use permit valid for one month. In this way, according to American "experts" providing highly paid technical assistance, Afghanistan can collect $30 million annually from its impoverished citizens and thereby decrease the foreign aid "burden" on the United States.

Jones asks, "Is it any wonder that foreign aid seems to ordinary Afghans to be something only foreigners enjoy?"

UPDATE BY FARIBA NAWA

Afghanistan, Inc. is a thirty-page report that digs deep into the corruption involved in the reconstruction of Afghanistan. The report focuses on US government-funded companies contracted to rebuild Afghanistan. The importance of this report is that it's the first serious look at corruption of aid money spending from a grassroots level. It includes an emphasis on various projects in villages and the cities and it covers all sides of the issue. It shows how big money is spent on bad work.

The report was first published in English through CorpWatch, a watchdog of corporations, on May 2, 2006. It was translated into the Persian languages of Dari and Pashto in September 2006. The companies investigated in the report continue to receive millions of dollars in contracts from the US government despite their incompetence and wasteful spending. Louis Berger, Bearing Point, Chemonics, and DynCorp are still taking American taxpayers' money and showing minimum results in Afghanistan.

Some of the mainstream press gave the report coverage, including NPR's *Morning Edition*, KRON Channel 4 news in San Francisco when it was first published, and later on, BBC radio and many other European outlets continue to call and ask the author about the report. However, that's a limited response to the fact that this was a groundbreaking report with important information for policy change. The report has been a source for many others researching the subject. If you'd like more information on corruption on reconstruction in Afghanistan, please refer to CorpWatch's website www.corpwatch.org. Integrity Watch Afghanistan is another organization that monitors corruption in the country and produces various reports.

UPDATE BY ANN JONES

Nine months later the conundrum I described—no peace, no security, no development—still pertains, and Afghan hopes sour.

The US still looks for a military solution. In the first five months of 2007, seventy-five coalition troops were killed (compared to fifty-three in the same period last year), including thirty-eight Americans. Civilian casualties were variously reported—some sources said "almost 1,800"—including 135 killed by US or NATO forces.

The US position on military "progress" against the Taliban, expressed by Defense Secretary Robert Gates on June 4, 2007, as he prepared to visit Afghanistan, remained "guarded optimism." Gates told reporters a goal of his trip was to insure close coordination of combat operations and development and reconstruction efforts. That's a switch, suggesting some clue that reconstruction may be a better way to "kill" the Taliban, but leaving unanswered the question of how to coordinate war and peaceful activity.

The real importance of "Why It's Not Working in Afghanistan" lies behind the front page military coverage—in what it reveals of the systemic scams and should-be scandals of American aid. The story makes news now and then when billions "disappear" from reconstruction projects in Iraq, but to my knowledge it has yet to be investigated by media or congress. What's discussed is the occasional budgetary black hole that suggests some random malfeasance, in much the same way that torture at Abu Ghraib was discussed as the work of a few "bad apples."

Maybe reporters don't want to take up the story because it's complicated. It's about numbers. Like Enron. Dreary, ho-hum, life-shattering stuff. I don't know. But one curious thing: when my book *Kabul in Winter* appeared in 2006, a very long section on this topic was the one part no reviewer touched.

Now bigger voices than mine speak out. Abdullah Abdullah, the distinguished former Foreign Minister of Afghanistan, recently complained that of every $100,000 promised to Afghan development, less than a third reaches the country. Matt Waldman, head of Afghanistan policy for Oxfam, one of the most respected humanitarian NGOs in the world, wrote in *The Guardian* (May 26, 2007) that "America is bankrolling Afghanistan" but "as in Iraq, a vast proportion of aid is wasted." And more to the point, "Close to half of US development assistance goes to the five biggest US contractors in the country." Waldman argues that too much aid money is lost to high salaries and living costs of international experts, purchase of non-Afghan resources, and corporate profits. He figures the cost of the average expat (read "American") expert at half a million dollars a year.

So why is it left to representatives of foreign governments, foreign humanitarian organizations, and foreign press to expose this fraud?

To keep up with news about Afghanistan see news@afghanistan-newscenter.com, a daily roundup of stories from the world's English language press. For policy issues see the Web site of New York University's Center on International Cooperation (www.cic.nyu.edu) or that of the Center's senior fellow and Afghanistan expert Barnett Rubin (brr5@nyu.edu). To keep an eye on the corridors of power see the website of the Center for Public Integrity (www.publicintegrity.org), and specifically for information on corporate scams see www.corpwatch.org.

Journalists should also be advised that several professional organizations are protesting the increasing difficulty of covering Afghanistan because of interference by US, Afghan, and ISAF forces.

They include IFJ (International Federation of Journalists), AIJA (Afghan Independent Journalists Association), and CPAJ (Committee to Protect Afghan Journalists). Currently Afghan journalists are also boycotting the Afghan Wolesi Jirga (lower house of Parliament) to protest its enactment of repressive media laws and the consequent imprisonment of journalists.

12

Another Massacre in Haiti by UN Troops

Sources:
HaitiAction.net, January 21, 2007
Title: "UN in Haiti: Accused of Second Massacre"
Authors: Haiti Information Project

Inter Press Service
Title: "Haiti: Poor Residents of Capital Describe a State of Siege"
Authors: Wadner Pierre and Jeb Sprague

Student Researcher: William Leeming
Faculty Evaluator: Dianne Parness

Eyewitness testimony confirms indiscriminate killings by UN forces in Haiti's Cité Soleil community on December 22, 2006, reportedly as collective punishment against the community for a massive demonstration of Lavalas supporters in which about ten thousand people rallied for the return of President Aristide in clear condemnation of the foreign military occupation of their country. According to residents, UN forces attacked their neighborhood in the early morning, killing more than thirty people, including women and children. Footage taken by Haiti Information Project (HIP) videographers shows unarmed civilians dying as they tell of extensive gunfire from UN peacekeeping forces (MINUSTAH).

A hardened UN strategy became apparent days after the demonstration, when UN officials stated they were entering Cité Soleil to capture or kill gangsters and kidnappers. While officials of MINUSTAH have admitted to "collateral damage," in the raids of December 2006, they say they are there to fight gangsters at the request of the René Préval government.

But many residents and local human rights activists say that scores of people having no involvement with gangs were killed, wounded, and arrested in the raids.

Although MINUSTAH denied firing from helicopter gunships, HIP captured more than three hours of video footage and a large selection of digital photos, illustrating the UN's behavior in Haiti.

An unidentified twenty-eight-year-old man, filmed by HIP, can be seen dying as he testifies that he was shot from a circling UN helicopter that rained gunfire on those below. HIP film also shows a sixteen-year-old, dying just after being shot by UN forces. Before dying he describes details of the UN opening fire on unarmed civilians in his neighborhood. The wounded and dying, filmed by HIP, all express horror and confusion.

IPS observed that buildings throughout Cité Soleil were pockmarked by bullets; many showing huge holes made by heavy caliber UN weapons, as residents attest. Often pipes that brought in water to the slum community now lay shattered.

A recently declassified document from the US embassy in Port-au-Prince reveals that during a similar operation carried out in July 2005, MINUSTAH expended 22,000 bullets over several hours. In the report, an official from MINUSTAH acknowledged, "given the flimsy construction of homes in Cité Soleil and the large quantity of ammunition expended, it is likely that rounds penetrated many buildings, striking unintended targets."

Frantz Michel Guerrier, spokesman for the Committee of Notables for the Development of Cité Soleil based in the Bois Neuf zone, said, "It is very difficult for me to explain to you what the people of Bois Neuf went through on Dec. 22, 2006—almost unexplainable. It was a true massacre. We counted more than sixty wounded and more than twenty-five dead, among [them] infants, children, and young people."

"We saw helicopters shoot at us, our houses broken by the tanks," Guerrier told IPS. "We heard detonations of the heavy weapons. Many of the dead and wounded were found inside their houses. I must tell you that nobody had been saved, not even the babies. The Red Cross was not allowed to help people. The soldiers had refused to let the Red Cross in categorically, in violation of the Geneva Convention." Several residents told IPS that MINUSTAH, after conducting its operations, evacuated without checking for wounded.

Following the removal of Haiti's elected Jean-Bertrand Aristide government (see *Censored 2005*, story #12), up to one thousand Lavalas political activists were imprisoned under the US-backed interim government, according to a Miami University Human Rights study.

A study released by the Lancet Journal of Medicine in August 2006 estimates that 8,000 were killed and 35,000 sexually assaulted in the greater Port-au-Prince area during the time of the interim government (2004-2006). The study attributed human rights abuses to purported "criminals," police, anti-Lavalas gangs, and UN peacekeepers.

HIP Founding Editor Kevin Pina commented, "It is clear that this represents an act of terror against the community. This video evidence shows clearly that the UN stands accused, once again, of targeting unarmed civilians in Cité Soleil. There can be no justification for using this level of force in the close quarters of those neighborhoods. It is clear that the UN views the killing of these innocents as somehow acceptable to their goal of pacifying this community. Every demonstration, no matter how peaceful, is seen as a threat to their control if it includes demands for the return of Aristide to Haiti. In that context it is difficult to continue to view the UN mission as an independent and neutral force in Haiti. They apparently decided sometime ago it was acceptable to use military force to alter Haiti's political landscape to match their strategic goals for the Haitian people."

UPDATE BY KEVIN PINA

Since President Jean-Bertrand Aristide and his Lavalas political party were ousted from power on February 29, 2004, accusations of gross human rights violations have persisted in Haiti. While the Haitian National Police (HNP) received training and assistance from the UN following Aristide's ouster, they were also accused of summary executions, arbitrary arrests, and the killing of unarmed demonstrators. The actions of the Haitian police became so egregious that even UN police trainers (CIVPOL) began to question the motives of their commanders and the mission's objectives. The Haiti Information Project (HIP) received the following correspondence in response to a May 8, 2005 article "UN accommodates Human Rights Abuses by police in Haiti."[1] This is the first publication of that correspondence:

> Just want to reinforce your observations as all being accurate.
>
> I am one of the 25 US CIVPOL here on the ground in

Haiti, having arrived last November. As a group we are frustrated by the UN's and CIVPOL's unwillingness to interpret
their mandate aggressively. I have been pushing them to
conduct investigations into all the shootings and other significant Human Rights violations with no success. The
Police Commissioner and command staff shows little interest and claim the mandate does not allow them to do this.
Unfortunately I have countless examples.

The corruption in the HNP is massive with little interest
in addressing the problem. Just keep up the pressure, I don't
know what else to do.

Stephen MacKinnon
Chief, Strategic Planning Unit
CIVPOL-MINUSTAH

Chief MacKinnon provided HIP with information and documents
that painted a disturbing picture of a UN operation more obsessed
with political embarrassment caused by mounting demonstrations
for Aristide's return than interest in reigning in human rights abuses
committed by the HNP.[2]

The United Nations Stabilization Mission in Haiti (MINUSTAH)
now stands accused of having itself committed several massacres in
the seaside shantytown of Cité Soleil. This area of the capital served
as a launching site for massive demonstrations demanding the
return of President Aristide and for an end to what they called the
foreign occupation of their country.

The Brazilian military has responsibility for leadership of the UN
military forces in Haiti and is authorized to use deadly force. They
are at the top of the command structure and their influence on the
overall mission should not be understated. More importantly, there is
a direct parallel between Brazilian military tactics utilized by UN
forces in Haiti and similar military-style assaults used by the police
in their own country.

The Brazilian military police have been accused of firing indiscriminately in the poor slums of Sao Paulo and Rio de Janeiro called
favelas. This was highlighted in an Amnesty International report
"Brazil: 'They come in Shooting': Policing socially excluded communities," released on December 2, 2005.[3]

This is similar to the tactics authorized by the Brazilian generals in Haiti. It has resulted in several high-profile massacres committed in the poor slum of Cité Soleil where protestors challenged the UN's authority by continuing to launch massive demonstrations demanding Aristide's return and condemning the UN's presence in Haiti. In each instance, the UN and the elite-run Haitian press demonized the entire community as being criminals and gangsters and/or collaborators of criminals and gangsters. While it is true that armed "gangs" operated in the neighborhood and a few claimed they were aligned with Aristide's Lavalas movement, these military raids had a clear correlation to the ongoing demonstrations and opposition to the UN presence in Haiti.

Cité Soleil was terrorized on July 6, 2005 when Brazilian commanders authorized a raid by UN forces with the stated aim of routing gangs in the area.[4] For Aristide supporters, the raid was a preemptive strike by the UN to dampen the impact of protests on Aristide's birthday, planned to take place only nine days later on July 15. It also represented the first time UN forces purposely sought to assassinate the leadership of armed groups claiming allegiance to Aristide's Lavalas movement.[5] By the time UN guns stopped firing, countless unarmed civilians lay dead with many having been killed by a single high-powered rifle shot to the head. Since then, documents obtained under the Freedom of Information Act show the US Embassy and various intelligence agencies, were aware of the excessive use of force by UN forces in Haiti on July 6, 2005.[6] Despite being heavily censored by US officials, what emerges is clear evidence of the disproportionate use of force by UN troops in Cité Soleil.

December 16, 2006 saw another large demonstration for Aristide that began in Cite Soleil and only six days later on December 22, Brazilian commanders would authorize a second deadly raid that residents and human rights groups say resulted in the wholesale slaughter of innocent victims. The unspoken parallel of Brazil's role in leading the UN's military strategy in Haiti is the fact that terror tactics such as these have been their modus operandi in their own country.

In the early morning hours of Feb. 2, UN forces entered Cité Soleil firing indiscriminately and their victims were two young girls killed as they slept in their own home.[7] Massive demonstrations were scheduled to take place five days later demanding the return of Aristide throughout Haiti on Feb. 7. While these demonstrations went largely unreported by the international corporate media, this stood in contrast, to the avalanche of news stories filed two days later on Feb. 9, when UN forces launched yet another deadly military operation in Cité Soleil.[8] Although these raids were ostensibly to rid the neighborhood of gangs, they followed the same pattern and relationship to demonstrations for Aristide's return and military tactics used by Brazilian commanders in previous UN operations.

The only rights organizations documenting the loss of life and destruction of property resulting from the UN raid on December 22, 2006, as well as previous and subsequent UN military operations, were the Institute for Justice and Democracy in Haiti (IJDH) and the Bureau des Avocats Internationaux (BAI).[9] HIP, the organization originally authoring the article being recognized by Project Censored, is a news agency that has extensive video evidence and interviews from Cité Soleil taken the same day these attacks by UN forces were executed. HIP offers any human rights organization the opportunity to view the documentary footage and evidence supporting the claims of Cité Soleil residents that massacres by UN forces have been committed against them. Unfortunately, Amnesty International, Human Rights Watch and the Inter-American Commission on Human Rights of the Organization of American States have remained conspicuously disinterested and silent about this evidence.

For further information and updates about Haiti, please visit www.haitiaction.net, www.ijdh.org, www.HaitiInformationProject.net, www.haitianalysis.com, www.canadahaitiaction.ca, and www.ahphaiti.org.

Notes

1. Haiti Information Project,"UN accommodates Human Rights Abuses by police in Haiti," May 8, 2005. See http://haitiaction.net/News/HIP/5_8_5/5_8_5.html.
2. Internet correspondence received from Steve McKinnon to HIP May 12, 2005.
3. Amnesty International Report, "Brazil: 'They come in Shooting': Policing socially excluded communities" December 2, 2005. See http://www.amnestyusa.org/document.php?lang=e &id=ENGAMR190252005
4. Haiti Information Project, "Evidence mounts of a UN massacre in Haiti," July 12, 2005. See http://www.haitiaction.net/News/HIP/7_12_5.html.
5. Haiti Information Project,"The UN's disconnect with the poor in Haiti," December 25, 2005. See http://haitiaction.net/News/HIP/12_25_5/12_25a_5.html.
6. Haiti Information Project, "US Embassy in Haiti acknowledges excessive force by UN," January 24, 2007. Article based on FOIA documents obtained by College of DuPage Geography Professor Keith Yearman. See http://haitiaction.net/News/HIP/1_23_7/1_23_7.html.
7. Haiti Information Project—February 2, 2007. UN terror kills Haiti's children at night http://haitiaction.net/News/HIP/2_2_7a/2_2_7a.html.

8. Haiti Information Project, "Massive demonstrations in Haiti catch UN by surprise," February 9, 2007. See http://haitiaction.net/News/HIP/2_9_7/2_9_7.html.
9. Haiti Information Project,"The UNspoken truth about gangs in Haiti," February 15, 2007. See http://haitiaction.net/News/HIP/2_15_7/2_15_7.html.
10. Video images documenting UN military operations on July 6, 2005 and December 22, 2006 were taken by HIP videographer Jean-Baptiste Ristil.

UPDATE ON HAITI BY JEB SPRAGUE AND WADNER PIERRE: Poor Residents of Capital Describe a State of Siege

Initially neither one of us thought of ourselves as journalists, but we were so shocked by events on the ground in Haiti (which were rarely being covered) that we felt compelled to write about them. In the dominant rhetoric of donor groups and corporate media coverage we found that the voices of grassroots civil society were absent. Of any country in the western hemisphere, Haiti's culture is filled with a vitality for democracy, personal interaction, and dialogue. Radio is the most popular form of communication partially because of economic accessibility and partially because it encourages discussion and debate. From researching our stories we've come to see that two civil societies exist, one tightly connected with foreign donors, the foreign embassies present in Port-au-Prince and the large media outlets; and another civil society, a pulsating grassroots that is usually ignored by foreign journalists and donors.

The testimonials and opinions of the donor and foreign government backed elite or middle class based civil society groups are propelled in the media spotlight as unbiased and independent, *the* Haitian civil society. These are the groups that have bilingual language skills, often higher education, and the technological tools to communicate their programs to a transnational audience. Aid groups fly them abroad to make presentations or provide them with training seminars in the Dominican Republic or Washington, DC.

In the slum- and rural-based communities another civil society exists outside of the international limelight. The members of this civil society are often broke and rarely make a profit from their positions. They are relatively unknown and unheard of by the outside world. These groups, popular and well organized on the ground, have broad participation. They carry out large mobilizations, they fill the streets with friends and family, they organize strikes, they are on the radio, and they organize co-ops, literacy centers, and community programs.

So in our articles we have tried to provide as many direct quotes and testimonials as possible from this grassroots civil society. At the same time we try to place this along side the official rhetoric, holding the official organs responsible, confronting them and asking them the hard questions (which they are often shocked to hear). But most important are the voices of the victims of violence, the wife and husband who lost their children, the unemployed man wounded on the side of the street; these are the people that are rarely heard in the mainstream media. Part of this is because corporate journalists choose to spend their time with elites, especially in developing countries, and part is because editors are dependent on their advertisers and don't see these stories as viable.

MINUSTAH's operations in Cité Soleil, since writing our article, have continued. But in recent months the killings have lessened (although a man just last week was shot and killed by UN troops/ early June 2007). Over the months that followed our article, MINUS-TAH was able to arrest one of the most well-known gang leaders, Evens Jeune, along with many of those within his group. MINUS-TAH has claimed to have set up hospital clinics in the buildings used by the gangs, but on-site visits have revealed empty houses with no hospital clinics and no UN staffers. Haitian government promises of job programs have been slow to materialize in Cité Soleil. UN officials have purposely downplayed or ignored the protests of the poor demanding reparations. However, a number of community schools and health organizations, such as the Lamp Foundation, continue to do good work in Cité Soleil. Some human rights groups, such as the GDP, BAI, CONODH, and AUHMOD, continue to be active in the neighborhoods, but other locally formed groups such as the HNVNPC have gone back to their jobs, mostly in churches and schools.

The population of Cité Soleil has suffered horribly, either caught in the crossfire or purposely targeted. The socio-economic situation and dire poverty in Cité Soleil is a direct result of the prolonged polices of wealthy countries and donor institutions; forcing and destabilizing out of power those elected Haitian governments that have advocated key policies of sovereignty and social investment, while opposing privatization and neoliberal adjustments whenever they can. Rarely told is how Haiti's police throughout the 1990's and early 2000's were systematically manipulated by the US embassy,

CIA, and Haitian elites—this had a direct result on the security situation in Haiti. Economic instability heightened by coups and prolonged political crises—promoted by elites unhappy with the popular electoral choice—have cost Haiti jobs and development. All of this has pushed Haiti further into the abyss.

When international institutions and governments are busy coordinating these kinds of egregious activities, we felt it the responsibility of journalists, activists, and academics (especially those lucky enough to have the resources) to investigate; all while speaking with the poor and finding out their concerns. From this experience we founded a website, haitianalysis.com, to connect foreign young journalists with young Haitian journalists in poor communities—with the specific purpose of covering poor communities and grassroots organizing. Soon after our IPS article appeared, members of the Haitian diaspora in New York were able to raise thousands of dollars to help in the funeral expenses of the two young Lubin daughters, Stephanie, seven, and Alexandra, four, killed by UN ammo according to their parents. Wadner's photos of the young girls have appeared in numerous Haitian newspapers and websites of various languages. The Lubin parents, distraught, wanted everyone to know about what had occurred on that night of February 1st 2007. To our knowledge, the United Nations has never launched an investigation into the killing of the two Lubin daughters. We will continue asking that they do.

For more information, we suggest that readers view websites such as ijdh.org, hurah.revolt.org, haitianalysis.com, pih.org, haiti.quixote.org, jubileeusa.org, and haitilabor.org.

13

Immigrant Roundups to Gain Cheap Labor for US Corporate Giants

Sources:

Truthout, January 27, 2007
Title: "Which Side Are You On?"
Author: David Bacon

The Nation, February 6, 2007
Title: "Workers, Not Guests"
Author: David Bacon

Foreign Policy in Focus, February 26, 2007
Title: "Migrants: Globalization's Junk Mail?"
Author: Laura Carlsen

Student Researcher: Fernanda Borras
Faculty Evaluator: Diana Grant, Ph.D.

The North American Free Trade Agreement (NAFTA) flooded Mexico with cheap subsidized US agricultural products that displaced millions of Mexican farmers. Between 2000 and 2005, Mexico lost 900,000 rural jobs and 700,000 industrial jobs, resulting in deep unemployment throughout the country. Desperate poverty has forced millions of Mexican workers north in order to feed their families.

The National Campesino Front estimates that two million farmers have been displaced by NAFTA, in many cases related to the increase in US imports. In 1994, the first year of the agreement, the United States exported $4.59 billion of agricultural products to Mexico, according to the Department of Agriculture. By 2006 the figure had risen to $9.85 billion—an increase of 114 percent. US exports of corn, Mexico's staple crop and largest source of rural employment, alone doubled to over $2.5 billion in 2006.

This combination of unemployment in Mexico, the huge gap between salaries in the United States and Mexico, and US demand for cheap labor to compete on global markets has created the current situation. The demand for undocumented labor in the US economy is structural. It is not just a few companies seeking to cut corners. These are not just jobs that "US workers won't take." Migrants work in nearly all low-paying occupations and have become essential to the US economy in the age of global competition.

The meatpacking industry provides a good example. The US meat industry as it went global shows a fast slide in working conditions over the past decades as a result of de-unionization, erosion of wages and benefits, and increasing safety and health hazards. Part and parcel of that slide has been the replacement of unionized US workers with migrants.

Aside from traditional employment in agriculture, another major use of migrant labor has been through the advent of subcontracting. This practice, well in place since the early 1980s, has contributed to the de-unionization of the workforce. It conveniently releases employees from direct responsibility for the legal status and treatment of workers in their employment.

In the wake of 9/11, Immigration Customs Enforcement (ICE) has conducted workplace and home invasions across the country in an attempt to round up "illegal" immigrants. ICE justifies these raids under the rubric of keeping our homeland safe and preventing terrorism. However the real goal of these actions is to disrupt the immigrant work force in the US and replace it with a tightly regulated non-union guest-worker program. This policy is endorsed by companies seeking permanent low-wage workers through a lobby group called Essential Worker Immigrations Coalition (EWIC). EWIC's fifty-two members include the US Chamber of Commerce, Wal-Mart, Marriott, Tyson Foods, American Meat Institute, California Landscape Contractors Association, and the Association of Builders and Contractors.

ICE now has Operation Return to Sender, a program, supposedly designed to target fugitive aliens. The program has resulted in the indiscriminate roundup of over 13,000 undocumented immigrants in cities throughout the United States.

Immigrant rights organizations have noted that the crackdown has led to serious human rights violations. Families are separated. Hearings are slow, and often families do not know for long periods of time where their loved ones are being held. A January 16 report from the Homeland Security Department's Inspector General of conditions at five detention centers identified frequent violation of federal standards, overcrowding, and health and safety violations.

The firings and raids highlight the vulnerability of immigrant workers under current US law. In 1986 Congress passed the Immigration Reform and Control Act, making it a federal crime for an employer to hire a worker without valid immigration documents. While few employers have ever faced penalties, in reality the law made it a crime for undocumented workers to hold a job. No current law requires employers to fire workers whose Social Security numbers don't jibe. But President Bush proposed a new administrative rule, which would tell employers to fire anyone with a no-match. The regulation has never been officially issued, but many companies claim they're already complying with it.

Both the enforcement and the agenda behind this crackdown are alarming many unions. In 1999 the AFL-CIO called for the repeal of employer sanctions, as well as for a generous legalization program, greater chances for family reunification, and enforcement of workplace rights. The federation was already on record opposing new guest worker programs. The Service Employees, and the two garment unions were among the first to push for this position. "We still call for the repeal of employer sanctions, as we have from the time it was passed," says Bruce Raynor, UNITE HERE president. "There are 12 million undocumented people living here, who are important to the economy," he fumes. "They have a right to seek employment, and employers have a right to hire them. The only way to deal with this is to give workers rights and a path to citizenship."

UPDATE BY DAVID BACON

"Which Side are you On?" and "Workers, not Guests" expose the way US immigration law is being transformed into a mechanism for supplying labor to some of the country's largest corporations. Immigration law is creating a two-tier society, in which millions of people are denied fundamental rights and social benefits, because they are recruited to come to the US by those corporations on visas that condemn them to a second-class status. Those guest workers face increased poverty and exploitation, and their status is being used to put pressure on wages, benefits and workplace rights for all workers.

"Workers, not Guests" describes the way that the Bush administration uses immigration raids to attack union organizing campaigns and efforts by immigrant workers to enforce basic workplace rights and protections. Further, the administration uses the raids to pressure Congress into adopting new, vastly expanded guest worker programs.

Both articles describe the way some groups have abandoned their historic opposition to contract labor programs. Instead, the National Council of La Raza, the National Immigration Forum, and other labor and religious organizations have developed a political alliance with some of the country's largest corporations, with the objective of passing new guest worker legislation. This legislation also includes provisions that will make future immigration raids much harsher and more widespread.

Since publication, the Bush administration and both Democratic and Republican senators have announced new proposals that go even further. They would end the ability of immigrant families to reunite in the US, and instead institute a corporate-driven point system intended to supply skilled labor to big companies. Raids and enforcement would become even harsher, with huge detention centers built on the border. The proposals would allow corporations to recruit as many as 600,000 contract guest workers a year.

The use of immigration policy to funnel labor to corporate employers is growing at the same time that Congress is debating new corporate trade legislation, including the renewal of fast track negotiating authority for the administration, and four new trade agreements—with South Korea, Peru, Panama, and Colombia. These bills would all increase the displacement of workers and farmers in other countries, sending many of them into the migrant stream to the US. This displacement is being coordinated with Congress's immigration proposals, which would then channel displaced workers into industries where their labor can be used profitably, and ensure that they can only remain in the US in a status vulnerable to exploitation.

The mainstream press has carried many articles about the proposals and raids. There has been very little coverage of the corporate backing for the immigration bills in Congress, however. Many reporters refer to the guest worker bills as "pro-immigrant" and "left." This has not only been inaccurate reporting, but has actually covered up the corporate domination of the immigration agenda in Congress. There has been virtually no coverage of the connection between US trade policy and immigration policy.

For more accurate information, readers can contact the National Network for Immigrant and Refugee Rights, www.nnirr.org. Global Exchange organized a national speaking tour on trade and immigration policy by David Bacon and Juan Manuel Sandoval, a leading

Mexican critic of NAFTA and US immigration policy. The presentations made during that tour are available on the Global Exchange website, www.globalexchange.org.

14

Impunity for US War Criminals

Source:

Congressional Quarterly, November 22, 2006
Title: "A Senate Mystery Keeps Torture Alive—and Its Practitioners Free"
Author: Jeff Stein

Student Researcher: Marley Miller
Faculty Evaluator: James Dean, Ph.D.

A provision mysteriously tucked into the Military Commission Act (MCA) just before it passed through Congress and was signed by President Bush on October 17, 2006 (see story #1), redefines torture, removing the harshest, most controversial techniques from the definition of war crimes, and exempts the perpetrators—both interrogators and their bosses—from prosecution for such offences dating back to November 1997.

Author Jeff Stein asks, "Who slipped language into the MCA that would further exempt torturers from prosecution?"

The White House denies any involvement or knowledge regarding the insertion of such language, leaving the origin of adjustments to this significant part of the MCA a mystery.

Motivation for this provision, however, leads clearly to leadership in the Bush administration, as the passage effectively rewrote the US enforcement mechanism for the Geneva War Crimes Act, which would have, upon sworn testimonies of Lieutenant General Randall M. Schmidt, Major General Mike Dunlavey, and US Brigadier General Commander, Janis Karpinski, held former Defense Secretary Donald Rumsfeld, Vice President Dick Cheney, and President George Bush guilty of active roles in directing acts of torture upon detainees held at Guantánamo and Abu Ghraib (see *Censored 2007*, Story #7) .

A spokesperson for the Center for Constitutional Rights comments, "The MCA's restricted definitions arguably would exempt certain US officials who have implemented or had command responsibility for coercive interrogation techniques from war crimes prosecutions . . . This amendment is designed to protect US government perpetrators of abuses during the 'war on terror' from prosecution."

Joanne Mariner of Human Rights Watch adds that the effect of this provision of the MCA is "that perpetrators of several categories of what were war crimes at the time they were committed, can no longer be punished under US law."

As a whole, the MCA evolved out of the need to override the June 2006 Supreme Court declaration that the administration's hastily assembled military commissions were unconstitutional. That momentous Supreme Court decision confirmed that all prisoners in US custody had to be held in accordance with the Geneva Convention's Article 3, which prohibits "outrages upon personal dignity, in particular, humiliating and degrading treatment." Through passage of the MCA, Congress and the President negated the corrective role of the courts in checking and balancing executive power.

A Senate aide involved in the drafting of the Senate version of the bill that was agreed upon by John McCain, Lindsey Graham, and John Warner, said, "We have no idea who [the extended impunity provision] came from or how it came to be." White House spokesperson Dana Perrino said the stealth changes didn't come from the counsel's office, "It could have come from elsewhere in the White House or Justice Department," she said, "but it didn't come from us."

Whatever the source, the amended provision was passed and is now a part of US law.

15

Toxic Exposure Can Be Transmitted to Future Generations on a "Second Genetic Code"

Source:
Rachel's Democracy & Health News, October 12, 2006
Title: "Some Chemicals are More Harmful Than Anyone Ever Suspected"
Author: Peter Montague

Student Researchers: Kristen Kebler and Michael Januleski
Faculty Evaluator: Gary Evans, M.D.

Research suggests that, contrary to previous belief, our behavior and our environmental conditions may program sections of our children's DNA. New evidence about how genes interact with the environment suggests that many industrial chemicals may be more ominously dangerous than previously thought. It is increasingly clear that the effects of toxic exposure may be passed on through generations, in ways that are still not fully understood. "This introduces the concept of responsibility into genetics and inheritance," said Dr. Moshe Szyf, a researcher at McGill University in Montreal, "This may revolutionize medicine. You aren't eating and exercising just for yourself, but for your lineage."[1]

The new field of genetic research, called epigenetics, involves what scientists are referring to as a "second genetic code" which influences how genes act in the body. If DNA is the hardware of inheritance, the epigenetic system is the software. The epigenetic system determines which genes get turned "off" or "on" and how much of a certain protein they produce.

It is this switching system that allows the genetic material in each cell to influence the creation of proteins—which ones are manufactured, in what sequence, and how many. Proteins are the building blocks of our bodies. The chemicals and hormones in our bodies are *proteins*. They determine, in large part, how we look, how we feel, even how we act.[1]

Now, it seems that this chemical switching system may also act in reverse. In most cases, epigenetic changes (changes to DNA from current environmental conditions) are not passed from parents to their offspring. Scientists are still not sure how—but genes seem to be "wiped clean" after a sperm fertilizes an egg. Based on the recent data, however, researchers are intrigued by the notion that some of the genetic changes influenced by our diet, our behaviors, or our environment, may be passed on from generation to generation.

On average, 1,800 new chemicals are registered with the federal government each year and about 750 of these find their way into products, all with hardly any testing for health or environmental effects. The bad news about chemical contamination is steadily mounting, while the number of new chemicals is steadily increasing. Many critics of the chemical and pharmaceutical industries are renewing their admonitions that government agencies practice the "precautionary principle"—the rule of "do no harm first" in the approval of new drugs and chemicals.

In 2005, the European Union responded to this situation by trying to enact a new law called Registration, Evaluation and Authorization of Chemicals (REACH), which requires that chemicals be tested *before* they are sold—not after. As they say in Europe, "No data, no market." At the same time, US and European chemical industries—and the White House—began working overtime to subvert the European effort to enact REACH. Their efforts failed, however, and the REACH act was adopted by the European Union in December, 2006.[2] Chemical companies throughout the US and Europe are still struggling with how they will respond to the new requirements.

Citations

1. Anne McIlroy, "Chemicals and Stress Cause Gene Changes That Can Be Inherited," *Globe & Mail*, March 11, 2006. See http://www.precaution.org/lib/06/prn_code_2.060311.htm.
2. "European Parliament OKs World's Toughest Law on Toxic Chemicals," *San Francisco Chronicle*, December 14, 2006.

UPDATE BY PETER MONTAGUE

Basically this story tells us that environmental influences (like our mother's diet and her exposure to toxic chemicals) are far more important to us than anyone suspected just a decade ago.

It turns out that environmental influences shape us from the moment of conception onward, and the earliest months and years of life are the most important ones. It is called "fetal programming" and it means our first environment (the womb) can determine what sorts of diseases will afflict us later in life. Furthermore, some of these early influences can be inherited by our offspring and even by their offspring. So your personal pattern of disease may have been set by your grandmother's diet, or by her exposure to toxicants.

These findings imply that keeping toxic industrial chemicals out of the environment is far more urgent than anyone has previously thought. With more than 1,000 chemicals presently entering commercial channels each year with almost no health or safety testing, this is not welcome news.

In May 2007, a group of two hundred scientists from five continents issued strongly worded consensus statement (the "Faroes Statement") saying that early exposure to common chemicals leaves babies more likely to develop serious diseases later in life, including diabetes, attention deficits, certain cancers, thyroid disorders, and obesity, among others.

Notably, the scientists urged governments not to wait for more scientific certainty but to take precautionary action now to protect fetuses and children from toxic exposures.

Most of the mainstream press continued to tiptoe around this story, with a few important exceptions, until May 2007 when the Faroes statement blew the story open. Now that it is out in the open, we'll have to see if the mainstream press has what it takes to explain the far-reaching ramifications of these findings.

The best source of information on this topic (and many others) is http://www.environmentalhealthnews.org. Search for "epigenetics," "fetal programming," or "gene expression."

16

No Hard Evidence Connecting Bin Laden to 9/11

Source:
The Muckraker Report, June 6, 2006, and *Ithaca Journal*, June 29, 2006
Title: "FBI says, 'No Hard Evidence Connecting Bin Laden to 9/11'"
Author: Ed Haas

Student Researcher: Bianca May and Morgan Ulery
Faculty Evaluator: Ben Frymer, Ph.D.

Osama bin Laden's role in the events of September 11, 2001 is not mentioned on the FBI's "Ten Most Wanted" poster.

On June 5, 2006, author Ed Haas contacted the Federal Bureau of Investigation headquarters to ask why, while claiming that bin Laden is wanted in connection with the August 1998 bombings of US Embassies in Tanzania and Kenya, the poster does not indicate that he is wanted in connection with the events of 9/11.

Rex Tomb, Chief of Investigative Publicity for the FBI responded, "The reason why 9/11 is not mentioned on Osama bin Laden's Most Wanted page is because the FBI has no hard evidence connecting bin Laden to 9/11." Tomb continued, "Bin Laden has not been formally charged in connection to 9/11." Asked to explain the process, Tomb responded, "The FBI gathers evidence. Once evidence is gathered, it is turned over to the Department of Justice. The Department of Justice then decides whether it has enough evidence to present to a federal grand jury. In the case of the 1998 United States Embassies being bombed, bin Laden has been formally indicted and charged by a grand jury. He has not been formally indicted and charged in connection with 9/11 because the FBI has no hard evidence connecting bin Laden to 9/11."

Haas pauses to ask the question, "If the US government does not have enough hard evidence connecting bin Laden to 9/11, how is it possible that it had enough evidence to invade Afghanistan to 'smoke him out of his cave?'" Through corporate media, the Bush administration told the American people that bin Laden was "Public Enemy Number One," responsible for the deaths of nearly 3,000 people on September 11, 2001. The federal government claims to have invaded Afghanistan to "root out" bin Laden and the Taliban, yet nearly six years later, the FBI said that it had no hard evidence connecting bin Laden to 9/11.

Though the world was to have been convinced by the December 2001 release of a bin Laden "confession video," the Department of Defense issued a press release to accompany this video in which Secretary of Defense Donald Rumsfeld said, "There was no doubt of bin Laden's responsibility for the 9/11 attacks even before the tape was discovered."

In a CNN article regarding the bin Laden tape, then New York Mayor Rudy Giuliani said that "the tape removes any doubt that the US military campaign targeting bin Laden and his associates is more than justified." Senator Richard Shelby, R-Alabama, the vice chairman of the Senate Intelligence Committee said, "The tape's release is central to informing people in the outside world who don't believe bin Laden was involved in the September 11 attacks." Shelby went on to say "I don't know how they can be in denial after they see this tape."

Haas attempted to secure a reference to US government authentication of the bin Laden "confession video," to no avail. However, it is conclusive that the Bush Administration and US Congress, along with corporate media, presented the video as authentic. So why doesn't the FBI view the "confession video" as hard evidence? After all, notes Haas, if the FBI is investigating a crime such as drug trafficking, and it discovers a video of members of a drug cartel openly talking about a successful distribution operation in the United States, that video would be presented to a federal grand jury. The participants identified in the video would be indicted. The video alone would serve as sufficient evidence to net a conviction in a federal court. So why, asks Haas, is the bin Laden "confession video" not carrying the same weight with the FBI?

Haas strongly suggests that we begin asking questions, "The fact that the FBI has no hard evidence connecting Osama bin Laden to 9/11 should be headline news around the world. The challenge to the reader is to find out why it is not. Why has the US media blindly read the government-provided 9/11 scripts, rather than investigate without passion, prejudice, or bias, the events of September 11, 2001? Why has the US media blacklisted any guest that might speak of a government-sponsored 9/11 cover-up, rather than seeking out those people who have something to say about 9/11 that is contrary to the government's account?" Haas continues. "Who is controlling the media message, and how is it that the FBI has no 'hard evidence' connecting Osama bin Laden to the events of September 11, 2001, while the US media has played the bin Laden-9/11 connection story for [six] years now as if it has conclusive evidence that bin Laden is responsible for the collapse of the twin towers, the Pentagon attack, and the demise of United Flight 93?"

UPDATE BY ED HAAS

On June 6, 2006 the Muckraker Report ran a piece by Ed Haas titled "FBI says, 'No hard evidence connecting bin Laden to 9/11.'" Haas is the editor and a writer for the *Muckraker Report*. At the center of this article remains the authenticity and truthfulness of the videotape released by the federal government on December 13, 2001 in which it is reported that Osama bin Laden "confesses" to the September 11, 2001 attacks. The corporate media—television, radio, and newspapers—across the United States and the world repeated, virtually non-stop for a week after the videotape's release, the government account of OBL "confessing."

However, not one document has been released that demonstrates the authenticity of the videotape or that it even went through an authentication process. The *Muckraker Report* has submitted Freedom of Information Act requests to the FBI, CIA, Department of Defense, and CENTCOM requesting documentation that would demonstrate the authenticity of the videotape and the dates/circumstances in which the videotape was discovered. CENTCOM has yet to reply to the FOIA request. After losing an appeal, the FBI responded that no documents could be found responsive to the request. The Department of Defense referred the *Muckraker Report* to CENTCOM while also indicating that it had no documents responsive to the FOIA request either.

The CIA however claims that it can neither confirm nor deny the existence or nonexistence of records responsive to the request. According to the CIA the fact of the existence or nonexistence of requested records is properly classified and is intelligence sources and methods information that is protected from disclosure by section 6 of the CIA Act of 1949, as amended. Therefore, the Agency has denied your request pursuant to FOIA exemptions (b)(1) and (b)(3).

Many people believe that if the videotape is authentic, it should be sufficient hard evidence for the FBI to connect bin Laden to 9/11. The *Muckraker Report* agrees. However, for the Department of Justice to indict bin Laden for the 9/11 attacks, something the government has yet to do, the videotape would have to be entered into evidence and subjected to additional scrutiny. This appears to be something the government wishes to avoid.

Some believe that the video is a fake. They refer to it as the "fat bin Laden" video. The *Muckraker Report* believes that while the videotape is indeed authentic, it was the result of an elaborate CIA sting operation. The *Muckraker Report* also believes that the reason why there is no documentation that demonstrates that the videotape went through an authenticity process is because the CIA knew it was authentic, they arranged the taping.

It is highly probable that the videotape was taped on September 26, 2001—before the US invaded Afghanistan.

17

Drinking Water Contaminated by Military and Corporations

Sources:

Environment News Service, March 24, 2006
Title: "Factories, Cities Across USA Exceed Water Pollution Limits"
Author: Sunny Lewis

AlterNet, August 4, 2006
Title: "Military Waste in Our Drinking Water"
Authors: Sunaura Taylor and Astor Taylor

Student Researchers: Jonathan Stoumen, Adrienne Magee, and Julie Bickel
Faculty Evaluator: Sasha Von Meier, Ph.D. and Steve Norwick, Ph.D.

Water is essential to life, contributing to blood circulation, digestion, metabolism, brain activity, and muscle movements. Yet reliably pure water is growing scarce, even in the United States. Despite the federal government's avowed commitment "to restore and maintain the chemical, physical, and biological integrity of the Nation's waters,"[1] corporations, municipalities, and the US military pollute our waters—often with little or no accountability.

"Polluters are using America's waters as their dumping ground," said US PIRG's Clean Water Advocate Christy Leavitt. (US PIRG is the national lobby office for the state Public Interest Research Groups, nonprofit public interest advocacy organizations.) "Troubled Waters: An Analysis of Clean Water Act Compliance," released by US PIRG in March 2006 shows that, between July 2003 and December 2004, over 62 percent of industrial and municipal facilities across the country discharged pollution into US waterways at rates above limits established by the Clear Water Act (CWA).

Using the Freedom of Information Act, US PIRG investigated major facilities' compliance—or *lack* of it—with established federal limits on pollution discharges. The average facility discharged pollutants in excess of its permitted limit by over 275 percent, nearly four times the legal limit. Nationally, 436 major facilities exceeded their limits at least half of the time during the study's timeframe. Thirty-five facilities exceeded their permits during every reporting period. Seven states allowed more than one hundred violations of at least

500 percent (Ohio, Indiana, Pennsylvania, New York, Tennessee, Texas, and Massachusetts). The study could not analyze facilities in California, Oregon, or Washington due to unreliable data.

Corn farming—think ethanol—is the crop most likely to leach chemical contaminants into waterways.[2] Atrazine, which several European nations have banned, is an herbicide widely used in agribusiness, especially on major crops such as corn. The EPA identifies atrazine as the second-most common herbicide in drinking wells. Maximum safe levels of atrazine in drinking water are three parts per billion, but scientists have found up to 224 parts per billion in Midwestern streams, and 2,300 parts per billion in Corn Belt irrigation reservoirs.

Today more than 40 percent of US waterways are unsafe for swimming and fishing, and, as shown by the PIRG study, industrial pollution of the nation's waters persists—despite the goals of the 1972 Clean Water Act to make all US waters safe for fishing, swimming, and other uses by 1983, and to eliminate the discharge of pollutants into waterways by 1985.

One reason for these ongoing failures is the Bush administration's consistent efforts to shortchange the Environmental Protection Agency's budget and to gut the Clean Water Act. In 2003, the Bush administration significantly weakened protections for small streams, wetlands, and other waters, despite Bush having declared 2002-2003 the Year of Clean Water.

However, opposition to environmental protection for clean waterways stems from not only the Bush administration but also the US military, whose pollution poisons the very citizens it is supposed to protect in the name of national security. Weapons production, by the US military and its private contractors, generates more hazardous waste annually than the five largest international chemical companies combined, accounting for one-third of the nation's toxic waste. Furthermore, the US military is among the most frequent violators of environmental laws.

The Department of Defense (DoD) has sought and received exemptions from a number of crucial public health and environmental laws. Dramatic increases in the amounts of trichloroethylene (TCE) in public aquifers have been one fatal consequence of these exemptions. TCE, a known carcinogen, is used commercially as a solvent. It is the most widespread industrial contaminant in US drinking water. Since the Korean War, military contractors, such as Hughes Missiles Systems (purchased by Raytheon in 1997), have used TCE to degrease airplane parts, and to clean fuel lines at missile sites.

Consequently, TCE contamination is especially common around military facilities. The Pentagon is responsible for the TCE contamination of over 1,400 properties. In 2001, the EPA sought to force the government to require more thorough cleanups at military sites, by lowering the acceptable limits on TCE from five parts per billion to one part per billion. In response, the DoD joined the Department of Energy and NASA in blocking the EPA's proposed action. The Bush administration charged the EPA with inflating TCE's risks, and called on the National Academy of Sciences to evaluate the EPA's claims. The Academy's 2003 report confirmed the EPA's assessment, linking TCE to kidney cancer, impaired neurological function, reproductive and developmental damage, autoimmune disease, and other human ailments. The Bush administration and the DoD have ignored these inconvenient findings. As a result, citizens, who pay for the military budget with their tax dollars, are also paying with their health and sometimes their lives.

Citations
1. Federal Water Pollution Control Act (33 USC. 1251 et seq), Section 101(a).
2. Sasha Lilley, "Green Fuel's Dirty Secret," *CorpWatch*, June 1, 2006.

UPDATE BY SUNNY LEWIS
Compliance with the Clean Water Act on the part of industrial and municipal water facilities and land developers is of utmost importance to the quality of America's waters—from wetlands, ponds, and small streams to mighty rivers and the Great Lakes.

The US Public Interest Research Group, US PIRG, which discovered the failure of 62 percent of facilities to comply with the law based on documents obtained through the Freedom of Information Act, intends to do more work on this subject later this year.

Christy Leavitt of US PIRG, quoted by ENS in the original article, says the group will issue another report based on updated figures obtained in May from the US Environmental Protection Agency.

As ENS reported, US PIRG recommended that all US waters be protected by withdrawal of what the group called "the Bush administration's 2003 No Protection" policy which excludes many small streams and wetlands from protection under the Clean Water Act.

Since the ENS report was published, the US Supreme Court handed down a ruling on the scope of the Clean Water Act that many water and environmental experts as well as Members of Congress believe has muddied the legal waters and made new legislation necessary.

In June 2006, the high court ruled in the case *Rapanos et ux., et at. v. United States* that there are limits to the federal government's authority to regulate wetlands under the Clean Water Act, but failed to agree on the confines of that power.

The consolidated case involved conflicts between developers who wanted to build condos and stores on wetlands and federal regulators, who refused to allow the developments under the authority of the Clean Water Act. The waters at issue were wetlands adjacent to ditches and drains that connected to "navigable waters" of the United States.

For a full discussion of the ruling, please see the ENS report, "US Supreme Court Decision Fails to Clarify Clean Water Act," at http://www.ens-newswire.com/ens/jun2006/2006-06-19-10.asp.

In 2001, the Supreme Court ruled in another case, *Solid Waste Agency of Northern Cook County v. Corps of Engineers*, SWANCC, that non-navigable, isolated, intrastate waters do not fall under the jurisdiction of the Clean Water Act.

On May 25, 2007, a bi-partisan bill was introduced in the House of Representatives that attempts to clarify the original intent of Congress in the 1972 Clean Water Act in the wake of these two decisions.

To achieve clarification, the new measure, the Clean Water Restoration Act, replaces the term "navigable waters of the United States" with the term "waters of the United States."

The Clean Water Restoration Act has 158 original cosponsors, and the endorsement of more than three hundred organizations representing the conservation community, family farmers, fishers, surfers, boaters, faith communities, environmental justice advocates, labor unions, and civic associations.

It replaces a bill mentioned in the original ENS report, the Clean Water Authority Restoration Act, that was not approved during the 109th Congress.

As ENS reported in March 2006, US PIRG recommended that the Clean Water State Revolving Fund be fully funded to help communities upgrade their sewer systems.

The Clean Water State Revolving Loan Fund guarantees loans for cities and towns so they can borrow for sewer projects at a lower interest rate, saving local taxpayers billions of dollars nationwide.

On March 8, 2007, ENS reported that the Bush administration's budget proposal to cut some $400 million from the Clean Water State Revolving Fund budget came under fire by members of both parties in the Senate Environment and Public Works Committee.

On March 9, 2007, ENS reported that the US House of Representatives passed the Water Quality Financing Act of 2007. For the first time in twenty years, the measure H.R. 720, would reauthorize the Clean Water State Revolving Funds. At press time, this measure had not come before the US Senate.

For its part, the US EPA Office of Enforcement and Compliance Assurance, OECA, says its actions to enforce Clean Water Act requirements in FY 2006 resulted in more than 283 million pounds of pollutants reduced.

Most of these reductions are the result of the EPA's "national priority efforts" to control overflows from combined sewer overflows and sanitary sewer overflows and contamination caused by surface runoff from stormwater and concentrated animal feeding operations, the agency said.

Working in partnership with states, OECA says it concluded major legal settlements with dozens of cities to bring critical sewer systems back into compliance.

The settlements require comprehensive plans to improve the maintenance and operation of systems to reduce overflows, and long-term capital construction projects to expand treatment capacity to ensure that sewage is properly treated before being discharged, the OECA said in the "EPA Fiscal Year 2006 Accomplishments Report."

The settlements concluded in FY 2006 will reduce overflows of untreated or inadequately treated sewage by 26 million pounds, with an estimated investment of $930 million in sewer system upgrades and improvements.

To find out more about the scope of the Clean Water Act and compliance with this law, visit:

US Public Interest Research Group: http://www.uspirg.org/

US EPA Office of Enforcement and Compliance Assurance: http://www.epa.gov/compliance/

US EPA Clean Water Act Compliance Assistance: http://www.epa.gov/compliance/assistance/bystatute/cwa/index.html

Clean Water Act State Revolving Fund: http://www.epa.gov/owm/cwfinance/cwsrf/index.htm

Stormwater Authority: http://www.stormwaterauthority.org

18

Mexico's Stolen Election

Sources:
AlterNet, August 2, 2006
Title: "Evidence of Election Fraud Grows in México"
Author: Chuck Collins and Joshua Holland

Revolution, September 10, 2006
Title: "Mexico: The Political Volcano Rumbles"
Authors: Revolution Newspaper Collective

Researchers: Bill Gibbons and Erica Haikara
Faculty Evaluator: Ron Lopez, Ph.D.

Overwhelming evidence reveals massive fraud in the 2006 Mexican presidential election between "president-elect" Felipe Calderón of the conservative PAN party and Andrés Manuel López Obrador of the more liberal PRD. In an election riddled with "arithmetic mistakes," a partial recount uncovered evidence of abundant stuffing and stealing of ballots that favored the PAN victory.

Meanwhile, US interests were significantly invested in the outcome of Mexico's election. Though neither candidate had any choice but to cooperate with the US agenda, important differences existed around energy policy, specifically with regard to foreign privatization of Mexican oil and gas reserves.

Though the energy sector of Mexico is already deeply penetrated by US capital, as it stands, the Mexican government owns and controls the oil industry, with very tight restrictions on any foreign investment. Petróleos Mexicanos (PEMEX), the fifth largest oil company in the world, exports 80 percent of its oil to the US. Sixty percent of its revenue ($30 billion per year) currently goes to the Mexican government, accounting for more than 40 percent of the Mexican government's annual revenues.

Calderón promises a more thorough and streamlined exploitation of Mexico's oil, demanding that Mexico remove barriers to private/foreign investment (which are currently written into the Mexican Constitution). Obrador, on the other hand, insisted on maintaining national ownership and control of the energy sector in order to build economic and social stability in Mexico.

In June 2005, Mexico signed an accord called Alliance for the Security and Prosperity of North America (ASPAN) with Canada and the US. The point was made that this accord would be binding on whoever became president of Mexico in the upcoming elections. Included in ASPAN is a guarantee to fill the energy needs of the US market, as well as agreements to forge "a common theory of security," allowing US Homeland Security measures to be implemented in Mexico.

Five months later, in November 2005, an "audition" was held with Mexican presidential candidates before members of the US Chamber of Commerce in Mexico City. All candidates were asked whether they would open the energy sector in Mexico, especially the nationalized oil company, PEMEX, to US exploitation.

Felipe Calderón received resounding applause when he answered that he is in favor of private investment in PEMEX, and of weakening the labor unions. He also received applause when he stated that he supported George Bush's guest worker program and that he agreed the border needed to be secured or militarized. Obrador said that he would not allow risk capital investment in PEMEX—but hastened to add that other sectors *would* be opened to investment.

Calderón won the audition, Obrador was granted the role of understudy. Former US Ambassador to Mexico Jeffrey Davidow told Obrador, "If you win the election, we will support you." But when Obrador appeared to be the front-runner in the election, PAN allied with forces in the US to launch a feverish campaign against him.

Though US laws prevent US influence in other countries' elections, anti-Obrador ads airing on Mexican TV were designed by US firms and illegally financed by business councils that included such transnationals as Wal-Mart and Halliburton. US election advisers Rob Allyn and Dick Morris were contracted to develop a media campaign that would foment fear that Obrador, with ties to Chavez and Castro, posed a dangerous Socialist threat to Mexico.

Outgoing president Vicente Fox violated campaign law by making dozens of anti-Obrador speeches during the campaign, as the PAN party illegally saturated airwaves with swift-boat style attack ads against Obrador. Under Mexican law, ruling party interference is a serious crime and grounds for annulling an election.

While Obrador's campaign and hundreds of independent election observers documented several hundred cases of election fraud in making their case for a recount, most Mexican TV stations failed to report the irregularities that surfaced. Days after the election *The New York Times* irresponsibly declared Calderón the winner, and Bush called to personally congratulate Calderón on his "win," even though no victor had been declared under Mexican law. Illegal media campaigns combined with grand-scale fraud had had their effect.

Dominant forces in the US thus had a strong presence behind the scenes of the 2006 Mexican election. As a consequence, Washington looks forward to working with Calderón, who promises tighter (repressive) control and cooperation on all matters of interest to the US, in an accelerated plan to put Mexico more directly under US domination.

Mexico has thus been denied the democratic election of a president who might have joined Latin America in standing up to aggressive US neoliberal policies.

19

People's Movement Challenges Neoliberal Agenda

Sources:

Trade Matters, American Friends Service Committee, May 3, 2006
Title: "Is the US Free Trade Model Losing Steam?"
Author: Jessica Walker Beaumont

International Herald Tribune, December 28, 2006
Title: "Economic Policy Changes With New Latin American Leaders"
Author: Mark Weisbrot

International Affairs Forum, March 31, 2007
Title: "Is Hugo Chavez a Threat to Stability? No."
Author: Mark Weisbrot

Student Evaluator: Toni Catelani
Faculty Evaluator: Phil Beard, Ph.D.

The US Free Trade model is meeting increasingly successful resistance as people's movements around the world build powerful alternatives to neoliberal exploitation.

This is particularly evident in Latin America, where massive opposition to US economic domination has demanded that populist leaders and parties take control of national governments in Venezuela, Bolivia, Ecuador, Argentina, Brazil, Nicaragua, and Uruguay.

Latin American presidents are delivering on promises to fix the mistake of twenty-five years of neoliberal reforms that resulted in the region's worst economic collapse in more than one hundred years. In the two decades preceding World Bank and International Monetary Fund (IMF) policies, 1960-1980, the region's income per person grew by 82 percent. By comparison it grew just 9 percent 1980–2000, and only 4 percent 2000–2005.

Strong ties between Venezuela's Hugo Chavez, Cuba's Fidel Castro, and Bolivia's Evo Morales, Ecuador's Rafael Correa, and Nicaragua's Daniel Ortega, along with cooperative relationships with major economies including Argentina and Brazil, are creating the real potential for autonomous alternatives to US-dictated economic policy in the Western Hemisphere.

In the past year alone several leaders have announced plans to cut ties with the World Bank and IMF. After a sweeping reelection in December 2006, Chavez announced April 30, 2007 that, having paid off debts to the World Bank and the IMF, Venezuela would cut ties with both institutions.[1] Chavez has been able to put his nation on a path of solid growth by fulfilling his 1998 campaign promise to renationalize Venezuela's oil industry (PDVSA). Though fierce US opposition to his move to end foreign privatization led to a failed US-backed military coup in 2002, nationalized oil is now the source of nearly half the Venezuela government's revenues and 80 percent of the country's export earnings. Venezuela's economy has grown 38 percent in the last three years.

Chavez plans to set up a new lending institution run by Latin American nations and has pledged to support it with Venezuela's booming oil revenues.[1] Venezuela's $50 billion in foreign exchange reserves is providing financial support to countries in the region without the exploitive policy conditions attached to WTO and World Bank lending. Leaders are thus able to deliver on promises to their people, contributing not only to stability but to the strengthening of Democracy in the region.

In April 2006, Evo Morales announced his rejection of the IMF and any future FTA with the US. He instead launched the Bolivian Peoples Trade Agreement (PTA), a socialist alternative to the neoliberal free trade model. The PTA emphasizes support of indigenous culture, reciprocity, solidarity, and national sovereignty. Above all the PTA emphasizes improved living conditions for the whole population as a result of international trade and investment. Bolivia's 2005 passage of a Hydrocarbons Law raised the royalties paid by foreign gas companies to the government of Bolivia. While infuriating US corporations, the resulting tens of millions of dollars in revenue have enabled Bolivia to pay off its IMF debt and begin to build social programs and national reserves.

In December 2006, Rafael Correa, who recently won the presidential election in Ecuador on an anti-privatization, anti-US military base platform, announced plans to restructure Ecuador's foreign debt in order to increase spending on crucial social programs. Ecuador has since paid its debt to the IMF and announced plans to sever ties to the institution. Nicaraguan President Daniel Ortega has also announced negotiations toward an IMF exit.

Argentina was one of the IMF's most publicized "successes" turned-crushing-failure at the end of the last century. From 1991 to 1998 the country adopted a host of IMF-recommended reforms including large-scale privatizations. The economy grew substantially during this period but went into a terrible downward slide beginning in mid-1998. At the end of 2001 the whole experiment fell apart, with the country defaulting on more than $100 billion of debt. The currency collapsed soon thereafter, and the majority of people fell below the poverty line in a country that had previously been one of the richest in Latin America.[2]

When Argentina's President Nestor Kirchner finally refused the IMF's debilitating repayment mandates, Argentina's economy began to rebound—and it hasn't stopped growing. In a remarkable expansion, which was never supposed to have happened according to IMF predictions, Argentina's economy has grown by 47 percent in the past few years, making it the fastest growing economy in the Western Hemisphere, and pulling more than nine million people (in a country of 36 million) out of poverty.[2] Argentina decided to make its break with the IMF in January 2006 by paying off its remaining $9.9 billion debt.

As of December 2005, Brazil is also free to make its own decisions, free from IMF interference, after paying off its debt two years ahead of schedule. "We repaid the money to show the world that this country has a government and it is the owner of its own nose," Lula said at the time, adding, "Brazil has been able to decide that it does not want another IMF deal."[3]

While it is an expanding reality that many strong and growing people's movements have not been so fortunate as to have representative governments—the people of India (see story #8), Mexico (see story #18), and Niger (see story #3) are but a few examples—more and more elected leaders in Latin America are providing models of true democratic leadership that is of, for, and by the people.

Citations

1. Jorge Rueda, "Venezuela Pulling Out of IMF, World Bank," Associated Press, May 1 2007.
2. Mark Weisbrot, "IMF's Fall From Power," Washington Post.com, April 13, 2007.
3. Xinhua, "Early Debt Payment Enables Brazil to Make Own Budget Decisions," Peoples Daily Online, December 16, 2005.

UPDATE BY JESSICA WALKER BEAUMONT

Written a year ago, the American Friends Service Committee article "Is the US Free Trade Model Losing Steam?" accurately predicted a growing resistance among Latin American and African leaders to the current "one-size-fits-all" US trade policy model.

Proponents of the current US free trade model seem willing to do whatever it takes to keep the free trade train moving down the track. However their time is literally running out, in part due to the looming July 1 expiration of "fast track" authority that gives the Bush administration the power to negotiate free trade agreements on behalf of Congress.

Although Bolivia, Ecuador and Southern Africa stand firm against US Free Trade Agreements (FTA), there remains a "coalition of the willing" lining up to get their trade agreements. Pending trade pacts for Congressional consideration include those with Colombia, Peru, Panama and Korea. Greasing the wheels to pass these FTAs is a new "breakthrough trade deal" with the Bush administration announced by Democratic leadership on May 10, 2007.

It is said that the deal would improve new free trade agreements by requiring that they include labor and environmental standards, and by insuring better access to essential medicines. Sounds good right? Well, the deal was negotiated in secret with only a handful of Congressional members, the legal text is still not released, and high-powered big business groups are supporters. The official outline of the deal reveals all that is excluded, ignoring a cry for substantial rethinking of US trade policy.

Meanwhile Bolivia continues to advance its People's Trade Agreement. In April, 2007 Bolivia (along with Venezuela and Nicaragua) decided to withdraw from the International Center for Settlement of Investment Disputes (ICSID) housed at the World Bank. This came out of the social movement started in 2001 against the US multinational Bechtel that sued Bolivia under the ICSID for $25 million after it was thrown out during the Cochabamba Water War. Dropping out of the ICSID sends a clear message that protecting private investment at the expense of the rights of the people will not be tolerated.

Ecuadorian President Rafael Correa, elected into power on an anti-FTA and anti-US military base agenda, is considering doing the same. In April Correa expelled the World Bank's representative in Quito, accusing him of withdrawing funds in protest over the government's oil sector reforms.

Costa Rica offers a new beacon of hope as they have yet to ratify the Central American Free Trade Agreement (CAFTA). Huge resistance to CAFTA grew as people learned it would require the dismantling of Costa Rica's public telecommunications sector that is funding education. On April 12, 2007 the Supreme Electoral Court approved a measure calling for a binding referendum on CAFTA, likely to take place in August or September. The CAFTA referendum will be Costa Rica's first public referendum since it gained independence from Spain in 1821 (*Inside US Trade*, May 4, 2007).

20

Terror Act Against Animal Activists

Sources:
Vermont Journal of Environmental Law, March 9, 2007
Title: "The AETA is Invidiously Detrimental to the Animal Rights Movement (and Unconstitutional as Well)"
Authors: David Hoch and Odette Wilkens

Green is the New Red, November 14, 2006
Title: "US House Passes Animal Enterprise Terrorism Act With Little Discussion or Dissent"
Author: Will Potter

Earth First! Journal, November, 2006
Title: "22 Years for Free-Speech Advocates"
Author: Budgerigar

Student Researcher: Sverre Tysl
Faculty Evaluator: Scott Suneson, MA

The term "terrorism" has been dangerously expanded to include acts that interfere, or promote interference, with the operations of animal enterprises. The Animal Enterprise Terrorism Act (AETA), signed into law on November 27, 2006, broadens punishment present under the Animal Enterprises Protection Act (AEPA) of 1992. One hundred and sixty groups, including the National Lawyers' Guild, the Natural Resources Defense Council, the League of Humane Voters,

Physicians' Committee for Responsible Medicine, and the New York City Bar Association, oppose this Act on grounds that its terminology is dangerously vague and poses a major conflict to the US Constitution.

The broad definition of an "animal enterprise," for example, may encompass most US businesses: *"any enterprise that uses or sells animals or animal products."* The phrase *"loss of any real or personal property,"* is elastic enough to include loss of projected profit. Concerns deepen as protections against *"interference"* extend to any *"person or entity having a connection to, relationship with, or transactions with an animal enterprise."*

A letter from the American Civil Liberties Union (ACLU) to Congress dated March 6, 2006, "on behalf of hundreds of thousands of activists and members and fifty-three affiliates nationwide," explains their opposition to AETA based on the concern that First Amendment activities such as demonstrations, leafleting, undercover investigations, and boycotts may be punishable as acts of terror under the overly vague and open-ended law.

The ACLU letter maintains, "Lawful and peaceful protests that, for example, urge a consumer boycott of a company that does not use humane procedures, could be the target of this provision because they 'disrupt' the company's business. This overbroad provision might also apply to a whistleblower whose intentions are to stop harmful or illegal activities by the animal enterprise. The bill will effectively chill and deter Americans from exercising their First Amendment rights to advocate for reforms in the treatment of animals."

Author Will Potter argues that the harsher amendments that AETA brings to its predecessor, AEPA, are hardly necessary, as AEPA was successfully used to disproportionately prosecute the SHAC 7— six animal rights activists organized to expose the illegal and inhumane operations of Huntingdon Life Sciences—for "animal enterprise terrorism." Budgerigar of *Earth First!* recounts that three of the defendants were charged under AEPA in September of 2006 with interstate stalking and conspiracy to commit interstate stalking for organizing demonstrations and running a website that published names and addresses of those involved in the vivisection industry. The group was collectively sentenced to twenty-two years in prison. "The supreme irony of this case," notes Budgerigar, "rests in the fact that these activists were convicted of conspiracy to damage the profits of an animal enterprise, but not of actually damaging it. Even so, the ever-so-honorable judge ordered the defendants to pay a total of $1,000,001 in restitution fees."

Yet Congress deemed that AEPA was not a serious enough tool for going after animal rights "extremists." David Hoch and Odette Wilkens of Equal Justice Alliance ask, "How did this bill [AETA] pass the House?"

Hoch and Wilkens explain that in spite of the fact that one hundred and sixty groups opposed its passage, the House Judiciary Committee placed AETA on the suspension calendar, under which process bills that are non-controversial can be passed by voice vote. The vote on the bill was then held hours earlier than scheduled, with what appears to have been only six (out of 435) Congresspersons present. Five voted for the bill, and Dennis Kucinich, who said that "[t]his bill will have a real and chilling effect on people's constitutionally protected rights," voted against it. Kucinich went on to say, "My concern about this bill is that it does nothing to address the real issue of animal protection but, instead targets those advocating animal rights."

Budgerigar concludes, "The message could not be more clear: run an effective activist campaign, and you will be vilified, criminalized, and imprisoned."

UPDATE BY DAVID HOCH AND ODETTE WILKENS

The Animal Enterprise Terrorism Act (AETA), whose recent passage received virtually no media coverage, will chill the first amendment rights of animal advocates and serve as a template for future limitations on the free speech of all activists. The Act subjects anyone who (1) uses interstate commerce, (2) with the intent to damage or interfere with an "animal enterprise" or with any person or entity associated with an animal enterprise, and (3) causes any economic damage or corporate profit loss or bodily injury or fear of bodily injury, or (4) conspires or attempts to do any of the foregoing, to prosecution for "animal enterprise terrorism."

AETA expands the Animal Enterprise Protection Act (AEPA), under which six animal activists were convicted and imprisoned for publicly advocating animal protection activities. The new law requires less serious conduct than the "physical disruption to . . . an animal enterprise" called for in AEPA, provides stiffer penalties for economic damage and subjects violators who cause no economic damage, bodily harm or fear of serious bodily harm, to as much as one year in prison, while also serving as a predicate for wiretapping.

AETA serves animal enterprises wishing to brand animal activists as criminals and treating dissent as terrorism, and indicates a trend toward treating dissent as terrorism, as evidenced by the Justice Department's current attempt to increase sentences up to twenty years through the application of a concept called "terrorism enhancement."

AETA violates the First and Fourteenth Amendments by proscribing formerly protected modes of expression and invidiously discriminating against animal activists through the imposition of harsher sanctions than those applied to similar or even more serious crimes under the 2005 federal sentencing guidelines. The Act is also unconstitutionally vague, due to the indecipherable ambiguity of statutory terms such as "interfere with" or "profit loss." That vagueness extends to declared exemptions for lawful boycotts and peaceful protests, which could involve the same conduct that would subject one to prosecution under AETA. A lawful boycott is, by definition, the intent to interfere with and cause economic damage to some enterprise.

Furthermore, an animal enterprise need not be acting lawfully to be protected under the Act. Illegal animal enterprise is not an affirmative defense for activities such as whistle-blowing or undercover investigations into animal cruelty, labor conditions, or environmental violations.

To pass AETA, the House invoked a technicality that allows non-controversial bills to be approved by a voice vote, and then voted when only six members were present, although the bill was highly controversial, with approximately one hundred sixty organizations opposing its passage. The Act is unjust, oppressive, and unconstitutional and the honorable thing would be for Congress to repeal it, but without public knowledge and pressure that is unlikely. Therefore, a more prudent strategy would be to increase public awareness until a critical mass convinces Congress to rescind the Act.

To learn more about AETA or become involved in the effort to repeal it, visit the Equal Justice Alliance website at http://noaeta.org/index.htm.

UPDATE BY WILL POTTER
Shortly after passage of the Animal Enterprise Terrorism Act, the Fur Commission USA distributed an announcement to supporters proclaiming "Mission Accomplished!" Corporations have been eager to

appropriate much of the "War on Terrorism" rhetoric against activists, but this was an interesting PR choice. Bush stood on the USS Abraham Lincoln in front of a banner proclaiming "Mission Accomplished" in 2003, only to be dogged by that hubris months, and now years, later.

It looks like corporations may be haunted by similar ghosts in this domestic front of the "War on Terrorism." Not only has the legislation not deterred illegal activity by underground activists, it may have actually added fuel to their fire. On January 5, 2007, the Animal Liberation Front—considered by the FBI to be the "number one domestic terrorist threat"—distributed an anonymous communiqué related to vandalism at the home of a University of Utah animal researcher. It concluded: "PS. To all the vivisectors we have yet to visit: don't bask in your recent legislative victory for too long. This new animal enterprise law means NOTHING. —ALF"

It wasn't an isolated incident. Just two days after the president signed the law, another communiqué claimed credit for vandalizing the windows of a pharmaceutical company, and underground activists signed it: "Dedicated to the SHAC 7!" (The SHAC 7 are a group of activists convicted under the original legislation. They were never accused of anything like breaking windows: they "conspired" to violate the law by running a website and vocally supporting both legal and illegal tactics against companies doing business with a controversial lab).

If the purpose of AETA is to go after underground activists, that mission is far from accomplished. And if the purpose of AETA is to go after "the above ground," activists are organizing to challenge that mission as well. Just a few weeks after the legislation passed, student activists protested outside the offices of US Rep. James P. McGovern in Massachusetts, naming and shaming him for not being present for a vote. McGovern's staff quickly stated publicly that he does not support the law, he would have voted against it if he had known about a vote, and he would advocate for repeal.

And then there were dozens of community events around the world to raise awareness about labeling activists as "ecoterrorists," from South Africa to Greece to Minneapolis, MN.

"Mission Accomplished"? Ahem.

To be clear, in some ways the mission of the Animal Enterprise Terrorism Act has been accomplished: it has instilled a level of fear in mainstream, above-ground, legal activists that they may one day be hit with the T-word in this ever-expanding "War on Terrorism."

But through my reporting I've found that an interesting thing happens when people learn about this "Green Scare" and the corporate and political interests behind it: that fear easily turns to rage. More than 140 comments have been posted on the article I wrote about the legislation passing the House. Some of them express fear and a bit of hopelessness. Many share the tenor of "Jersey" who wrote: "do they really think everyone is going to crawl into the woodwork and stand for this?"

Since the law passed, I have been speaking regularly in public forums like the New York City Bar Association, Yale Law School, activist conferences, and with both mainstream and alternative press, and I've been able to see that phenomenon over and over again: questioning and investigating the legislation, and the money behind it, demystifies the law. It declaws it.

That knowledge is what ultimately worked against Senator Joseph McCarthy, succeeding where the "loyalty oaths" and the "naming names" failed. It can work now, too. If reporters do their jobs, and expose these issues to the general public, people can stop being afraid and start being pissed.

For more information, please visit www.GreenIsTheNewRed.com.

21

US Seeks WTO Immunity for Illegal Farm Payments

Sources:
Oxfam International, June 29, 2006
Title: "US Seeks 'Get-Out Clause' for Illegal Farm Payments"

Financial Times UK, January 9 2007
Title: "Canada Launches WTO Case on US Subsidies"
Author: Eoin Callan

Student Researcher: Cedric Therene
International Business Evaluator: Tim Ogburn

On July 24, 2006, after nearly five years of global trade negotiations, talks at the meetings of the World Trade Organization collapsed—

perhaps permanently, say some economic analysts. In January of 2007, trade ministers from the United States, the European Union, Brazil, India, Japan, and Australia said they remained hopelessly stalemated, mostly on the contentious issue of farm trade. US negotiators blamed the breakdown on E.U., India, and Japan for balking at the unrestricted opening of markets to agricultural products.[1]

What went uncovered in mainstream news sources was any analysis of the content of the negotiations—what exactly the countries involved were offering, and what they expected in return.

Of utmost importance to the Bush Administration was that the US receive immunity from lawsuits by poor countries before Bush's special "fast track" trade negotiating powers expired at the end of June, 2007.

In a last-minute proposal, one not included on the original agenda, the US suddenly insisted that all trade agreements include a special clause called a "Peace Clause" that would make its use of illegal farm subsidies immune from prosecution by the countries affected. Between 1994 and 2003, such a Peace Clause had denied developing nations any legal recourse in the face of the "dumping" of cheap foreign products that had devastated their agricultural communities.

According to international NGOs such as Oxfam International, the Peace Clause gives rich countries like the US and the European Union free rein to provide huge subsidies to their farmers. Such practices benefit the economies of already-wealthy nations, while damaging the agricultural communities of poorer nations. According to a 2003 Oxfam report, thirty-eight developing countries have suffered from unfair competition as a result of illegal subsidies in the US and EU.

Events following expiration of these legal protections make it clear why the US was so eager to reintroduce a new version of the Peace Clause (and why it was done so slyly). Following its expiration in 2003, Brazil took the US to the WTO court charging that US cotton subsidies had depressed world prices, hurting cotton producers in Brazil and around the world—and Brazil won! In 2005, the WTO agreed with Brazil's charge, ordering that the US immediately discontinue its distribution of illegal agricultural subsidies. Fearing that other developing nations would follow suit, US negotiators were driven to reintroduce the proposal for protections they had enjoyed under the Peace Clause.

More recently, following the July 2006 collapse of the Doha trade talks, Canada has asked the WTO to review charges that the US is continuing to use illegal and "trade-distorting" agricultural subsidies. The charges focus on payments made to American corn farmers, but also challenge the total level of US agricultural subsidies. This is the most significant challenge to the structure of US agricultural subsidies since the landmark WTO ruling in favor of Brazil in 2005.

In June of 2007, The Canadian government asked the WTO to establish a dispute settlement panel to investigate the allegation.[2] Under WTO rules, the United States can provide up to $19.1 billion annually in subsidies that are considered trade-distorting. Canada says the United States broke the rules every year from 1999 to 2005 except for 2003.

Gretchen Hamel, a spokeswoman for the US trade representatives, parroted the position taken previously by US officials addressing the Brazil dispute. She said, "Negotiation, not litigation, is the path to removing trade distortions in agriculture and improving opportunities for farmers and producers all around the world."[2] The US says that it needs the Peace Clause renewed in order to protect itself from litigation while it "is in the process of reducing its trade-distorting subsidies." But Oxfam notes that, proposals included in the new Peace Clause would actually allow the US to increase its farm support from under $20 billion to almost $23 billion. The EU proposal would allow an increase in farm subsidies from $23 billion to $33 billion. Poor countries, with no surplus to supplement their farmers' income shortfalls, would have nothing to respond with—no global support, no economic power, and no legal appeals.

Citations

1. Paul Blustein, "Trade Talks Fail After Stalemate Over Farm Issues; Collapse Comes With Finger-Pointing," *Washington Post*, July 25, 2006.
2. Phillip Brasher, "Canada attacks US subsidies at WTO," *Des Moines Register*, June 8, 2007.

22

North Invades Mexico

Source:
TomDispatch.com, September 19, 2006
Author: Mike Davis
Title: "Border Invaders: The Perfect Swarm Heads South"

Student Researcher: Rachel Icaza and Erica Haikara
Faculty Evaluator: Francisco Vazquez, Ph.D.

The visitor crossing the Mexican border from Tijuana to San Diego these days is immediately confronted by a huge sign, "Stop the Border Invasion!" Sponsored by allies of the anti-immigrant vigilante group, the Minutemen, the same signs insult Mexican citizens at other border crossings in Arizona and Texas. The ultimate irony is that a crisis invasion is indeed occurring, but the signs, it seems, may be pointed the wrong direction.

Author Mike Davis points out that, in a "reality stood on its head," few people—at least outside Mexico—have bothered to notice that while all the nannies, cooks, maids, and gardeners have been heading north to tend the luxury lifestyles of irate republicans, the Gringo masses have been rushing south to enjoy glorious budget retirements and affordable second homes in Mexico.

The number of North Americans living in Mexico has soared from 200,000 to 1 million (one-quarter of all US expatriates) in the past decade. With more than 70 million American baby-boomers expected to retire in the next two decades, experts predict "a tidal wave" of migration to warmer—and cheaper—climates. Baby-boomers are not simply feathering nests for eventual retirement, but also increasingly speculating in Mexican resort property and gated communities, complete with Hooters, Burger King, and Starbucks. The land rush is sending up property values to the detriment of locals whose children are consequently driven into slums or forced to emigrate north, only to face increasing "invasion" charges.

The Gringo footprint is largest (and brings the most significant geopolitical consequences) in Baja California, an epochal process that, if unchecked, will produce intolerable social marginalization and ecological devastation.

Indeed, the first two stages of informal annexation have already occurred. Under the banner of NAFTA, Southern California has exported hundreds of its sweatshops and toxic industries to the *maquiladora* zones of Tijuana and Mexicali. The Pacific Maritime Association, representing the West Coast's major shipping companies, has joined forces with Korean and Japanese corporations to explore the construction of a vast new container port at Punta Colonel, 150 miles south of Tijuana, which would undercut the power of Longshore unionism in San Pedro and San Francisco.

Secondly, tens of thousands of US retirees and winter-residents are now clustered at both ends of the peninsula. Along the northwest coast from Tijuana to Ensenada, a recent advertisement for a real estate conference at UCLA boasts that "there are presently over fifty-seven real estate developments . . . with over 11,000 homes/condos with an inventory value of over $3 billion . . . all of them geared for the US market."

Meanwhile, at the tropical end of Baja, a US expatriot enclave has emerged in the twenty-mile strip between Cabo San Lucas and San Jose de Cabo. Los Cabos has become an archipelago of real-estate hot spots where continuous double-digit increases in property values pull in speculative capital. Judging from the registration of private planes at the local airport, Cabos has essentially become a resort suburb of Orange County—the home of the most vehement Minutemen chapters.

Davis points out that many wealthy Southern Californians evidently see no contradiction between fuming over the "alien invasion" with one's conservative friends at the Newport Marina one day, and flying down to enjoy their Cabos investment properties the next.

One of several multi-billion dollar real estate projects being developed for the US market is the Villages of Loreto: another 6,000 homes for expatriates in colonial-Mexico motif on the Sea of Cortez. The $3 billion Loreto project boasts that it will be the last word in green design, exploiting solar power and restricting automobile usage. It will, coincidently, balloon Loreto's population from its current 15,000 to more than 100,000 in a decade, with the social and environmental consequences of a sort that can already be seen in the slum peripheries of Cancun and other mega-resorts.

One of the irresistible attractions of Baja is that it has preserved a primordial wildness that has disappeared elsewhere in the West. Local residents, including a very eloquent indigenous environmental movement, cherish this incomparable landscape, as they do the survival of an egalitarian ethos in the peninsula's small towns and fishing villages.

However, thanks to the silent invasion of the baby-boomers from the north, much of the natural history and frontier culture of Baja could be swept away in the next generation. The problem is, as Tom Engelhardt of *Tomdispatch* points out, "Fences don't work if you've got your own plane."

23

Feinstein's Conflict of Interest in Iraq

Source:
North Bay Bohemian, January 24, 2007
Title: "Senator Feinstein's Iraq Conflict"
Author: Peter Byrne

Student Researcher: David Abbott, Amanda Spigut, and Ann Marie O'Toole
Faculty Evaluator: David McCuan, Ph.D.

Dianne Feinstein—the ninth wealthiest member of congress—has been beset by monumental ethical conflicts of interest. As a member of the Military Construction Appropriations Subcommittee (MILCON) from 2001 to the end of 2005, Senator Feinstein voted for appropriations worth billions of dollars to her husband's firms.

From 1997 through the end of 2005, Feinstein's husband Richard C. Blum was a majority shareholder in both URS Corp. and Perini Corp. She lobbied Pentagon officials in public hearings to support defense projects that she favored, some of which already were, or subsequently became, URS or Perini contracts. From 2001 to 2005, URS earned $792 million from military construction and environmental cleanup projects approved by MILCON; Perini earned $759 million from such projects.

In 2000, Perini earned a mere $7 million from federal contracts. After 9/11, Perini was transformed into a major defense contractor. In 2004, the company earned $444 million for military construction work in Iraq and Afghanistan, as well as for improving airfields for the US Air Force in Europe and building base infrastructures for the US Navy around the globe. In a remarkable financial recovery, Perini shot from near penury in 1997 to logging gross revenues of $1.7 billion in 2005.

It is estimated that Perini now holds at least $2.5 billion worth of contracts tied to the worldwide expansion of the US military. Its largest Department of Defense contracts are "indefinite delivery-indefinite quantity" or "bundled" contracts carrying guaranteed profit margins. As of May 2006, Perini held a series of bundled contracts awarded by the Army Corps of Engineers for work in the Middle East worth $1.725 billion. Perini has also been awarded an open-ended contract by the US Air Force for military construction and cleaning the environment at closed military bases.

In 2003 hearings, MILCON approved various construction projects at sites where Perini and/or URS are contracted to perform engineering and military construction work. URS's military construction work in 2000 earned it a mere $24 million. The next year, when Feinstein took over as MILCON chair, military construction earned URS $185 million. On top of that, the company's architectural and engineering revenue from military construction projects grew from $108,726 in 2000 to $142 million in 2001, more than a thousand-fold increase in a single year.

Beginning in 1997, Michael R. Klein, a top legal adviser to Feinstein and a long-time business partner of Blum's, routinely informed Feinstein about specific federal projects coming before her in which Perini had a stake. The insider information, Klein said, "was intended to help the senator avoid conflicts of interest." Although Klein's admission was intended to defuse the issue, it had the effect of exacerbating it, because in theory, Feinstein would not know the identity of any of the companies that stood to contractually benefit from her approval of specific items in the military construction budget—until Klein told her.

Feinstein's husband has profited in other ways by his powerful political connections. In March 2002, then-Governor Gray Davis appointed Blum to a twelve-year term as a regent of the University of California, where he used his position as Regent to award millions of dollars in construction contracts to URS and Perini. At the time, he was the principal owner of URS and had substantial interests in Perini. In 2005, Blum divested himself of Perini stock for a considerable profit. He then resigned from the URS board of directors and divested his investment firm of about $220 million in URS stock.[1]

Citation

1.   Peter Byrne, "Blum's Plums" *North Bay Bohemian*, February 21, 2007.

UPDATE BY PETER BYRNE

Shortly before my expose of Senator Dianne Feinstein's conflict of interest was published in January 2007, Feinstein, who had declined to substantively comment upon serious allegations of ethical misconduct as reported in the story, resigned from the Military Construction Subcommittee. I then wrote three follow-ups, including a news column on her resignation, an expose of her husband Richard Blum's conflict of interest as a regent of the University of California, and an expose of Blum's business partner, Michael R. Klein. With Blum's financial backing, Klein, a war contractor, operates a non-profit called The Sunlight Foundation that awards millions of dollars to reporters and government watchdog groups to research government ethics.

In March, right-wing bloggers by the thousands started linking to and commenting upon these stories—agitating for a Congressional investigation of Feinstein. In just two days, the stories got 50,000 online hits. Michael Savage and Rush Limbaugh did radio segments on my findings. I declined to appear on their shows, because I do not associate with racist, misogynist, homophobic demagogues. Fox News' Bill O'Reilly invited me to be on his national TV show, but quickly uninvited me after I promised that the first sentence out of my mouth would frame Feinstein as a neoconservative warmonger just like O'Reilly.

As the storm of conservative outrage intensified, Joe Conason, from The Nation Institute, which had commissioned the Feinstein investigation, asked to have the tag thanking the Nation Institute for funding removed from my stories because, he said, Katrina vanden Heuval, *The Nation's* editor and publisher, did not want the magazine or its non-profit institute to be positively associated with Limbaugh. I told Conason that not only was I *required* to credit The Nation Institute under the terms of our contract, but that *The Nation's* editors should be proud of the investigation and gratified by the public reaction.

The back story to that encounter is that, in October, vanden Heuvel had abruptly killed the Feinstein story, which had been scheduled to run as a cover feature before the November 2006 election in which Feinstein was up for reelection. *The Nation's* investigative editor, Bob Moser, who worked closely with me on the project from start to finish, wrote that I had done a "solid job," but that the magazine liked to have a political "impact," and since Feinstein was "not facing a strong challenge for reelection," they were not going to print the story. Moser added that there was no "smoking gun," which amazed me, since Klein's admission that he was funneling defense contracting wish lists developed by Feinstein's husband's company directly to the senator, who was in a position to make those wishes come true, was a hot and smoking fact pointing toward corrupt practices. Subsequently, vanden Heuval wrote an editorial praising women leaders of the newly-empowered Democratic Party, including Feinstein: go figure.

I then sold the story to Salon.com, who abruptly killed it right before publication, too. This time the editor's explanation was that "someone talked to the Sunlight Foundation" and that Salon no longer saw the matter as a serious conflict of interest. So, I pitched the story to *Slate*, *The New Republic*, *Harper's*, the *Los Angeles Times* and, by way of experiment, to the neoconservative *American Spectator* and *Weekly Standard*. Most of the editors praised the reporting, but turned down the story. I cannot help but believe that, considering the precarious balance of power in the post-election Senate, some of these editors were not eager to critique the ethics of a Democrat. As for rejection by the neoconservatives, I theorize that they secretly adore Feinstein, who has consistently supported Bush's war and homeland security agenda and the illiberal Patriot Act.

So I sold the tale to the *North Bay Bohemian*, which, along with its sister papers in San Jose and Santa Cruz ran it on the cover—complete with follow-ups. After it appeared, the editors and I received a series of invective-filled emails from war contractor Klein (who is also an attorney) but, since he could show no errors of fact in the story, he did not get the retraction that he apparently wanted. In March, the story crested a Google tidal wave generated by left- and right-wing bloggers wondering why the mainstream media was ignoring the Feinstein scandal. After two dozen newspapers ran a McClatchy wire service article in April observing that no one had found any factual faults in my reporting, the lefty group Media Matters attacked me on its Web site as a right-wing pawn, without even calling me for comment, nor finding any errors in my reporting. I parried their fact-free insults with facts and they were compelled to correct the inaccurate rant.

On April 30, *The Hill* newspaper in Washington D.C. ran a highly-visible op-ed by a conservative pundit quoting from my story and comparing Feinstein (unfairly) to convicted felon and former

Congressman, Duke Cunningham. As the Feinstein investigation gained national traction, mostly outside the realm of the mainstream media, one of Klein's employees at the Sunlight Foundation posted a "critique" of my story, which was loaded with personal insults, but contained no factual substance. Not coincidentally, Feinstein's press office distributes, upon request, a similarly-worded "rebuttal," which insults my personal integrity, finds no factual errors, and does not address the damning fact, reported in the story, that four non-partisan ethics experts based in Washington D.C. found the senator had a conflict of interest after reviewing the results of my investigation.

Also, in April, CODEPINK and The Raging Grannies held a demonstration in front of the Feinstein-Blum mansion in San Francisco demanding that she return her war profits to the Iraqi people. That was my proudest moment.

Five months after the story was printed, opinion-floggers across the political spectrum continue to loudly ask why the mainstream media has not reported on Feinstein's ethical problem. Some say that the hurricane of opinion raised by the investigation has killed Feinstein's chance for a spot on the Democratic Party's presidential ticket in 2008. Klein has continued to send me e-mails full of verbal abuse, misspellings, and implied threat of lawsuit.

Blissfully, I delete them.

24

Media Misquotes Threat From Iran's President

Sources:

Global Research, January 20, 2007
Title: "Wiped Off The Map—The Rumor of the Century"
Author: Arash Norouzi

Information Clearing House, May 9, 2006
Title: "Full Text: The President of Iran's Letter To President Bush"
Translated by *Le Monde*

Student Researchers: Becky Bazell
Faculty Evaluator: Peter Phillips, Ph.D.

Across the world a media story has spread that Iran's President Ahmadinejad has threatened to destroy Israel, by saying that,

"Israel must be wiped off the map." Contrary to general belief, this statement was actually a misinterpretation. However, it was the Islamic Republic News Service in Iran that first mistranslated the quote. Iran's Foreign Minister attempted to clarify the statement, but the quote ended up having a life of its own in the corporate media.

Amid heated wrangling over Iran's nuclear program and the threat of preemptive strikes by the US, the quote has been continually used to reinforce the idea that Iran is being run by extremists seeking the total destruction of Israel.

So what did Ahmadinejad actually say? To quote his exact words in Farsi:

"*Imam ghofi een rezhim-e ishghalgar-e qods bayad az safheh-ye ruzgar mahv shavad.*"

Rezhim-e is the word "regime," pronounced just like the English word with an extra "eh" sound at the end. Ahmadinejad did not refer to Israel the country or Israel the landmass, but the Israeli regime. This is a vastly significant distinction, as one cannot wipe a regime off the map. Ahmadinejad did not even refer to Israel by name, he instead used the specific phrase "*rezhim-e ishghalgar-e qods*" (regime occupying Jerusalem).

A similar statement by Ahmadinejad in December 2006, "As the Soviet Union disappeared, the Zionist regime will also vanish and humanity will be liberated," has also been misinterpreted.

In May of 2006 President Ahmadinejad published an open letter to President Bush clearly asking for peace and the mutual respect of human rights. He warns that Western media, through contrived and deceptive information, has intensified the climate of fear that leads to attacks on innocent peoples. The letter was not reported in the US news media. Ahmadinejad began the letter writing, "Mr. George Bush, For some time now I have been thinking, how one can justify the undeniable contradictions that exist in the international arena . . . Can one be a follower of Jesus Christ (PBUH), the great Messenger of God, Feel obliged to respect human rights, Present liberalism as a civilization model, Announce one's opposition to the proliferation of nuclear weapons and WMDs, Make "War on Terror" his slogan, And finally, Work towards the establishment of a unified international community—a community which Christ and the virtuous of the Earth will one day govern, But at the same time, have countries attacked; The lives, reputations and possessions of people destroyed and on the slight chance of the . . . of a . . . criminals in a village city, or convoy for example the entire village, city or convey set ablaze."

EVALUATOR COMMENT

Ahmadinejad declared that Zionism is the West's apparatus of political oppression against Muslims. He says the "Zionist regime" was imposed on the Islamic world as a strategic bridgehead to ensure domination of the region and its assets. This position is viewed as threatening to many in the West. While threats and counter-threats escalates tensions in the Persian Gulf, I believe it is important for the media to publish both sides of issues and be as accurate as possible by seeking to build understanding rather than fear and anger.
—Peter Phillips

UPDATE BY ARASH NOROUZI

In May 2007, the US House of Representatives unanimously passed a resolution calling on the U.N. Security Council to charge Ahmadinejad with the crime of inciting genocide "because of his calls for the destruction of the State of Israel"—a violation of the U.N.'s 1948 Genocide Convention—specifically citing the false "wiped off the map" quote from October 2005. It also called for the U.N. to prevent Iran from obtaining nuclear weapons, with the "potential means to the end of carrying out President Mahmoud Ahmadinejad's threats against Israel."

This misquote has become a key component of the push for war with Iran, a war that would make Iraq look like the cakewalk it was predicted to be. Attacking Iran would result in massive death and destruction, affect world oil supplies, provoke terrorism, could initiate the next World War, and might even include the use of nuclear weapons for the first time since WWII. In this heated atmosphere, an accurate narrative is essential in averting the next cataclysmic Mideast intervention. When President Bush emphasizes the importance of taking the words of America's enemies seriously, that process begins with first determining just what exactly those words *are.*

Yet my article is about more than just clarifying a mistranslated statement. It's about the media, propaganda, plagiarism, language, false assumptions . . . Functioning much like a puzzle, it engages readers by allowing them to deconstruct the quote and its meaning themselves. This self-verification process adds a compelling aspect in which credibility becomes largely obsolete. The article's 'punchline' demonstrates undeniably that members of the mainstream media knowingly spread this rumor, and readers are challenged to check for themselves by comparing linked sources proving this claim.

The idea is not merely to contest a single misquote, but to also promote skepticism about all pre-war intelligence. If this quote is false, then it's logical to assume that other accusations against Iran could be wrong too—just as they were with Iraq.

The overwhelming ubiquity of this misquote has deterred others from correcting what they probably view as a lost cause. Yet my article alone has been viewed by millions, translated into at least half a dozen languages, garnered radio interviews, inspired videos on YouTube, and become the subject of an entire article in *The Bangkok Post*. It got the attention of people at the BBC, *Washington Post*, IAEA, State Department, United Nations, and the Islamic Republic itself. It's been quoted by numerous journalists, authors and academics, in published letters to the editor, and on call-in TV shows such as on C-SPAN. The Associated Press has now begun citing the "vanish from the page of time" phrase, adding that "independent analysts" have refuted the "map" quote; and Dennis Kucinich was prepared to correct the rumor when asked about the subject on TV recently.

These are hopeful signals that underscore the importance of alternative voices in the media, and their potential effectiveness in influencing the discourse. If the first casualty of war is the truth, then it's up to the truth tellers—whomever they may be—to enlighten us.

25

Who Will Profit from Native Energy?

Source:
LiP Magazine, June 5, 2006
Title: "Native Energy Futures"
Author: Brian Awehali

Student Researchers: Ioana Lupu and Mayra Madrigal
Faculty Evaluator: Dolly Freidel, Ph.D.

Energy on Native American land is becoming big business. According to the Indigenous Environmental Network, 35 percent of the fossil fuel resources in the US are within Indian country. The Department of the Interior estimates that Indian lands hold undiscovered reserves of almost 54 billion tons of coal, 38 trillion cubic feet of natural gas, and 5.4 billion barrels of oil. Tribal lands also contain enormous amounts of alternative energy. "Wind blowing through Indian reservations in just four northern Great Plains states could support almost 200,000 megawatts of wind power," Winona LaDuke told *Indian Country Today* in March 2005, "Tribal landholdings in the southwestern US . . . could generate enough power to eradicate all fossil fuel burning power plants in the US."

The questions to be answered now are: what sort of energy will Indian lands produce, who will make that decision, and who will end up benefiting from the production?

According to Theresa Rosier, Counselor to the Assistant Secretary for Indian Affairs, "increased energy development in Indian and Alaska Native communities could help the Nation have more reliable homegrown energy supplies." This, she says, is "consistent with the President's National Energy Policy to secure America's energy future."

Rosier's statement conveys quite a lot about how the government and the energy sector intend to market the growing shift away from dependence on foreign energy. The idea that "America's energy future" should be linked to having "more reliable homegrown energy supplies" can be found in native energy-specific legislation that has already passed into law. What this line of thinking fails to take into account is that Native America is not the same as US America. The domestic "supplies" in question belong to sovereign nations, not to the United States or its energy sector.

So far, government plans to deregulate and step up the development of domestic (native) energy resources is being spun as a way to produce clean, efficient energy while helping Native Americans gain greater economic and tribal sovereignty. Critics charge, however, that large energy companies are simply looking to establish lucrative partnerships with tribal corporations, which are largely free of regulation and federal oversight.

For example, in 2003, the Rosebud Sioux of South Dakota, in partnership with NativeEnergy, LLC, completed the first large-scale native-owned wind turbine in history. The project was billed as a way to bring renewable energy–related jobs and training opportunities to the citizens of this sovereign nation, who are among the poorest in all of North America.

NativeEnergy's President and CEO Tom Boucher, an energy industry vet, financed the Rosebud Sioux project by selling "flexible emissions standards" created by the Kyoto Protocol. These are the tax-deductible pollution credits from ecologically responsible companies (or in this case, Native American tribes), which can then be sold to polluters wishing to "offset" their carbon dioxide generation without actually reducing their emissions.

Since the Rosebud test case proved successful, NativeEnergy moved forward with plans to develop a larger "distributed wind project," located on eight different reservations. NativeEnergy also became a majority Indian-owned company in August 2005, when the *pro-development* Intertribal Council on Utility Policy (COUP) purchased a majority stake in the company on behalf of its member tribes.

The COUP-NativeEnergy purchase just happened to coincide with the passage of the 2005 Energy Policy Act. The act contains a number of native energy–specific provisions in its Title V, many of which set alarming precedents.

Most outrageously, it gave the US government the power to grant rights of way through Indian lands without permission from the tribes—if deemed to be in the strategic interests of an energy-related project. Under the guise of "promoting tribal sovereignty," the act also released the federal government from liability with regard to resource development, shifting responsibility for environmental review and regulation from the federal to tribal governments. Also, according to the Indigenous Environmental Network, the act "rolls back the protections of . . . critical pieces of legislation that grassroots indigenous peoples utilize to protect our sacred sites." Some critics have derided the 2005 act as a fire sale on Indian energy, characterizing various incentives as a broad collection of subsidies (federal handouts) for US energy companies.

America's native peoples may attain a modicum of energy independence and tribal sovereignty through the development of wind, solar, and other renewable energy infrastructure on their lands. But, according to Brian Awehali, it won't come from getting into bed with, and becoming indebted to, the very industry currently driving the planet to its doom.

UPDATE BY BRIAN AWEHALI

I believe the topic of this article was important and urgent because sometimes all that glitters really is gold, even if the marketing copy says it's green. The long and utterly predictable history where indigenous peoples and US government and corporate interests are both concerned shouldn't be forgotten as we enter the brave new green era. Marketing for-profit energy schemes on Indian lands as a means of promoting tribal sovereignty is both ludicrous and offensive, as are "green" development plans intrinsically tied to the extraction of fossil fuels in the deregulated Wild West of Indian Country. Energy companies are only interested in native sovereignty because it means operations on Indian lands are not subject to federal regulation or oversight. This is why I included a discussion in my article about the instructive example of the Alaska tribal corporations and the ways they've mutated into multi-billion dollar loophole exploiters. (My brief examination of Alaska tribal corporations drew heavily from an excellent *Mother Jones* article, "Little Big Companies," by Michael Scherer). It's also my belief that the probably well-intentioned idea of "green tags," carbon offset credits, and market-enabled "carbon neutrality" should be examined very closely: Why are we introducing systems for transferring (or trading) the carbon emissions of "First World" polluters to those who contributed least to global warming? I would argue that this is merely a nice-sounding way for the overdeveloped world to purchase the right to continue its pathologically unsustainable mode of existence, while doing little to address the very grave ecological realities we now face.

It's very hard to know what the impact of this story was, or to gauge mainstream response to it. In my experience, the so-called mainstream has a difficult time absorbing and understanding Native American issues, not least because this mainstream tends to think of indigenous peoples in North America in historical, rather than contemporary, terms. I am, however, encouraged by the number of journalists and writers who are beginning to ask critical questions about greenwashing, and I see my story as adding to that collective body of work.

For more information about energy policy and its impact on indigenous communities of North America, I recommend visiting the Indigenous Environmental Network (www.ienearth.org), and checking out their Native Energy Campaign.

CENSORED 2008 HONORABLE MENTIONS

Citibank Aids in Tax Evasion for World's Elite

Source:
The New Internationalist, August 2006
Title: "Confessions of a Citibanker"
Author: Lucy Komisar

Citibank, one of the largest financial services conglomerates in the world, operates branches in seventeen of the world's seventy tax havens, providing banking services and investments returns on billions of dollars of unreported income for the world's elite. Citibank helps Argentina's rich shelter billions in illicit capital in offshore accounts where interest earnings remain unreported. Argentina's government reported in 2002 that over $127 billion of national money, being held abroad in unreported income accounts. In Spain, Citibank offers people with over $1 million to invest International Personal Banking accounts (IPBs), which allow for the movement of funds to other Citibank off-shore accounts. Private banking systems in the world are estimated to hold over $11.5 trillion in assets offshore. Income from these assets would earn as much as $860 billion a year. Much of this income remains unreported in the account holders home countries, thus avoiding potential annual taxes of some $255 billion worldwide.

Injured Soldiers Sent Back to War

Sources:
Salon, March 11, 2007
Title: "The Army is ordering injured troops to go to Iraq"
Author: Mark Benjamin

Clamor Magazine, Fall 2006
Title: "The New Wartime Body: Amputee Vets Return from Iraq"
Author: Socket

The military is redeploying troops who doctors say are medically unfit for battle, some with serious injuries including multiple amputations. Division and brigade surgeons have summarily downgraded soldiers' injury profiles without medical exams in order to redeploy them. Injured vets often come back to civilian life owing money in the face of increased medical expenses. Returning to active duty is the only option for many who can't afford civilian medical care. Injured personnel face a culture that encourages them to go back to war, and no alternative training is being offered to them.

MEFTA: Target, Wal-Mart Profit off Jordanian Slavery

Sources:
Inter Press Service, May 3, 2006, June 29, 2006, September 28, 2006
Titles: "US, Israel, Jordan Pact Created Havens for Servitude"
  "US, Oman Pact Nixes Israel Boycott"
  "US Union, Business Group Slam Jordan Sweatshops"
Author: Emad Mekay

Major US companies, including Wal-Mart, Target, Kohl's, Victoria's Secret and L.L. Bean, are buying apparel from sweatshops in Jordan under a three-way trade deal that binds the Arab nation to Israel and the United States. The National Labor Committee (nlcnet.org) has released a report saying that the Jordan Free Trade Agreement (FTA) has descended into human trafficking and involuntary servitude. A similar US Middle East FTA with Oman is going through despite several protests over Oman's record on labor standards, human rights abuse, and the environmental destruction. Both the United States and Israel are seeking to replicate this model in numerous trade deals with other countries in the Arab world, under President George W. Bush's plan for a Middle East Free Trade Area (MEFTA), which would tie all twenty-two Arab states with the US and Israel in a trade deal by 2013.

Scientists Paid to Dispute Climate Study

Source:
The Guardian/UK, February 2, 2007
Title: "Scientists Offered Cash to Dispute Climate Study"
Author: Ian Sample

Scientists and economists have been offered $10,000 each by lobbyists, American Enterprise Institute (AEI)—funded by ExxonMobile—

to undermine the major climate change report published by the UN's Intergovernmental Panel on Climate Change (IPCC). The AEI has received more than $1.6m from ExxonMobile and more than twenty of its staff have worked as consultants to the Bush administration. Ben Stewart of Greenpeace said: "The AEI is more than just a think tank, it functions as the Bush administration's intellectual Cosa Nostra. They are White House surrogates in the last throes of their campaign of climate change denial. They lost on the science; they lost on the moral case for action. All they've got left is a suitcase full of cash."

Tough Immigration Laws Revive Private Prison Industry

Source:

In These Times, September 4, 2006
Title: "Follow the Prison Money Trail"
Author: Silja J. A. Talvi

According to the Institute on Money in State Politics, private prison companies are campaigning hard to sign contracts with poor states that have the toughest sentencing laws—and are most likely to come up with the bodies to fill prison beds. Those states are also the ones most likely to have passed the "three-strikes" laws that were pushed by conservative think tank, American Legislative Exchange Council (ALEC), some of whose members come from the ranks of private prison companies. Leaders in the private prison industry, CCA (Corrections Corp of America) and The GEO Group, have paid tens (if not hundreds) of thousands of dollars in exchange for a privileged position on ALEC's Criminal Justice Task Force (which CCA chairs). ALEC, in turn, promotes prison privatization. In addition CCA and GEO spend millions on campaign contributions at both the federal and state level. They especially focus on impoverished states—where a little money goes a long way. At the federal level, GEO and CCA have perfected the art of the "very tight revolving door" which involves snapping up former corrections administrators, PAC lobbyists, and state officials to serve as consultants to private prison companies.

Supermarket Consolidation

Source:
The Oakland Institute, February 14, 2007
Title: "Retail Consolidation Threatens US Food Security"
Authors: Katy Mamen, Anuradha Mittal

The top five food retailers control more than half of all grocery sales in the US. Corporate consolidation in food retail has put our access to a reliable supply of healthy and affordable food at risk and supermarkets are abandoning low-income communities where profit margins are lower. Labor standards are being forced down by the anti-union actions of competitive corporate food giants.

Fake News Still Happening

Sources:
Center for Media and Democracy, November 14, 2006
Title: "Still Not the News: Stations Overwhelmingly Fail to Disclose VNRs"
Authors: Diane Farsetta and Daniel Price

Democracy Now! November 14, 2006
Title: "Corporate Propaganda Still On the News: Study Finds Local Stations Overwhelmingly Fail to Disclose VNRs"
Author: Amy Goodman

Video news releases (VNR) are pre-packaged broadcast segments designed to look like news, that are funded by and scripted for corporate or government clients. In April 2006, the Center for Media and Democracy released a comprehensive report detailing TV newsrooms' use of VNRs. In August 2006 the FCC launched an investigation of the seventy-seven stations implicated. Follow-up by the Center for Media and Democracy indicates that viewers are still routinely deceived by fake TV news as television networks continue to air VNRs (see chapter 9).

World Bank Promotes Labor Abuse

Source:
Common Dreams, March 23, 2006
Title: "World Bank Trade Strategy Has Not Adequately Helped the Poor"
Authors: Friends of the Earth International

The International Confederation of Free Trade Unions strongly criticized the new edition of the World Bank's highest-circulation publication, *Doing Business*, for recommendations that governments do away with labor regulations in order to make it easier to "do business." Countries that establish minimum wages above a certain very low level, set maximum weekly hours below sixty-six hours, require any advance notice for dismissal, or specific procedures for job termination are considered to have rules that hinder investment. Countries are ranked according to their "ease of doing business" indicators. Critics have charged that the report encourages countries to violate internationally recognized labor standards.

New International Trade Union

Sources:
Asheville Global Report, November 1, 2006
Title: "A new international trade union confederation is born"
Authors: ITUC

AFL-CIO Now, November 1, 2006
Title: "International Free Trade Union Group Merges, Re-Emerges as New Organization" Author: Mike Hall

A new international trade union was created on November 1, 2006. The International Confederation of Free Trade Unions (ICFTU) joined with the World Confederation of Labor (WCL) to form the new union that will represent more than 190 million workers around the globe. With some four hundred affiliates in more than 150 countries, the International Trade Union Confederation (ITUC) sees a chance to tackle the new challenges of economic globalization that are having a devastating effect on millions of workers. "The creation of the ITUC will solidify the trade union movement's capacity at the national and international levels," declared Guy Ryder, General Secretary of the ITUC, "Stronger, we will exert more influence on companies, governments, and the international financial and trade institutions." Willy Thys, the former General Secretary of the WCL, said: "There is no doubt that the ITUC will become an effective countervailing force in a society that has changed enormously, with workers' rights being flouted under the pressure created by the current trajectory of 'race to the bottom' globalization."

Stock Market Regulation

Source:
Dissident Voice, March 4, 2007
Title: "Juicing the Stock Market"
Author: Mike Whitney

Some Wall Street analysts are concerned that a small group of top-level Executive Branch insiders (the "Working Group on Financial Markets") are manipulating global markets to prop up a shaky and failing American economy. In February 2007, when an 8 percent freefall on the Chinese stock exchange triggered a 416-point drop in the US stock market, it sent tremors through the global economy and drew sudden attention to deeply rooted systemic problems in the US economy. In apparent contradiction to their "free market" ideology, it is believed that members of the supragovernment group worked with lenders to force a market turnaround. By buying stock index futures or using other methods to keep American stock markets afloat, they set stock values artificially and dangerously high (seemingly "competitive"). Author Mike Whitney fears that such manipulations disrupt natural corrections that are a normal, and healthy, part of the business cycle.

CHAPTER 2

Censored Déjà Vu
What Happened to Previous Censored Stories

by Peter Phillips and the Project Censored writing team

During the thirty-one years of Project Censored's existence, few stories, if any, have generated more controversy than our inclusion of physicist Dr. Steven E. Jones's research on the collapse of the World Trade Center buildings on September 11, 2001 as story number eighteen in *Censored 2007*. Debates over the relevance of Jones's work, not to mention the validity of the US government's version of what happened on 9/11, have proven fractious again and again. The story is so sensitive that many people simply refused to even consider its investigation. Two of Project Censored's esteemed national judges resigned because we included this story in the 2007 yearbook.

Dr. Jones is a founding member of Scholars for 9/11 Truth (www.scholarsfor911truth.org) an organization of over two hundred researchers who question the veracity of the US government's official 9/11 Commission Report.

Scholars in the group have addressed a number of questions regarding 9/11 that remain unanswered: Why did the US government ignore numerous prewarnings from multiple sources, including a team of US military data experts? Why did NORAD fail to intercept the hijacked jets despite more than adequate time to intercede? What is the likelihood that the nineteen alleged terrorists acted without significant US or inside assistance?

Dr. Jones's research focuses on the collapse of World Trade Center building 7 (WTC7) at 5:20PM on 9/11. Project Censored recognized Dr. Jones for this specific research in our *Censored 2007* yearbook and invited him to speak at Sonoma State University (SSU). At SSU, Jones addressed over 250 people, and he emphasized that WTC7 was never hit by an airplane, suffered only minor debris damage from Tower 1, and fires burned on only a few of its floors. Yet, all twenty-four steel support columns in the building collapsed simultaneously, bringing the forty-seven-story building down in 6.6 seconds (at free-fall speed) in its own footprint. Dr. Jones believes that demolition by military-grade thermite is the only possible explanation for the building's sudden, complete collapse. He reported that research on molten metal from the debris and analysis of WTC dust reveal chemical traces indicative of thermite reactions. At his SSU lecture, Dr. Jones was clear and adamant in stating that he does not know who placed thermite in the building. He has no conspiracy theory regarding who was involved.

Some scientists in the US (including two at our University) have challenged Dr. Jones's research, but few have actually read or analyzed his work. Instead many prematurely dismiss Jones as a crazy conspiracy theorist, unworthy of consideration.

To the contrary, Dr. Jones has strong support from numerous academic researchers. The Scholars for 9/11 Truth Web site identifies two dozen structural engineers, chemists, and physicists who support his demolition hypothesis. Furthermore, two professors of structural analysis and construction from The Swiss Federal Institute of Technology in Zürich (ETH)—the Swiss equivalent of Cal Tech or MIT—have expressed their support for Jones's conclusions.

Additionally, over sixty US architects and engineers have petitioned for an independent investigation with subpoena power in order to uncover the full truth surrounding the events of 9/11/01—specifically the collapse of the World Trade Center Towers and Building 7. They believe that there is sufficient doubt about the official story and therefore that the 9/11 investigation must be reopened and must include a full inquiry into the possible use of explosives that may have been the actual cause behind the destruction of the World Trade Center Towers and WTC Building 7. (See http://www.ae911truth.org/.)

Nonetheless, the troubling implications of Dr. Jones's work have triggered widespread challenges, including our local *New York Times*-owned *Press Democrat*. On November 4, 2006, the *Press Democrat* ran a front-page article that labeled Jones a "discredited academic."

When scientists dispute the interpretation of data regarding matters as important as the events of 9/11, it seems appropriate to us at Project Censored that the dispute be covered as a national news story and that a full review of the evidence take place. Including this story in our *Censored* yearbook and inviting Jones to present his work for public consideration at Project Censored's annual Media Accountability Conference is what any university seeking truth in scholarship should do. Media organizations—both corporate and independent—must not shy away from the responsibility to report on serious issues, regardless of the public pressure and the controversial nature of the story (see Chapter 7).

For a video view of a recent Steven E. Jones lecture May 24, 2007 see: http://video.google.com/videoplay?docid=2327190455851154008&q=America+Rebuilding&hl=en

Censored #18, 2007
Physicist Challenges Official 9/11 Story

Research on the events of 9/11 by Brigham Young University physics professor Dr. Steven E. Jones concludes that the official explanation for the collapse of the World Trade Center buildings is implausible according to laws of physics. Dr. Jones is calling for an independent, international scientific investigation "guided not by politicized notions and constraints but rather by observations and calculations."

Sources:
Deseret Morning News, November 10, 2005
Title: "Y. Professor Thinks Bombs, Not Planes, Toppled WTC"
Author: Elaine Jarvik

Brigham Young University Web site, Winter 2005
Title: "Why Indeed Did the WTC Buildings Collapse?"
Author: Steven E. Jones

Deseret Morning News, January 26, 2006
Title: "BYU professor's group accuses US officials of lying about 9/11"
Author: Elaine Jarvik

UPDATE ON RESEARCH CHALLENGING THE OFFICIAL STORY OF 9/11 BY STEVEN E. JONES, JUNE 8, 2007

In my first peer-reviewed paper regarding the events of 9/11,[1] I challenged the "official story" that two hijacked planes alone were sufficient to cause the complete and rapid collapses of three Manhattan skyscrapers, the Towers and World Trade Center 7. The straight-down collapse of WTC 7 is particularly startling since it was not even hit by a jet, yet it collapsed at nearly free-fall speed at 5:20 p.m. on 9/11. The 9/11 Commission Report failed to mention the collapse of this forty-seven-story building in downtown Manhattan, a remarkable oversight. The FEMA report on its collapse admitted, "Our best hypothesis [fire plus some damage] has only a low probability of occurrence."[2]

Meanwhile, structural engineers and professors have added their voices challenging the official story during the past year. For example, structural engineer Joseph Phelps (who is on the editorial board for the *Journal of 9/11 Studies*) wrote, "the airplane couldn't cause this . . . Something is cutting the columns, it's called controlled demolition." Hugo Bachmann, a structural professor at ETH in Switzerland, stated, "In my opinion WTC7 was with the highest probability brought down by controlled demolition done by experts."[3] Likewise, structural professor Jörg Schneider stated: "WTC7 was with great probability brought down by explosives."[4] A group of architects and engineers who challenge the official 9/11 story has emerged during the past year along with a group of jet pilots.[5]

One of the most compelling recent finds is that of many iron-rich microspheres in the WTC dust.[6] The presence of metallic spherules implies that these metals were once molten, so that surface tension pulled the droplets into a roughly spherical shape. Then the molten droplets solidified in air, preserving the information that they were once molten in the spherical shape as well as chemical information.

Iron melts at 1538°C (2800°F), so the presence of these numerous iron-rich spheres implies a very high temperature in the WTC to form them. Too hot in fact for the fires in the WTC buildings since jet fuel (kerosene), paper, and wood furniture—and other office materials—cannot reach the temperatures needed to melt iron or steel. The iron-rich component of the WTC dust sample was analyzed in some detail by scanning electron microscopy (SEM) and X-ray energy dispersive spectroscopy (X-EDS).[7] Using these advanced probes, we have determined that many of the spheres contain high aluminum and sulfur contents as well as high iron. (The presence of significant aluminum and sulfur in droplets rules out melted-steel as the source of these spherules.) Iron-aluminum-sulfur rich spheres are seen in both the WTC dust and in spherules produced in thermate-control reactions.[8] Details of the spherules and comparisons will appear in a forthcoming paper. The information borne by these previously-molten microspheres found in large numbers in the WTC dust is striking—the spheres tell us much about what took place that remarkable day in history.

In addition to the work described above, research challenging the "official story" of 9/11 has advanced broadly in the past year as reflected in publications in the *Journal of 9/11 Studies*.9 Physicists, chemists, engineers, pilots, historians, and others have researched and published significant contributions in the *Journal*. A notable paper by Professor David Ray Griffin is entitled: *The American Empire and 9/11*.10 Physics Professor and Fellow of the American Physical Society, David Griscom, wrote a stern response to an article in *Counterpunch* that belittled 9/11 research.11 Mechanical engineer Gordon Ross and architect Eric Douglas performed analyses strongly challenging the NIST report. There are over sixty peer-reviewed publications in the *Journal* published during the past year and 9/11 research and teaching continues around the globe at a rapid pace.

Sources:

1. See http://journalof911studies.com/volume/200609/Why_Indeed_Did_the_WTC_Buildings _Completely_Collapse_Jones_Thermite_World_Trade_Center.pdf.
2. FEMA, "World Trade Center Building Performance Study," May 2002, http://www.fema.gov/ library/wtcstudy.shtm.
3. Joseph M. Phelps, private communication.
4. See http://tagesanzeiger.ch/dyn/news/ausland/663864.html (See also 5).
5. See http://www.danieleganser.ch/e/zeitungsartikel/index.htm and http://journalof911studies .com/articles/Intersecting_Facts_and_Theories_on_911.pdf.
6. See http://ae911truth.org/ and http://www.pilotsfor911truth.org/.
7. See http://journalof911studies.com/volume/200704/JonesWTC911SciMethod.pdf.
8. See http://journalof911studies.com.
9. See http://journalof911studies.com/volume/200704/DavidRayGriffin911Empire.pdf.
10. See http://journalof911studies.com/letters/e/hand-waving-the%20physics-of-911-by-david-griscom.pdf.
11. See http://journalof911studies.com/volume/200704/NISTandDrBazant-SimultaneousFailure-WTCCollapseAnalysis2.pdf and http://journalof911studies.com/volume/200612/NIST-WTC-Investigation.pdf.

UPDATE BY KEVIN STOLLE

Since our article came out in *Censored 2007*, Brigham Young University put Dr. Jones on paid leave. Six weeks later he decided to retire so he could "spend more time speaking and conducting research of my own choosing," Jones said in a statement released by the university. More evidence has come to light, raising additional questions about the official narrative of 9/11. Several videos have surfaced on the Internet showing BBC journalists reporting that

Building 7 had collapsed well before it had actually done so. Not only was the broadcast time-stamped at 21:54 (4:54PM EST), a full twenty-six minutes before the event had actually occurred, but the building in question was still standing clearly in the background. According to FEMA, WTC 7 collapsed at 5:20pm on the afternoon of 9/11. CNN also reported that Building 7, "has collapsed or is collapsing," at 4:15pm. That was over an hour before it actually fell.

After the commotion over the BBC clips, Google removed the footage from Google Video. Google and the BBC are in an "advanced stage of talks" to share content on Google Video.

Another video that surfaced on the Internet is a clip of the PBS documentary "America Rebuilding." The clip depicts Larry Silverstein, owner of three WTC buildings that collapsed. In the clip he says, "I remember getting a call for the Fire Department commander, telling me they were not sure they were gonna be able to contain the fire. I said 'ya know, we've had such terrible loss of life. Maybe the smartest thing to do is pull it. And they made the decision to pull and we watched the building collapse." "Pulling it" is jargon for controlled demolition. According to FEMA, NIST, and Frank Fellini, the Assistant Chief responsible for WTC 7 at that time, there were no firefighters in the building at the time. He couldn't have been referring to "pulling" the firefighters.

Many have also come forward stating that they had been forewarned of the demolition of the building. A New Jersey EMT has gone public on how emergency workers were told that Building 7 was going to be "pulled," before a twenty second demolition countdown broadcast over radio preceded its collapse. A former NYPD police officer, Craig Bartmer, had helped with rescue efforts on 9/11. He was in the immediate vicinity of building 7 when it collapsed and claims to have heard explosions.

Censored # 3, 2006
Another Year Of Distorted Election Coverage

Story #3 in *Censored 2006* was about the uncovered controversy surrounding the presidential election of 2004. The unusual ten million-vote discrepancy between actual vote counts and exit polls in this election brought up the question of fraud. Almost two years later factors such as the purge of black voters, the million missing ballots cast but not counted, and the malfunctioning voting machines all added to the likelihood of fraud and corruption in the 2004 election.

Sources:

Steve Freeman and Josh Mitteldorf, "A Corrupted Election," *In These Times*, February 15, 2005.

Greg Palast, Rev. Jesse Jackson, "Jim Crow Returns To The Voting Booth," *Seattle Post-Intelligencer*, January 26, 2005.

Bob Fitrakis, Harvey Wasserman, "How a Republican Election Supervisor Manipulated the 2004 Central Ohio Vote," www.freepress.org, November 23, 2004.

PROJECT CENSORED UPDATE TO OUR 2005 REPORTS QUESTIONING THE VERACITY OF THE 2004 US PRESIDENTIAL ELECTION BY STEVE FREEMAN

When we first began investigating suspicious results and processes in the 2004 US Presidential Election, the possibility of a stolen presidential election seemed far-fetched, fantastic, staggering. Yes, there were widespread anecdotal reports of voting problems, the highly curious phenomenon of electronic voting, and the strangely suspect exit polls. But it was difficult to imagine that actual vote counts could be so dramatically altered. Florida 2000 was one thing, but a discrepancy of millions of votes that goes uncontested by the would-be victors, unreported in the media, and which goes unchallenged by scores of political experts, pollsters, and pundits, in what was probably the world's most closely watched election in half a century—that was an entirely different matter. Surely, some institution in the world's strongest democracy would prevent—or at least challenge— a crime of this magnitude.

But though American institutions systematically certified the results as legitimate, doubts about neither process nor outcome were resolved. Rather, the more we investigated, the more insistent those doubts became.

In presentations to the American Statistical Association, the American Association for Public Opinion Research, and the American Academy for the Advancement of Science, we showed how an overwhelming preponderance of evidence indicates that had the votes been counted as cast, Bush would have been denied a second term. Rather than providing him with a 120,000-vote plurality, Ohioans rejected Bush's reelection by 500,000 votes. Had the votes been counted as cast, Bush would have lost Nevada, New Mexico, almost certainly Florida, and several other states as well. Rather than reelecting Bush by three million votes, a national plurality of six million Americans tried to vote Bush out of office.

The evidence proving these numbers are carefully and inescapably laid out in *Was the 2004 Presidential Election Stolen? Exit Polls, Election Fraud, and the Official Count* by Freeman and Joel Bleifuss (Seven Stories Press, June 2006. See www.electionintegrity.org/book). Further documentation of the exact mechanisms by which half a million votes were stolen in Ohio has been produced by Bob Fitrakis, Harvey Wasserman, and Richard Hayes Phillips. Greg Palast has documented additional "lost" Democratic votes around the nation. Marc Crispin Miller added other examples nationwide and explained how and why the media ignore election theft and other critical issues.

It's scandalous, of course, that the media has never reported these findings. Yet despite the continued neglect of evidence of election theft by the mainstream media, many positive developments have taken place.

First, there has been something of a break in media reporting. Although they haven't been willing to take on election theft, electronic voting has been widely attacked. The *Washington Post* ran a full page graphic in March 2006 with the headline "How to Steal an Election" reproducing a chart from Freeman and Bleifuss contrasting the safeguards on Las Vegas slot machine versus the lack of any meaningful assurance on America's voting machines. *Post* Editor noted that "Americans protect their vices more than they guard their rights."(See http://www.washingtonpost.com/wp-dyn/content/graphic/2006/03/16/GR2006031600213.html.)

Second, a newly skeptical public has woken up to official dissimulation and the failure of media, only 45 percent of Americans say they are confident that Bush really won the last election. This despite any reports in the media of election fraud.

Third, the values battle is secure. A Zogby poll commissioned by election defense attorney, Paul Lehto, indicated that Americans support the idea of transparent counts by 92 percent-4 percent. Such margins are virtually unheard of in public opinion polls. Essentially, the concept of open, transparent election processes enjoys far more support among Americans than even baseball, hot dogs, or apple pie. Moreover, there has been no abatement of official rhetoric of democracy. If anything it has been upped. That's one of the main reasons we're fighting in Afghanistan and Iraq after all.

Fourth, we have seen success elsewhere. E-voting abandoned in Holland; machine voting has been abandoned in entirety in Ireland, partly on the basis of our reports about what has happened here in the US.

And perhaps most important, a new Election Integrity movement has been born. "Election integrity" was not a term in use prior to the work that we began to publish in the aftermath of the 2004 election. But since December 2004, hundreds of groups have formed around the nation. We probably had a material impact in 2006. For the first time in many election cycles, those who had been continually more emboldened in producing more and more fanciful results, may well have been restrained. In states such as Ohio, Pennsylvania, and California, where our groups have been most active, egregious past results have not been repeated and proponents of election reform have won.

UPDATE BY JOSH MITTELDORF

We've seen much progress in the last year for mainstream recognition that the system that counts our votes needs cleaning up. As I write this, there is legislation under consideration in Congress, and there are articles, hearings, and open public debate on the subject. What is still missing is any recognition that this is not a potential problem for the future: that elections have been stolen in the past, and that the Bush regime in particular has no legitimacy. On the editorial pages of the "liberal media," there is an eerie sense that solutions are being proposed, even as no problem is being defined. Of course, it's all being done in the name of public confidence, to secure our democracy, not to rescue it.

In August 2005, the silence of the mainstream press was first broken. *Harper's* published an article by Mark Crispin Miller, an eloquent compilation of the evidence that the 2004 presidential election had been stolen, framed in a meditation on the failure of the press to take note (http://www.harpers.org/ExcerptNoneDare.html). Newsstands sold out. The article turned into a book in October: *Fooled Again: How the right stole the 2004 election, and how they'll steal the next one too unless we stop them*, published by Basic Books in September 2005.

Eight months later, an article came out in *Rolling Stone* by Robert

F Kennedy, Jr., reaching a much wider audience, both because of the circulation of *Rolling Stone* and the name recognition of the author. Some of the article was based on interviews with Steve Freeman about exit polls and other evidence that the election had been corrupted (see http://www.rollingstone.com/news/story/10432334/was_the_2004_e lection_stolen). Freeman's book, *Was the 2004 Presidential Election Stolen?* was published by Seven Stories Press in June, and Kennedy wrote a follow-up article that appeared in *Rolling Stone* last October (see http://www.rollingstone.com/politics/story/11717105/robert_f _kennedy_jr_will_the_next_election_be_hacked/print).

By that time, much of the public had leapfrogged the newspapers and the politicians, and was suspicious of the electoral machinery. In a September Zogby poll, only 45 percent expressed confidence that Bush had won re-election 'fair and square' (see http://www.scoop .co.nz/stories/HL0609/S00346.htm).

Rep. Rush Holt (D-NJ) introduced a bill to Congress that will demand paper receipts from electronic voting machines, and which specifies a random audit procedure in an attempt to spot-check the honesty of those machines. But many people in the election integrity movement have already moved beyond the audit approach. As activist-attorney Paul Lehto has said, they've taken away the openness and transparency of a public vote count, and they want to give us in return a window through which some kinds of vote tampering can be detected. (As I write this, Holt's bill is moving through committee in the 110th Congress as HR 811.)

Meanwhile, another election has come and gone. In 2006, Democrats took control of both houses of Congress. Many in the public were reassured, and took the Democratic victory as an indication that the people's will was served. But the logic of this deduction is not so clear. In fact, the nationwide Democratic margin in November, 2006 was lower by 5 percent than preelection polls and election-day exit polls would indicate. Jonathan Simon of the Election Defense Alliance estimates that, were it not for broad manipulation of the vote count, the Democrats might have won forty-seven seats, instead of twenty-seven (see http://electiondefensealliance.org/land-slide_denied_exit_polls_vs_vote_count_2006).

In April, 2007, the Bob Fitrakis and Harvey Wasserman's The Free Press Web site dropped a bombshell. Internet records for web address assignment indicate that the votes in the pivotal 2004 Ohio election were counted not on the official server of the Ohio Department of State, but on a private server, owned by a company that leases space to the Republican National Committee. This may explain how hundreds of thousands of votes could have been switched electronically from Kerry to Bush, turning the state of Ohio red, and assuring Bush's reelection. Once again, Democrats in Congress took no note, and the mainstream press was silent (see http://www.freepress.org/departments/display/19/2007/2553).

All in all, we are in a curious situation indeed. The mainstream press has systematically declined to cover the issue of election theft. The American people—perhaps a majority—seem to have bypassed the press, and they suspect the truth that elections are being systematically subverted. In a sense, the truth has not been so well dissembled, but a key instrument for organizing and establishing legitimacy is AWOL, and our representatives in Congress feel little pressure to change the system that got them "elected."

UPDATE BY KRISTINE MEDEIROS

In 2005, Rep. John Conyers asked the Government Accountability Office (GAO) to examine allegations of election fraud and corruption in the 2004 election. In September 2005 the GAO concluded that, while there is no evidence that the election was rigged, the US election system has a number of serious weaknesses. It found that electronic voting systems "have caused local problems in federal elections resulting in the loss of votes or miscounts of votes."

One of the major concerns with electronic voting systems, the GAO reports, is that inadequate security systems make then vulnerable to hacking. The report cited a number of examples. On Diebold's Accu-Vote-TS, the voter may touch the screen for one candidate and the vote will be recorded and counted for another. In Florida, security reviews showed that someone with access to an optical scan system could falsify election results without any record of the deed. Other computer security experts (in a test environment) used smart cards and memory cards to improperly access administrator functions, vote multiple times, change vote totals and produce false elections reports. "It is incumbent upon Congress," concluded Rep. Conyers, "to respond to this problem and to enact much needed reforms such as a voter verified paper audit trail that protects all Americans rights to vote."

In the 2000 election two million African Americans votes were not cast and Kerry vowed to the NAACP that it would not happen again. But nearly 3 million votes were cast and not counted in the 2004 election. Journalist Greg Palast predicted what happened in 2004, and he is predicting it for the 2006 and 2008 elections. Behind the 2000 felon purge lists and behind the 2004 caging lists were databases from the same companies that now have homeland security contracts.

Palast claims that there is a pattern to the manipulation of national elections. This includes "spoiling" ballots (such as the hanging chads), rejecting "provisional ballots," voters finding themselves at the "wrong" precinct or wrongly "scrubbed" from voter rolls, "caging" lists used to challenge voters with "suspect" addresses, not counting absentee ballots, and delayed registrations. Many of these were tactics used during the Jim Crow era following the Civil War. They are also tactics that the US has chastised dictatorships and rogue nations for using.

Meanwhile, for 2006 and 2008, the GOP is pushing new Voter ID requirements that, if passed, could quadruple the number of voters turned away from the polls for "wrong" ID (like a missing middle initial on your voter registration).

To learn more about Palast's forecasts for the 2006 and 2008 elections, read *Armed Madhouse* by Greg Palast (see gregpalast.com). For more information about the controversy over the 2004 presidential election, read "Was the 2004 Election Stolen?" by Robert Kennedy Jr. in the June 1, 2006 edition of *Rolling Stone* and "Was the 2004 Election Stolen? NO" by Fahad Manjoo on Salon.com, June 6, 2006.

Sources:

Joel Bleifuss, "Ghosts in the Voting Machines," *In These Times*, December 29, 2005.

Greg Palast, "How They Stole Ohio and the GOP 4-step Recipe to 'Blackwell' the USA in 2008, Abracadabra: Three million votes vanish," Buzzflash.com, June 2, 2006.

Greg Palast, *Armed Madhouse*, 2006.

Robert Kennedy Jr., "Was the 2004 Election Stolen?" *Rolling Stone*, June 1, 2006.

Fahad Manjoo, "Was the 2004 Election Stolen? NO" Salon.com, June 6, 2006.

Censored #1 2007
Future of Internet Debate Ignored by Media

Sources:
Buzzflash.com, July 18. 2005
Title: "Web of Deceit: How Internet Freedom Got the Federal Ax, And Why Corporate
News Censored the Story"
Author: Elliot D. Cohen, Ph.D.

Throughout 2005–2006, a large underground debate raged regarding the future of the Internet. Groups advocating "Net Neutrality" want a legal mandate that would require cable companies to allow Internet service providers (ISPs) free access to their cable lines (called a "common carriage" agreement). This was the model used for dial-up Internet, and it is the way content providers want to keep it. They also want to make sure that cable companies cannot screen or interrupt Internet content without a court order.

The Battle Over Net Neutrality Continues
By Steve Anderson

The discussion of Net Neutrality in our last edition left off noting that on June 8, 2006, the House Energy and Commerce Committee passed the Communications Opportunity, Promotion, and Enhancement (COPE) Act (HR 5252) with a 321-101 vote, without the accompanying Network Neutrality Act (HR 5273). The Net Neutrality Act would have essentially made Net Neutrality an enforceable law.[1]

After the Cope Act passed the House, the bill moved to Senate, with advocates on either side engaging in a fierce battle to sway this critical vote. Supporters of the COPE Act claimed the bill would support innovation and freedom of choice. Net Neutrality advocates say that its passage would make Internet Service Providers (ISP's) gatekeepers of the Internet.

The June 28, 2006 Senate vote on a Net Neutrality–friendly amendment offered by Sens. Olympia Snowe (R-Maine) and Byron Dorgan (D-N.D.) fell to a 11–11 tie, shortly after US Senator Ron Wyden (D-Ore.) placed a "hold" on the COPE Act legislation essentially stalling the bill until changes were made.[2]

Shortly before the Senate voted on the COPE Act Alaska Republican Ted Stevens, head of the Senate Commerce Committee, made this fateful remark: "The Internet is not something that you just dump something on. It's not a big truck. It's, it's a series of tubes." The statement was humorously conveyed on *The Daily Show*, and even remixed into a techno song, which was widely distributed online.3 Shortly after the Ted Stevens debacle the SavetheInternet.com coalition received a further boost when Internet pioneer Sir Tim Berners-Lee forcefully argued in favor of Net Neutrality in a *New York Times* interview.4

Over the summer hundreds of Web users concerned about Net Neutrality inundated the Internet with videos and blog entries encouraging fellow citizens to get involved in the issue. As the Senate's August recess drew to a close citizens supporting Net Neutrality rallied in twenty-five cities nationwide, delivering SavetheInternet petitions to their senators and urging them to oppose the phone and cable companies' attempts to gut Net Neutrality. The citizen-led movement is what Salon would later describe as "a ragtag army of grassroots Internet groups, armed with low-budget videos, music parodies, and petitions."5 The telecoms employed Mike McCurry, Clinton's former press secretary, to lead their lobbying effort with an industry funded group called Hands Off the Internet. The group produced its own online videos poking fun at the SavetheInternet.com coalition and relaying their view of Net Neutrality.

The HR 5252 bill died with the end of 109th Congress, and the situation looked positive for Net Neutrality proponents with the new Democrat-controlled House and Congress. On December 28, AT&T officials agreed to adhere to strict Network Neutrality if allowed to complete an $85 billion merger with BellSouth. The SaveTheInternet.com coalition called it "A victory we can hang our hats on."6

Over the course of 2006 the nation's largest phone and cable companies spent more than $100 million on DC lobbyists, think tanks, ads and campaign contributions to defeat Network Neutrality.7 At the same time The SavetheInternet.com coalition grew to 850 groups including National Religious Broadcasters, the Service Employees International Union, the American Library Association, EDUCAUSE, Gun Owners of America, Future of Music Coalition, Parents Television Council, the ACLU, and every major consumer group in the country. The coalition also includes thousands of bloggers and hundreds of small companies that do business online. This diverse coalition resulted in more than 1.5 million Americans contacting their representatives urging them to support net neutrality.[8]

A Victory With Historic Proportions

If the SavetheInternet.com coalition succeeds in making Net Neutrality, law citizens will have scored a victory "of historic proportions," according to Geov Parrish of WorkingforChange.com.[9] "Name the last time a lobby with that much power and money was stymied in its top legislative priority by a citizen movement," Parrish wrote."Offhand, I can't think of any examples at all. And this during the most corrupt, lobbyist-pliant Congress in recent American history."[10]

In keeping with past success SaveTheInternet.com launched the latest manifestation of the campaign with an online video called *Save The Internet: Independence Day*. The video outlines how everyday Internet users and grassroots organizations can save Internet freedom. *Save The Internet: Independence Day* quickly made its way around the net through users sharing the video with friends and family. Also crucial to the circulation of this video are independent media outlets and bloggers, who are also threatened by a closed Internet.

Making Net Neutrality Law and More

In the new year The SaveTheInternet.com coalition began pushing congress to make Net Neutrality law. Using their (now award-winning) "Independence Day" video, the coalition began campaigning for a faster, more open, and accessible Internet. On January 8, Sen. Byron L. Dorgan (D-S.D.) and Sen. Olympia J. Snowe (R-Maine) sponsored the Internet Freedom Preservation Act of 2007, which would protect net neutrality.

On June 11, 2007 at the SavetheInterent "Party for the Future" celebration of Net Neutrality victories, the SavetheInternet.com coalition unveiled the "Internet Freedom Declaration of 2007." The Declaration sets forth a plan not just for winning Net Neutrality in Congress, but establishing faster, universal, and affordable broadband for everyone. The declaration calls for "world-class quality through competition," "an open and neutral network," and "universal affordable access." The declaration is a big step in media reform, changing the terms of debate from defending against further media deregulation, to demanding a truly public media infrastructure.[11]

In March 2007 SavetheInternet.com supporters rallied for "in-district" meetings with members of Congress and their staff. The rallies resulted in several members pledged to support Net Neutrality legislation when it came to a vote in Congress.[12]

On March 15, 2007, all five FCC Commissioners were brought before the House Subcommittee on Telecommunications and the Internet to testify about their decisions regarding Net Neutrality. Members of the House pressed FCC Chairman Kevin Martin to take a stronger position in support of Net Neutrality. The hearing was the first time in three years that commissioners had appeared before the Subcommittee.[13]

In May 2007 an "Ad Hoc Public Interest Spectrum Coalition" made a proposal to the FCC on how the auction of the valuable 700 MHz spectrum should be conducted. The 700 MHz spectrum can be used to offer wireless Internet, and the proposal asserted the auction should provide "new entrants [with] the opportunity to enter the market in competition with incumbent providers." The coalition includes the Consumer Federation of America, Consumers Union, EDUCAUSE, Free Press, Media Access Project, New America Foundation, and US Public Interest Research Group.[14] As of June 4, a quarter-million people have contacted the FCC urging the agency to use the 700 MHz spectrum to offer a more open and competitive Internet service ecology.[15]

On March 22, 2007 The Federal Communications Commission (FCC) unanimously voted to seek public comment on the possibility of adding a network neutrality principle to its 2005 Internet Policy Statement.[16] The comment period ends on June 15, 2007, and already tens of thousands have made submissions.[17]

Democratic candidates Hillary Clinton, John Edwards, Barack Obama, and Bill Richardson, among others, have all stated their strong support for legal protections for Net Neutrality. Supporters were joined by GOP candidate Mike Huckabee (R-Arkansas), who told a collection of bloggers that Net Neutrality must be preserved.[18]

Steve Anderson is the Founder of The Center For Information Awareness and is the Publisher at COA News.

Citations

1. See http://www.buzzflash.com/contributors/05/07/con05238.html.
2. See http://www.sourcewatch.org/index.php?title=Network_neutrality_legislation.
3. See http://networks.silicon.com/webwatch/0,39024667,39160962,00.htm.
4. See http://www.nytimes.com/2006/09/27/technology/circuits/27neut.html?ref=circuits.
5. See http://www.salon.com/tech/feature/2006/10/02/slayers.
6. See http://www.savetheInternet.com/blog/2006/12/29/a-victory-we-can-hang-our-hats-on/.
7. See http://mediacitizen.blogspot.com/2006/07/senators-respond-to-grassroots.html.
8. See http://www.freepress.net/press/release.php?id=188.
9. See http://www.workingforchange.com/article.cfm?ItemID=21498.
10. See http://www.workingforchange.com/article.cfm?ItemID=21498.
11. See http://www.freepress.net/docs/netfreedomdeclaration-front.pdfvv.
12. See http://www.savetheInternet.com/blog/2007/04/25/neutrality-supporters-swarm-congress-in-spring-07/.
13. See http://www.infoworld.com/article/07/03/14/HNdemocratsgrillfcc_1.html.
14. See http://www.publicknowledge.org/node/962.
15. See http://www.freepress.net/news/23612.
16. See http://www.Internetnews.com/infra/article.php/3667481..
17. See http://www.savetheInternet.com/blog/2007/06/07/net-neutrality-an-american-experience/.
18. See http://republicanrace08.blogspot.com/2007/05/blogger-interview-with-mike-huckabee.html.

UPDATED BY ZOE HUFFMAN

The battle over "network neutrality" on the Internet continued to rage in 2006. In the last year, some triumphs have been made to protect Net Neutrality, yet the fight is far from decided. The House passed the Communications Opportunity, Promotion, and Enhancement (COPE) Act (HR 5252) last year but the Act still sits in the Senate. In tandem with this Act, the Internet Freedom Preservation Act (S 215) was introduced into the Senate on January 9, 2007. As of this writing, no final vote had been taken and the Act still awaits analysis in the Commerce, Science, and Transportation Committee. This Act would amend the Communications Act of 1934, protecting net neutrality against Internet providers who would limit access based on fees garnished by content providers.[1]

Additionally, as part of the merger of AT&T and BellSouth, there was a stipulation that AT&T maintains Net Neutrality for at least the next two years.[2] This may seem to be good precedent for future companies to uphold Net Neutrality, but as the Chairman of the FCC, Kevin Martin, clarifies, this is not meant to be enforceable on other companies and he "would oppose such policies in the future."[3] The contest over Net Neutrality has also achieved greater prominence in mainstream society since 2008 Democratic presidential candidates have helped position it among the issues to be covered in the race.[4]

This is coupled with Internet grassroots organizations taking part in the debate, such as MoveOn.org and SaveTheInternet.com. The fight marches on and is it yet to have any permanent resolution.

Citations

1. For full text of Act, see http://thomas.loc.gov/cgi-bin/query/D?c110:1:./temp/~c110xzIU57::.
2. Tom Abate, "Net neutrality advocates hail AT&T's concessions," *San Francisco Chronicle*, January 7, 2007.
3. Stephanie Kirchgaessner, "Net neutrality will not be enforced, says head of FCC AT&T AGREEMENT," *Financial Times* (London), February 2, 2007.
4. Charles Babington, "Neutrality On the Net Gets High '08 Profile," *Washington Post*, February 20, 2007.

UPDATE: JUNE 12, 2007
Maine Is First State in Nation to Pass Net Neutrality Resolve

A diverse coalition of Mainers applauded the enactment today of the first Net Neutrality resolve in the nation. The resolution, LD 1675, recognizes the importance of "full, fair and non-discriminatory access to the Internet" and instructs the Public Advocate to study what can be done to protect the rights of Maine Internet users.

"Maine is the first state in the nation to stand up for its citizens' rights to a nondiscriminatory Internet," said Senator Ethan Strimling, the original sponsor of LD 1675. "The rest of the nation should follow suit and study what can be done to protect net neutrality."

"This important legislation puts Maine first in affirming that Internet providers should not be allowed to discriminate by speeding up or slowing down Web content based on its source, ownership or destination," said Tony Vigue of the Community Television Association of Maine.

Source: http://www.acmecoalition.org/

Censored #2 2007
Halliburton Charged with Selling Nuclear Technologies to Iran

Sources at Halliburton allege that, as recently as 2005, Halliburton sold key components for a nuclear reactor to an Iranian oil development company. Leopold says his Halliburton sources have intimate knowledge of the business dealings of both Halliburton and Oriental Oil Kish, one of Iran's largest private oil companies.

Source:
Global Research.ca, August 5, 2005
Title: "Halliburton Secretly Doing Business With Key Member of Iran's Nuclear Team"
Author: Jason Leopold

UPDATE BY DON NELSON

Much has been made about the swirling controversy and connection between the current Bush Administration and Halliburton. It is widely known that Vice President Dick Cheney was the CEO of Halliburton from 1995–2000, before he came into office. Less known are allegations by sources of journalist Jason Leopold that Halliburton sold materials used in building nuclear reactors to an Iranian oil development company as recently as January 2005.

Federal law prohibits US companies from trading directly with Iran because of its ties to terrorist organizations. This federal law was enacted after Bush's infamous declaration of Iran being a part of the "Axis of Evil." However foreign subsidiaries are allowed to do business with Iran, as long the foreign business is independent of the US business.

Halliburton Products & Services Ltd., the foreign subsidiary in Iran, recently quit operations after current CEO David Lesar announced on Monday April 9, 2007 that the company would not take any more business in Iran. Several of these reasons included a poor business environment and low profit, as well as safety concerns. Halliburton's announcement came on the same day that Iranian President Mahmoud Ahmadinejad said that his country was now capable of producing nuclear fuel on an industrial scale.

"Halliburton had to be dragged kicking and screaming out of Iran," said Senator Frank R. Lautenberg (D-NJ). "If Halliburton wasn't pressured by Congress, they would still be doing business in Iran," he added.

Halliburton and its former KBR Inc. division have been heavy targets of criticism because of KBR's more than $19 billion in Pentagon contracts as the sole provider of food and shelter services to the military in Iraq and Afghanistan. In April 2007, Lesar announced the sell-off the KBR construction and services unit, which has been under heavy scrutiny for overcharging the US military in Iraq.

Lesar decided to move the headquarters of his large oil industry to

Dubai. According to a press release on the Halliburton Web page, Lesar announced on March 11, 2007 that he would move the company to Dubai to further the company's efforts in growing Halliburton's business in the Eastern Hemisphere. He also said that over the next five years that Halliburton would shift 70 percent of its capital investment, which includes oil and gas zones in the Middle East, Russia, Africa, the North Sea and East Asia.

Halliburton is the first major western corporation to move its chief executive to Dubai. The Dubai office allows him to be closer to the world's largest oil companies, such as Saudi Aramco and Abu Dhabi National Oil Co. Halliburton will continue to pay taxes on its global earnings and will remain a US-registered company trading on the New York Stock Exchange.

The move of the headquarters to Dubai is of great concern for the reason that this potentially allows for breaking of US sanctions, and potential illegal dealings that would help Iran or other such rogue nations to further develop their nuclear program.

Sources

David Ivanovich, "Halliburton Prepares for Iran Work," *Houston Chronicle*, January 11, 2007.

John Porretto, "Halliburton Completes Oil Field Projects in Iran," Associated Press, May 23, 2007.

Jim Krane, "Halliburton Embraces Mideast," Associated Press, June 8, 2007.

Editorial, "Exploiting a Loophole," *Daily Press*, June 6, 2007.

Censored #3 2007
Oceans of the World in Extreme Danger

Oceanic problems once found on a local scale are now pandemic. Data from physical oceanography, marine biology, meteorology, fisheries science, and glaciology assert the seas are changing in every way. The world ocean is growing warmer and atmospheric litter has altered its chemistry radically. Thousands of toxic compounds poison marine creatures and devastate propagation, creating dead zones and laying waste to coastal nurseries, coral reefs, and kelp forests. Reckless fishing practices have ramped up, dredged ocean bottoms, and driven species toward extinction. Human failure in governance of the world's largest public domain threatens critical elements of the global life support system.

Source

Mother Jones, March/April, 2006
Title: "The Fate of the Ocean"
Author: Julia Whitty

UPDATE BY JOCELYN THOMAS

In 2006, researchers from around the globe—including staff from the Zoological Society of London, and the Deep Sea Conservation Coalition—called on the United Nations to ban dredging ocean bottoms. As of June 2007, the effort has seen little success.

In July of 2006, a study was published by the US National Center for Atmospheric Research showed continued over-acidification of the world's oceans. The report claimed that since 1800 there has been a huge influx of carbon dioxide in the oceans. Now, in addition to warming the oceans, that influx has also being linked to rising acidity in the ocean waters, according to the researchers. According to one of the research team leaders, the ocean is currently experiencing "the most dramatic changes in marine chemistry in the past 650,000 years."[1] This increase in acidity is causing the breakdown of coral reefs, so much so that a 2004 study estimated that one-fifth of the world's coral reefs are completely destroyed.[2]

In November of 2006, the journal *Science* published a report that the "progressive unraveling of entire marine ecosystems . . . could lead to the 'collapse' of all commercial species."[3] The researchers' findings were used as backbones for stories in the *New York Times*, the *San Diego Union-Tribune*, the *Baltimore Sun*, the *Los Angeles Times*, the *Sacramento Bee*, and the *San Francisco Chronicle*.

Citations

1. David Perlman, "Greenhouse gas turning oceans acidic; Carbon dioxide hampers ability of food chain to thrive, federal report finds," *San Francisco Chronicle*, July 6, 2006.
2. Craig Pittman, "Study: Acidity engenders ocean life," *St. Petersburg Times*, July 6, 2006.
3. "Troubled Seas," *The New York Times*, November 14, 2006.

Censored #4 2007
Hunger and Homelessness Increasing in the US

The number of hungry and homeless people in US cities continued to grow in 2005, despite claims of an improved economy.
Increased demand for vital services rose as needs of the most destitute went unmet, according to the annual *US Conference of
Mayors Report*, which has documented increasing need since its
1982 inception.

Sources:
The New Standard, December 2005
Title: "New Report Shows Increase in Urban Hunger, Homelessness"
Author: Brendan Coyne

OneWorld.net, March, 2006
Title: "US Plan to Eliminate Survey of Needy Families Draws Fire"
Author: Abid Aslam

UPDATE BY REGINA MARCHESCHI
According to the most recent report by the Conference of Mayors
(December 2006) more people were homeless and hungry in 2006
than in 2005, with children making up a quarter of the homeless in
emergency shelters.

In 2006 civic and government groups received 7 percent more
requests for food than in 2005, with 74 percent of the cities registering an increase. Additionally, emergency assistance for the elderly
increased by 18 percent. Of the emergency food requests, 23 percent
were unmet, and 18 percent of the requests for emergency assistance
were also unmet. Twenty-nine percent of requests made by homeless
families (children and parents) were unmet in 2006. Additionally,
86 percent of the emergency shelters had to turn away homeless
families, along with having to turn away 77 percent of other homeless people. People remain homeless an average of eight months in
the survey cities. Thirty-two percent of the cities said that the length
of time people were homeless increased during the last year.

The outlook for 2007 was bleak, as the Mayors' Report expected
an increase in requests for emergency food assistance and emergency shelters nationwide. Major media in the US again ignored the
Mayors' Report. A few regional newspapers such as the *Boston Globe*,

that reported on January 11, 2007 that Project Bread, a nonprofit that is active in working to end hunger, recently issued a status report on hunger in Massachusetts finding that hunger was a serious problem in thirty-five cities and towns in the Commonwealth.

Source: See http://usmayors.org/uscm/hungersurvey/2006/report06.pdf.

Censored #5 2007
High-Tech Genocide in Congo

In the Congo six to seven million have died since 1996 as a consequence of invasions and wars sponsored by western powers trying to gain control of the region's mineral wealth. At stake is control of natural resources that are sought by US corporations—diamonds, tin, copper, gold, and more significantly, coltan and niobum, two minerals necessary for production of cell phones and other high-tech electronics; and cobalt, an element essential to nuclear, chemical, aerospace, and defense industries.

In 1996 US-sponsored Rwandan and Ugandan forces entered eastern Democratic Republic of Congo. By 1998 they seized control and moved into strategic mining areas. The Rwandan Amy was soon making $20 million or more a month from coltan mining. The mineral is shipped abroad, mostly through Rwanda then sold to companies like Nokia, Motorola, Compaq, Sony and other manufacturers for use in cell phones and other products. The process is tied to major multinational corporations at all levels. These include US-based Cabot Corporation, OM Group, GE, Boeing, Raytheon, and Bechtel.

Sources:
The Taylor Report, March 28, 2005
Title: "The World's Most Neglected Emergency: Phil Taylor talks to Keith Harmon Snow"

Earth First! Journal, August 2005
Title: "High-Tech Genocide"
Author: Sprocket

Z Magazine, March 1, 2006
Title: "Behind the Numbers: Untold Suffering in the Congo"
Authors: Keith Harmon Snow and David Barouski

UPDATE BY JEFF HULING

In 2005, the Democratic Republic of Congo's (DRC) transitional government under Joseph Kabila established a commission to uncover fraud in wartime contracts. Congolese lawmaker Christophe Lutundula headed the investigation panel.

The Lutundula Commission report investigated mining and other business contracts that rebels and government authorities signed between 1996–2003, uncovering illegal natural resource exploitation, profiteering from armed conflict, and fraud by international mining companies. The report denounces contracts signed by recently elected (November 2006) President Joseph Kabila, and it advises that others be renegotiated or canceled.

The World Bank has been reluctant to act on the commission's recommendations. In February 2006, NGO Rights and Accountability in Development (RAID) called on World Bank president Paul Wolfowitz to investigate the Bank's inadequate program for restructuring the DRC's mining sector. RAID asked for the Bank's nomination of an independent group of experts to examine the legality of mining contracts since 2003. So far the Bank has failed to heed RAID's recommendation.

In November 2006, a confidential World Bank memo leaked to the *Financial Times* revealed that three of the DRC's biggest mining contracts over which the World Bank had oversight were approved with "a complete lack of transparency." Craig Andrews, the World Bank's principal mining specialist, wrote the memo to Pedro Alba, the country director for Congo, saying that the deals had not undergone a "thorough analysis, appraisal, and evaluation" before being approved. The contracts, between state-owned Gécamines and three international mining groups, signed away 80 percent of Gécamines's mineral asset base to private mining companies.

The World Bank's country manager in Congo, Jean-Michel Happi, said legal and financial audits would proceed. Paul Fortin was appointed by World Bank to manage Gécamines, but President Kabila's allies on Gécamines's board have veto power on any recommendations made by Fortin.

Patricia Feeney, executive director of Rights and Accountability in Development, a British-based NGO, said it would be "a huge battle" to end corruption. "The group that has benefited the most from these mining contracts has been Kabila's entourage."

In October 2006, Sierra Leone's mineral resource minister Mohamed Swarray Deen revealed that coltan (and platinum reserves) were discovered in the region. International companies have already submitted bids to extract the minerals.

Sources:

"Sierra Leone discovers coltan, platinum reserves," Agence France-Presse, October 4, 2006.

Senegal Dakar, "VOA News: Democratic Republic Of Congo's Kabila Faces Unruly, Corrupt Mining Sector," *US Fed News*, December 15, 2006.

"DR Congo: End Illegal Exploitation of Natural Resources," Human Rights Watch, February 21, 2006, http://hrw.org/english/docs/2006/02/20/congo12692.htm.

"Congo: mining, conflict and complicity," *Bretton Woods Project*, January 31, 2007, http://www.brettonwoodsproject.org/art.shtml?x=549090.

Michelle Faul, "Congo Gov't Must Bring Order to Mines," Associated Press Online, November 12, 2006.

Censored #6 2007
Federal Whistle-blower Protection in Jeopardy

Special Counsel Scott Bloch, appointed by President Bush in 2004, is overseeing the virtual elimination of federal whistle-blower rights in the US government. The US Office of Special Counsel (OSC), the agency that is supposed to protect federal employees who blow the whistle on waste, fraud, and abuse is simply dismissing hundreds of cases. According to the Annual Report for 2004 (which was not released until the end of 1st quarter FY 2006) less than 1.5 percent of whistle-blower claims were referred for investigation while more than 1,000 reports were closed before they were even opened.

On March 3, 2005 OSC staff members joined by a coalition of whistle-blower protection and civil rights organizations filed a complaint against Bloch. His own employees accused him of violating the very rules he is supposed to be enforcing. The complaint specifies instances of illegal gag orders, cronyism, invidious discrimination, and retaliation by forcing the resignation of one-fifth of the OSC headquarters legal and investigative staff.

Source:

Public Employees for Environmental Responsibility Web site.
Titles: "Whistle-blowers Get Help from Bush Administration," December 5, 2005;

"Long-Delayed Investigation of Special Counsel Finally Begins," October 18,2005; "Back Door Rollback of Federal Whistle-blower Protections," September 22, 2005
Author: Jeff Ruch

UPDATE BY TONI CATELANI

The Office of the Special Counsel (OSC) is the government agency mandated to protect federal whistle-blowers and is also in charge of policing whether federal employees are engaging in political activity on the job. Scott Bloch, the head of the OSC, has been the subject of an ongoing investigation by the Office of Personnel Management Inspector General at the behest of the Bush White House, because of a whistle-blower complaint alleging a host of misconduct charges against him by his own staff.

As this investigation reaches its final stages, Bloch has announced that he will investigate the White House over the firing of US Attorneys, missing Karl Rove e-mails, and political briefings for General Services Administration managers. "It makes no sense for Scott Bloch to investigate the White House while the White House investigates Bloch" according to PEER Executive Director Jeff Ruch. Indeed, it seems unlikely that the OSC will be able to conduct a thorough investigation into the White House while Scott Bloch is under investigation himself. However, questions remain about whether OSC has the jurisdiction and legal authority to launch this type of investigation.

OSC has become a "black hole" for whistleblower disclosures and incidence of retaliation has increased exponentially under the Bush administration according to watchdog groups. On March 14, 2007, Congress finally got on board by passing H.R. 985, The Whistleblower Protection Enhancement Act of 2007, by a vote of 331-94. Included in the bill is protection for employees in scientific agencies, and for CIA and FBI employees who have no federal whistle-blower protection under the original 1989 legislation. CIA and FBI employees have undergone extensive background investigations, obtained security clearances, and handled classified information on a routine basis, yet they receive no protection when they come forward to identify abuses that undermine national security. H.R. 985 is currently in Senate Committee and the White House has threatened to veto, citing national security concerns.

For more information and updates regarding this issue please visit the following websites:

http://www.peer.org/federal/federal_info.php?row_id=23
http://www.truthout.org/docs_2006/052207K.shtml
http://www.motherjones.com/washington_dispatch/2007/04/bloch.html

Sources:

Public Employees for Environmental Responsibility Web site OSC page: http://www.peer.org/federal/federal_info.php?row_id=23
Author: Jeff Ruch

Mother Jones, "Karl Rove's Least Likely Interrogator: Scott Bloch and the Office of Special Counsel," April 25, 2007, Schulman, Daniel.
http://www.motherjones.com/washington_dispatch/2007/04/bloch.html

Truthout, "Whistleblowers Charge Retaliation, More Protections Sought," May 22, 2007. Fisher, William. http://www.truthout.org/docs_2006/052207K.shtm

www.whistleblowers.org

Censored # 7 2007
US Operatives Torture Detainees to Death in Afghanistan and Iraq

On October 25, 2005, the American Civil Liberties Union released documents of forty-four autopsies held in Afghanistan and Iraq. Twenty-one of those deaths were listed as homicides. "These documents present irrefutable evidence that US operatives tortured detainees to death during interrogation," said Amrit Singh, an attorney with the ACLU. "The public has a right to know who authorized the use of torture techniques and why these deaths have been covered up."

The Department of Defense released the autopsy reports in response to a Freedom of Information Act request filed by the ACLU, the Center for Constitutional Rights, Physicians for Human Rights, and Veterans for Common Sense and Veterans for Peace.

An overwhelming majority of the so-called natural deaths covered in the autopsies were attributed to "arteriosclerotic cardiovascular disease" (heart attack). Persons under extreme stress and pain may have heart attacks as a result of their treatment as detainees.

The Associated Press carried the story of the ACLU charges on their wire service. However, a thorough check of Lexus-Nexus and Proquest electronic databases, using the keywords ACLU and autopsy, showed that fewer than two percent of US daily papers reported the story.

Sources:
American Civil Liberties Web site, October 24, 2005
Title: "US Operatives Killed Detainees During Interrogations in Afghanistan and Iraq"

Tom Dispatch.com, March 5, 2006
Title: "Tracing the Trail of Torture: Embedding Torture as Policy from Guantanamo to Iraq"
Author: Dahr Jamail

UPDATE BY REGINA MARCHESCHI

Since *Censored 2007* appeared, only two newspapers—The Targeted News Service (May, June, and July of 2006) and the *Miami Herald* (June 2006)—covered these atrocities. Notably, however, the *Herald* reported that the detainees committed suicide, and did not report the actual autopsy findings. By contrast, The Targeted News Service stated that these atrocities violated domestic and international law, that the Defense Department allowed these abuses to flourish, and that some of the techniques used, such as stress positions, were similar to those authorized in Guantánamo in 2002 by Defense Secretary Rumsfeld. However, the perpetrators of these atrocities along with senior officials who sanctioned them, such as Rumsfeld, have escaped accountability.

This has not changed. In September 2006, President Bush defended torture, stating that it was an "alternative set of [interrogation] procedures" (Human Rights Watch 2007). In October of 2006, the US Congress, "acting on behest of the Bush administration, denied Guantánamo detainees the possibility of challenging their detention in court via the right of habeas corpus" (Human Rights Watch 2007). Secretary Rumsfeld stated that [any] "government official who authorizes or condones torture is entirely immune from suit and cannot be held accountable for his actions" (Human Rights First Press Release, March 6, 2006).

More than 100,000 documents that have been turned over to the ACLU as a result of the Freedom of Information Act litigation are available at www.aclu.org/torture.

The ACLU released a full report on US torture to the United Nations Committee Against Torture in April of 2006. The report, "Enduring Abuse: Torture and Cruel Treatment by the United States at Home and Abroad," states that: "The United States has failed to comply with its obligations under the Convention Against Torture at home and abroad. To justify torture and abuse in the 'global war on terrorism,' the government narrowly defined torture and argued that the prohibition against cruel, inhuman or degrading treatment does not apply outside the United States. Its selective interpretation of the Convention justified the development of interrogation techniques that violated the treaty, created a climate of confusion among US soldiers, and led to widespread torture and abuse of detainees in Guantánamo Bay, Iraq, and Afghanistan."

The report goes on to state that

> [T]his abuse was the direct result of policies promulgated from high-level civilian and military leaders and the failure of these leaders to prevent torture and other cruel, inhuman or degrading treatment by subordinate the widespread and systemic nature of the torture and abuse, the United States has refused to authorize any independent investigation into the abuses. No high-level official involved in developing or implementing the policies that led to torture and abuse has been charged with any crime related to the abuses. The government continues to assert that the abuse was simply the actions of a few rogue soldiers.

A provision was quietly tucked into the Military Commissions Act just before it passed through Congress and was signed into law by President Bush on October 17, 2006. It redefines torture, removing the harshest, most controversial techniques from the definition of war crimes, and exempts the perpetrators—interrogators and their bosses—from punishment all the way back to November 1997. The provision could keep Bush Administration officials and former officials—such as Donald Rumsfeld—from prosecution for war crimes (see Chapter 1, Censored Story #14).

To stay current on this critical topic, please visit the following websites regularly:

http://www.amnesty.org/
http://www.hrw.org/
http://www.ccr-ny.org/v2/home.asp

Censored #9 2007
The World Bank Funds Israel-Palestine Wall

Despite the 2004 International Court of Justice (ICJ) decision that called for tearing down the Israel-Palestinian Wall and compensating affected communities, Israel has accelerated construction of the Wall. The barrier's route runs deep into Palestinian territory, aiding Israeli annexation and fracturing Palestinian territorial continuity.

In December 2004, the World Bank outlined the framework for a Palestinian Middle East Free Trade Area (MEFTA) policy. Central to World Bank proposals were the construction of massive industrial zones where Palestinians imprisoned by the Wall and dispossessed of land could be put to work for low wages. The MEFTA vision also set forth a plan for the construction of high-tech military gates and checkpoints along the Wall, allowing for complete control over the movement of Palestinians and exports. The project would be financed by the World Bank and other donors and controlled by the Israeli Occupation.

Sources:
Left Turn Issue #18
Title: "Cementing Israeli Apartheid: The Role of World Bank"
Author: Jamal Juma'

Al-Jazeera, March 9, 2005
Title: "US Free Trade Agreements Split Arab Opinion"
Author: Linda Heard

UPDATE BY JONATHAN KAUFMANN

In March 2007, the World Bank released an assessment of Gaza and the West Bank's poor economic climate. The study stated that the Wall was the biggest impediment to growth in Palestine's private sector, but omitted any mention of the barrier's illegality. The report cited the over five hundred "checkpoints and obstacles" within the West Bank as the major challenges to economic development there, and said that the Occupied Territories' industry was doomed to fail unless restrictions on Palestinian movement were relaxed.

The following April, a progress report written by the United

Nations Relief and Works Agency for Palestine Refugees in the Near East (UNRWA) recorded a significant decline of living conditions in the occupied territories between July and December of 2006. Unemployment was at 28.4 percent, and an estimated 165,000 employees in the public sector received reduced wages. As a result, the number of Palestinians living on less than a dollar a day increased to 40 percent in the West Bank and 80 percent in Gaza.

The Palestinian dependency on humanitarian assistance has grown, but the electoral victory of the Hamas party in January 2006 caused a boycott that froze international aid to the Palestinian Authority. According to the Integrated Regional Information Networks (IRIN), agencies have been struggling to raise funds necessary to assist Palestinians. Many aid workers have said that in order to solve the financial problems of the Occupied Territories, a long-term political solution is needed.

Works Cited

"West Bank and Gaza Investment Climate Assessment: Unlocking the Potential of the Private Sector," World Bank Report No. 39109—GZ, March 20, 2007, http://siteresources.worldbank.org/INTWESTBANKGAZA/Resources/294264-1166008938288/ICA2007.pdf.

"Israel-OPT: Humanitarian Situation Got Worse in 2006, Says UN Agency," IRIN Middle East, May 15, 2007, http://www.irinnews.org/Report.aspx?ReportId=71857.

"Emergency Appeal Progress Report July-December 2006," United Nations Relief and Works Agency for Palestine Refugees in the Near East, April 2007, http://domino.un.org/pdfs/UNRWAreport31.pdf.

Censored #10, 2007

Deadly strikes by US warplanes are seen as a way to improve dramatically the combat capabilities of even the weakest Iraqi combat units. However, the overall level of violence and the number of Iraqi fatalities has increased dramatically.

Sources:

Tom Englehardt, "Tomgram: Dahr Jamail on the Missing Air War in Iraq," TomDispatch.com, January 2006, http://www.tomdispatch.com/index.mhtml?pid=42286.

Seymour M. Hersh, "Up in the Air," *The New Yorker*, November 28, 2005, http://www.newyorker.com/printables/fact/051205fa_fact.

UPDATE BY DON NELSON

When the US entered into war with Iraq in 2003, few expected the ongoing war to last four years. Many speculated that, because of the President's diminishing approval ratings—including resistance from military leadership and within his own party—the US would begin to withdraw American troops from Iraq in 2006. This was not the case, of course, and in mid-2007 the President appears intent on escalating the US troop commitment in Iraq while intensifying air attacks.

According to the Associated Press, during the first four and a half months of 2007, American aircraft dropped 237 bombs and missiles in support of ground forces in Iraq. This surpasses the 229 expended in all of 2006. After the 2003 "shock and awe" invasion where thousands of missiles and bombs were dropped, US airpower has settled down a bit. Air Force figures show that there were 285 munitions dropped in 2004, 404 in 2005, and 229 in 2006. These totals don't include warplanes' often devastating use of 20mm and 30mm cannon or rocket fire, or firing by Marine Corps aircraft. Army Lt. Col Bryan Cox, a ground-forces liaison at the regional air headquarters says that the number of Air Force and Navy "close air support" missions, which usually involve a flyover show of force or surveillance work, rather than bombing, also has grown by 30 to 40 percent in spring 2007.

Iraq Body Count, a London based anti-war research group maintains a database compiling news media reports on Iraqi war deaths. In their report of Iraqi casualties from US air strikes, they found that Iraqi civilian deaths averaged just a few a month in early 2006 while climbing to forty a month by year's end, and averaging more than fifty a month thus far in 2007.

The US military doesn't record death totals for Iraqi civilians. "Air operations over Iraq have ratcheted up significantly, in the number of sorties (in the air)" said Col. Joe Guastella, the Air Force's operations chief for the region. "It has a lot to do with increased pressure on the enemy by the MNC—the Multinational Corps—Iraq combined with more carriers."

Reducing the number of troops in Iraq seems to be the furthest thing from President Bush's mind. He aims to send at least another 28,000 troops to Iraq, mainly in the area of Baghdad as part of the US-led security plan. The plan involves moving troops from fortified bases to closer contact with civilians and insurgents. This has resulted in a higher number of casualties and is evident in the statistics that show that in April and May of 2007 that 231 US forces were killed. The 231 fatalities is the largest two-month total for US deaths, exceeding the 215 that died in April–May 2004 when US troops fought insurgents in Fallujah. In January of 2007, Bush said there would be more than 150,000 troops in Iraq by the end of June. According to AP military writer Robert Burns, as of May 23, 2007 the U.S troop level stands at 147,000. Another 10,000 are scheduled to arrive over the course of the next month.

The most recent death tolls of American soldiers reflect fighting in areas south and east of Baghdad, with Diyala being a province northeast of the capital where a lot of the fighting is happening. The increased presence of aircraft carriers and the availability of fighter planes are largely responsible for the increased use of an air war strategy. A US Navy aircraft carrier on station since February in the Persian Gulf has added about eighty warplanes.

Sources:
Charles J. Hanley, "US Air Attacks in Iraq More than Double From 2006 Total," *Houston Chronicle*, June 6, 2007.

"US Drops Bombs on Iraq at Twice Last Year's Rate," *Augusta Chronicle*, June 6, 2007.

"219 Killed is Highest Total over 2 Months; Iraq Security Push Drives US Deaths," *USA Today*, May 30, 2007.

Hanley, "US Forces Step Up Air War—Bombing Runs More than Double from '06," Associated Press.

Robert Burns, "Tactics Change, Iraq Strategy the Same," *San Francisco Chronicle*, May 24, 2007.

Censored #12, 2007
Pentagon Plans to Build New Land Mines

The Pentagon has requested $1.3 billion for two new antipersonnel land mines, the first of which could roll out as early as 2007. The United States has not used antipersonnel land mines since the first Gulf War when 100,000 mines were scattered by plane across Iraq and Kuwait. This move would end a moratorium on land mine use signed into law by George H. W. Bush in 1992 and would call into question the United States' previous intention to join the 145 country 1997 Mine

Ban Treaty. There have been reports of US use of landmines in the war in Iraq, but the Pentagon has yet to either confirm or deny this claim. Human Rights Watch (HRW) has estimated that such weapons kill and maim five hundred people, mostly civilians, per week.

Source:

Inter Press Service, August 3, 2005
Title: "After 10-Year Hiatus, Pentagon Eyes New Landmine"
Author: Isaac Baker

Human Rights Watch Web site, August 2005
Title: "Development and Production of Landmines"

UPDATE BY DAVID ABBOTT

The Pentagon's 2006 budget request nearly tripled the previous year's allotment, asking for nearly $90 million for each of the next three years. The Pentagon expects to spend $390 million on production of Track I (spider) land mines through fiscal year 2011. Research, development, and production of the Track I land mine system alone is approaching and will likely surpass $1 billion.[1]

For the first time in nearly a decade, the Bush administration plans to begin production of a new generation of antipersonnel mines. Seeking to avoid the images of soldiers in wheelchairs and dismembered children associated with land mines, the administration has renamed these particular land mines "networked munitions systems." Wrapping land mines in a new name—removing the stigma they deserve—makes selling them to Congress and the public easier. Still, these networked munitions systems are nothing but high-tech land mines, whose purpose, as before, is to maim and kill humans.

Fortunately Congress is not that easily fooled. On August 1, 2006 Senators Patrick Leahy (VT) and Arlen Specter (PA) introduced the bipartisan Victim-Activated Landmine Abolition Act of 2006. The bill prohibits the procurement of any victim-activated weapon, whether called a land mine or something else.[2]

In a related matter in February 2007, forty-six countries attended the Oslo Conference on Cluster Munitions in order to launch a treaty-negotiating process signing onto the Oslo Declaration's pledge to reach an international agreement to ban cluster munitions by the end of 2008. On May 25, sixty-eight states gathered in Lima, Peru for the second meeting of the so-called Oslo Process to ban the use, production, stockpiling, and transfer of the weapons, although some states proposed exempting large categories of submunitions from the ban, such as those that have self-destruct mechanisms or a specific reliability rate.

The world's leading producers of cluster bombs—the United States, Russia and China—did not attend the Oslo or Lima conferences, nor did Israel, which was criticized for using cluster munitions in Lebanon during the most recent Middle East conflict. The next full meeting in the Oslo Process will be in Vienna from December 5-7, 2007.

In September 2006, US Senators Dianne Feinstein (D-Calif.) and Patrick Leahy (D-Vt.) introduced an amendment to the annual defense spending bill that would have prevented US tax dollars from being used to "buy, use or transfer US-made cluster bombs until the Pentagon adopts rules of engagement ensuring the weapons are not used near any large concentrations of civilians." The amendment failed in the Senate by a vote of 30-70, but in February 2007 the senators reintroduced the bill as Legislation (S. 594). However, the legislation allows the president authority to "waive this provision if he certifies that it is vital to protect the security of the United States."

Cluster bombs were used heavily in the most recent war between Israel and Lebanon, where it is estimated that 100,000 Israeli bombs failed to detonate, and UN figures estimate that 26 percent of south Lebanon's cultivatable land is affected by the ordinance.

The proposed ban could have an impact on the 2008 US presidential election, as Washington's main ally in the Middle East has taken harsh international criticism for its use of the weapons, and it is perceived to be a sensitive issue for Jewish-American voters.

The Leahy/Feinstein Legislation detailed the extent of the use of cluster munitions in recent conflicts:

➤ Combining the first and second Gulf Wars, the total number of unexploded bomblets in the region is approximately 1.2 million. An estimated 1,220 Kuwaitis and 400 Iraqi civilians have been killed since 1991.

➤ In Iraq in 2003, 13,000 cluster bombs with nearly 2 million bomblets were used.

➤ In Afghanistan in 2001, 1,228 cluster bombs with 248,056 bomblets were used. Between October 2001 and November 2002, 127 civilians were killed, 70 percent of them under the age of eighteen.

➤ Between nine and 27 million unexploded cluster bombs remain in Laos from US bombing campaigns in the 1960s and 1970s.

Approximately 11,000 people, 30 percent of them children, have been killed or injured since the war ended. Most recently, it is estimated that Israel dropped 4 million bomblets in southern Lebanon, and 1 million of these bomblets failed to explode. Reports indicate that Hezbollah retaliated with cluster bomb strikes of their own.

Citations

1. See http://www.fcnl.org/issues/item.php?item_id=1988&issue_id=9.
2. See http://www.fcnl.org/issues/item.php?item_id=2044&issue_id=9.

Censored #25, 2007
US Military in Paraguay Threatens Region

Five hundred US troops arrived in Paraguay with planes, weapons, and ammunition in July 2005, shortly after the Paraguayan Senate granted US troops immunity from national and International Criminal Court (ICC) jurisdiction. Neighboring countries and human rights organizations are concerned that the massive air base at Mariscal Estigarribia, Paraguay is a potential site for US military regional expansion.

The Mariscal Estigarribia air base is within 124 miles of Bolivia and Argentina, and two hundred miles from Brazil, near the Triple Frontier where Brazil, Paraguay, and Argentina meet. Bolivia's natural gas reserves are the second largest in South America, while the Triple Frontier region is home to Guarani Aquifer, one of the world's largest fresh water sources.

Sources:

Upside Down World, October 5, 2005
Title: "Fears mount as US opens new military installation in Paraguay"
Author: Benjamin Dangl

Foreign Policy in Focus, November 21, 2005
Title: "Dark Armies, Secret Bases, and Rummy, Oh My!"
By Conn Hallinan

International Relations Center, December 14, 2005
Title: US Military Moves in Paraguay Rattle Regional Relations"
Sam Logan and Matthew Flynn

UPDATE BY KAT PAT CRESPÁN

The Paraguayan government revoked US immunity from the ICC on

October 2, 2006. According to Thomas Shannon, Assistant Secretary of State for Western Hemisphere Affairs, the US will not continue to provide military support without immunity for its soldiers. Yet, a day later President Bush signed a waiver allowing military aid in twenty-one countries that have refused to sign immunity, including Paraguay.

The US military has had increased interaction with the Paraguayan police and military, advising them on how to deal with farmer groups who protest the 90,000 poor families who have been forced off their land and displaced by the rapidly expanding soy industry. US military exercises have also been correlated with civilian deaths around the country, in areas where many farmer organizations operate. In Concepción, there have been eleven deaths and three US military exercises and near the Triple Frontier region, an area where intelligence officials initially believed to be terrorist activity by fundamentalist Islamic groups, there have been twelve deaths and three exercises. The US conducts training and classes to teach Paraguayan troops how to fight insurgency and internal enemies. However, the US Embassy rejects all claims that the US military is linked to the increased repression against political groups, and that the training missions are medical related. Yet, according to deputy speaker of the Paraguayan parliament, Alejandro Velazquez Ugarte, of the thirteen exercises only two are of civilian nature. Paraguayan officials use the threat of terrorism to justify their transgressions against campesino resistance leaders.

In October 2006, FBI director Robert Mueller arrived in Paraguay to check on preparations for a permanent FBI office in Asunción. Although journalist Hugo Olazar reported that in September 2006 US troops were operating out of Mariscal Estigarribia, the United States denies the allegation. The US said the same before operating an $80 million air base in Manta, Ecuador, which had been described as a "dirt strip." Although the US stance on Mariscal Estigarraibia remains the same, the correlation of the military exercises to the deaths of landless farmers raise human rights concerns as the US continues to be heavily involved training Paraguayan armed forces.

THE CONTROVERSIAL CASE OF MUMIA ABU JAMAL

Honoring *Censored 2000* Introduction by Mumia Abu Jamal

UPDATE BY BILL GIBBONS

Mumia Abu Jamal may be the most renowned political prisoner in the world today. He has been on Pennsylvania's death row since he, as many believe, was falsely convicted and railroaded for the murder of Police Officer Daniel Faulkner in 1982. Mumia is a revolutionary journalist who continues to pursue his craft from behind bars in solitary confinement at Pennsylvania's Penitentiary. In 2000, Mumia honored the pages of *Censored* by writing our introduction.

In May of 2007 a three-judge panel of the Federal Circuit Court of Appeals began hearing oral arguments on a retrial for Mumia's case. Each day the court was packed with supporters, including people like former Congresswoman Cynthia McKinney and a delegation from Europe. Hundreds more protesters stood out side the court hearings. The Mumia case is highly controversial—supporters of the police have vilified him. But people who examine the trial with an open mind have found Judge Albert Sabo's court to be one of the most discredited courts in US history. Around the world Mumia is so beloved that a suburb of Paris has named a street after him, an important avenue which leads to France's Olympic stadium.

At the time of Mumia's arrest he was already a well-known revolutionary journalist, radio commentator, and former Black Panther Minister of Information—at age 15. Shortly before dawn, on December 9, 1981, Mumia was moonlighting as a cab driver in downtown Philadelphia. He came upon a scene involving a confrontation with a white police officer and Mumia's brother William Cook. Shortly thereafter Mumia was found lying on the sidewalk, shot in the chest, and Officer Faulkner lay dying from bullet wounds. The Police charged Mumia with murder.

Recently released crime scene photos reveal that the Police changed evidence. During oral arguments at the Third Circuit Court of Appeals, photos taken by press photographer Pedro P. Polakoff III show police actively manipulating evidence at the homicide scene. For example, they moved the officer's hat from the roof of Billy Cook's vehicle to the sidewalk to make the scene more emotionally dramatic. One photograph shows Police Officer James Forbes holding both pistols found at the scene in one hand, bare-handed, getting his fingerprints all over the evidence and smudging existing prints. Forbes was caught lying on the witness stand because he had testified that he had not handled the firearms in a manner that would have gotten finger prints on the trigger or butt of the pistol, or smudged existing fingerprint evidence. The newly release photos show that he was not telling the truth to the courts.[1]

Photos also show the cab driver Robert Chobert was not parked behind Mumia's vehicle and Faulkner's squad car. The witness was nowhere near where the prosecution says he was. Again, as with other witnesses, the police were caught using terror to coerce a witness to give false testimony.[2]

Journalist Michael Schiffman found from researching the newly released photos that a .38 revolver would leave divot holes, or ricochet marks, on the sidewalk had the defendant fired rounds at the prone officer Faulkner and missed as the prosecution had claimed. The photos do not show these marks.

A mass protest movement prevented Mumia's execution in 1995, but he still was denied justice and remains locked away on Death Row. Mumia's case became an international issue. The European Parliament, human rights groups like Amnesty International, and others have called for a new trial.

In 2001 a federal district court judge upheld Mumia's conviction but overturned the death sentence hanging over his head on technical grounds. It was on the 2001 decision that the current federal appeals court is hearing arguments. Mumia's defense team is asking for a new trial while prosecutors are asking that the death sentence be reinstated. The principal legal issues are whether the prosecution in the 1982 trial had deliberately excluded black jurors and whether the verdict form given the jurors misled them on how to decide a possible death sentence.

During the period of Mumia's trials, the Philadelphia DA's office produced a training tape for new assistant DAs on how to exclude black jurors. A federal district judge has already found that the jury form was biased and federal courts, because of blatant racism and bias, have overturned a long list of Philadelphia convictions.

The appeals court, which may not rule for several months, may grant a new trial, order a new evidentiary hearing or reject the appeal, in which case Mumia would face execution within a short period.[3]

Through twenty-five years in solitary confinement, Mumia Abu

Jamal has held his head high despite the viciousness of the Philadelphia police, prison system and courts, and repeated threats of execution. Mumia's books, weekly columns, and radio commentaries inspire not just people in the United States, but even encourage people across the globe.

Citations

1. "Michael Schiffman Presents Part 1," http://www.abu-jamal-news.com/audio/j4m/schiff1.mp3.
2. "Michael Schiffman on Polakoff's Crime Scene Photos," http://www.abu-jamal-news.com/audio/j4m/schiff2.mp3.
3. "Abu-Jamal seeks new US murder trial, claims racism," Reuters, May 17, 2007.

CHAPTER 3

Junk Food News and News Abuse

by Jocelyn Thomas, Toni Faye Catelani, Jenni Leys, Christina Carey, and Kate Sims

Regular readers of Project Censored are familiar with our annual list of Junk Food News, in which Project volunteers and interns select a list of the dumbest, least important, most overplayed stories of the year. Project Censored founder Carl Jensen introduced the chapter as a response to charges from some in the mainstream media that the Top 25 Censored list was nothing more than a skewed interpretation of the journalism and editing process. After all, the news can't print (or air) everything. Stories the Project referred to as "Censored," they said, were simply those that had been set aside to make room for more deserving, consequential news.

So every year, Project Censored researchers scour the daily press outlets, hoping to find evidence that the news is so littered with deep, meaningful stories of great importance that they could not possibly have found the space (or time) to cover our "relatively inconsequential" top twenty-five. We have yet to find that evidence.

Junk Food News stories for Censored 2008:

1. Britney Spears has a meltdown
2. Anna Nicole has a baby
3. Brad Pitt & Angelina Jolie have a baby and adopt others
4. Jon Benet's "killer" is found to be a fraud
5. The rise and fall of O.J. Simpson's book
6. The feud between Donald Trump and Rosie O'Donnell
7. Miss USA Tara Conner's drug abuse
8. Paul McCartney's divorce
9. An astronaut wears a diaper to attack her romantic rival
10. Madonna adopts an African baby

Other nominations that didn't make the final list include Lindsay Lohan's stint in rehab, Prince Harry's trip to Iraq, the Paris Hilton/Nicole Richie tussle, Paula Abdul's drunk behavior on *American Idol*, *American Idol* contestant(s) in nudie pictures on the Internet, Hillary Clinton and violent video games, the Superbowl Mars Bar kiss between two men, Mayor Gavin Newsom's affair with his aide's wife, the Kate Hudson/Owen Wilson relationship, Cheney's gay daughter has a baby, James Brown's widow fights for inheritance, the "war" on Christmas and Easter, consumers camping out to get a PS3 game system, and the lawsuits against the movie *Borat*.

1. Moving up from number seven last year to number one on this year's Junk Food list is the long-suffering paparazzi target Britney Spears. On February 17, Ms. Spears was photographed in a Los Angeles salon giving herself a buzz cut. The media (including the news media) went into frenzied overdrive, offering incessant speculation on why poor Britney might be coming unglued. While possibly important to thirteen-year-olds, adults might have preferred to hear about the newly released analysis of 2005 census figures showing that nearly 16 million Americans are currently living in deep or severe poverty. About one in three severely poor people are under age seventeen, and nearly two out of three are female. Mainstream news anchors took the time to wonder if Ms. Spears was too young and immature for the pressures of motherhood. They weren't able to squeeze in, however, the fact that female-headed families with children account for the lion's share of the severely poor.

Perhaps even more troubling, during the week of February 17, 2007, TV news found little time to examine an appeals court ruling that bolstered the Bush Administration's bid to hold prisoners indefinitely. The decision upheld part of a tough anti-terrorism law that took away the rights of Guantánamo prisoners to challenge their detention before federal judges.

Sources

"Britney Spears Shaves Head, Gets new Tattoo," Fox News and Associated Press, February 17, 2007.

Tony Pugh, "US Economy leaving record numbers in severe poverty," *McClatchy Newspapers*, February 23, 2007.

"Law restricting Guantánamo appeals upheld," Reuters, February 20, 2007.

2. On September 7, 2006, Anna Nicole Smith gave birth to a baby girl and everyone held their breath for the ultimate piece of the puzzle—who was the father? For those of you who missed it, the birth certificate listed none other than Anna Nicole's personal attorney Howard K. Stern.* Now, for those of you who kept up to date regarding the Anna Nicole goings-on, here's what you did miss: A September 2006 report found that the Iraq violent death toll for August was three times larger than the preliminary count. The final tally disproved official US and Iraqi claims that a "security crackdown" had led to a drop in the number of deaths that month. At the same time, scientists in the arctic were warning of a new global warming "time bomb." Glacier scientists found that the global warming gasses trapped in the permafrost were bubbling out in much larger amounts than anticipated and voiced concerns about what this likely indicated.

Sources

Seth Borenstein, "Scientists Find New Global Warming 'Time Bomb,' Associated Press, September 7, 2006.

Rawya Rageh, "Iraq Deaths Multiply in New August Count," Associated Press, September 7, 2006.

3. After the "Brangelina" roller coaster of 2005 and the frenzy of rumor and innuendo it sparked, hadn't we heard enough about the private lives of Brad Pitt and Angelina Jolie? The answer, it would seem, was no. On May 27, 2006, the day of their baby Shiloh's birth, the media went into paparazzi overdrive to obtain photos of the "most beautiful baby in the world." They weren't as interested, however, in another set of photos released that day. These photos depicted US Marines killing Iraqi civilians "execution-style." The unearthed photographs, taken by a Marine intelligence team, convinced military investigators that a single unit had killed as many as twenty-four unarmed Iraqis in an insurgent stronghold after a roadside bomb had killed an American in November of 2005. While this shocking story did eventually break the surface of mainstream coverage, it never attained the breadth of coverage so eagerly showered on Brad and Angelina.

---

* After Anna Nicole Smith's death in February 2007, DNA testing showed the father was former boyfriend Larry Birkhead.

Sources

Tony Perry, Julian E. Barnes, and Tom Lasseter, "Photos Indicate Civilians Slain Execution-Style: An official involved in an investigation of Camp Pendleton Marines" actions in an Iraqi town cites "a total breakdown in morality," *Los Angeles Times*, May 27, 2006.

"Iranian-Backed Militia Groups Take Control of Much of Southern Iraq," Knight Ridder Newswire, May 27, 2006.

4. On August 16, 2006, it was reported that officials had arrested a man by the name of John Marc Karr who was suspected in the infamous murder of Jon Benet Ramsey, the six-year-old pageant winner from Colorado. When Karr confidently proclaimed that, yes, he had indeed been involved in the crime, the national news media couldn't get enough. Cable and network outlets spent the better part of two weeks obsessed with a story that in the end turned out to be a dead duck: DNA tests proved Karr wasn't their man. So was this the best that network producers could find to report? As August is the height of the summer vacation season, the five million yearly visitors to our national parks might have been interested to hear a new report that a dozen of the most popular national parks are becoming increasingly susceptible to climate change. Mt. Rainier has more glacial ice than the rest of the Cascades combined and is among the best studied sites in the nation. Rainier's glacier cover shrank by more than a fifth from 1913 to 1994 and the volume of the glaciers by almost one-fourth, leaving scientists very concerned.

Sources

Les Blumenthal, "Washington State's Glaciers are Melting, and that Has Scientists Concerned," *McClatchy Newspapers*, August 29, 2006.

"Exclusive: Secret Tapes of John Marc Karr," ABC News, August 22, 2006.

Unmesh Kher and Simon Montlake, "John Mark Karr's Strange Life as a Teacher," *Time Magazine*, August 18, 2006.

5. On November 15, 2006 O.J. Simpson returned, once again, to the spotlight, this time wearing sequins and tap shoes. Simpson announced that he was going to publish a novel posing the 'hypothetical" that if he did murder his wife and his wife's friend then he would have done it in this way, or that way. The press had a field day—and so did the public. It wasn't long before there was a TV

movie to go along with the book. And then suddenly both were canceled. The publishers dismissed the idea as ill-contrived and family members of the victims moved into the spotlight. In the end, Simpson insisted that the book was written by a ghostwriter, and that he killed no one. Surprise.

Meanwhile, were we missing the bigger picture? During the O.J. Simpson reporting, President George Bush told his senior advisors that he wanted to send 20,000 more troops to Iraq instead of pulling troops out. The rest of his new plan would involve pursuing the diplomatic cooperation of nearby countries through international conferences or the like, reuniting the Shia and the Sunni by creating a magical political framework and allocating more resources to Iraq. The London *Guardian* made this known in November 2006. Funny how the mainstream news wasn't able to pick up on this report until January 2007.

Sources

Simon Tisdall, "US Plans Last Big Push in Iraq: Strategy Document Calls for Extra 20,000 Troops, Aid for Iraqi Army and Regional Summit," *Guardian/UK*, November 16, 2006, http://www.commondreams.org/headlines06/1116-06.htm.

6. On December 20, 2006, Rosie O'Donnell criticized billionaire Donald Trump on *The View* after he told reporters that he would allow Miss USA, Tara Conner, to continue with her duties despite her violation of pageant guidelines (see JFN #7). O'Donnell went on to claim that Trump was not a good moral authority for young people in America. In response, Trump began a media blitz in which he called her several unflattering, and perhaps even defamatory, names. This prompted a media blitz that lasted for weeks. Every day mainstream news shows provided an "important update" to the ongoing feud.

One can only hypothesize the number of important, groundbreaking stories that might have emerged if not for the over-hyped, and ultimately boring, celebrity clash.

One that certainly received less attention than its due, was a shocking new study about the extreme discrepancies between the world's wealthiest and the poorest. According to a newly updated study released by the Helsinki-based World Institute for Development Economics Research of the United Nations University, the richest two percent of adults in the world now own more than half the world's wealth (up from 5 percent just three years ago). By contrast, the assets of half of the world's adult population account for barely 1 percent of global wealth. The study's authors say their work is the most comprehensive study of personal wealth ever undertaken.

Sources

Mark Dagostino, "Rosie Slams Trump, The Donald Fires Back," *People*, December 20, 2006.

Aaron Glantz, "Richest 2 Percent Own Half the World's Wealth," OneWorld.net, December 22, 2006.

7. On December 16, 2006, it was reported that the reigning Miss USA, Tara Conner from Brussel Springs, Kentucky, was under scrutiny from the Miss USA pageant because of published reports of underage drinking, cocaine use, and allegations of sexual escapades. As America wondered if she would keep her crown or be forced to resign in disgrace, the mainstream media failed to pick up on a startling Associated Press report that hundreds of prisoners have been transferred from Guantánamo Bay to other countries, and then set free. The prisoners had been arrested during the nationwide sweep that took place after 9/11. Donald Rumsfeld labeled them as "among the most dangerous, best-trained, vicious killers on the face of the Earth." The decision to suddenly release so many of the former detainees raised questions about whether they were really as dangerous as the United States claimed. Either that or some of America's staunchest allies in the "War on Terror" had suddenly decided to set hundreds of terrorists and militants free.

Sources

Fox News, Inewsnetwork, December 16, 2006.

"Will Trump Dump Miss USA? Winner of Pageant he runs is in Trouble," *Chicago Sun-Times*, December 17, 2006.

"Most Gitmo Detainees Freed Elsewhere," Associated Press, December 16, 2006.

8. On May 17, 2006 Heather Mills and Paul McCartney announced their impending separation, just prior to Paul's sixty-fourth birthday. It was announced via the couple's Web sites that the two were to separate. If media speculation in the weeks prior to this had been intense, it was ten-fold after the announcement.

The following day, television news outlets missed two stories that may have been slightly more important to the daily lives of the American public. First, the *New York Times* announced that the Bush administration was planning to solve the US/Mexican border problem by privatizing border control. They have begun providing huge subsidies to their cronies at Raytheon and Lockheed Martin to do less work for more money (so much for the efficiency of private enterprise). Second, according to Canada's National Farmer's Union, global food supplies are near the breaking point. Rising population, water shortages, climate change, and the growing costs of fossil fuel-based fertilizers point to a calamitous shortfall in the world's grain supplies in the near future.

Sources

Marilyn Stowe, "My advice to Sir Paul? Pay up now—and get a gagging order," *The Times* (London), October 18, 2006.

Eric Lipton, "Bush Turns to Big Military Contractors for Border Control," *New York Times*, May 18, 2006.

Stephen Leahy, "Global Food Supply Near the Breaking Point," Inter Press Service, May 18, 2006.

9. On Feb. 5, 2007, United States Navy Capt. Lisa Nowak, the famously diaper-clad astronaut, was arrested in Florida and charged with, among other things, attempted murder, attempted kidnapping, burglary, and battery. This sparked a free-for-all during which the mainstream media covered every minute detail of the astronaut's life and loves. It certainly beat out the trial of First Lt. Ehren Watada, the US soldier who refused to go to Iraq, that began the same day that Nowak was arrested. Watada's decision to battle the military system rather than the people of Iraq received virtually no notice from the mainstream television and press outlets.

Sources

Jean-Louis Doublet, "Trial of US Soldier Who Refused to Go to Iraq Opens Monday," Agence France Presse, February 4, 2007.

Tomas Alex Tizon, "Instead of Iraq, a Battle All His Own," *Los Angeles Times*, February 5, 2007.

10. On October 11, 2006, it was reported that pop star Madonna had adopted a one-year-old boy in Malawi. Madonna said she hoped to

highlight the problem of AIDS in the southern African nation. Controversy erupted four days later when the boy's father said he had felt confused and powerless in the face of the singer's determination to take his only surviving child, whose mother had passed away.

Of less concern that week was a new national poll revealing people's attitudes toward the challenges facing modern families. According to the survey, Americans said that they are anxious about the forces that threaten family. Americans point to divorce as the biggest challenge to stable family life today, rising above other factors such as same sex or dual career couples. According to the new data, 88 percent of US adults say divorce has negative impacts on maintaining a stable American family life. Only 53 percent said that same sex couples were a negative impact and only 50 percent said dual career households negatively impact families.

Sources

"Madonna adopts child in Africa," BBC News, October 11, 2006.

Angella Johnson, "Madonna's adopted baby's father tells how he was powerless to stop her," *The Daily Mail*, October 15, 2006.

"Divorce Seen As Biggest Challenge to Stable American Family Life, New Survey Reveals," *Redbook*, October 18, 2006.

NEWS ABUSE

In 2001, addressing concerns that some of the stories overplayed in the media could not appropriately be called Junk Food, Project Censored writers added a list of stories we call News Abuse—potentially valid news stories that eventually consumed more space and air time than their importance would seem to warrant.

The News Abuse stories for 2008:
1. Death of Anna Nicole Smith
2. Death of Steve Irwin
3. Mel Gibson's drunken rant
4. Duke University lacrosse team's alleged involvement in a rape
5. Michael Richards's racist comments

1. In the early afternoon of February 8, 2006, the tabloid it-girl Anna

Nicole Smith was found unresponsive in her hotel room, rushed to the hospital, and pronounced DOA at 2:49 pm. During that same week, the former US Ambassador of Iraq failed to explain what happened to $12 billion in newly printed, shrink-wrapped $100 bills that he had flown to Baghdad, and had since misplaced. Also on that day, Iran's top authority said that the Islamic Republic would target "US interests around the world" if its nuclear program was challenged. Iran's leader reminded all listening that "The enemies know well that any aggression will lead to a reaction from all sides in the Iranian nation on the aggressors and their interests around the world."

Sources

Joseph L. Galloway, "Billions and Billions of Dollars Just Disappear in Iraq," McClatchy Newspapers, February 8, 2007.

Parisa Hafezi, "Iran Says It Will Target US Interests if Attacked," Reuters, February 8, 2007.

2. The death of crocodile hunter Steve Irwin took over news on September 4, 2006. The icon of wildlife adventurers was reportedly taping a new documentary off of the Australian north coast, when a stingray that he was swimming with stung him right in the heart.

While the US obsessed over the loss of the *Crocodile Hunter*—his death, his death tape and his documentary—news outlets neglected to tell us that China had begun working on a nuclear deal with Pakistan. So what's the big deal that Pakistan, sworn enemy of India (who by the way is getting nuclear weapons from the US), is getting nuclear power from the China National Nuclear Corporation? So Pakistan is becoming more powerful and China is in the nuclear trading business. No big deal. Nothing bad will come of it.

Source

Antoaneta Bezlova, "Snubbed by US, Pakistan doing Nuclear Deal with China," Inter Press Service, September 4, 2006, http://www.commondreams.org/head-lines06/0904-01.htm.

3. On July 28, 2006 Mel Gibson was arrested for speeding down the Pacific Coast Highway in a drunken haze. Described as cooperative until arrested, Gibson then became threatening, shouting anti-Semitic remarks and asking "Are you a Jew?" to the arresting officer (who is in

fact, Jewish). The incident sparked an almost immediate media hub-bub, prompting two separate public apologies from Gibson.

Ironically, mainstream media outlets spent that weekend studiously ignoring all but the most banal stories following the Israeli attack on Lebanon. They neglected to mention reports from AP and the *Guardian* that sixty people, including thirty-four children, had been killed during an Israeli attack on Qana. Widely publicized throughout Europe, Americans were ignorant of the fact that the death toll in Lebanon was as much as twice the official figure reported in the US. Prior to the attack, Israeli commanders had announced, "If You Haven't Left, we will consider you Hezbollah." According to the London *Guardian*, global outrage called the Qana attack a "War Crime" by Israel. US rearming flights, headed for Israel, were forced to avoid a Scottish Airport after being denied entry by local authorities. Another report highlighted the fragility of the ecosystem in Lebanon, calling Lebanon's trees, air, and sea "Casualties of War."

Sources

Dahr Jamail, "Death Toll Could Be Twice the Official Figure," Inter Press Service, July 28, 2006.

Hassan M. Fattah, "Casualties of War: Lebanon's Trees, Air, and Sea," *New York Times*, July 29, 2006.

Gaith Abdul-Ahad, Jonathan Steele and Clancy Chassay in Qana; Rory McCarthy at the Israel-Lebanon border; Wendell Steavenson in Beirut, and Julian Borger in Washington, "They Found Them Huddled Together," *The Guardian/UK*, July 31, 2006.

4. On April 11, 2007, the North Carolina Attorney General announced that all charges against the three lacrosse players charged with rape in 2006 had been dropped. The obviously weary Duke University students said they were looking forward to leaving the entire incident behind them. But this was not to be. The dropping of the charges produced perhaps as large a media firestorm as had the original charges. Cable and network news shows worked feverishly to beat each other out for the most "in-depth" and "hard-hitting" interviews.

It is interesting to note that on that same day, April 11, 2007, the research database LexisNexis and Information Analytics Group launched their new software, AIS—Advanced Investigative Solutions—designed to help law enforcement "locate and monitor non-compliant sexual predators." The new software enables investigators to more quickly respond to child abductions and supports law enforcement agencies with their efforts to enforce the Adam Walsh Child Protection and Safety Act, which mandates strict registration requirements for sex offenders. The AIS "leverages critical information, link analysis, mapping and alerts needed to rapidly identify and locate sexual predators." More than 6,000 federal, state, and local government and law enforcement agencies have already begun using its investigative solutions every day to locate suspects, track down fugitives, and solve crimes.

Sources

"Duke Rape Suspects Speak Out," *60 Minutes*, October 11, 2006.

LexisNexis Media Relations Press Release, "LexisNexis Risk & Information Analytics Group Launches Solution to Help Tackle National Sex Predator Problem," April 11, 2007.

5. On November 20, 2006 actor Michael Richards let loose on a couple of so-called hecklers in the audience of one of his stand-up comedy shows. He shouted racist remarks at them, including the N-word, and said that in the past they would have been "hanging from a tree" by now. This not-so-funny outburst made headlines across the United States, labeling Richards (or as we all know him, Kramer from *Seinfeld*) to be a racist. His garbled and unconvincing apology on the Letterman show did little to assuage the situation. While the incident caused a small flurry of mainstream debate on the "state of racism in America," the coverage was, for the most part, shallow and disingenuous.

During this time there was a meaningful protest in Indonesia that was almost completely ignored. The Indonesian people protested the arrival of George W. Bush, his presence there and his war against terrorism—with 2,000 marching to show their disdain for the Bush administration, its practices, and its war in Iraq. The normally peaceful resort town was turned into a military state by the US-backed autocratic government.

Source

Greg Stohr, "Bush Faces Storm of Protest in Indonesia," Agence France-Presse, November 20, 2006, http://www.commondreams.org/headlines06/1120-07.htm.

CHAPTER 4

10 Signs of Hope
Stories of Action and Change We Didn't Hear about in 2006 and 2007

by Kate Sims and Project Censored, with help from the people of *YES! Magazine*

Whether mainstream or independent, coverage of news is often characterized as depressing and overwhelming. People frequently complain that the information we receive imparts a sense of hopelessness and powerlessness, rather than clarity and a sense of involvement.

At the same time, from the perspective of many professional journalists, 'real news' is, appropriately, that which keeps us up to date on what's going wrong in the world—the crimes, the wars, the political corruption. As Carl Jensen said in 1993, "the news should warn us about those things that make our society ill, whether economically, politically, or physically."

For the most part, positive news stories are placed in the category of fluff pieces, scattered among the real news stories to keep readers from tuning out completely. Beyond the usual escapist celebrity exposes, these stories generally take the form of feature articles that highlight the actions of a local hero, a school project, or someone who has overcome adversity. Positive stories may address the delivery of care packages to our troops in Iraq or the successful cleanup of a local stream, but they tend to steer clear of the victories that address the deeper social and structural problems facing the global citizenry. It is rare that we see a story about the productive actions people have taken to address the national health care crisis, the crumbling of our democratic institutions, or the corruption of our voting system.

Is it simply that there are no stories about people making meaningful change? Are there no signs that people are taking on the challenges that threaten to undermine the values we care most about—like democracy, global justice, opportunity for all, a healthy planet? Based solely on the daily news, one might reasonably conclude that it is just too late for citizens of the earth to generate the great mobilizations necessary for our species' and our planet's survival.

For years, careful readers of Project Censored's Top 25 have noted that many of the stories highlight not only the negative consequences of a particular event or trend, but also the positive responses that are sparked by these situations. But still, it is vital that negative stories of great consequence not be ignored simply because they are painful to consider. It would be irresponsible (and hypocritical) for us to downplay (or sugarcoat) the huge stories of political corruption, bad legislation, and global violence that are so consistently underplayed in the corporate media.

And yet, the marginalizing of stories about positive change can be as great a tragedy as the under-coverage of the trends that threaten us. Without such coverage, people can't know that their peers are taking the action that they themselves yearn for, but are afraid to embark on alone. Plus, those who are ready to become active are denied important information about which actions are most effective, which are not, and how they might want to get involved.

We are told that the world—especially the world outside US borders—is a scary, confusing, incurable mess. We don't know—or we forget—that social movements can create change with surprising speed. History shows us that, while efforts to change can seem ponderous (and maddeningly slow), once a critical mass is reached, large positive, even revolutionary changes can be made with startling rapidity. What is scoffed at as fringe and radical one moment can be embraced by the mainstream as within the bounds of "rational debate" the next. Writer David Korten says that these positive changes have the potential to bring about a deep cultural transformation he calls "The Great Turning"—the title of his most recent book (May 2006).

So, is it necessary that good investigative journalism act only as an alarm bell, warning citizens of current or potential threats to our security and liberty?

Likewise, is it good journalism to narrowly reflect the perspective of those in charge, consigning grassroots leaders, social movement organizers, and cultural trend setters to the back of the media bus? With such behavior, it is little wonder that the mainstream was caught by surprise when the city of Seattle was virtually shut down during the WTO summit in 1999—they simply hadn't known there was a story there.

Can hard-hitting journalism also apprise us of the actions that rejuvenate our political health, the people who are building positive movements in a negative world, the events that allow global citizens to build more powerful coalitions?

For years, Project Censored researchers have looked to *YES! Magazine* as the standard for this emerging trend, or force, in journalism. Since 1996, the people of *YES!* have done the deep investigations and dug up the stories around the world which remind people that the possibilities for change are not just an abstraction, they are real and happening.

Few of the stories from *YES!* hit the mainstream—or at least the positive movements that underlie them get ignored. But their work has helped spark an underground movement that isn't waiting for the mainstream to catch up.

Perhaps the best "censored" news is a theme that runs through every issues of *YES!* The big secret is that, throughout the world, there are millions of people actively engaged in moving toward the formation of just and peaceful societies. Yes, there are extremists in every country who will take advantage of desperate and bitter situations (and that includes *every* country). And increasing economic insecurity and violence tends to move people in the direction of extremism and various forms of fundamentalism, both religious and secular.

But increasingly (and encouragingly), people are rediscovering their power and right to live in dignity, and taking on the urgent questions of our time—how to end poverty, how to build peaceful and just societies, how to live within the carrying capacities of our environment. While our most powerful leaders are at a loss in the face of these historic challenges—or are too corrupted by corporate money and bankrupt policies to provide real leadership—social movements, grassroots leaders, organizations at every level from the local to the global, are moving ahead with solutions. And they are joining forces.

The World Social Forums, and their regional counterparts, which began just six years ago, are weaving together movements, organizations, and approaches from around the world and showing that another world is possible. The Internet is building bridges of understanding and communication among those working for change. Meanwhile *YES!* and other forward-thinking members of the independent press are reporting on this transformation, as it is happening in the United States and throughout the world.

• • •

In 2006, *YES! Magazine* celebrated its tenth anniversary by releasing "The Ten Most Hopeful Trends of the Last 10 Years"—ten signs that change is happening both within our national borders and outside of our "American bubble." Being big list-makers ourselves, Project Censored thought we would "borrow" this idea and select what we thought were the most inspiring signs of change and hope that occurred within our 2006-2007 research cycle. While most of these stories have been uncovered by the people at *YES!*, Project Censored added in a couple others we liked as well:

10 STORIES OF HOPE AND CHANGE IN 2006 AND 2007

1. The Global "free trade" agenda is losing steam

Throughout the 1990s, and into the 2000s, global lending institutions such as the World Bank and the International Monetary Fund (IMF) pushed hyper-capitalist, "free-trade" agendas ostensibly to help developing nations alleviate poverty and develop into modern democracies. Third World citizens quickly noticed that the new programs caused greater suffering than the afflictions they were designed to ease. These programs reoriented developing economies to a focus on exports rather than meeting local needs, and benefited foreign corporations and the wealthy elites while undermining local economies. Sustained and consistent activism over the last decade or so is now bearing fruit as pro-corporate global trade policies are starting to unravel.

Activists win big at WTO

Beginning with the Zapatista uprising as NAFTA took effect in 1994, and continuing with the uprising against the WTO in Seattle in 1999, activists have gathered around the world to press for an end to this hyper-capitalism. With the slogan, "No deal is better than a bad deal," activists joined hands on the streets and in the corridors of power to protest WTO trade deals they said would harm people and the planet—and they won big.

On July 24, 2006, the WTO's director general announced a halt to all global trade negotiations under way at the WTO. The "Doha 'Development' Round," launched two years after the Seattle WTO, ostensibly to focus on the needs of the poorest countries, was suspended until further notice.

Stopping the Doha Round shows the growing strength of civil society when communities come together to work for a world where people matter more than trade. How these networks and the wider global justice movement — in all of its contradictions and complexities—evolve will set the course not only for trading relations between nations, but for humanity's ability to create a more equitable and sustainable future.

Mark Randazzo, "No Deal," YES! #40, Winter 2007. http://www.yesmagazine.org/article.asp?ID=1592

Bolivia Stands up to Global Lenders

This article is also listed as one of the Top 25 Censored stories of 2008 (#19). However, its impact as an important sign of hope in the movement for global equity cannot be overlooked:

In 2006, Bolivia's President Evo Morales confirmed his refusal to sign agreements with the IMF or a Free Trade Agreement with the US. In April, Morales released the Bolivian Peoples Trade Agreement (PTA), an alternative to the neo-liberal free trade model being pushed by the IMF and World Bank. The PTA fosters an indigenous vision of development, emphasizing solidarity, national sovereignty, and well-being of the whole population. Along with negotiating to recover state stock control of private enterprises, these actions reverse a situation in which foreign corporations defined policies and strategies of resource ownership, control, and trade. This model is the fruit of a strengthening movement against corporate globalization, not only throughout Latin America, but across the globe.

"Is the US Free Trade Model Losing Steam?" American Friends Service Committee, Trade Matters, May 3, 2006, http://www.afsc.org/trade-matters/trade-agreements/LosingSteam.htm.

2. A tide of change is sweeping Latin America

Any large-scale social transition that affects an entire continent will be perceived differently by different people. Such is the case with the sweeping political changes we are witnessing in the Southern

Hemisphere. In the conservative and, to a smaller extent, mainstream press, there has been much worried hand-wringing over the rise of Venezuelan President Hugo Chavez and the spread of the left within the countries of South America. But for the poor of the hemisphere, it looks a lot more like the rise of a new democracy.

The YES! Magazine *summer 2007 issue #42 (released in May of 2007) did an excellent job of examining and highlighting this subject. Entitled "Democracy: Latin America Leaps Ahead," it details the extraordinary changes taking place throughout the southern hemisphere in the middle 2000s—from Venezuelan worker co-ops to Cuba's ambitious global health care mission; from the impact of a woman president on gender roles in Chile to the "recuperated" factories of Argentina.*

In 2006, poor people's candidates swept many of the Latin American elections. With the January inauguration of a new president of Ecuador, a comeback president in Nicaragua, and a re-elected president in Venezuela, the tide of change in Latin America appears unstoppable. A year ago, Bolivia's first indigenous president, Evo Morales, took office, and Brazil's left-leaning president, Luiz Inácio Lula da Silva, was reelected in October. Nicaraguan President Daniel Ortega has signed on to Venezuelan President Hugo Chavez's Bolivarian Alternative for the Americas (ALBA), a trade pact that includes Bolivia and Cuba, and is widely seen as an alternative to the US-supported Free Trade Area of the Americas.

Meanwhile, in Oaxaca, native women played a central part in the movement against autocratic rule in Mexico. Putting their personal lives on hold, women in the Mexican state of Oaxaca helped shut down the government, took over a TV station, and stood up to police violence. Following the election of Governor Ulises Ruiz Ortiz in 2004, a group of women (called "urban guerillas" by the Ruiz government) formed neighborhood protest groups and participated in the marathon discussions that guided the protesters' actions.

Sarah van Gelder, "Poor People's Candidates Sweep Latin American Elections," *YES! Magazine* #41, Spring 2007. http://www.yesmagazine.org/article.asp?ID=1674#latinamerica.

John Gibler, "In Oaxaca, Women Rise," *YES! Magazine* #41 Spring 2007 http://www.yesmagazine.org/article.asp?ID=1637.

3. In the midst of chaos, civic leaders aren't waiting for the US to bring peace and democracy; they are moving forward now

Members of the Iraqi Freedom Congress don't like the occupation or the militias, but neither are they signing up with political or religious extremists. Instead, these Iraqis are claiming the space to live with their neighbors in peace. The Iraqi Freedom Congress (IFC), founded in March 2005, is bringing together labor unions, student groups, women's rights organizations, and neighborhood assemblies to defend civil society against the occupation troops and the profusion of armed factions. The IFC is working to establish a parallel governance structure to that of the US-backed regime and armed militias linked to ethnic and religious groups. In the war-torn city of Kirkuk, Iraq's civil resistance movement is building a new model for a secular society that puts equal citizenship ahead of ethnic or sectarian identity. The working model for this program is a Kirkuk neighborhood, dubbed Al-Tzaman ("Solidarity"). In a starkly divided city, it has become a haven for peaceful coexistence.

Bill Weinberg, "In Iraq: A Place To Be Human, First" *YES! Magazine* #38, Summer 2006, http://www.yesmagazine.org/article.asp?ID=1458

4. A new International Confederation of Trade Unions has formed to support global workers

November 1, 2006 saw the dawn of a new International Trade Union Confederation. The largest of its kind, The ITUC represents 168 million workers through 306 affiliated organizations within 154 countries and territories. The goal of the union is to keep labor standards high and to make it harder for transnational corporations to play employees in different countries against one another. At the founding congress in Vienna, the new General Secretary of the ITUC declared, "The creation of the ITUC will solidify the trade union movement's capacity at the national and international levels . . . we will exert more influence on companies, governments, and the international financial and trade institutions. The founding of the ITUC is an integral part of the process of uniting the power of trade unionism." Some international observers see this as the beginning of a small shift in the balance of global power.

"A new international trade union confederation is born" ITUC Media Release (*Asheville Global Report*) Winter 2006, http://www.ituc-csi.org/spip.php?article16.

"International Free Trade Union Group Merges, Re-Emerges as New Organization" Mike Hall, *AFL-CIO Now*, 11/1/2006, http://blog.aflcio.org/2006/11/01/international-trade-union-group-merges-re-emerges-as-new-organization/.

5. Worldwide opposition to genetically modified organisms (GMOs) is beginning to pay off

Since the beginning of corporate-sponsored genetic modification of ancient crop seeds, grassroots movements throughout the world have questioned and criticized the fundamental alteration of staple foods—and warned of its potentially devastating legacy. Over the last couple of years, these efforts have begun to pay off.

In Brazil, after protests by more than 1,000 farmers in the GMO-free state of Parana, the Brazilian Environmental Protection Agency fined the Syngenta company one million Reals ($466,000) for its experimental GMO-crop cultivation near Iguaçu National Park.

In Mali, a group of farmers acting as Africa's first "citizen jury" voted, in February 2006, against the introduction of GMO crops. After debate and consultation with international experts, the jury proposed focusing research and training on local varieties and organic farming methods instead of using GMOs. Although the jury's vote is not binding on the government, it is at the forefront of a growing movement throughout Africa.

And finally, in an important development, a United Nations panel has upheld a global moratorium on "terminator" plants (genetically engineered to prevent farmers from using the seeds from their harvests for the next crop, forcing them to buy from seed companies like Monsanto). The moratorium, enacted under the UN Convention on Biological Diversity, passed despite fierce pressure from Australia, New Zealand, and Canada and the US along with seed corporations Monsanto and Syngenta. A broad coalition of farmers, indigenous people, environmental and social justice activists, and local and regional governments defended the moratorium.

Lilja Otto, "UN Panel Upholds 'Terminator Plant' Moratorium," *YES! Magazine* #38 Summer 2006, http://www.yesmagazine.org/article.asp?ID=1487#gmo.

6. American communities have begun to reclaim their voting rights

Bipartisan activists in New Mexico and California's Humboldt County remind us, once again, that the price of liberty is eternal vigilance. These communities are demonstrating that protecting your right to vote requires that you know what is happening in your state—before, during, and after Election Day—and are willing to hold your leaders accountable.

In New Mexico, citizen activists, disgusted by systematic vote disappearance, demanded change—and got it. In 2005, Voter Action, a group of motivated citizens, some jumping into activism for the first time, sued the state of New Mexico over the bad machines and the failure to count the vote. The activists invited the Greg Palast investigations team to lay out their findings to huge citizens' meetings in Albuquerque and Santa Fe. It worked. Voter Action, successful in New Mexico, is now pursuing lawsuits in seven states to stop the Secretaries of State from purchasing electronic voting systems that lack paper trails and therefore cannot be audited.

Humboldt County ejected outside corporations from election meddling by declaring corporations "non-persons." On June 6, 2006, voters in Northern California's Humboldt County decided by a 55–45 margin that corporations do not have the same rights of "personhood" as a citizen, especially when it comes to participating in local political campaigns. One Eureka resident explained, "Every person has the right to sign petition recalls and to contribute money to political campaigns. Measure T will not affect these individual rights."

Greg Palast, "Recipe for a Cooked Election," *YES! Magazine* #39, Fall 2006, http://www.yesmagazine.org/article.asp?ID=1511.

John Nichols, "Citizens 1, Corporations 0," *The Nation*, June 7, 2006, http://www.thenation.com/blogs/thebeat?bid=1&pid=89125.

7. Health care activism, quietly but powerfully, is moving toward change

Below the radar, a movement for universal health care is sweeping the nation, and the wins are beginning to roll in. Polls show that the overwhelming majority of Americans—75 percent, according to the latest Harris Poll—want what people in other wealthy countries have: single-payer or universal health insurance.

In the 1930s, Canadians and Americans had similar health levels—until Canadians adopted a single-payer health care system and left Americans in the dust. Today, in Canada, there is no association between income inequality and mortality rates—none whatsoever. But in the US, poor people die younger. And an estimated 18,000 die each year because of lack of health care coverage. A recent UC San Francisco study estimates that the US would save over $161 billion every year in paperwork alone if it switched to a single-payer system like Canada's.

What has changed about the national movement is that this time things are taking off at the state level. Health care justice groups are becoming reenergized; faith, labor groups and social service organizations are all coming together. Their work can be seen in a number of state efforts emerging around the country; six have already passed meaningful legislation.

Rev. Linda H. Walling, "A Growing Movement," YES! Magazine #39, Fall 2006, http://www.yesmagazine.org/article.asp?id=1507.

Doug Pibel and Sarah van Gelder, "Health Care: It's What Ails Us," YES! Magazine #39, Fall 2006, http://www.yesmagazine.org/article.asp?id=1498.

Holly Dressel, "Has Canada Got the Cure?" YES! Magazine #39, Fall 2006, http://www.yesmagazine.org/article.asp?id=1503.

8. Latin American countries are breaking ties to their military past, refusing to send trainees to the School of the Americas

In yet another sign of a changing Southern Hemisphere, new efforts to attain peace are beginning to heal the wounds of a violent past. In the spring of 2006, several Latin American countries moved away from this military legacy and their ties to the United States. Argentina announced that the government would make public all secret military archives to help uncover human rights violations during that country's "dirty war" of 1976—in which 30,000 people allegedly were tortured and disappeared.

Argentina and Uruguay also joined Venezuela in deciding to end the practice of sending troops to train at the US-run School of the

Americas, now renamed the Western Hemisphere Institute for Security Cooperation (WHINSEC). Bolivia has agreed to reduce the number of troops it sends to WHINSEC. It was here, in the repressive dictatorships of the 1970s and 1980s, that many members of the military received training.

Lisa Garrigues, "Latin America Breaks Ties to Military Past," *YES! Magazine* #38, Summer 2006, http://www.yesmagazine.org/article.asp?ID=1487#latinamerica.

9. Local food systems are building health and community wealth

More Americans than ever before are thinking about where their food comes from and how far it travels, and they're increasingly choosing to eat local. Over the last decade, the number of farmers' markets has more than doubled to 3,700. Many families are buying through "Community Supported Agriculture" (CSAs) that deliver directly from the farmer to their home. Chefs have caught on to the fresh taste and seasonal interest of local foods, and their popularity. So have caterers. Ranches have switched from servicing the global market to selling local, cutting out the intermediaries that swallow profits. Community gardens, youth gardens, and school gardens are springing up in rural and urban areas. Community kitchens are allowing start-up entrepreneurs to try out a new food-product business before making a huge investment in a private kitchen that meets public health standards. This movement is strengthening local economies, providing opportunities for young entrepreneurs, helping people get to know their neighbors and appreciate the diverse offerings of their local ecosystems, supporting local farmers, and improving the health and nutrition of those involved. Yet, despite the rapid growth of local food projects throughout North America, their contributions to wealth and health at the community level still fail to register with most of the media or with many conventional businesspeople and economic development officials. Perhaps this is because the annual growth in food sales for a corporation such as Wal-Mart or Whole Foods is easy to measure. It's harder to track the diffuse growth of the local foods movement—whose participating markets may collectively have a higher growth rate in the United States than the big stores—

but where the majority of benefits do not flow back to a single, distant corporate headquarters.

Gary Nabhan, "Food to Stay," *YES! Magazine* #40, Winter 2007, http://www.yesmagazine.org/article.asp?ID=1581.

10. Emerging World Social Forums are building a global movement

World Social Forums (WSFs) have been taking place around the world since 2001, when organizers, principally from Latin America and Europe, brought together 20,000 people in Porto Alegre, Brazil. The idea was to go beyond protesting outside the World Economic Forum, where the rich and powerful set a global agenda. The social forums have since grown, with well over 100,000 people attending. And local and regional forums are springing up around the world, all of them open to those working to create a more just and sustainable world. Some have criticized the WSFs for perpetuating an elitist agenda itself. Political writer and speaker, Arundhati Roy criticized the WSF for undergoing an "NGO-ization" after its inception—embracing what she charged was a top-down hierarchical model, with panelists that talked much and did little.

Others, however, still consider the forums to be a rich source of dialoguing and coalition-building. Writer Ingmar Lee says the WSFs justify themselves simply in the act of getting so many activists together, "many for the first time to see each other's projects, to recognize the importance of dissent, and to feel solidarity with their neighbours . . . There is a desperate need for a new political paradigm, and that's what needs to be discussed at these kinds of Forums."

North America is the last region of the world to host a national or regional social forum, and, up to now, few Americans have attended the global events. The WSF International Council encouraged US organizers to hold a national social forum, but organizers felt it important to lay the groundwork first. The Southeast Social Forum was a test to see if a US forum was possible. The organizers exceeded their goals on all counts. Close to six hundred people came, nearly a third of whom were youth, and 80 percent people of color. "We are the ones we've been waiting for," said one participant. "This is the time for transformation on a larger scale."

Spurred on by this success, organizers from the Southeast and the Southwest (primarily people of color) headed up the organizing of the first US Social Forum that took place in Atlanta in June 2007.

Sarah van Gelder, "Southern Revival," *YES! Magazine* #39, Fall 2006, http://www.yesmagazine.org/article.asp?ID=1528.

Ingmar Lee, "Last Reflections On The World Social Forum, Karachi," Countercurrents.org, April 5, 2006, http://www.countercurrents.org/lee050406.htm.

Increasing knowledge about movements toward change on a global scale can, to some degree, "inoculate" us against the mainstream, consumer-focused cynicism that is so pervasive today. We hope that the stories listed in this chapter help to further this knowledge and to show that the wisdom reflected in the celebrated phrases *"si se puede"* and "we shall overcome," are at work in the world, now more than ever.

People who want to learn more about *YES! Magazine*, the stories they cover and the work that they do, are encouraged to visit their excellent website at www.yesmagazine.org.

CHAPTER 5

Into the Labyrinth
Perspectives from the 2007 National Conference for Media Reform, Memphis

by Kat Pat Crespán, Jenni Leys, Regina Marcheschi, Donald Nelson, and Andrew Roth

In January 2007, nearly 3,500 activists, students, politicians, policy-makers, and journalists gathered for the third National Conference for Media Reform in Memphis, Tennessee. The size and diversity of the gathering—nearly double the attendance of the first conference in 2003—led keynote speaker Bill Moyers to proclaim, "This is a movement bursting at its seams." Activist Jane Fonda urged the creation of "media that is powerful, not a media that serves the interests of the powerful." The Reverend Jesse Jackson criticized the corporate media's "lockout of people of color."[1] And FCC Commissioner Michael J. Copps proposed a new "American Media Contract," defining what broadcasters owe the public in return for use of the nation's airwaves:

1. A right to media that strengthen our democracy.
2. A right to local stations that are actually local.
3. A right to media that looks and sounds like America.
4. A right to news that isn't canned and radio playlists that aren't for sale.
5. A right to programming that isn't so damned bad so damned often.[2]

In addition to attending featured addresses, conference participants worked together in over one hundred panels and workshops, on topics ranging from civil rights and women's rights to fair elections and Net Neutrality.

A team of seven represented Project Censored in Memphis: Censored Interns Camelia Gannon-Patino, Zoe Huffman, Jeff Huling, and Jenni Leys; Censored alumna and filmmaker Sandy Brown; and faculty members Peter Phillips and Andy Roth. This team spread the word about Project Censored and its current activities, visited the National Civil Rights Museum, and dined on Memphis's famed barbeque (including portabella mushrooms for the vegetarians). After long but exhilarating days at the Conference, the Censored team returned to Pilgrim House Hostel, where we sometimes ended the evening by walking the Hostel's outdoor labyrinth.

Though the team's Memphis experiences deserve a story of their own, this chapter reports on interviews conducted by Project Censored at the Media Reform Conference. Leys and Roth conducted thirteen formal interviews, which Huling and Brown filmed; team members supplemented these interviews with numerous informal conversations. We interviewed (in alphabetical order):

➤ Robin Andersen, professor of Communication and Media Studies at Fordham University, where she directs the Peace and Justice Studies Program;

➤ Joel Bleifuss, editor of *In These Times*;

➤ Jeff Chester, executive director of the Center for Digital Democracy;

➤ Mark Cooper, director of consumer research for the Consumer Federation of America;

➤ Michael Copps, FCC Commissioner;

➤ Deborah Frazier, community radio advocate and broadcaster, Bloomington, IN;

➤ Peter Hart, the activism director at Fairness and Accuracy in Reporting (FAIR);

➤ Elizabeth Kucinich, British humanitarian and spouse of presidential candidate Rep. Dennis Kucinich (D-OH);

➤ Sarah Olson, independent journalist and radio producer;

➤ Anna Belle Peevey, journalist for the *Asheville Global Report* and coanchor, coeditor of *AGR-TV*;

➤ Federico Subervi, professor in the School of Journalism and Mass Communication, Texas State University-San Marcos, and director, Latinos and Media Project;

➤ Sunsara Taylor, World Can't Wait: Drive Out the Bush Regime, and writer for *Revolution* newspaper;

➤ Al White, director, Action Communication and Education Reform, Duckhill, Mississippi.

We sought our interviewees' perspectives on:
> why media reform matters,
> what citizens need to know to be "media literate" in the twenty-first century,
> what role diversity plays in the media reform movement, and
> the effects of media consolidation on democracy.

Our interviewees all agreed that, "real news is democracy's oxygen."3 In the remainder of this chapter, we report in more detail their answers to our questions.

MEDIA LITERACY: INTERNET AND OTHER DEVELOPING TECHNOLOGIES

We asked our interviewees, "In the twenty-first century, what do citizens need to know to be media literate?" Many responded in terms of understanding new technology, and especially the Internet. New technologies have made the access to information and "the production of media very simple and very cheap," according to Anna Belle Peevey of the *Asheville Global Report* (AGR). "We have so much at our fingertips and it's just a matter of networking and collaborating enough to get it out there." Peavey's work in helping to launch AGR's weekly television news program is one case in point.4

Mark Cooper (Consumer Federation of America) argues that the Internet "will be the dominant means of communication in the twenty-first century."

> Just as in the twentieth century, if you didn't have a telephone, you couldn't fully participate in our society; in the twenty-first century, if you don't have access to the Internet, particularly high speed Internet, you will not be able to participate.

Cooper described the 1934 Telecommunications Act, which promoted affordable telephone service for all, and called for a similar approach to the Internet today:

> When [Congress] declared that goal, two-thirds of the

American people did not have a telephone. It was genuinely a progressive goal in the sense that it set a target, an aspiration, for every American to have access, for a reasonable price, to the major means of communication in the twentieth century, the telephone. In the twenty-first century, the equivalent is high-speed Internet service, which is even more important than the telephone.

Cooper emphasized that, while telephone was primarily a method of personal communication, the Internet is more than that: it is also a vehicle of mass communication, which Cooper pointed out, the telephone was not. Thus, Cooper (and others) argue that the high-speed Internet represents "the convergence of mass communication and personal communication," making it "an essential ingredient for being media-enabled in the twenty-first century."[5] Deborah Frazier (WKSU, Kent, Ohio), Peter Hart (FAIR), and Al White (Action Communication and Education Reform) all expressed hope that newly developing media technologies would favor the public, save equality, and improve the political climate for social change.

Interviewees consistently stressed that, in its present state, no one *owns* the Internet. It is the first time in US history that a form of mass communication is *not* privately owned and, since the creation of the Federal Communication Commission, *not* regulated by the FCC. Because the Internet, in its present form, is neither owned nor regulated, most of its material is created and posted by common citizens. This distinguishes the Internet from other media. According to Cooper,

> Sixty percent of the content on the web is produced by people. If you look at television, it's almost zero. If you look at radio—talk radio—sometimes you get call-in shows, but it's a small percentage. If you look at the print media, letters to the editor, et cetera, [it is more like] one percent.

Increasingly, citizens access news and information, not through traditional media (for example newspapers), but through the Internet.

In consequence, Cooper argues that, "The corporations and government have lost control of speech. This scares them. They spend all their time trying to regain control of speech." Major corporations are moving online to counter this. This is one reason why it is so important (again, in Cooper's words) to "fight to prevent people from stopping us from speaking inside cyberspace."

For similar reasons, numerous interviewees expressed concern over the future of Net Neutrality.[6] Thus, Federico Subervi (professor of Journalism and Mass Communication at Texas State University-San Marcos) understands the goal of Internet access for all as means of including "more segments of society in the process of making decisions about their lives—economic, political, social, cultural decisions." Robin Andersen (professor of Communication and Media Studies at Fordham University) described the Internet as a resource for expression of multiple perspectives, which must be heard and evaluated before we can make our own decisions. Joel Bleifuss echoed this point. Unfortunately, most of the corporate media present only "one side of the world," which they try to sell to the public as "hard and fast reality." If Net Neutrality is preserved, the Internet provides an alternative to this commodified, one-sided version of news. Specifically, the Internet can be one means that alternative media employ to put pressure on corporate media, "to have them re-do stories that were inaccurately told," says Anderson, noting counts of participants at antiwar demonstrations as one case in point. A robust, Internet-based press can push coverage of "stories that are important for the future of life on earth in many ways," says Bleifuss, putting the corporate press "on notice that they're being watched, that there are people who are doing these stories."

Our interviewees also noted that new technology also has a potential down side. Jeff Chester (Center for Digital Democracy) notes that new digital media are designed "to enhance the power of the advertising/entertainment system" so that the public is increasingly "assaulted by sophisticated interactive technologies designed to trivialize us as people."[7] Similarly, Mark Cooper (Consumer Federation of America) expressed concern that blogging, which has flourished on the Internet, should not be understood as a substitute for investigative reporting. (For more on this, see a subsequent section of this chapter, "What is [and isn't] 'Journalism'?").

AN (ILL-) INFORMED PUBLIC?

Our Memphis interviewees agreed that people must be informed to act effectively as citizens and community members. Conference attendees recognized a crucial gap, widened by disinformation and spin, between how informed the public *believes* it is and how informed it *really* is. We asked our interviewees what they understood as the sources of this disconnect, and how people can make themselves more media literate.

Sarah Olson told us that she "often hears journalists describe that they could not run a particular story because their editors said it was not something the audience would like. . . . There's a demand for entertainment as well as the perception of a demand." Al White also acknowledged that the corporate media have become more focused on entertainment rather than information. He added that "corporate media has control over what the public sees. . . . Whoever controls the resources, controls who has access to it." Thus, when we asked him about corporate media's coverage of a number of sensitive topics (for example, the truth about 9/11, vote fraud, impeachment) he answered each question with a terse "Control and domination."

Another interviewee, Anna Belle Peevey (*Asheville Global Report*) also emphasized the danger of people turning to media only for entertainment. She said that she had received an e-mail from a man who wrote that there was "no better cure for insomnia than to watch our show, because [we're] so dull." And I wanted to ask him, "Which particular story did you find dull? The fact that the United States just bombed Somalia with no pretense . . . or the fact the United States is selling oil rights to Iraqi crude? Which one of those was dull?

This made Peevey think, "Oh, of course, he finds it dull because we didn't mention Rosie O'Donnell and we didn't mention the lady who had sex with her."

Several interviewees invoked *Democracy Now!* as an exemplar of how independent media can inform and mobilize increasingly large audiences. In particular, Peter Hart (FAIR) discussed how, six or seven years ago, *Democracy Now!* was just "a local show with a little bit of national distribution. Now it's probably more known as a national show." In its current form, most people "do not identify it as a *local* radio show at all." Hart emphasized how this makes him hopeful: hard-hitting, truthful news will reach large audiences, when it is done correctly. Of course, there's still the problem of people saying that they don't want to listen to that kind of radio with their morning coffee.

So the American public is used to being entertained. How to inform them and ourselves? Luckily, we asked our interviewees that question, too.

Federico Subervi believes that the public needs to know "the impact of the marketing and advertising on their lives, the impact of the limited information about the politics in their daily lives, and [how] the decision makers got elected without [the public's] full participation in the process." Similarly, Sarah Olson advocates directing "attention to who and what is covered and how in the media—both the alternative and mainstream media, both commercial and independent press," and increasing our "awareness of language." If people only knew how much information is skewed or simply withheld from us, we would be enraged. The people would do something.

Robin Andersen told us that she thinks the real problem is that too many people in the country "assume that the media is fair, that it's objective and telling a [single] story." Instead, Anderson continues, "The media seems to be aligned by a very small group of people at the top who seem to be directing the country." She suggests that conferences like Memphis help to sort out what is wrong, what we are missing, and what can be done. As the panels at the Media Conference made clear, there are numerous stories, interests, and processes that the corporate media do not make known.

Deborah Frazier takes a different approach. She articulates how the public "own[s] the airwaves and they need to take them back. No one ever told them that." If the people just realized that they do, in fact, own the airwaves, then they just might do something constructive with their newfound ownership. Frazier advocates a vision of "community" in its most profound sense, advising us that,

> We have to reach out to our friends and neighbors and to our communities on all levels, whether it is our politicians, whether it is our keepers of the gate as it were, in terms of the FCC and the different organizations that regulate the media, or corporations. All of those contacts are important,

but we have to educate each other and ourselves. That means talking to each other, that means writing your newspaper, putting a letter to the editor in your local newspaper. That means not being afraid to speak out and to try to talk in terms that people can understand, because it really does affect their everyday lives.

Frazier also warned us about the FCC. She says that if people actually knew what the FCC was up to and what their policies were, they would not want them. If we want change, we have to meet in our town halls and vote.

Whether we're changing the media through voicing an opinion on the radio or by telling our neighbor about the latest information on Lebanon, we know there is something to be done. With so many options it is hard to believe that not enough has been done to educate our friends and family. So arm yourselves with information.

WHAT IS (AND ISN'T) "JOURNALISM"?

Although we did not directly ask our Memphis interviewees this question, a number of them held strong, revealing opinions on what counts as "journalism," as displayed in their responses to other questions. The Media Reform Conference participants that we interviewed regularly used the word "journalism" as a moral term, defining what is good and desirable. Our interviewees thus distinguished journalism from other forms of mass mediated discourse.

Many of our interviewees provided a *negative* definition of journalism by identifying what does not count as journalism. For example, as previously noted, many of our interviewees distinguished between journalism and entertainment. Sarah Olson, told us,

There is a perception that all there is in the media is entertainment. They [corporate media] work together to give you a really dumbed-down version of the news. . . . I personally don't think it's about entertainment. I think that most people here at the conference don't think it is about entertainment either.

Instead, journalism requires (in Sunsara Taylor's words) "real reporting" that satisfies the public's hunger for "the truth" and "a real discussion of what's at stake in the world." Olson and Taylor establish a contrast between the values of truth and those of entertainment. By blurring the boundaries between news and entertainment, the news media fail in their responsibility to inform citizens.[8]

Entertainment values situate news viewers and readers as *consumers*, rather than as citizens, a theme that Joel Bleifuss, editor of *In These Times*, spoke passionately about. Bleifuss told us that it is important for people "to realize that they are not consumers," and that too often the mass media "objectifies" them as such. As a result, it can seem that "your role in society is to buy and maybe to vote." Instead, Bleifuss believes that journalism must nurture citizens' awareness so that we "begin to question [our] place within the system."

Mark Cooper (Consumer Federation of America) echoed these sentiments when he spoke critically about the increasingly prominent position of blogging,

> The blog is an extension of something that has always existed. It's the water cooler conversation; it's the garden fence; it's the street corner chat, right? But it's now blown up in scale, because you can talk to so many more people. But by itself, it's not enough. I don't have investigative journalism in the blogosphere. Almost all of it is editorial opinion. Who's going to investigate the politicians? Not just opine on what they did. So, blogging is great as a form of expression, but we really have a tremendous challenge in creating and sustaining an institution of journalism that gives me reporters digging up facts and editors checking the facts. There's not a lot of that in the blogosphere.

Journalism, then, requires "digging up" and "checking the facts," activities that may characterize some blogs, but are central to the work of investigative journalism.

Investigative reporting requires autonomy and independence, which Elizabeth Kucinich found lacking in the corporate media's coverage of the onset of the war in Iraq:

When we look at the war with Iraq, we see how the media chose a position. They chose merely to repeat what people in authority said. They didn't question, they didn't analyze. There was a lack of journalism.

Thus, Kucinich links journalism with autonomous analysis of actual evidence.

Reporter Sarah Olson told us about her work on the story of Lieutenant Ehren Watada's case, as an example of how government action can encroach on journalistic autonomy. At the time we spoke with her, Olson faced the likelihood of a subpoena in the military's prosecution of Lt. Watada for his refusal to participate in the Iraq War. Based on her interviews of Watada, Olson expected to be called to testify in the case against him.[9] She told us,

The idea of asking a journalist to participate in the prosecution of political speech is absolutely inimical to the idea of a free press . . . I'm concerned that this is an instance where they are asking a journalist to participate in suppression of this kind of speech. I don't think it's a reasonable thing to do. Also I don't think asking journalists to participate in the prosecution of their sources is something that is, under basic journalist principles, an agreeable thing.

Instead, journalism requires free speech. Though many of our interviewees defined journalism in terms of what it is not, they also spoke affirmatively about what it is (or should be).

For Sunsara Taylor, good journalism requires a broad spectrum of information and opinion to identify the truth. Thus journalism

addresses a broader spectrum of political debate than that defined by the Republicans and Democrats. . . . If the discourse in the popular media is between the Republicans and Democrats, and that is what is legitimate, then that is a very narrow discourse, and the criteria is not the truth.

This theme resonates with the findings of David Croteau and David Hoynes's 1994 study of interviewed guests on ABC's *Nightline* and PBS's *NewsHour*. Croteau and Hoynes found that both programs presented a narrow spectrum of political perspectives, while giving the impression of rigorous debate.[10]

Peter Hart (FAIR) spoke about the significance of Al Jazeera and the launch of its English-language broadcasts,

> When you look at things like Al Jazeera it had become kind of synonymous with telling a different story. These are journalists, they do journalism. But it looks very different from the journalism we know. Why is that? It provokes a kind of discussion that I think is really helpful for our movement.

Again and again in our conversations and interviews in Memphis, we heard people asserting the importance of journalism representing a broad spectrum of voices, topics, and issues. This notion of a "broad spectrum" is currently being exploited by MSNBC in its "fuller spectrum of news" brand campaign.[11] But in Memphis, the people we spoke with about the future of journalism were less interested in branding, and more concerned with what sociologist Herbert Gans has characterized as a commitment to "multi-perspectival news."[12]

"THE CLAMP": MEDIA OWNERSHIP AND DIVERSITY

Our interviewees agreed that ongoing consolidation of media ownership remains one of the greatest threats to the realization of multi-perspectival news. Robin Andersen connected ownership and diversity succinctly: "The media is increasingly owned by a small group of people, designed around profit," which exacerbates the need for "far more diversity and multiplicity of voices throughout." She describes the consolidation, monopoly, and lack of regulation as a "clamp": "We've had this clamp on American media for so long, centered around a kind of 'mainstream' view of America and certainly portrayed in the English language." This clamp has "detached" the nation's political leadership "from the grassroots of this country."

"Clearly we need media as diverse as the population," Mark Cooper asserted. He pointed to the fact that "the average American citizen lives in a state today that is 50 percent more diverse than it was thirty years ago. . . . Foreign language diverse media is critically necessary to reflect the diversity that is America." Jeff Chester (Center for Digital Democracy) echoed this in expressing hope that the media reform movement would become an increasingly "multi-lingual, multi-culturally diverse movement." Similarly Peter Hart (FAIR) asserted that "it's difficult for those of us who only speak English to really appreciate what's going on around the world."

Several interviewees described the importance of Spanish-language radio in mobilizing immigrant communities during Fall 2006. Commenting on these successes, Sunsara Taylor (World Can't Wait, *Revolution*) urged "progressive, responsible people in the English media to learn from what happened in the Spanish media." Along similar lines, Federico Subervi (School of Journalism and Mass Communication, Texas State University-San Marcos) called for "studying Latino media at every level"—from children's television to consumer issues to advertising to politics to ownership—as "indispensable" to media reform and democracy.

"If you just put the media out in one language," Elizabeth Kucinich told us, "then you only communicate one line of thought, your only communicate with one community, the English-speaking community. As you can see, America is made up of hundreds of ethnic groups and that should be embraced." Anna Belle Peevey (*Asheville Global Report*) also understands the issue of media diversity in terms of community:

> It's all about building community, about networking. As immigration becomes a larger issue every single day, and Hispanics are a part of our community (as well as other ethnic groups, but primarily Hispanics), then we need to find ways to network and work together to spread the word. There needs to be a lot of education and that can only happen with the proliferation of media. It sure as hell isn't being said on NBC or Fox News.

Media Matters for America's May 2007 report substantiates Peevey's criticism that the corporate media (e.g., NBC and Fox) do not support this type of community. "Locked Out: The Lack of Gender and Ethnic Diversity on Cable News Continues" reports that "cable news remains an overwhelmingly white and male preserve." The report concludes: "If the cable news networks want their guests to represent the full spectrum of Americans, they have a long way to go."[13]

Our Memphis interviewees anticipated this critique, consistently calling for news that represents (in Robin Andersen's words) "a multiplicity of voices and perspectives."

COVERAGE OF THE NATIONAL CONFERENCE FOR MEDIA REFORM

A version of the "clamp" described by Anderson seemed to restrict corporate media coverage of the Memphis conference itself. We tracked corporate media coverage of the National Conference for Media Reform and found very little.

We used the Lexis-Nexis database, searching January 5-21, 2007 (a week before and a week after the conference). Using this time frame, we initially searched "general news" as the LexisNexis category and "major papers" as our source. We used "National Conference" and "Media Reform" as search terms. This produced just two news stories related to the Conference. A subsequent search, on "National Conference for Media Reform" yielded nothing. Using the terms "Media Reform" and "Memphis," generated the same two stories.

The first of the two stories "Bashed, Thrashed and Encouraged," ran in the *Seattle Times* on January 19, 2007. The second story, "Reports Show Future Looks Strong for Media," appeared in the January 12, 2007 issue of *USA Today*. These two articles seem to be polar opposites: The *Seattle Times* article focused on how mainstream journalists are portrayed as the cause of all problems in the media. Ryan Blethen's report begins:

> I did not go to Memphis to get mugged. But that is what it felt like sitting through the National Conference for Media Reform. The conference might have felt like an assault against a journalist like me who works at a metropolitan newspaper.

By contrast, the *USA Today* article emphasized an economic upside for TV and newspapers, despite the wave of new media. Using the same search terms and date range, we searched for coverage in magazines and journals. This search yielded nothing, as did a search of LexisNexis's "Ethnic News" sources. We also searched for news transcripts, locating nine broadcasts that mentioned the Media Reform Conference. Most of these were brief reports.

The local media paid a little more attention to the conference. We searched "US News" with a focus on Tennessee news sources. This search yielded nine articles. The first two of these, "Veteran Washington Reporter Criticizes War Coverage" and "Critics of 'Big Media' Warn About Internet Freedom at Forum," originated from the Associated Press's State & Local Wire. A third article, "Media Reform Movement Chooses Memphis for Conference," appeared, in advance of the conference, in Memphis' trade paper, *The Commercial Appeal*. The *Memphis Flyer* ran six stories on the conference.

By contrast, numerous video clips from the 2007 Memphis Conference can be found on the YouTube.com Web site. When we used "NCMR" as a search term, no fewer than sixty video clips popped up from this year's conference alone. (YouTube.com also includes videos from the previous two Media Reform conferences.) Using the search phrase "National Conference for Media Reform" produced eighty hits. These clips mostly depict featured speakers, including numerous "celebrities" within the media reform movement: Bill Moyers, Amy Goodman, Jane Fonda, Rev. Jesse Jackson, Danny Glover, Representative Dennis Kucinich, Senator Bernie Sanders, and Project Censored's own Peter Phillips.

The general findings of this research suggest that there was little to no corporate news coverage of the National Conference for Media Reform. It is alarming that a group forum addressing issues as important as the ones regarding today's media was not given the coverage that it deserved. By contrast, the ready availability on the Internet (via YouTube.com and also the Free Press website) of video and audio recordings from the conference underscores our interviewees' points about the importance of the Internet and Net Neutrality for truly democratic media.

CONCLUSION

In Plato's *Euthydemus*, Socrates likens a discussion of "the kingly art" of politics to a labyrinth: just as the goal is in sight, the argument turns back on itself, leaving seekers of truth back "at the beginning, having still to seek as much as ever." Our interviews with participants in the National Conference for Media Reform suggested a similar dynamic. Progress on issues such as media literacy and inclusivity, ownership and Net Neutrality bring us still closer to the goal of truly democratic media. But, as in a labyrinth, the path turns, and what seemed close at hand recedes into the distance: struggles remain, as all our interviewees agreed.

However, it is noteworthy, for both Socrates' point and ours, that the chosen image is a *labyrinth*, rather than a *maze*. Although a maze includes paths that lead to dead ends, a true labyrinth contains a single path that eventually reaches its goal, despite the apparent turns and setbacks. At the end of the day, then, the image of a labyrinth, rather than a maze, best reflects the *optimism* of our Memphis interviewees. The path is long, and not always clear, but working together we will reach the common goal of more democratic media.

ACKNOWLEDGMENTS

We are grateful to Robin Andersen, Joel Bleifuss, Jeff Chester, Mark Cooper, Michael Copps, Deborah Frazier, Peter Hart, Elizabeth Kucinich, Sarah Olson, Anna Belle Peevey, Federico Subervi, Sunsara Taylor, and Al White for sharing their time and ideas with us. Sandy Brown and Jeff Huling filmed the interviews, which Jenni Leys and Andy Roth conducted.

Citations

1. Media Reform News, "National Conference for Media Reform Rocks Memphis." http://www.freepress.net/content/newsletter_v2n2_a1.
2. See Michael J. Copps, "American Media Contract," http://www.freepress.net/docs/new_american_media_contract.pdf.
3. See "Media Reform News: Media Reform in Five Words." http://www.freepress.net/content/newsletter_v2n2_a7.
4. See http://www.agrnews.org/?section=tv for online episodes of Asheville Global Report TV.
5. Cf. Robert Greenwald's observation that the Internet is the "most profound revolution since the printing press." See Bailey Malone, Kristine Medeiros, Jessica Rodas, and Andrew Roth, "The Ongoing Contest: Media Reform and Democracy," pp. 231-245 in *Censored 2007: Media*

Democracy in Action, edited by Peter Phillips and Project Censored. New York: Seven Stories Press, 2006; quote at p. 242.

6. See Chapter 2, "Censored Deja Vu," above, for an update on net neutrality, the #1 story from *Censored 2007*.

7. See also Jeff Chester, *Digital Destiny: New Media and the Future of Democracy*. New York: New Press, 2007.

8. On the important but increasingly blurred distinction between "news" and "entertainment," see Samuel Winch's underappreciated study, *Mapping the Cultural Space of Journalism: How Journalists Distinguish News from Entertainment*. Westport, CT: Praeger, 1997.

9. See, e.g., "Sarah Olson, The Pentagon, and the First Amendment," by Doug Ireland. http://www.zmag.org/content/showarticle.cfm?ItemID=11978. See also http://www.source-watch.org/index.php?title=Sarah_Olson#Articles_By_Sarah_Olson.

10. David Croteau and William Hoynes, *by Invitation Only: How the Media Limit Political Debate*. Monroe, ME: Common Courage, 1994.

11. See, e.g., http://www.primenewswire.com/newsroom/news.html?d=116604.

12. Herbert Gans, Jr. *Deciding What's News: A Study of CBS Evening News, NBC Nightly News, Newsweek, and Time*. Chicago: Northwestern University Press, 2005[1979].

13. See Media Matters for America, "Locked Out: The Lack of Gender and Ethnic Diversity on Cable News Continues" (7 May 2007). http://mediamatters.org/CableDiversity.

CHAPTER 6

Corporate Media Bias and the Case of the Cuban Five

by Jeffrey Huling

"The case of the Cuban Five is a shameful example of
injustice in our country"
—Howard Zinn

INTRODUCTION

In 1998, the FBI arrested five Cubans in Miami for engaging in
"espionage activity." Oddly, the US government did not use the
arrests to publicly demonize Castro; instead they stifled the potential
political firestorm by placing the Five in solitary confinement for seventeen months—a violation of penitentiary regulations stipulating
that isolation can be applied for a maximum of sixty days. Despite the
prosecution's lack of evidence, the Five were convicted in 2001 and
placed in five different prisons deliberately spread across the US
(California, Colorado, Wisconsin, Texas, and Florida). These tactics—
the pre-trial use of solitary confinement and the dispersion of the
Five after the trial—are such that anticipate and actively seek to stifle
real or potential opposition. The fact that the Five are hailed in Cuba
as heroes and freedom fighters intimates the US Government's
interest in quieting the case.

Although ostensibly arrested for engaging in espionage activity,
the evidence presented at the trial clearly showed that the Five had no
intention to gather US "intelligence." Rather, they had attempted to
infiltrate Miami-based terrorist organizations, gathering intelligence
to prevent further attacks, both covert and overt, on Cuba. Since
Castro overthrew Batista in 1959, Cuban exile communities have terrorized Cuba with assassination attempts, propaganda, and economic subversion—crop burnings, sugar mill bombings, and violent
campaigns to disrupt Cuba's tourist industry. More than four thousand violent incidents have occurred against Cuba since the 1959 rev-

olution. Many of the terrorist organizations responsible operated with the sanction of the US government, as they still do today. Yet, not many people are paying attention or have the ability to pay attention—blame this on the media.

In general, the corporate media (and some independent media) has failed to adequately cover the case of the Cuban Five. When the case is "covered," the reports are jaundiced and uninformed. They also lack the deep investigation that would implicate the Bush dynasty in the sanction and production of known terrorists, therefore exposing the hypocrisy of the Bush administration's "War on Terrorism."

To properly understand the plight of the Cuban Five and why the US government continues to harbor terrorists, a brief history of US-Cuba relations is necessary.

US-SPONSORED TERRORISM IN CUBA

The US obsession with Cuba dates back to the American Revolution. It was John Quincy Adams, while Secretary of State, who said that taking Cuba is "of transcendent importance" to the political and commercial future of the United States.[1]

By the turn of the twentieth century, Cuba was economically dependent on the US. This dependence aggrandized during the 1950s when Cuban sugar, through a quota system, was guaranteed a market in the US above world market price. The US purchased more than half of the sugar produced in Cuba and controlled 40 percent of its production. It also owned half of the arable land and controlled 90 percent of Cuba's utilities. The US had investments in mining, oil refineries, rubber by-products, livestock, cement, tourism, and one-fourth of all bank deposits. Eighty percent of Cuba's imports were procured from the US. Most Cubans identified themselves with the American way of life and their sense of progress was measured by their ability to purchase American goods. Despite an Americanized economy, one-third of Cuba's population remained impoverished. Economic stagnation coupled with American discrimination and racism towards Cubans led to a growing disenchantment with and resentment of the US.[2]

With the revolution of 1959, Castro sought to weaken Cuba's economic dependence on the US while promoting a Cuban identity removed from American influence. Tax policies and agrarian reforms were passed in order to reduce economic inequality while favoring Cuban over foreign investments. US businesses opposed the wage increases, labor, and land reforms. Relations quickly deteriorated as many powerful US interests lost land to the Cuban government. For example, US sugar companies were threatened with the loss of over 1.5 million acres of land.

After Castro visited the US in April 1959, Vice President Richard Nixon suggested to his colleagues that a force of Cuban exiles be armed immediately to overthrow Castro.4 By May, the CIA began arming guerillas inside of Cuba while supervising bombing and incendiary raids piloted by exiled Cubans based in Miami.5 The next year "Castro and his rebel army fought counterrevolutionary groups . . . who used air bases in southern Florida to engage in assassination attempts . . . [to] burn crops, bomb sugar mills, and attack ships bound for Cuba. The US failure to disavow these groups and prevent their activities was enough evidence for Castro to assert US complicity in these actions."6

The Eisenhower administration secretly made a formal decision to conquer Cuba, but in such a way that the US hand would not be evident.7 With Cuba's nationalization of all US businesses by August 1959, Eisenhower allotted $13 million for guerilla warfare training to between four and five hundred Cuban exiles in Guatemala.8 These same US-trained Cuban exiles were employed in April of 1961 for the failed Bay of Pigs invasion under the Kennedy administration. Following the invasion, Kennedy continued his program of international terrorism, most notably Operation Mongoose, which, according to Ray Garthoff, a former State Department specialist on the Soviet Union, included sending sabotage units into the country.9 During the height of the Cold War, the CIA's Operation Mongoose team blew up a Cuban factory, killing four hundred people, according to Castro.

During the 1970s, the CIA continued to fund the exile community. On October 6, 1976 exiles blew up a Cubana Airlines plane after it departed from Barbados, killing seventy-three people, among them, the entire Cuban championship fencing team. The CIA, headed by George Bush, Sr., knew of the bombing in advance, but failed to warn Havana.10 Orlando Bosch, imprisoned with Luis Posada Carriles for the bombing, was released from a Venezuela prison in 1987 under pressure from US ambassador Otto Reich. Bosch then traveled to Miami where he was detained for a 1974 parole violation (Bosch was convicted in 1968 for firing a bazooka at a Cuban-bound freighter in Miami). Citing FBI and CIA reports that Bosch has caused "indiscriminate injury and death," including thirty acts of terrorism, the US Justice Department ruled that Bosch should be deported because of his terrorist activities. In spite of this, Bosch was pardoned by President Bush in 1989, after a campaign was launched to reverse the Justice Department's decision. Leading the effort was now current House Representative for Florida's 18th Congressional district, Republican Ileana Ros-Lehtinen, who at the time was running for Congress (her campaign manager was Jeb Bush, son of the president).[11] Raoul Cantero, grandson of former dictator Fulgencio Batista, was Bosch's lawyer and primary spokesman—he now resides as a Florida Supreme Court Justice. Although widely regarded as one of the most dangerous terrorists in the western hemisphere,[12] Bosch walks freely in Miami and even appears in television and radio programs bragging that he is still preparing attacks against Cuba.

Throughout the 1990s, the tourist industry became the main target for Miami-based terrorist organizations, with the bombing of tourist buses and hotels. The 1997 bombing that killed an Italian tourist was committed by Salvadoran terrorists financed in Miami, under the command of Luis Posada Carriles. Posada had escaped from a Venezuelan prison in 1985 (prison authorities were bribed), where he was charged along with Bosch for the Cubana airliner bombing of 1976.[13] He was then secretly flown to El Salvador where he worked to ferry weapons to the Contras, an operation run by White House aide Oliver North.[14]

In 2000, Posada was imprisoned in Panama for plotting with three Cuban exiles to assassinate Fidel Castro while the leader was visiting Panama City during the Ibero-American Summit. After serving half of an eight year sentence, Posada was pardoned by outgoing Panamanian President Mireya Moscoso "as a favor to Bush, whose reelection in November 2004 was riding on the continued backing of Miami Cubans."[15] In May 2005, Posada was detained in El Paso, Texas, for attempting to enter the US illegally. Despite declassified CIA documents detailing Posada's connection to the 1976 bombing, the US refused to prosecute or extradite Posada to Venezuela, violating three international treaties signed with this country. Instead, a US federal grand jury indicted Posada in January 2007 on immigration violations and transferred him to a New Mexico prison. But in April he was released by US District Judge Kathleen Cardone, despite a government request to keep him jailed pending an appeal.[16] On May 8, all charges were dropped against Posada, inciting a public uproar in Cuba. Dagoberto Rodriguez Barrera, chief of the Cuban Interest Section in Washington, blamed the White House for having "made all the efforts necessary to protect the bin Laden of the hemisphere, [out of] fear that he could have talked and recount the whole history about the US government links with his terrorists' activities."[17] President Hugo Chávez of Venezuela demanded "that they extradite that terrorist and murderer to Venezuela, instead of protecting him."

THE TRIAL OF THE CUBAN FIVE

Because of the constant threat of terrorism, the Cuban Five monitored the terrorist activities of exile groups and reported back to Cuba. They were arrested in Miami, Florida in September 1998, and charged with twenty-six counts of violating US Federal Law. The two main charges were conspiracy to commit espionage and conspiracy to commit murder, while the other twenty-four were minor and technical offenses, alleging the use of false names and the failure to register as foreign agents.

The first conspiracy charge alleged that three of the Five had agreed to commit espionage. A conspiracy is an illegal agreement between two or more persons to commit a crime—it need not occur. Circumstantial evidence is enough to demonstrate that there *must have been* an agreement to commit a crime, actual and direct proof is not necessary. The prosecution admitted that the Five lacked possession of a single page of classified government information, although the law requires the presence of national defense information in order to prove the crime of espionage.

The prosecution relied on the fact that Antonio Guerrero worked in a metal shop of a Navy training base in Southern Florida, implying that he was attempting to access national defense information. But the Navy base was completely open to the public, and Guerrero had never applied for a security clearance, had no access to restricted areas, and had never tried to enter any. The FBI had Guerrero under surveillance for two years before the arrests, but there was no testimony from the agents about any wrongdoing.

Antonio Guerrero's mission was to "discover and report in a timely manner the information or indications that denote the preparation of a military aggression against Cuba on the basis of what he could see by observing open public activities."[18] This information was available to any member of the public, which cannot form the basis of an espionage persecution. However, the jury still made the conviction.

The conspiracy to commit murder charge alleged that Gerardo Hernandez conspired with other non-indicted Cuban officials to shoot down two planes flown by the exile group Brothers to the Rescue (BTTR). BTTR had repeatedly crossed Cuban airspace during the 1990s to drop propaganda pamphlets. Cuba subsequently warned the US that they were committing airspace infractions, but US officials remained indifferent and BTTR continued to fly. In 1996, two BTTR planes were shot down by the Cuban Air Force, killing four men. Cuba alleges the planes crossed into Cuban airspace, ignoring verbal warnings. The US maintains they were shot down over international waters. In a recording played at the trial of the Five, "the pilot of one of the planes could be heard laughing as the planes deliberately violated the order to turn back [from the Cuban Air Force]."[19]

Gerardo Hernandez and his colleagues were advised by Cuba to stay off BTTR planes for a few days, during which the planes were shot down. This coincidence was enough for the prosecution to argue that Hernandez was involved in a conspiracy to kill the men in the planes, although no evidence of this was presented. The trial judge ruled that in order to convict Hernandez, the prosecution had to prove that before the planes took off, Hernandez was involved in a plot to down the planes before they reached Cuban waters. In response, the prosecution conceded it had no evidence and that the ruling "created an insurmountable obstacle for conviction."[20] The jury still convicted Hernandez.

In June 2001, after only five days of deliberation, twelve jurors in a Miami Court returned guilty verdicts on all twenty-six counts. The defense's request for leniency was ignored, and all were given the maximum sentences. Gerardo Hernandez received two life sentences plus fifteen years, Antonio Guerrero and Ramon Labanino received life in prison plus ten years and eighteen years respectively, Fernando Gonzalez received nineteen years, and Rene Gonzalez fifteen years.

After the convictions, all five immediately appealed. In March 2004, they met with three judges from the US District 11th Court Circuit, who, after considering the bias in Miami towards Cuban nationals, granted the defense a change of venue and a new trial on August 9, 2005. But the court decision was quickly stifled when the US government—in a very rare review process—had the appellate case reheard by all members of the 11th Circuit, who subsequently overturned the three judges' original ruling for appeal, thus ignoring the bias which undermined the legitimacy of the original court decision.

Florida International University professor Dr. Lisandro Perez comments that "the possibility of selecting twelve citizens of Miami-Dade County who can be impartial in a case involving acknowledged agents of the Cuban government is virtually zero."[21] A poll taken in 2000 shows that 49.7 percent of Cuban-Americans in Miami-Dade wanted direct US military action against Cuba, as opposed to only 8.1 percent of Americans nationwide.[22] Law dictates that if a fair trial is impossible in the location given, the venue must be changed.[23]

In May 2005, the Working Group on Arbitrary Detention of the United Nations Human Rights Commission declared the Five's imprisonment as arbitrary, urging the US government to resolve the situation. Pleas from other international human rights organizations such as Amnesty International, and support committees in ninety-seven countries have also sought the release of the Five. Many consider them political prisoners, who had only attempted to defend their country from terrorism.

Organizations have also condemned the US's refusal to grant visas to Olga Salanueva and Adriana Pérez, wives of René González and Gerardo Hernández. On June 25, 2002, after waiting five years to visit her husband, Adriana was finally granted a visa. However, upon her arrival in the US, Adriana was arrested by the FBI, interrogated for eleven hours and expelled to Cuba.

In 2006, Amnesty International sent an open letter to the government of the United States, disapproving of their refusal to grant visas to Olga Salanueva and Adriana Pérez, stating that "in the absence of a clear and immediate threat posed by such visits, this measure is unnecessarily punitive and contrary both to standards for the humane treatment of prisoners and to states, obligation to protect family life."[24] The letter also raised questions about the guarantee of due process in the Miami trial.

Despite worldwide support for the Cuban Five, the US has maintained its harsh position. The Five remain incarcerated in five separate prisons throughout the US, while ex-CIA mercenaries Orlando Bosch and Luis Posada Carriles—widely considered the two most dangerous terrorists in the Western Hemisphere—are provided sanctuary by the US government.

CONTENT ANALYSIS: CORPORATE NEWS COVERAGE OF THE CUBAN FIVE

The fact that hardly anyone in the US knows about the case of the Cuban Five is telling enough of its coverage. Not only are the corporate media outlets to blame, but some of the independents are as well, like *In These Times*, *The Progressive*, and *Mother Jones*. In the corporate news coverage—rare as it is—there are observable tendencies of bias against Cuba. The tone of the articles tend to demonize the Five, while the information presented often neglects Cuba's opposing viewpoint and defense of their actions.

The *New York Times'* reporting is bereft of context and glaringly one-sided—Cuba's perspective is apparently unworthy of consideration. Since the 1996 incident, Cuba has maintained that the downing of the two BTTR planes occurred over Cuban airspace,[25] not over international waters as the US asserts. The *New York Times* obsequiously assumes the planes were shot down over international waters.[26] An excerpt from one article reads: "F.B.I. officials said their investigation of Cuban intelligence gathering in South Florida began after Brothers to the Rescue, known for making mercy flights between Florida and Cuba searching for people in boats fleeing Cuba, lost two planes in an attack by Cuban fighter jets in 1996."[27] There is vital information missing from the article, thus misleading readers. Brothers to the Rescue (BTTR) were not shot down while rescuing refugees,[28] as readers might assume, they were seeking to penetrate Cuban airspace for political motives. To their credit, one

New York Times article mentions that "Cuba has vigorously defended five of the spies who fought and lost their cases in federal court . . . insisting that the men sought only to thwart terrorism by radical exiles, like a spate of Havana bombings in 1997 that killed an Italian tourist."[29] But the *New York Times* takes the issue no further.

The Associated Press (AP), a wire service providing articles for many newspapers, covered the case of the Cuban Five relatively well. Profiles of the Five are provided along with most of the developments in the court case. Context is there, as well as the Cuban perspective. For instance, AP includes various arguments from the Five's defense team, who contend that Cuban-American relations are in such a state that this alone would affect the outcome of the trial. The Five were necessary to Cuba as the "United States was either unwilling or unable to prevent them from supporting terrorist attacks in Cuba." Attorney Mendez cited a "string of eight bombings in Cuba over a four-month period in 1997" as "only part of a 40-year history of raids, bombings, and arms smuggling missions that justified the agents' undercover work in South Florida."[30] AP also reports that jurors heard evidence of Miami-based terrorist organizations that "bomb Cuban hotels and smuggle weapons into Cuba," while the warnings of those attacks were "forwarded to the FBI about Miami-based support and financing for terrorism in Cuba."[31]

AP also describes the charges against Hernandez and the proper context surrounding the 1996 incident, making it explicit that BTTR were flying into Cuban territory on "a mission to drop 500,000 political leaflets."[32] Defense attorney Paul McKenna "offered evidence the attack was in Cuban airspace and insisted Cuba was concerned only with its own territory after repeated incursions by the Miami group for nearly two years."[33]

Since the arrest of the Cuban Five, the *Washington Post* has mentioned them in nine articles. Only two of the articles made the front page, while the rest were buried deep within section A, the exceptions being one article on the front of the Style section and one on the front of the Metro section. Most of WP articles lack in context and balance, implicating the Five as gang of spies, while others make efforts to provide Cuba's viewpoint.

The article published September 15, 1998 quotes US attorney Thomas E. Scott twice, who says the Five were determined "to strike at the very heart of our national security system." Unfortunately,

Cuba's viewpoint is not presented. It is not until the convictions in June of 2001 that another major article appears. This one appears on page 12 of section A, which reports the guilty convictions of the Five as "a committed band of spies working to infiltrate South Florida's military installations and Cuban exile community." *Post* reports that "there were no Cuban Americans or anyone with close ties to the large Cuban American community here on the twelve-member jury, which deliberated for five days," but the article does not mention the anti-Castro bias prevalent in Miami-Dade County. *WP* does include that the defendants considered themselves "Cuban patriots, trying to protect their country from Cuban American extremists in South Florida." It is also reported that their "spying" on military installations did not actually threaten any national security.

One article to make the front page in 2006 headlined "Cubans jailed in U.S. as spies are hailed at home as heroes." The article reports that "American officials tend to paint Cuban agents as infiltrators bent on undermining U.S. national security. But the Cuban government asserts they are men of courage, sent to the U.S. to ferret out terrorism plots by Cuban exile groups waging war against President Fidel Castro." This is the kind of balanced reporting that should encompass every article. There are other quotes from Cuba, expressing anger at the continued incarceration, as Antonio Lage was quoted: "'Hypocrites, that's what Bush and the Americans are—hypocrites,' he said. 'They talk about fighting terrorism, but they keep these heroes in prison for trying to stop the terrorists in Miami.'"

Throughout the nine articles in the *Post*, there is a general demonizing of the Cuban Five as terrorists, clandestine agents, and enemies of the State. There are redeeming points like the June 2006 article, which shows both opposing viewpoints of the case. But much is being left out of the story, such as the context surrounding the 1996 incident, which implicated Gerardo Hernandez in the conspiracy to commit murder charge.

The television coverage of the case is virtually non-existent. CBS and CNN aired brief reports, but nothing comprehensive. CNN featured US attorney Tom Scott (quoted by the *Washington Post*) who said, "the spy ring was tasked by the Cuban government to strike at the very heart of our national security system." But no defense lawyer was included on behalf of the Cuban Five, no opposing viewpoints presented.

CONCLUSION

The Case of the Cuban Five should be known to every American concerned with injustice or the actions of their government. But that information must be available for the public to obtain. If it is not, then freedom of thought is undermined—it narrows with the closing limits of obtainable knowledge. When the mainstream media is influenced by corporate interests and entertainment, and the independent media is too timid to confront controversial issues, the outcome is an uninformed public with a distorted perspective.

Media coverage in general and its priorities are reflected in the lack of both quantity and quality of coverage of the Cuban Five. To provide the proper context of the case would be to implicate the US government in the sanction of known terrorists like Bosch and Posada, and to expose their connections to the Bush administration. This should call into question the legitimacy of Bush's War on Terrorism. Not to mention the legitimacy of the US judicial system in general, that exonerates terrorists like Posada and Bosch while condemning the Cuban Five who fight against terrorism.

For almost nine years, the Cuban Five have waited in prison for a fair trial. Adriana Perez, the wife of Gerardo Hernández, is still prevented by the US government from seeing her husband. The media are responsible, not only to the Cuban Five and their families, but to the American public, who depend on and put faith in their news outlets for fair, objective, and comprehensive reporting. The failure of the media deserves the harshest censure, while the Cuban Five deserve nothing less than the loudest cries of social protest.

Jeffrey Huling is a graduate student in English at Sonoma State University.

Project Censored Research Interns assisting with this study include: Zoe Huffman, Jenni Leys, Jocelyn Thomas, and Erica Haikara.

Citations

1. Chomsky, Noam. "Cuba and the United States: A Near-Half Century of Terror." *Superpower Principles*. Ed. Salim Lamrani. New York: Common Courage Press, 2005. 28.
2. Staten, Clifford L. *The History of Cuba*. New York: Palgrave Macmillan, 2005. 84.
3. Roberts, J M. *Twentieth Century*. New York: Penguin, 1999. 657.

4. Thomas, Hugh. *Cuba: The Pursuit of Freedom*. New York: Harper and Row, 1971, p. 1210.

5. Chomsky, Noam. "Cuba and the United States: A Near-Half Century of Terror" in *Superpower Principles*. Ed. Salim Lamrani. New York: Common Courage Press, 2005, p. 29.

6. Staten, Clifford L. *The History of Cuba*. New York: Palgrave Macmillan, 2005. 92.

7. Chomsky, Noam. "Cuba and the United States: A Near-Half Century of Terror" in *Superpower Principles*. Ed. Salim Lamrani. New York: Common Courage Press, 2005, p. 29.

8. Staten, Clifford L. *The History of Cuba*, p. 96.

9. Dobbs, Michael. "Document Details '62 Plans on Cuba; U.S. Weighed Military Move to Oust Castro." *Washington Post* 27 Jan. 1989: A14.

10. Blum, Willam. "The Unforgivable Revolution." *Superpower Principles*. Ed. Salim Lamrani. New York: Common Courage Press, 2005. 52. William Blum cites these sources: a) *Washington Post*, 1 November 1986, pp. A1, A18. b) Jonathon Kwitny, *The Crimes of Patriots* (New York, 1987), p. 379. c) William Schaap, "New Spate of Terrorism: Key Leaders Unleashed," *Covert Action Bulletin* (Washington), No. 11, December 1980, pp. 4-8. d) Dinges and Landau, pp. 245-6. e) Speech by Fidel Castro, 15 October 1976, reprinted in Toward Improved US-Cuba Relations, House Committee on International Relationsm Appendix A, 23 May 1977. f) The CIA documents declassified by the Agency, sent to the National Archives in 1993, and made available to the public. Reported in *The Nation* (New York), 29 November 1993, p. 657.

11. Franklin, Jane . "Terrorist Connections Resurface In Florida." *ZNet* 29 June 2002. <http://www.zmag.org/content/showarticle.cfm?ItemID=2049>.

12. Chomsky, Noam. "Cuba and the United States: A Near-Half Century of Terror" in *Superpower Principles*. Ed. Salim Lamrani. New York: Common Courage Press, 2005, p. 42.

13. According to Noam Chomsky (*Superpower Principles*, 42), the airline bombing was financed by Jorge Mas Canosa, head of the tax-exempt Cuban-American National Foundation (CANF). CANF is a Miami-based anti-Cuba lobby group, dedicated to overthrowing the Cuban Government of Fidel Castro.

14. Barger, Brian. "Posada: accused airline bomber still at large." *United Press International* 4 Sep. 1998.

15. Williams , Caroll J. "Cuban jet bombing suspect ordered free on bail in U.S." *LA Times* 7 Apr. 2007.

16. Williams , Caroll J. "Cuban jet bombing suspect ordered free on bail in U.S." *LA Times* 7 Apr. 2007.

17. "Judge throws out charges against anti-Castro militant." *CNN* 8 May 2007. <http://www.cnn.com/2007/LAW/05/08/posada.charges/index.html>.

18. Weinglass, Leonard. "The Trial of the Cuban Five." *Superpower Principles*. Ed. Salim Lamrani. New York: Common Courage Press, 2005, p. 120.

19. Ibid., p. 121.

20. Ibid., p. 122.

21. Weinglass, Leonard. "The Trial of the Cuban Five." *Superpower Principles*. Ed. Salim Lamrani. New York: Common Courage Press, 2005.

22. Smith, Wayne S. "A Sad Day in the History of American Justice: The Trial of the Cuban Five." *Superpower Principles*. Ed. Salim Lamrani. New York: Common Courage Press, 2005.

23. Weinglass, Leonard. "The Trial of the Cuban Five." *Superpower Principles.* Ed. Salim Lamrani. New York: Common Courage Press, 2005.

24. Lee, Susan. "An Open Letter to the State Department: The US is Violating the Rights of the Cuban Five." *Counterpunch* 26 Jan. 2006.

25. Rohter, Larry. "Cuba Blames U.S. in Downing of Planes." *The New York Times* 27 Feb. 1996: 14.

26. See June 9, 2001 article "5 Cubans Convicted in Plot to Spy on U.S," December 13, 2001 "Leader of Cuban Spy Ring Given Life in Prison," and August 10, 2005 "New Trial Ordered For 5 Accused Spies."

27. Navarro, Mireya. "10 People Are Charged With Spying for Cuba." *The New York Times* 15 Sep. 1998: 18.

28. Three other NYT' articles mislead readers in the same vein. See the May 8, 1999 article "Cuban Spy Suspect Faces Murder Charges," November 27, 2000 "Spy Trial to Start for Five Accused of Aiding Cuba" and December 13, 2001 "Leader of Cuban Spy Ring given Prison."

29. Golden, Time. "White House Wary of Cuba's Little Spy Engine That Could." *The New York Times* 5 Jan, 2003: 3.

30. *Prosecutor: Spy ringleader helped Cuba attack Miami planes,* Associated Press, Catherine Wilson, May 30, 2001.

31. *Defense: Agents never ordered to get US secrets and didn't,* Associated Press, Catherine Wilson, May 31, 2001.

32. *Cuba: five convicted agents were heroes protecting their nation,* Associated Press State & Local Wire, Anita Snow, June 20, 2001.

33. *Chance for conviction clouded in shadowy world of spies,* Associated Press, Catherine Wilson, June 6, 2001.

Left Progressive Media Inside the Propaganda Model

by Peter Phillips and Project Censored

INTRODUCTION

In *Manufacturing Consent* (Chomsky and Herman, 1996) Ed Herman and Noam Chomsky claim that because media is firmly imbedded in the market system, it reflects the class values and concerns of its owners and advertisers. According to Herman and Chomsky, the media maintains a corporate class bias through five systemic filters: concentrated private ownership; a strict bottom-line profit orientation; overreliance on governmental and corporate sources for news; a primary tendency to avoid offending the powerful; and an almost religious worship of the market economy, strongly opposing alternative beliefs. These filters limit what will become news in society and set parameters on acceptable coverage of daily events.

The danger of these filters is that they make subtle and indirect censorship all the more difficult to combat. Owners and managers share class identity with the powerful and are motivated economically to please advertisers and viewers. Social backgrounds influence their conceptions of what is "newsworthy," and their views and values seem only "commonsense." Journalists and editors are not immune to the influence of owners and managers. Journalists want to see their stories approved for print or broadcast, and editors come to know the limits of their freedom to diverge from the "common-sense" worldview of owners and managers. The self-discipline that this structure induces in journalists and editors comes to seem only "commonsense" to them as well. Self-discipline becomes self-censorship—independence is restricted, the filtering process hidden, denied, or rationalized away.

Chomsky (1989) points out that the propaganda model is a structural theory that shows how large or significant interests in society influence decision making by simply being powerful in their own right. He does not claim that government or corporate media owners directly and systematically dictate news coverage perspectives to editors and producers.

Numerous media advocacy organizations including Fairness and Accuracy in Reporting (FAIR), Project Censored, and the Center for Media Democracy have maintained an ongoing analysis of corporate media biases and continuing structural censorship in the US for at least the past two decades. Books like *Into the Buzzsaw* document overt situational censorship inside corporate media (Borjesson, 2002). Continuing research leaves little doubt that the propaganda model still serves us well as a theoretical understanding of why important news stories fail to appear, contain obvious bias, or lack socio-historical context.

In this study researchers at Project Censored explore the degree to which the propaganda model of understanding self-censorship extends throughout the media culture including left-of-center independent media organizations. We examine the deepening propaganda model pressures inside the corporate media and hypothesize the potential for these pressures to impact left progressive media in the US.

TWENTY YEARS OF THE PROPAGANDA MODEL AND ACCELERATED MEDIA CONCENTRATION IN THE CONTEXT OF 9/11

Examining the propaganda model today requires full consideration of the structural influence of media consolidation and the sensitivities of a post-9/11 media culture. Both have strongly influenced how media works in the US today.

Consolidation of media has brought the total news sources for most Americans to less than a handful, and these news groups have an ever-increasing dependency on prearranged content. Since the passage of the Telecommunications Act of 1996, a gold rush of media mergers and takeovers has been occurring in the US. Over half of all radio stations were sold in the first four years of the Act, and the repeatedly merged AOL-Time-Warner-CNN has become one of the largest media organizations in the world. Less then ten major media corporations now dominate the US news and information systems. Giant companies, such as Clear Channel, own over 1,200 radio stations. Ninety-eight percent of all cities have only one daily newspaper and these are increasingly controlled by huge chains (Bagdikian, 2004).

The twenty-four-hour news shows on MSNBC, Fox, and CNN are closely interconnected with various governmental and corporate sources of news. Maintenance of continuous news shows requires a constant feed and an ever-entertaining supply of stimulating events and breaking news bites. Advertisement for mass consumption drives the system and prepackaged sources of news are vital within this global news process. Ratings demand continued cooperation from multiple-sources for ongoing weather reports, war stories, sports scores, business news, and regional headlines. Print, radio, and TV news also engage in this constant interchange with news sources.

The preparations for and the following of ongoing wars and terrorism fit well into the kaleidoscope of preplanned news. Government public relations specialists and media experts from private commercial interests provide ongoing news feeds to the national media distributions systems. The result is an emerging macro-symbiotic relationship between news dispensers and news suppliers. Perfect examples of this relationship are the press pools organized by the Pentagon both in the Middle-East and in Washington DC, which give prescheduled reports on the war in Iraq to selected groups of news collectors (journalists) for distribution through their individual media organizations.

Embedded reporters (news collectors) working directly with military units in the field must maintain cooperative working relationships with unit commanders as they feed breaking news back to the US public. Cooperative reporting is vital to continued access to government news sources. Therefore, rows of news story reviewers back at corporate media headquarters rewrite, soften, or spike news stories from the field that threaten the symbiotics of global news management.

Journalists who fail to recognize their role as cooperative news collectors will be disciplined in the field or barred from reporting, as in the recent celebrity cases of Geraldo Rivera and Peter Arnett during the early invasion of Iraq in 2003.

Symbiotic global news distribution is a conscious and deliberate attempt by the powerful to control news and information in society.

The Homeland Security Act, Title II Section 201(d)(5) specifically asks the directorate to "develop a comprehensive plan for securing the key resources and critical infrastructure of the United States including...information technology and telecommunications systems (including satellites) . . . emergency preparedness communications systems."

Corporate media today is perhaps too vast to enforce complete control over all content 24 hours a day. However, the government's goal is the operationalization of total information control, and the continuing consolidation of media makes this process even easier to achieve.

Newly expanded public relations firms in service to governments and private corporations support and feed the post-9/11 media system. The public relations industry has experienced phenomenal growth since 2001 after several years of steady consolidation. There are three publicly traded mega-corporations, in order of largesse: Omnicom, WPP, and Interpublic Group. Together, these firms employ 163,932 people in over 170 countries. Not only do these monstrous firms control a massive amount of wealth, they possess a network of connections in powerful international institutions with direct connections to governments, multinational corporations, and global policy-making bodies.

Omnicom maintains an enormous group of subsidiaries, affiliates, and quasi-independent agencies such as BBDO Worldwide, DDB Worldwide, and TBWA Worldwide, GSD&M, Merkley Partners, and Zimmerman Partners along with more than 160 firms through Diversified Agency Services division, including Fleishman-Hillard, Integer, and Rapp Collins.

WPP, a UK-based conglomerate, also touts an impressive list of subsidiaries such as Young and Rubicam, Burson-Marsteller, Ogilvy and Mather Worldwide, and Hill and Knowlton along with numerous other PR, advertising, and crisis management firms.

Before the first Gulf War, a propaganda spectacle took place courtesy of Hill & Knowlton. Hill & Knowlton helped create national outrage against Iraq by the recounting of horrifying events supposedly caused by Iraqi soldiers in Kuwait. A young woman named Nayirah claimed in Congressional testimony and before a national audience that she saw "Iraqi soldiers come into the [Kuwait] hospital with guns, and go into the room where fifteen babies were in incubators. They took the babies out of the incubators, and left the babies on the cold floor to die." What the public was not told is that Nayirah was the daughter of Sheikh Sand Nasir al-Sabah, Kuwait's ambassador to the US. The public also wasn't told that her performance was coordinated by the White House and choreographed by the public relations firm Hill & Knowlton on behalf of the Kuwait government.

The big PR forms are closely interconnected with corporate media. Four members of the WPP group sit on the Council on Foreign Relations. One Omnicom board member holds a position at Time Warner, and another holds a lifetime trustee position at PBS.

The public relations company Rendon Group is one of the firms hired for the PR management of America's preemptive wars. In the 1980s, the Rendon Group helped form American sentiment regarding the ousting of President Manuel Noriega in Panama. They shaped international support for the first Gulf War, and in the 1990s organized the Iraqi National Congress and handpicked Ahmed Chalabi. The Rendon Group created the images that have shaped support for a permanent War on Terror, including the toppling of the statue of Saddam, Private Jessica Lynch's heroic rescue, and dramatic tales of weapons of mass destruction.

Public relations contracts during the George W. Bush administration, compared to the Clinton years, increased from millions to billions. In 2000, the last full fiscal year of the Clinton Administration, the federal government spent $38.6 million on sixty-four contracts with major public relations agencies. In 2001, the first year of the Bush administration, the federal government spent $36.6 million on sixty-seven contracts with major public relations agencies. By 2002, the first fully budgeted year of the Bush administration, federal spending on PR contracts increased to $64.7 million on sixty-seven contracts. Upon realization that the Bush administration had indiscriminately paid people to represent the "No Child Left Behind" campaign, Rep. Henry Waxman requested a GAO investigation into the use of funds for media efforts. The report concluded that from 2003 through half of 2005, the administration spent $1.6 billion on 343 contracts with public relations firms, advertising agencies, media organizations, and individual members of the media. The biggest spender was the Department of Defense with $1.1 billion in contracts.

Certainly media consolidation, 9/11 tensions, and the expanding PR industry are shaping the media in ways that we are only beginning to understand.

INDEPENDENT MEDIA RESPONDS

Media Democracy activists have been merging as an international movement for media reform and grassroots news (Chomsky and Hackett, 2001). Central to this movement is the understanding that corporate media undermines freedom of information, and that democracy can only be maintained with full governmental and corporate transparency (McChesney, 1999). Several national media reform conferences have occurred in the US since 1997 and independent media outlets on the web have mushroomed worldwide (www.freepress.net). Indymedia sites now exceed 160, and *Democracy Now!* is broadcasted on over five hundred stations (Phillips, 2003, 2004; Project Censored 1999, 2003). The success of independent media is significant. However, the question becomes, to what extent are the independent media themselves imbedded in the propaganda model? Are independent media strong enough to operate outside the dominant filters of corporate media in the US?

RESEARCH QUESTIONS

This study examines corporate media's culture of compliance with governmental and corporate PR efforts and the post-9/11 atmosphere of media cooperation with the War on Terror. The questions for this study include: To what extent does this transformation impact liberal independent media? Does the propaganda model extend to the liberal press in areas where news stories are seriously denigrated or ignored by the corporate media? Do these news stories become too sensitive or difficult for liberal independent media to cover? Do labels like "conspiracy theory" deter liberal media from covering the factual aspects of key news stories? Are some news stories so sensitive that coverage is deemed too costly to independent media's credibility?

Researchers at Project Censored have examined these questions by conducting a content analysis of ten well-known liberal media sources on eight key news stories denigrated or ignored by the corporate media. In addition we interviewed thirteen media reform experts at the National Media Reform Conference in Memphis in January 2007, asking them why certain news stories just don't seem to make it into the media.

We have great respect for each of these independent media organizations in this study. We consider them some of the strongest advocates for democratic media reform, governmental transparency, and grassroots empowerment in the US today. This is the reason we hope that by doing this research the best can improve for the betterment of all.

THE NEWS STORIES

Corporate Media Distorts Israel-Palestine Death Rates

IfAmericansKnew.org has conducted extensive content analysis of corporate media reporting on the Israel-Palestine conflict. They undertook a statistical analysis of the *New York Times,* NBC, CBS, ABC, and Associated Press in various years from 2001-2004, looking at the number of Israeli and Palestinian deaths reported. They focused on the headlines and lead paragraph. They found that there is a strong correlation between corporate media coverage of a person's death and that person's nationality. For example, in 2004 there were 141 reports of Israeli deaths in AP headlines and lead paragraphs, while in reality there were only 108 Israeli deaths. The difference comes from reporting a death more than once. During this same period, the AP reported Palestinian deaths at 543, but at the time in reality 821 Palestinians had been killed. The ratio of actual Israeli conflict deaths to Palestinian conflict deaths in 2004 was 1:8. Corporate media tends to reported deaths of Israelis to Palestinians at a 2:1 ratio. For example, AP reported 131 percent of Israeli deaths, whereas they only reported 66 percent of Palestinian deaths in 2004.

Source: www.ifamericansknew.org

Physicist Challenges Official 9-11 Story

Research into the events of 9/11 by former Brigham Young University physics professor, Steven E. Jones, concludes that the official explanation for the collapse of the World Trade Center (WTC) buildings is implausible according to laws of physics. In debunking the official explanation of the collapse of the three WTC buildings, Jones cites the complete, rapid, and symmetrical collapse of the buildings; the horizontal explosions (squibs) evidenced in films of the collapses; the fact that the antenna dropped first in the North Tower, suggesting the use of explosives in the core columns; and the large pools of molten metal observed in the basement areas of both towers.

Other findings among the reports:

➤ No steel-frame building, before or after the WTC buildings, has ever collapsed due to fire. But explosives can effectively sever steel columns.

➤ WTC 7, which was not hit by hijacked planes, collapsed in 6.6 seconds, just 0.6 of a second longer than it would take an object dropped from the roof to hit the ground.

➤ With non-explosive-caused collapse there would typically be a piling up of shattered concrete. But most of the material in the towers was converted to flour-like powder while the buildings were falling.

➤ Steel supports were "partly evaporated," but it would require temperatures near 5,000 degrees Fahrenheit to evaporate steel—and neither office materials nor diesel fuel can generate temperatures that hot.

➤ Molten metal found in the debris of the WTC may have been the result of a high-temperature reaction of a commonly used explosive such as thermite.

Two professors of structural analysis and construction from The Swiss Federal Institute of Technology in Zurich (ETH)—the Swiss equivalent of Cal Tech or MIT—have recently expressed their support for Jones's conclusions. Dr. Hugo Bachmann stated on September 9, 2006 that, "WTC7 was, with the utmost probability, brought down by controlled demolition done by experts." Dr. Jörg Schneider also interprets the available videos of the building's collapse as indices that WTC7 was brought down by explosives.

Sources:
Deseret Morning News, November 10, 2005.
Title: "Y. Professor Thinks Bombs, Not Planes, Toppled WTC"
Author: Elaine Jarvik

"Why Indeed Did the WTC Buildings Collapse?"
Author: Steven E. Jones, http://www.wtc7.net/articles/stevenjones_b7.html

Deseret Morning News, January 26, 2006
Title: "BYU professor's group accuses US officials of lying about 9/11"
Author: Elaine Jarvik

The Cuban Five and Media Bias in the US

The Cuban Five are a group of five Cuban men sent by the Cuban government to Miami to infiltrate anti-Castro terrorist groups. Their main objective was to join Cuban exile groups who had been regularly challenging Cuba with violent attacks, airspace intrusions, and broadcasted and aerial-dropped propaganda. Over 4,000 violent incidents have occurred against Cuba since the 1959 revolution including bombing, assassinations, and biological warfare. Cuba had informed the US multiple times of these infractions, yet the US did nothing. Cuba felt infiltration were necessary in order to prevent further attacks.

The US Government arrested the Cuban Five in September of 1998 and charged them with twenty-six different crimes, including fraud, the use of false names, and not registering as agents from another country, and conspiracy to commit espionage. The Five were charged with actual espionage, as not one piece of confidential US information was ever found to have been collected. They were convicted and languish in US Federal prisons today.

Corporate media coverage of the Cuban Five since 1998 is brusquely one-sided; Cuba's viewpoint is deemed unworthy of consideration and the context of the events surrounding the trial is poorly reported.

Source: *Superpower Principles*, 2005, edited by Salim Lamrani, Media Bias and the Cuban Five: By Jeff Huling, Chapter 6.

US Operatives Torture Detainees to Death in Afghanistan and Iraq

The American Civil Liberties Union released documents of forty-four autopsies held in Afghanistan and Iraq October 25, 2005. Twenty-one of those deaths were listed as homicides. The documents show that detainees died during and after interrogations by Navy Seals, Military Intelligence, and other government agency (OGA). "These documents present irrefutable evidence that US operatives tortured detainees to death during interrogation," said Amrit Singh, an attorney with the ACLU. "The public has a right to know who authorized the use of torture techniques and why these deaths have been covered up."

Additionally, ACLU reports that in April 2003, Secretary Rumsfeld authorized the use of "environmental manipulation" as an interrogation technique in Guantánamo Bay. In September 2003, Lt. Gen. Sanchez also authorized this technique for use in Iraq. So responsibility for these atrocities goes directly to the highest levels of power.

A press release on these deaths by torture was issued by the ACLU on October 25, 2005 and was immediately picked up by Associated Press and United Press International wire services, making the story available to US corporate media nationwide. A thorough check of LexisNexis and ProQuest electronic databases, using the keywords "ACLU" and "autopsy," showed that fewer than a dozen of the 1,700 daily papers in the US picked up the story.

Sources:
American Civil Liberties Web site, October 24, 2005
Title: "US Operatives Killed Detainees During Interrogations in Afghanistan and Iraq"

TomDispatch.com, March 5, 2006
Title: "Tracing the Trail of Torture: Embedding Torture as Policy from Guantánamo to Iraq"
Author: Dahr Jamail

Widespread Voter Fraud in 2004 Election

The official vote count for the 2004 election showed that George W. Bush won by three million votes. But exit polls projected a victory margin of five to seven million votes for John Kerry. This ten-million-vote discrepancy is much greater than any possibility of error margin. The overall margin of error should statistically have been under one percent. But the official result deviated from the poll projections by more than five percent—a statistical impossibility. The discrepancy between the exit polls and the official count was considerably greater in the critical swing states.

This exit poll data is a strong indicator of a corrupted election. But the case grows stronger if these exit poll discrepancies are interpreted in the context of more than 100,000 officially logged reports of irregularities and possible fraud during Election Day 2004.

Sources: Freeman, Steven and Josh Mitteldorf, "A Corrupted Election," *In These Times,* February 15, 2005.

Loo, Dennis, "No Paper Trail Left Behind: The Theft of the 2004 Election," *Censored 2006,* Seven Stories Press, 2006.

Freeman, Steven and Joel Bleifuss, *Was the 2004 Presidential Election Stolen?*, Seven Stories Press, 2006.

National Impeachment Movement Developing in US

Impeachment advocates are widely mobilizing in the US. Thousands of letters to the editors of major newspapers have been printed in the past year asking for impeachment. William Dwyer's letter in the *Charleston Gazette* says, "Congress will never have the courage to start the impeachment process without a groundswell of outrage from the people." City councils, boards of supervisors, and local and state level Democrat central committees have voted for impeachment including the California Democratic Party in April 2007. The city and county of San Francisco, voted "Yes" on February 28, 2006. The New Mexico State Democratic Party convention rallied on March 18, 2006 for the "impeachment of George Bush and his lawful removal from office." The national Green Party called for impeachment on January 3, 2006.

Polls show that a growing majority of Americans favor impeachment. In October of 2005, Public Affairs Research found that 50 percent of Americans said that President Bush should be impeached if he lied about the war in Iraq. A Zogby International poll from early November 2005 found that 53 percent of Americans said, "If President Bush did not tell the truth about his reasons for going to war with Iraq, Congress should consider holding him accountable through impeachment."

New avenues of resistance are emerging to challenge the illegal occupants in the White House. On February 17–18, 2007 some twenty-five organizations met in New York for an emergency impeachment conference. The result of the weekend planning was the formation of a new coalition of activists to pursue the impeachment of Bush and Cheney through an increase in public pressure, lobbying, media activism, advertising, creative actions, and civil disobedience. Impeachment was the theme at massive marches in major cities on March 17-18, as well as a chain store shopping boycott April 15 (tax day) to April 22 (Earth Day).

Sources: www.worldcantwait.org, www.wearenotbuyingit.org, www.a28.org

US Government Had Extensive Prewarnings of the 9/11 Attack

While news stories about 9/11 prewarnings were covered in the corporate media, there has been no follow-up on the likelihood that the Bush

Administration actually knew in advance that the 9/11 attacks were imminent. Afghanistan, Argentina, Britain, Cayman Islands, Egypt, France, Germany, Israel, Italy, Jordan, Morocco, Russia, as well as the US intelligence community all warned of imminent terrorist attacks.

9/11 prewarnings include:

➤ June of 2001: German intelligence warned the CIA, Britain's intelligence agency, and Israel's Mossad that Middle Eastern terrorists were planning to hijack commercial aircraft and use them as weapons to attack "American and Israeli symbols which stand out." (*Frankfurter Allgemeine Zeitung*, 9/11/01; *Washington Post*, 9/14/01; Fox News, 5/17/02)

➤ June 28, 2001: George Tenet wrote an intelligence summary to Condoleezza Rice stating, "It is highly likely that a significant al-Qaeda attack is in the near future, within several weeks." (Washington Post, 2/17/02)

➤ June-July 2001: President Bush, Vice President Cheney, and national security aides were given briefs with headlines such as "Bin Laden Threats Are Real" and "Bin Laden Planning High Profile Attacks." The exact contents of these briefings remain classified but, according to the 9/11 Commission, they consistently predicted attacks that would occur "on a catastrophic level, indicating that they would cause the world to be in turmoil, consisting of possible multiple—but not necessarily simultaneous—attacks." (*9/11 Commission Report*, 4/13/04 B])

➤ July 26, 2001: Attorney General Ashcroft stopped flying commercial airlines due to a threat assessment. (CBS, 7/26/01) The report of this warning was omitted from the 9/11 Commission Report. (Griffin 5/22/05)

➤ Aug 6, 2001: President Bush received a classified intelligence briefing at his Crawford, Texas ranch, warning that bin Laden might be planning to hijack commercial airliners, entitled "Bin Laden Determined to Strike in the United States." The entire memo focused on the possibility of terrorist attacks inside the US and specifically mentioned the World Trade Center. (*Newsweek*, 5/27/02; *New York Times*, 5/15/02, *Washington Post*, 4/11/04, White House, 4/11/04, Intelligence Briefing, 8/6/01)

➤ August, 2001: Russian President Vladimir Putin warned the US that suicide pilots were training for attacks on US targets. (Fox News, 5/17/02) The head of Russian intelligence also later stated, "We had clearly warned them" on several occasions, but they "did not pay the necessary attention." (Agence France-Presse, 9/16/01)

▶ September 10, 2001: a group of top Pentagon officials received an urgent warning that prompted them to cancel their flight plans for the following morning. (Newsweek, 9/17/01) The 9/11 Commission Report omitted this report. (Griffin, 5/22/05)

Sources: Phillips, Peter, Bridget Thornton, Lew Brown, and Andrew Sloan, "A Sociological Case for Impeachment of George W. Bush and Richard Cheney," *Impeach the President*, Seven Stories Press, 2006.

Griffin, David Ray and Peter Dale Scott, *9/11 and American Empire*, 2006.

NORAD's Failure to Prevent the 9/11 Attacks

North American Aerospace Defense Command (NORAD) failed to prevent the attacks on 9/11 and has given us three contradictory explanations for this failure. The military's first story was that no planes were sent up until after the Pentagon was hit. This would mean that the military leaders had left their fighters on the ground for almost ninety minutes after the FAA had first noticed signs of a possible hijacking. Within a few days, the military had put out a second story, saying that it had sent up fighters to intercept the airliners, but that, because the FAA had been very late in notifying the military about the hijackings, the fighters arrived too late. Even assuming the truth of late notification, the military's fighters still had time to intercept the hijacked airliners before they hit their targets. To try to defend the military against this accusation, *The 9/11 Commission Report* gave a third version, according to which the FAA, after giving the military insufficient warning about the first hijacked airliner, gave absolutely no notification about the other three airliners until after they had crashed.

Source: Griffin, David Ray, "9/11, The American Empire and Common Moral Norms," *9/11 and American Empire*, 2006.

Liberal Media Coverage of the Stories

These news stories have been ignored or heavily denigrated by the corporate media in the US. In each case either the stories were covered in an extremely biased fashion, ignored all together, or dismissed as conspiracy theories or worse. Each story has factual content that contributes to its appropriateness as a contemporary news story.

Project Censored's research team has verified the accuracy of the news stories. We do not make judgments on the implications of the stories such as NORAD failures and voter fraud. The news stories stand alone. If correct, there may be actors contributing to the implementations of the events, but interpretations in that regard must remain for further investigation and discovery. Nonetheless, we believe that freedom of information is necessary in a democratic society and that it is inappropriate for media both corporate and independent to ignore stories because of implications that reach beyond the specifics of the events.

The following chart describes the coverage of these news stories by ten liberal media outlets:

Liberal Media Coverage of Sensitive News Stories

Sources	Death Rates	9/11 Bldg 7	Cuban Five	US Torture	2004 Voter Fraud	Impeach Movement	9/11 Pre-Warn	NORAD Failure
In These Times	No	Yes-N	No	No	Yes	Yes	No	No
Buzz-Flash	No	No	Yes-P	No	Yes	Yes	Yes	No
The Progressive	Yes-P	Yes-N	No	No	Yes-P	Yes	Yes-N	Yes-N
Mother Jones	Yes	Yes-P	No	Yes	Yes	Yes	Yes-P	No
AlterNet	No	Yes-N	Yes	No	Yes	Yes	Yes-P	Yes-N
The Nation	No	Yes-P Yes-N	Yes	No	Yes-P	Yes	Yes-P Yes-N	Yes-P Yes-N
Truth Out	No	Yes-P	Yes	Yes	Yes	Yes-P	Yes-P	Yes-P
Common Dreams	Yes-P	Yes-P Yes-N	Yes	Yes	Yes	Yes	Yes Yes-N	Yes Yes-N
Democracy Now!	No	No	Yes	No	Yes	Yes	Yes-D	Yes-D
ZNet	No	No	Yes	Yes	Yes-P	Yes	No	Yes-N

Table Codes
Yes: Coverage of the core issues
No: Did not cover the story
Yes-P: Partial coverage of the story but left out key points
Yes-N: Opinion statement against the story or negative coverage
Yes-D: Coverage of the story as a debate between antagonists

The results of our research show a mixed coverage of the eight news stories by the ten liberal media organizations. Voter fraud and impeachment are by far the best-covered issues among the sample stories. This is encouraging in that the corporate media has essentially dismissed any coverage of widespread fraud in the 2004 election as unsubstantiated, while liberal media widely covered vote fraud issues in Ohio, but full coverage of the depth of election fraud in numerous other states was not highlighted in all articles.

The impeachment movement is still ignored by the corporate media, as evidenced by the lack of coverage of the California Democratic Party resolution for impeachment April 28, 2007. Finding solid coverage from the ten liberal media organization is a positive step to recognizing the importance of liberal media addressing issues outside of the two party system of power.

Puzzling to us is the failure of six of ten liberal media outlets to cover ACLU's torture story, especially since the evidence was so widely available through Associated Press, and completely ignored by the corporate media in the US. The ACLU report provides absolute proof of widespread torture in Afghanistan and Iraq at multiple sites during 2002–2004. We must question if some of the same propaganda model pressures at work within the corporate media are extending to the editorial processes within liberal media as well. Torture is a sensitive story in that it totally contradicts the generally held belief that abuse of human rights is seldom deliberately perpetrated by US troops abroad. The public wants to believe that crimes against humanity only occur in times of extreme pressure and in individual situations in which a few solders overstep the boundaries of human decency. Torturing someone to death is not part of the traditional American value system and the learning of such news is upsetting to the sensitivities of most people. By covering such a story, a news source is running the risk of being challenged as unpatriotic and threatening to the values of the United States of America. This risk was surely a consideration for some of the 97 percent of the corporate media editors/producers who ignored the story completely, and it may well be a factor in why six of ten liberal media groups didn't cover the story as well.

Equally sensitive is the coverage of Israel-Palestine death rates. Eight of ten of the liberal media groups did not cover the massive imbalance of deaths occurring in the recent Intifada. Two liberal media groups did partially cover the story, but corporate media and most of the liberal media provided coverage that relayed messages of equal death rates between Israel and Palestine.

"The Israel Lobby" (Mearsheimer and Walt, 2006) examines the historical unwavering US support for Israel. According to Noam Chomsky the "Israel lobby gets it inputs in large part because it happens to line up with powerful sectors of domestic US power" (1991). Given this overlap it seems that the propaganda model explains editorial decisions inside the corporate media when covering the Israel-Palestine conflict, but it leaves a question regarding why most liberal media ignore this story as well. The Israel lobby includes the ability to influence campaign contributions and donations among the broad Jewish communities in the US. Perhaps a concern of losing Jewish community donations is influencing liberal publication editorial decisions?

The US corporate media has widely denigrated the Cuban Five for years (see Chapter 6). However, the case of the Cuban Five has only recently been covered by *The Nation* in a special report on Cuba (May 14, 2007) and it is unclear why three major liberal media organizations have not found this story newsworthy over the five years the events have been occurring.

The corporate media in the US has widely supported the 9/11 Commission's report and ignored, denigrated or openly challenged the questioning of events around 9/11 as loony conspiracy theories. The three stories related to 9/11 in our sample contain factual information to more than substantiate the legitimate reporting of these stories and conducting of additional investigative research on the events. Yet, we see an almost uniform response inside the liberal media to the difficulties of covering 9/11 news stories. When partial cover occurs as in the case of Building 7 with four liberal outlets, there is counter-balancing negative coverage on the same story from three of them. The *Progressive* takes denial lead by dismissing all three stories as conspiracy theories at their worst. *Democracy Now!* distinguishes itself by covering two of the stories as a debate. The label of conspiracy theory by the corporate media seems to make it particularly difficult for left liberal media to cover 9/11-related news stories. Widespread support for the 9/11 Commission's report within corporate media seems to extend the propaganda model pressures to left liberal media as well.

MEDIA REFORM CONFERENCE INTERVIEWS ON DIFFICULT TO COVER STORIES

Project Censored research staff conducted thirteen interviews at the Media Reform Conference in Memphis in January of 2007. We asked interviewees why our sample stories, voter fraud, impeachment, and 9/11 issues where so difficult to cover.

Robin Andersen, associate professor of Communications Media Studies, Fordham University, on 9/11: "Whatever we think about its veracity, we need to have those stories out into the public sphere because the public should be allowed to apply their own judgment . . . based on the evidence, not based on opinions arguing it's completely implausible."

Joel Bleifuss, editor of *In These Times,* on voter fraud: "[T]o question the legitimacy of the 2004 presidential election, or the 2000 presidential election for that matter, is something the mainstream press and even some of the independent press is afraid to do . . . it is sort of a taboo topic and so people become accepting of the boundaries of permissible thought."

On 9/11: "We basically think that while there is a lot that can still be said about the knowledge the administration had and the failures of intelligence prior to 9/11, we've been fairly skeptical of some of the 9/11 theories that are out there."

Jeff Chester, Center for Digital Democracy, on 9/11: "The US system of journalism has failed the public countless times. It failed to warn the US public prior to 9/11 . . . [media] consolidation leaves laid-off journalists and closed bureaus . . ."

Sarah Olson, independent radio producer, Oakland, CA, on voter fraud: "It was largely . . . the corporate media saying there is nothing. The independent media saying there was massive fraud, unfortunately it has become an 'us versus them' debate."

On 9/11: ". . . no one really covers it terribly seriously except the people . . . who believe it isn't true. Very often people dismiss the questions around 9/11 in a way that's probably isn't helpful. Good journalism always fosters meaningful debates. That is something that hasn't happened well on any of the subjects you brought up."

Anna Belle Peevey, *Asheville Global Report*, Asheville, North Carolina, on impeachment: "the coverage has been very slim, it is probably marketed as a crazy decision by the liberal people of the world and liberal media to throw a monkey wrench in the administration's plan to win the War on Terror and protect America's freedom. Independent publications . . . offer a much different stance . . . and are the voice of the people."

On 9/11: "The major news media dispels the exact same information that the government did, which was these people came, they attacked us, and we fought back . . ."

Sunsara Taylor, World Can't Wait, Reporter for *Revolution Newspaper*, on voter fraud: "They said, this is a loony conspiracy theory and . . . there was no engaging the substance what was very well-documented investigation on voter fraud."

On 9/11: "I definitely think that there has not been a truthful, unencumbered search exploring the questions . . . the Bush administration would have no hesitancy to do harm to people around the world or people in this country if they felt it was politically expedient."

What was consistent among the people interviewed in Memphis was a general belief that the corporate media has failed or refused to cover issues around voter fraud, impeachment, and 9/11. To varying degrees the independent press has attempted to address some of the issues but some major gaps still exist.

CONCLUSION

Based on the evidence presented we conclude that media concentration, PR consolidation, and post-9/11 sensitivities have all contributed to the continuation of strong support for the propaganda model theory as a significant way to understand corporate media in the US. We understand also that this theory may contribute to the news story selection process inside the left liberal media as well.

Further investigation of this evidence will likely continue to develop over the next decade of media research.

Project Censored researchers assisting with this study include: Andrew Roth, Assistant Professor of Sociology, and research interns: Sarah Randle, David Abbott, Courtney Wilcox, Zoë Huffman, Jeff Huling, Jenni Leys, Jocelyn Thomas, Erica Haikara, Michael B Jangles Jr., Jessica Rodas, Mike Spiff, Erik Jilburg.

Bibliography

Bagdikian, Ben H. *The New Media Monopoly*. Boston: Beacon Press, 2004.

Borjesson, Kristina. *Into the Buzzsaw*. Prometheus Books, 2002.

Chomsky, Noam & Edward Herman. *Manufacturing Consent: The Political Economy of the Mass Media*, Pantheon, 1988.

Chomsky, Noam. *Necessary Illusions: Thought Control In Democratic Society*. Boston: South End Press, 1989.

Chomsky, Noam, "The New World Order," Speech at UC Berkeley, March 16, 1991.

Freeman, Steven and Joel Bleifuss. *Was the 2004 Election Stolen?* Seven Stories Press, 2006.

Hackett, Robert, "Building a Movement for Media Democratization," *Censored 2001*, Seven Stories Press, 2001.

McChesney, Robert, *Rich Media, Poor Democracy*, New York: The New Press, 1999.

Mearsheimer, Walt, and Walt, Stephen. "The Israel Lobby," *London Review of Books*, March 23, 2006.

Phillips, Peter. "Rebuild Democracy with Grassroots Community News," *Censored 2003*, New York: Seven Stories Press, 2002.

Phillips, Peter. "Media Democracy in Action," *Censored 2004*. New York: Seven Stories Press, 2003.

Phillips, Peter. *Censored 2006*. New York: Seven Stories Press, 2005.

Project Censored. *Progressive Guide to Alternative Media and Activism*. New York: Seven Stories Press, 1999 and 2003.

Covering War's Victims
A Content Analysis of Iraq and Afghanistan War Photographs in the *New York Times* and the *San Francisco Chronicle*

by Andrew Roth, Zoe Huffman, Jeffrey Huling, Kevin Stolle, and Jocelyn Thomas

> "The lie in war is almost always the lie of omission."
> Chris Hedges, *War is a Force that Gives Us Meaning*

Sparing use of photographs is central to the management of war news. Consider two cases in point. In May 2004, photographs from Abu Ghraib of US captors abusing Iraqi detainees made torture starkly real to many US citizens. On May 7, 2004, before the *Washington Post* published a series of the photographs, Secretary of Defense Donald Rumsfeld told the Senate and House Armed Service Committees that the images in question showed "blatantly sadistic, cruel and inhuman" torture of Iraqis. He worried publicly that, "If these are released to the public, obviously it's going to make matters worse."[1] In September 2005, US District Judge Alvin K. Hellerstein ordered release of additional Abu Ghraib photographs, asserting that "the freedoms we champion are as important to our success in Iraq and Afghanistan as the guns and missiles with which our troops are armed."[2]

In 2004–2005, Russ Kick (editor, *The Memory Hole*) and Ralph Begleiter (professor of communication, University of Delaware) used the Freedom of Information Act (FOIA) to make public over seven hundred photographs of flag-draped coffins containing US military personnel killed overseas.[3] The Pentagon and the Bush administration had strenuously resisted news coverage and photography of dead soldiers' homecomings on all military bases. Professor Begleiter called the government's release of the Dover Air Force Base photographs an important victory for the American people, for the families of troops killed in the line of duty during wartime, and for the honor of those who have made the ultimate sacrifice for their country. . . . This significant decision by the Pentagon should make it difficult, if not impossible, for any US government in the future to hide the human cost of war from the American people.4

If, as Susan Sontag suggests, most contemporary citizens' knowledge of war is "camera-mediated," rather than experiential, then photographic images from Dover Air Force Base, not to mention Abu Ghraib, are necessary to the US public's full understanding of war's human cost.5

This chapter presents a case study in how two major national newspapers present photographic images of war in Iraq and Afghanistan to the US public. Analyzing front-page coverage in the *New York Times* and *San Francisco Chronicle*, we have examined, coded, and analyzed twenty-five months of photographs related to the wars in Iraq and Afghanistan.

Visuals, including news photographs, play a crucial role in how readers experience newspapers and engage the stories that they contain. For example, the Poynter Institute's ongoing "Eyes on the News" study demonstrates that: 90 percent of readers enter pages through large photographs or other visual images; running a visual element increases the likelihood by three times that the reader will read at least some of the accompanying text; and readers' comprehension and recall increase when photographs or other visuals accompany stories. Overall, under ideal circumstances, readers take in 75 percent of the photographs in a newspaper. By comparison, they are aware of only 25 percent of the paper's text, and read just 13 percent of its stories in any depth. This research shows that readers' experience of newspapers is holistic and visual.6

This study focuses on news photographs appearing on the front pages of the *Times* and the *Chronicle* during two periods, March–December 2003 and January 2006–March 2007. Examining these data, we ask:

➤ how frequently do front-page news photographs depict war in Afghanistan or Iraq? And,

➤ to what extent do these photos portray the *human cost* of those wars?

Based on content analysis of over 6,000 front-page news photos spanning 1,389 days of coverage, we find that only 12.8 percent of the photos analyzed relate in some way to the wars in Afghanistan and Iraq. A mere 3.3 percent of those front-page news photos represent war's most fundamental human cost, by depicting dead, injured, or missing humans. We find an enormous gap between the number of actual deaths in Afghanistan and Iraq during this time span, which numbers in the tens of thousands (and hundreds of thousands, by some estimates) and the number of deaths depicted visually, through front-page photographs—just forty-eight images of human death, in our data collection.

Based on this evidence, we argue that front-page news photographs "cover" the human cost of war in ways that run contrary to popular understandings of the press's role and responsibilities in a democratic society.

In journalism "to cover" a story usually means to be responsible for reporting an event, with the aims of drawing attention to it, and enhancing public understanding of it. However, "to cover" can also mean to put something (like a blanket) over something else, to hide, protect, or decorate it. We argue that the corporate media's coverage of the human cost of war in Afghanistan and Iraq amounts to the second—and, for journalism, problematic—meaning of the action, "to cover." When only 202 of the 6,037 front-page news photographs we analyzed depict the human cost of war, we conclude that the *Times* and the *Chronicle* do more to hide that cost from the public, rather than bring it to their attention.

The absence of front-page news photographs depicting bodily injury and death contributes to what Elaine Scarry describes as "the disappearance of the body" in contemporary war, despite the fact that "injuring is, in fact, the central activity of war," its "obsessive content." This central fact, Scarry notes, "often slips from view."[7] The body's disappearance allows the state and the press to direct the public's attention to the "mythic reality" of war, rather than its "sensory reality" in which "we see events for what they are" and "war is exposed for what it is—organized murder."[8]

Our analysis proceeds by considering perspectives on the political values and journalistic conventions that shape contemporary war photography, a review of our data and methods, and more detailed presentation of our findings. The concluding discussion raises important questions about the social significance of this limited coverage.

POLITICAL AND JOURNALISTIC VALUES

Institutions, as much as individuals, produce and present news photographs. Political and journalistic values strongly influence the content and placement of news photographs.9 However, as Barbie Zelizer has argued, standards regarding the usage of images in news "remain generally unarticulated in the journalistic community."10 During wartime, when the topic of death becomes the focus of news images, the lack of consensus becomes pronounced:

> Arguments—about our dead versus their dead; about civilian versus military dead; about showing the faces of the dead; about class, race, and the dead; about identifying the dead before their next of kin are notified—inevitably draw in news editors, media ombudsmen, and readers in letters to the editor, suggesting at a fundamental level that Western journalism has no problem using words in news to verbally recount the stories of death in war time but it has many problems using news pictures showing those who have died. In this respect, journalists' decisions about what to do with images of death reflect more broadly on the role and function of journalism as a whole.11

By and large, however, Zelizer argues that news organizations tend to depict war as "clean, heroic and just" by limiting images of war "to those that are consonant with prevailing sentiments about the war." These images "tend not to be graphic."12

US government restrictions limit the type of images that photojournalists make, both overseas and at home, in covering the Afghanistan and Iraq wars. The Pentagon's fifty-point Coalition Forces Land Component Command (CFLCC) Ground Rules Agreement (known informally as the "embed rules") specifically prohibits:

➤ "photographs or other visual media showing an enemy prisoner of war or detainee's recognizable face, nametag or other identifying feature or item" (point #40)

➤ "photographs or other visual media showing a deceased service member's recognizable face, nametag or other identifying feature of item" (#43)

➤ Photographs of patients in medical facilities are allowed "only with the consent of the attending physician or facility commander and with the patient's informed consent, witnessed by the escort. 'Informed consent' means the patient understands his or her picture and comments are being collected for news media purposes and they may appear nationwide in news media reports" (#48 & #49).[13]

These restrictions' impact on photojournalists' ability to report the war cannot be overstated. Consider, for example, the account of Michael Kamber, a photographer for the *New York Times*:

> The embedded restrictions have tightened up considerably since I was last here. You now need written permission from a wounded soldier to publish his photo if he is in any way identifiable and even if his face is not visible. If unit insignias or faces of others soldiers are visible, that also disqualifies a photo from being used, according to one of the highest-ranking PAO's (Public Affairs Officer) in Iraq. . . . When I was here in '03 and '04, the military was much more welcoming. I was invited to shoot memorials (now off limits) and when I embedded with the 1st Cav, they just invited me out. No papers to sign, no written conditions. They just asked that I show respect for the soldiers if they were killed, which I would do anyway. Now there are these new restrictions make it nearly impossible to shoot the dead and wounded. . . . I seriously question who these restrictions are for. . . . The question I pose is: What would have happened to our visual history if Robert Capa and Gene Smith were running around the battlefield during WWII trying to get releases signed as they worked? What if this had been required in Vietnam? Or any war?[14]

Testimony by other war photographers, including the *New York Times's* Tyler Hicks and the *Los Angeles Times's* Pulitzer Prize winner Carolyn Cole, corroborate this account.[15]

Of course, US government regulations also impose limits on

images of war dead at home, as indicated by the Pentagon's resistance to the efforts of Russ Kick and Ralph Begleiter, mentioned above, to secure release of photographs from Dover Air Force Base, depicting the flag-draped coffins containing US military personnel killed overseas.

Many factors—including restricted access, hazardous logistics, and professional ethics—combine to limit the number and type of news photographs of war's victims. We sought to evaluate quantitatively the extent of this limitation by asking: 1. how frequently do front-page news photographs depict war in Afghanistan or Iraq? And, 2. to what extent do these photos portray the *human cost* of those wars?

DATA AND METHODS

We examined two newspapers, the *New York Times* and the *San Francisco Chronicle*, as our primary data sources. We chose the *Times* as the widely acknowledged national paper of record, and the *Chronicle* as a major metropolitan newspaper. We focused on the front page of the *Times* and the *Chronicle* for two periods, 1. the first calendar year of the war in Iraq, from 19 March to 31 December, 2003, and 2. the most recent year up to the four year anniversary of the Iraq conflict, i.e., from 1 January, 2006 to March 20, 2007. We have coded a total of 1,389 days of front-page coverage from the *Times* and the *Chronicle*, including 708 days of the *Times* and 681 of the *Chronicle*.[16] We conducted a content analysis of the front pages of the *Times* and the *Chronicle*, coding for the number of *days* that included stories on Iraq and/or Afghanistan, the total *number of photographs* appearing on the front pages for those days, and the frequency with which those photographs depicted the wars in Afghanistan or Iraq. We intentionally employed broad definitions of what counted as a story or photograph related to Iraq or Afghanistan to maximize the counts for each of these categories. Thus, for example, a photograph of President Bush speaking at a press conference about congressional funding for the war in Iraq, was counted as a war photo, even though it does not depict actual combat or its aftermath.

For photographs depicting Iraq or Afghanistan, we also coded the location of the photograph on the front page (above or below the fold), and whether the photograph depicted dead, injured or missing humans. For those photographs that did portray the human cost of war, we also coded the age, gender, nationality of the victim(s) photographed. We also sought to determine the status of dead, injured, or missing persons as "official" (i.e., combatants) or "unofficial" (non-combatants, i.e., civilians). If photographs depicted dead humans, we coded whether the image revealed the face of the victim.

Our coding framework included not only images of actual human bodies, but also images that symbolically represented dead or missing human bodies. For example, in some news photographs, a grave marker, a soldier's empty boots, or a life portrait held by a relative might stand as a symbolic representation of a dead or missing human.

Finally, for each war photograph we noted its accompanying caption and, when applicable, the headline of the news story associated with the photograph.

Working as a team to code this enormous data corpus, we were concerned with the reliability of our coding. Therefore we attempted to develop coding categories that required a minimum of subjective interpretation. At the project's onset, we met regularly to compare coding decisions and to refine our sense of how to code complicated, "borderline" cases. This effort paid off with a high degree of inter-coder reliability. Even our most difficult, "interpretive" categories (for example, official vs. unofficial status) produced inter-coder reliability rates greater than 90 percent, and our reliability reached 100 percent for more "objective" categories (e.g. number of photographs, location above/below the fold, etc.) Thus, we report the following findings with the highest degree of confidence in their reliability.

FINDINGS

For the two periods we coded (March 19, to December 31, 2001, and January 1, 2006 to March 20, 2007), the *New York Times* and the *San Francisco Chronicle* devoted considerable attention to the war in Iraq, but less to the ongoing war in Afghanistan. Overall 71 percent of the days we coded included stories on Iraq. During the same period, only 6 percent of the coded days included stories on the war in Afghanistan. In the *New York Times*, over 84 percent of the days coded included some coverage of the war in Iraq; and the war in Afghanistan appeared on the *Times*' front page on 9 percent of the days coded. The *San Francisco Chronicle* included coverage of the war in Iraq on 58 percent percent of the coded days, and Afghanistan on three percent of the days analyzed.

During this time span we counted a total of 6,037 news photographs on the front page of the *Times* (N=2487) and the *Chronicle* (N=3550). We coded 774 of these front-page photographs as depicting persons or events related to the wars in Iraq or Afghanistan. Table 1 summarizes these findings:

Table 1: Front Page News Photos, by News Source

	ALL NEWS PHOTOS	IRAQ & AFGHAN	IRAQ ONLY
NY TIMES	2487	408 (16%)	396 (16%)
SF CHRONICLE	3550	366 (10%)	357 (10%)
TOTAL	6037	774 (13%)	753 (12%)

Over 16 percent of the photographs on the front page of the *New York Times* depict either the wars in Iraq or Afghanistan. The figure is slightly greater than 10 percent for the *San Francisco Chronicle*. Overall, combining the two papers' coverage, just 12.8 percent of the front-page photographs relate to conflict in Iraq or Afghanistan. This is a remarkably small figure given both the global importance of the wars in Iraq and Afghanistan and our coding framework's inclusive definition of what counted as photographs related to Iraq or Afghanistan. The war in Afghanistan is especially invisible, accounting for less than 1 percent of front-page news photographs in the *Times* and the *Chronicle*.

If images of the wars in Iraq and Afghanistan appear infrequently on the front pages of the newspaper, then images depicting the human cost of war are even less common. Most photographs related to the wars depict them in *political* terms (see, for example, Figure 1). In our data, we counted just 202 images that depicted the *human cost of war*, by representing dead, injured, or missing humans. Put another way, on average, just one out of four front-page photographs depicting the wars in Afghanistan or Iraq also depicted dead, injured, or missing bodies; overall, just three percent of the front page news

Figure 1: Casual Update: President Bush, joined by Condoleezza Rice, Defense Secretary Donald H. Rumsfeld, Vice President Dick Cheney and Gen. Richard B. Myers, walked to a news conference at his Texas Ranch yesterday. He reported "good progress" in Iraq but said more work needed to be done. (*New York Times*, August 9, 2003) AP

Most news photographs depicting war in Iraq (or Afghanistan) depict it as a political matter. Note how the image, in tandem with the language of "more work . . . to be done," obscures the human cost of war.

photographs in our data depict the human cost of war in Afghanistan or Iraq. Table 2 summarizes these findings.

Table 2: Front Page News Photos Depicting Human Cost of War, by News Source

	WAR PHOTOS	HUMAN COST PHOTOS	DEATH PHOTOS
NY TIMES	408	115 (28%)	73 (18%)
SF CHRONICLE	366	87 (24%)	48 (13%)
TOTAL	774	202 (26%)	121 (16%)

Of the 6,037 front-page news photographs we coded, including 774 that depicted war in Iraq or Afghanistan, just 121 depict dead humans. Most of these photographs (N=86) are *symbolic representations* of human death—for instance, the life portrait of a deceased US soldier in the presence of the soldier's surviving family members, or the beheaded body of a child's doll lying in blood in an Iraqi marketplace after a car bomb detonated. Only thirty-five of the "death" photos depict actual, dead human bodies. Table 3 summarizes our findings regarding photographs that depict US and Iraqi dead.

Table 3: Photographs Depicting US, and Iraqi Dead, by News Source*

	US DEAD			IRAQI DEAD		
	Total	Actual	Symbolic	Total	Actual	Symbolic
NY TIMES	25	5 (20%)	20 (80%)	34	16 (47%)	18 (53%)
SF CHRONICLE	21	0 (0%)	21 (100%)	22	11 (50%)	11 (50%)
TOTAL	46	5 (11%)	41 (89%)	56	27 (48%)	29 (52%)

*Note: The sum for photographs of US and Iraqi dead in this table (112) is less than the total for photos of the dead, reported in Table 2, because a number of photos depict either (i) fatalities from other nations (for example, Afghani, or Coalition Forces from the UK) or (ii) dead whose national identity we could not determine with certainty.

Images of actual Iraqi dead (N=27) appear far more frequently than images of actual US dead (N=5); US dead are more likely to appear in photographs that represent them symbolically.

Table 4 summarizes our findings regarding the combatant status, gender, and age of the dead humans depicted.

Table 4: Photographs Depicting Official Status, Gender, and Age of Dead; by Nationality*

	OFFICIAL STATUS			GENDER			AGE			
	Total	Uniform	Not Uni.	Total	Male	Female	Total	Adult	Teen	Child
US DEAD	46	42 (91%)	4 (9%)	34	30 (88%)	4 (12%)	46	38 (83%)	4 (9%)	0 (0%)
IRAQI DEAD	56	16 (29%)	21 (38%)	58	28 (48%)	3 (5%)	56	25 (45%)	2 (4%)	2 (4%)
TOTAL	102	58 (52%)	25 (22%)	92	58 (63%)	7 (8%)	102	64 (57%)	6 (5%)	2 (2%)

*Note: Due to photos where the status, gender, or age of the dead could not be determined with certainty, sums are not identical and percentages do not necessarily total 100 percent.

Predictably, images of US dead depict uniformed, official combatants, with just four exceptions: In these cases, all from the *Chronicle*, photographs depict the life portraits of US military personnel, not in uniform. Notably, none of the photos of US dead in

Figure 2: US troops guard the body of a soldier killed in an attack by rocket propelled grenades on a convoy on the main road west of Baghdad. (*New York Times*, July 17, 2003) AP

A rare photograph of a dead US soldier in the battlefield. Note how the soldier's body is obscured, by both a blanket and the fencepost, and heavily protected.

our data depict civilian contractors, despite increasing public awareness and concern regarding this aspect of contemporary war.[17]
Images of Iraqi dead are a mixture of civilian (N=21) and combatant
(N=16), with a comparable number (N=19) indeterminate, based on
the image and its accompanying caption. Images of US dead comprise thirty men, four women, with fourteen indeterminate; images
of Iraqi dead include twenty-eight men, three women, with twenty-
seven indeterminate. The front-page war photographs rarely depict
child fatalities (N=2).

The most graphic—and controversial—war photographs depict
the faces of the dead. Images of this type are exceedingly rare in our
data set (N=67). Table 5 summarizes our findings regarding these
photographs:

Table 5: Images Depicting Faces of the Dead, by News Source

	Total	Life Portrait	Face Obscured By Camera Angle	Covered	Face Visible
NY TIMES	31	9 (29%)	4 (13%)	12 (39%)	6 (19%)
SF CHRONICLE	37	26 (70%)	2 (5%)	9 (24%)	0 (0%)
TOTAL	68	35 (51%)	6 (9%)	21 (31%)	6 (9%)

By far, most photographic images of the dead took the form of life
portraits (N=35), largely due to the *Chronicle's* use of this image type.
Twenty of these depicted US military personnel, nine Iraqis, and two
other (coalition troops from the U.K., and Brazil.) Six times in our
data, the photographer framed her/his shot so that the face of the victim, which might have otherwise been visible, was obscured. These
were evenly divided between US and Iraqi casualties. All six photographs where the victim's face is visible depict Iraqi casualties.

ANALYSIS

Journalists value photographs as evidence of "having been there,"
establishing their authority as eyewitnesses; newspaper publishers
value photographs because they compel public attention, officials
and politicians regard images as "tools for shaping public opinion
and justifying policy in wartime," and members of the US public see

Figure 3: The body of a man lay in the street of Falluja, Iraq, yesterday after American soldiers clashed with demonstrators for a second time this week. (*New York Times*, May 1, 2003) AP

Camera angle obscures the victim's face, but in contrast with Figure 3, above, the Iraqi fatality is shown unattended.

news photographs as "a way of coming to grips with the news of war."[18] Each of these four groups, Zelizer contends, "has been consistent in its assumption that seeing is believing." Of course, as she subsequently shows, news photographs of war not only *denote*—depicting the world as "it is"—they also *connote*, depicting that world "in a symbolic frame that helps us recognize the image as consonant with broader understandings of the world."[19]

Our findings raise questions about *both* the denotations and connotations of front-page war photographs in the *New York Times* and *San Francisco Chronicle*. The (in)frequency with which the *Times* and *Chronicle's* front-pages include photographs depicting the human cost of war diverges radically from the frequency with which humans have killed or injured one another in Afghanistan and Iraq. During the two periods that we coded, comprising twenty-five months of coverage, photographs on the front page of the *New York Times* depicted US dead twenty-five times and Iraqi dead thirty-four times; and, for the same time span, photos on the front page of the *San Francisco*

Chronicle depicted US dead twenty-one times and Iraqi dead twenty-two times. This contrasts sharply with even the most conservative publicly available mortality figures: For example, during the same time period, the Department of Defense reports 1,531 US military fatalities.[20]

Our findings substantiate and elaborate the results of the *Los Angeles Times'* six-month study of six newspapers and two newsmagazines.[21] The *Times'* study included photographs from all pages of the newspapers studied, not just the front pages; this study covered the period between September 2004 and February 2005. Table 6 summarizes the *Times'* findings for photographs depicting US and Iraqi dead and wounded:

Table 6: Newspaper Photographs of US and Iraqi Dead and Wounded, by News Source (*Los Angeles Times* Study, September 2004–February 2005)

	US		IRAQI	
	Dead	Wounded	Dead	Wounded
Atlanta Journal-Constitution	0	4	3	9
Los Angeles Times	0	10	22	19
New York Times	0	10	30	25
St. Louis Post-Dispatch	0	6	8	7
Seattle Times	1	4	5	5
Washington Post	0	6	5	13
TOTAL	1	40	73	78

At first glance, the *Times'* findings may be interpreted as conflicting with ours (recall Table 3, above). The *Times* data shows newspapers overwhelmingly more likely to publish photos of Iraqi dead (N=73) than US fatalities (N=1). From this perspective, our data *contrast* with the *Los Angeles Times'* findings: Photographs on the front page of the *San Francisco Chronicle* depict roughly equal Iraqi (N=21) and US (N=22) fatalities, and though the *New York Times* publishes more photographs of Iraqi (N=34) than US deaths (N=25), this difference is less than for any of the newspapers examined in the *L.A. Times* study.

Differences among specific newspapers' coverage of war's human cost certainly matter, and such comparative analyses deserve further attention. However, to emphasize differences—between either the findings of the *L.A. Times* study and ours, or the *San Francisco Chronicle* and the *New York Times* in our study—is to obscure more fundamental similarities. In both studies, the most striking finding is how infrequently newspapers publish photographs that depict the human cost of war. This is so despite the conventional wisdom (often mobilized as a critique of news content) that "if it bleeds, it leads." This also runs contrary to Barbie Zelizer's argument that, during wartime journalism is characterized by a "turn to the visual."[22]

Instead our findings (and those of the *L.A. Times* study) support Elaine Scarry's argument. Recall that Scarry contends that 1. "[t]he main purpose and outcome of war is injuring" and 2. this fact "may disappear from view simply by being omitted."[23] Though Scarry's argument focuses on the uses of *language* (for example, the active reformulation of actions or events, as in the phrase "neutralizing the target"), she tells us that, when discourse about war *does* acknowledge injury to "the sentient tissue of the human body," the body is *"held in a visible but marginal position."*[24] This aptly describes the use of front-page photographs in the newspapers we have examined. Overall, the *New York Times* and *San Francisco Chronicle* front pages *omit* photographic representation of the wars in Afghanistan and Iraq. When front-page photographs include images related to these wars—which, in our data, occurs only 12 percent of the time—these images tend to portray war in *political terms*, i.e., as a policy matter (recall, for example, Figure 1) or a domestic contest between Republican and Democratic politicians. Front-page photographs of the human cost of war, as depicted through images of dead, injured, or missing humans, are exceedingly rare, constituting in our data, as we have seen, just three percent of the front-page photographs published by the *Times* and *Chronicle*. Thus, we conclude that the human cost of war is permitted a visible but marginal position on the front pages of US newspapers.

CONCLUSION

"What does it mean to protest suffering, as distinct
from acknowledging it?"
Susan Sontag, *Regarding the Pain of Others*

Photographs shape our understandings of the world and our place in it. This is especially true of war. In wartime, publishing photographs that depict injury and death may be the closest that newspapers can come to depicting for their readers what Chris Hedges calls "the sensory reality of war."

Amid public discussion of how the government's rules for "embedding" journalists impacts news coverage of the wars in Afghanistan and Iraq, journalists within the corporate press have raised concern about the absence of newsworthy war photographs appearing in newsprint.[25] Of course there are exceptions to these claims. The cover of the *New York Times'* "2006: The Year in Pictures" featured a dramatic series of fifteen photos, by Tyler Hicks, depicting in vivid, grim detail the wounding and eventual rescue of US Marine Lance Corporal Juan Valdez-Castillo;[26] on April 2, 2007, *Newsweek's* special "Voices of the Fallen" edition featured life portraits of US military personnel, in and out of uniform, who have since been killed in the Iraq war, accompanied by poignant testimony from their letters, journals, and e-mails. Images and text such as these do much to convey to the US public the true costs of the war.

Furthermore, visual representations of the human cost of war need not be limited to photographs. Adrianna Lins de Albuquerque and Alicia Cheng's "31 Days in Iraq" exemplifies the potential of original, clear graphics to bring home the magnitude of human injury in ways that mere numbers do not. In a paragraph preceding their "31 Days" graphic, Albuquerque and Cheng note: "While the daily toll [of soldiers, security officers and civilians killed] is noted in the newspapers and on TV, it is hard for many Americans to see these isolated reports in a broader context." Their graphic, centered on a map of Iraq, visually depicts the number of American, Coalition, and Iraqi forces, as well as police officers and civilians killed in Iraq in the month of January 2006, locating the dead geographically and identifying the cause of death (e.g., "car bomb," "accidental death," "US strike," etc.).[27]

Assisting the public to "see in a broader context" and to understand beyond "isolated reports" should be a fundamental job and a basic responsibility of news media in democratic societies such as the United States. Governmental regulation—taking the form of the "embed rules" for journalists with the US military in Iraq and Afghanistan—constitutes one primary *external* constraint on the ability of the press to fulfill its duty to the US public; self-censorship—often in the name of "taste" and "decorum"—and inadequate funding comprise two *internal* constraints on this.[28] Thus, a truly informed public needs to understand not only the human cost of war, but also the political and journalistic forces that may limit, or prevent, news organizations from reporting the real human cost of war.

Photographs of dead bodies constitute the most blunt form to depict visually war's human cost. In the case of the current wars in Afghanistan and Iraq, given constraints of access imposed by the US military, we might have expected journalists to respond—and, perhaps, even resist—by creating new, innovative means of conveying the human loss that war entails. Instead, as this study demonstrates, the press has chosen to "cover" the casualties of war by essentially hiding them from the public's view.

Of course, active opposition to war "does not necessarily require an accurate perception or description of the relation between injuring and political goals."[29] However, in the absence of news photos and stories that depict the sensory reality of war—including the significance of injuring as its central activity—acceptance of war, with varying degrees of attention to its human cost, becomes much more likely.

Acknowledgments: We are grateful to Kathryn Jeon and Paula Hammett, from Sonoma State University's Schulz Information Center; without their assistance the task of data collection would have been much more difficult. Colleagues in the School of Social Sciences Brown Bag lecture series, as well as Nick Wolfinger and Elizabeth Boyd provided welcome encouragement and constructive criticism at previous stages in this project's development.

Citations

1. Testimony of Secretary of Defense Donald H. Rumsfeld before the Senate and House Armed Services Committees, http://armed-services.senate.gov/statemnt/2004/May/Rumsfeld.pdf.

2. Greg Mitchell, "Judge Orders Release of Abu Ghraib Photographs." *Editor and Publisher*, 29 September 2005, http://www.editorandpublisher.com/eandp/news/article_display.jsp?vnu-content_id=1001218842.

3. See National Security Archive, "Return of the Fallen: Pentagon Releases Hundreds More War Casualty Homecoming Images," http://www.gwu.edu/~nsarchiv/NSAEBB/NSAEBB152/index.htm. and also The Memory Hole, "Photos of Military Coffins (Battlefield and Astronaut Fatalities) at Dover Air Force Base." http://www.thememoryhole.org/war/coffin_photos/dover/.

4. National Security Archive, "Return of the Fallen," op cit.

5. Susan Sontag, *Regarding the Pain of Others*. New York: Farrar, Straus & Giroux, 2003; quote at p. 24.

6. See, for example, Monica L. Moses, "Readers Consume More of What They See," Poynter Online (January 17, 2001), http://www.poynter.org/content/content_view.asp?id=4763. We are indebted to Melinda Milligan for bringing the Poynter Institute data to our attention.

7. Elaine Scarry, "The Structure of War," pp. 60-157 in *The Body in Pain: The Making and Unmaking of the World*. New York: Oxford University Press, 1985; quotes at pp. 67 & 80. See also John Taylor, "The Body Vanishes in the Gulf War," pp. 157-192 in *Body Horror: Photojournalism, Catastrophe and War*. New York: New York University Press, 1998.

8. Chris Hedges, *War is a Force that Gives Us Meaning*. New York: Random House, 2002; quote at p. 21. Hedges adapts the distinction between the "mythic" and "sensory" realities of war from psychologist Lawrence LeShan.

9. In addition to Sontag and Scarry, cited above, see Stuart Hall, "The Determination of News Photographs," pp. 226–43 in *The Manufacture of News: Social Problems, Deviance and the Mass Media*, rev. ed., edited by Stanley Cohen & Jock Young. London: Constable, 1981[1972].

10. Barbie Zelizer, "Death in Wartime: Photographs and the 'Other War' in Afghanistan." *The Harvard International Journal of Press/Politics* v. 10, n. 26 (2005): pp. 26-55; quote at p. 27.

11. Ibid., p. 27. See also, Barbie Zelizer, "Which Words Is a War Photo Worth? Journalists Must Set the Standard," *USC Annenberg Online Journalism Review* (April 28, 2004). http://www.ojr.org/ojr/ethics/1083190076.php.

12. Zelizer, "Death in Wartime," p. 31. Zelizer's observation that newspapers' use of photographs in war coverage is "consonant with prevailing sentiments about the war" echoes Daniel Hallin's study of televised news coverage of the Vietnam War. Hallin shows that US television news media did not adopt an oppositional stance toward the war until after Congress became divided in its support for the war. See Daniel C. Hallin, "The Media, the War in Vietnam, and Political Support: A Critique of the Thesis of an Oppositional Media," *Journal of Politics*, v. 46, n. 1 (1984), pp. 2-24.

13. For the full text of the CFLCC Ground Rules Agreement, see http://www.rsf.org/article.php3?id_article=5334. The "embed rules" also appear in Susan D. Moeller, *Shooting War: Photography and the American Experience of Combat*. New York: Basic Books, 1989; pp. 218-221.

14. Michael Shaw, "Reading the Pictures: *Have We Just Seen the Last Combat Injury in Iraq,"* The Huffington Post (June 6, 2007). http://www.huffingtonpost.com/michael-shaw/reading-the-pictures-em_b_50927.html?view=print. A slideshow of Michael Kamber's photographs, titled "The Reach of War: A Deadly Search for Missing Soldiers," with his narration, can be see at http://www.nytimes.com/packages/khtml/2007/05/22/world/20070523_SEARCH_FEATURE.html. We are grateful to David Abbott for bringing Kamber's comments to our attention.

15. See James Rainey, "Portraits of War: Unseen Pictures, Untold Stories," *Los Angeles Times*, May 21, 2005. http://www.latimes.com/news/nationworld/nation/la-na-warphotos21may21,0,625844.story?coll=la-home-headlines

16. The number of days' coverage for each paper is not identical because certain days were not available to us in any of the three formats required for our coding: microfilm, online with images, or hard copy.

17. See, for example, Peter W. Singer, "Outsourcing War: Understanding the Private Military Industry," *Foreign Affairs* (March 1, 2005), http://www.brookings.edu/views/articles/fellows/singer20050301.htm. Casualties.org documents a minimum of 398 civilian contractor deaths in Iraq, through May 2, 2007, in a list that is flagged as "incomplete." See http://icasualties.org/oif/Civ.aspx.

18. Zelizer, "Death in Wartime," pp. 29-30.
19. Ibid, p. 31; see also Stuart Hall, "Determination of News Photographs," op cit.
20. "Military Casualties: By Month" http://icasualties.org/oif/ (accessed June 5, 2007).
21. James Rainey, "Portraits of War," op cit.
22. Barbie Zelizer, "When War is Reduced to a Photograph," pp. 115-135 in *Reporting War: Journalism in Wartime*, edited by Stuart Allan and Barbie Zelizer. London and New York: Routledge, 2004.
23. Elaine Scarry, "The Structure of War," op cit., at pp. 63, 64.
24. Ibid., p. 80, emphasis in original.
25. See, for example, James Rainey, "Portraits of War," op cit., and, more recently, David Carr, "Not to See the Fallen Is No Favor," *New York Times* (May 28, 2007) pp. C1, 6.
26. See www.nytimes.com/picturesoftheyear.
27. Adrianna Lins de Albuquerque and Alicia Cheng, "31 Days in Iraq," *New York Times* (February 6, 2006) p. A23. See http://www.nytimes.com/imagepages/2006/02/06/opinion/20060206_IRAQ_GRAPHIC.html.
28. In *Regarding the Pain of Others* (p. 68) Susan Sontag warns that "good taste" is "always a repressive standard when invoked by institutions."
29. Elaine Scarry, "Structure of War," p. 64.

An Epidemic of Fake TV News Gets Swept under the Carpet

by Diane Farsetta

"Hurricane seasons for the next twenty years could be severe. But don't blame global warming," television news anchor Tom Daniels told viewers of WTOK-11 in Meridian, Mississippi, on May 31, 2006.

The ABC affiliate then showed Dr. William Gray, who was identified as one "of the nation's top weather and ocean scientists." Gray denied that there's any link between global warming and the severity of recent hurricane seasons. "We don't think that's the case," he said, speaking from behind a podium. "This is the way nature sometimes works." The segment concluded that the hurricanes that had devastated Gulf Coast communities located just hours away from WTOK viewers could easily be explained by "the cycle of nature."

The claims were not accurate. And the segment was not news—it was a public relations video, funded by and scripted for oil company lobbyists.

In fact, an increasing body of data connects climate change and hurricane severity. "No one doubts that since the early 1990s storms have increased in their intensity and no one doubts that average sea temperatures have increased slightly over the past thirty years," explained Andrew Buncombe in an August 2006 article for the *Independent*. "Whether there is a link between these two phenomena remains unanswered."

Peer-reviewed scientific studies on the issue have reached conflicting conclusions, though an in-depth analysis reported in September 2006 found "a large human influence" on rising sea-surface temperatures, which leads to stronger hurricanes. The same month, *Nature* magazine wrote about a position paper from federal scientists that linked intensified hurricanes to global warming. The document was reportedly quashed by the Bush administration. In 2007, the world's top climate scientists concluded, in the fourth assessment report by the Intergovernmental Panel on Climate Change, that the increase in hurricane and tropical cyclone strength since 1970 was, "more likely than not," due to global warming.

These and other inconvenient truths are regularly under assault by the oil industry and its allies in government. Companies like Exxon Mobil fund scientists, think tanks, and organizations that in turn dutifully challenge the large, varied, and growing base of evidence of climate change and its likely repercussions. In doing so, the oil industry has adopted the tactics of Big Tobacco, whose long and remarkably successful campaign to obscure the health dangers of smoking can be summed up by an infamous internal company memo stating, "doubt is our product."

Environmental and media watchdog groups have repeatedly documented the oil industry funding behind many climate change skeptics. The use of PR video to insert climate change skeptics directly into newscasts, presenting them as impartial experts, is a shocking new twist. But when that story was broken in November 2006 (in a report that I coauthored), news coverage of it was limited to a smattering of regional outlets, independent media, and the broadcast and PR industry trade press.

THE FAKE NEWS CYCLE

The public expects, rightly, that "news" is information that has been gathered and verified by a journalist acting as a fair observer. Journalists have their own points of view, of course, but should avoid—or at least fully disclose—any potential, perceived, or real conflict of interest.

"Fake news" occurs when public relations practitioners adopt the practices and/or appearance of journalists, in order to insert persuasive messages into news media. While fake news is obviously bad news, it's very good PR. For example, praise for Brand X has much more credibility when it's relayed by a seemingly independent reporter or commentator, rather than an actor in a commercial or a Brand X spokesperson in any setting. PR practitioners have dubbed this widely used tactic the "third party technique."

Video news releases (VNRs) are the dominant form of fake news.

VNRs are sponsored, prepackaged video segments and additional footage created by PR firms, or by publicists within corporations, government agencies, or organizations. A VNR presents the client's message using a format and tone that mimic independent television news reports. For the vast majority of VNRs, nothing in the material for broadcast identifies the segment as a VNR or discloses the client behind it. (One PR firm's minor exception to this rule is discussed below.) Though they imitate—and are aired as—news, VNRs are payola, not journalism. They provide favorable "reporting," in return for payment.

PR firms produce VNRs in order to burnish a client's image, improve product sales, respond to negative developments, or support policies favorable to the client. The "Global Warming and Hurricanes" segment described above was a VNR produced by the major PR firm Medialink Worldwide. Medialink's client was TCS Daily Science Roundtable. TCS Daily is a website published by Tech Central Station and was run by the Republican lobbying and PR firm DCI Group at the time the segment was released. (DCI Group sold the website in October 2006.) Exxon Mobil—one of the DCI Group's clients—gave the Tech Central Science Foundation $95,000 in 2003, for "climate change support."

Sadly, WTOK communicated none of these affiliations, caveats, or complexities when it aired as "news" an edited version of the "Global Warming and Hurricanes" VNR. Viewers were led to believe that the segment was a fully vetted product of the station's own reporting. Viewers were also not informed that the esteemed Dr. Gray had told the *Denver Post* in June 2006 that global warming is a "hoax," something that "they've been brainwashing us [about] for 20 years."

Such is the power of VNRs, which have been used to sell nearly everything, from pharmaceuticals to wars. Clients willing and able to pay tens of thousands of dollars per segment use VNRs to displace unflattering "real" news and/or create favorable media coverage.

PR firms distribute and promote VNRs to television newsrooms using satellite and online video channels, as well as the video feeds of such major news companies as CBS, FOX, CNN, and Associated Press. In its 2003 annual report, Medialink Worldwide boasted that its materials "reach more than 11,000 newsrooms" and "more than 11,000 online multimedia newsrooms." On its website, the firm D S Simon Productions promises to maximize TV broadcasts of its VNRs with "300 targeted pitch calls to broadcast networks, network affiliate news feeds, national cable outlets, regional cable networks, and syndicated shows, as well as local network affiliates and independent TV stations."

Thanks to resource-strapped—and sometimes ethically challenged—newsrooms, VNRs are routinely incorporated into newscasts, without any disclosure to viewers. The impact on the modern information environment is significant, as television remains the most popular news source in the US.

WHO'S BEHIND YOUR NEWS?

Television stations' use of VNRs appears to be near universal. Nielsen studies in 1992, 1996, and 2001 found that 100 percent of TV stations surveyed aired VNRs. In 2003, Medialink Worldwide chair Larry Moskowitz told a radio reporter, "Every television station in America with a newscast has used and probably uses regularly this material from corporations and organizations that we provide as VNRs."

In the 1990s and early 2000s, many TV stations increased the amount of time allotted to news programming while either decreasing newsroom budgets or simply maintaining them at previous levels. This trend made VNRs increasingly popular among newsroom staff. "Local broadcasters are being asked to do more with less, and they have been forced to rely more on prepackaged news to take up the slack," explained Tom Rosentiel, director of Project for Excellence in Journalism, and Marion Just, political science professor, in a March 2005 *New York Times* op-ed.

The number of VNRs produced and delivered to TV newsrooms is significant. An academic study from December 2000 credited Medialink Worldwide with producing one thousand VNRs annually, "roughly double the number of its nearest competitor." That study, by Mark Harmon and Candace White at the University of Tennessee, also stated that "a typical newsroom may have ten to fifteen VNRs available per day." In 1990, the magazine of the Society of Professional Journalists estimated that "5,000 to 15,000 VNRs are distributed each year." Undoubtedly, the numbers are higher today.

VNRs usually arrive in TV newsrooms via the station's satellite or online video feeds, and are often just a channel or folder away from "real" news. Subsequently, some TV newsroom personnel have claimed that they've aired VNRs by mistake. However, video providers claim to have clearly segregated VNRs from real news in their feeds, following the controversy over Bush administration VNRs in 2004 and 2005 (see below). In addition, as they enter newsrooms, nearly all VNRs list their clients in the opening frames. These frames are used to inform newsroom personnel only; they are not intended or formatted for broadcast. Nonetheless, PR executives often point to them as evidence that they have done their ethical duty.

Despite these measures and despite journalistic codes and TV station policies that call for clear identification of all VNR footage, disclosure to news audiences is exceedingly rare. In a two-part study that tracked nearly seventy VNRs released in 2005 and 2006 (which I coauthored), the Center for Media and Democracy documented 140 VNR broadcasts during TV news programming. In *only two* of those 140 broadcasts did the station clearly disclose the source of the video to its viewers.

Peter Simmons, an Australian academic with Charles Sturt University's School of Communication, maintains that "individual journalists and public relations practitioners perceive their work to be enhanced when news release material is used *without disclosure*" (emphasis added). Another finding of the Center for Media and Democracy supports his assertion. When the firm D S Simon Productions started mentioning the clients at the end of its prepackaged VNRs, using on-screen labels and verbal statements, TV stations removed these notifications and *still* failed to provide any disclosure to viewers in twelve out of the fifteen instances documented.

Other major findings of the Center for Media and Democracy (CMD) study include:

VNR usage is widespread. By tracking less than 2 percent of the total number of VNRs produced over sixteen months, CMD identified more than one hundred television stations that had aired VNRs. These include stations in major markets, such as New York City, Los Angeles, Boston, Chicago, and Miami. Collectively, the identified stations broadcast to more than half of the US population.

VNRs are usually the sole source for news segments. Nearly 85 percent of the VNR broadcasts documented by CMD were segments from which all of the video and information presented had been derived from a VNR package.

Corporations fund the vast majority of VNRs. Corporations funded more than 90 percent of the VNRs tracked by CMD. Most corporate VNRs promoted specific products. Others featured services or information related to products offered by the client, such as a General Motors VNR on online car shopping. Corporate VNRs with subtler sell-jobs focused on the client's good deeds, such as a Capitol One VNR touting the bank's efforts to protect seniors against financial scams. Other VNRs associated the client with a desirable profession or a cutting-edge product.

Health-related VNRs are especially popular—and problematic. CMD documented news broadcasts of numerous VNRs that overstated or misrepresented the benefits of health products. For example, the major New York City station WCBS-2 aired a VNR promoting over-the-counter supplements to treat arthritis pain, after an independently funded medical study found they "did not reduce pain effectively." Several other TV stations aired VNRs promoting prescription drugs, after totally removing or greatly minimizing the risk information included in the VNR package—information that must be included in drug advertisements, under Food and Drug Administration regulations.

THERE OUGHT TO BE A LAW

Much of the debate over disclosure has focused on VNRs from the US federal government. In 2004, it was revealed that the Bush administration funded VNRs on such controversial topics as the "No Child Left Behind" education policy and the Medicare prescription drug plan. A March 2005 *New York Times* exposé detailed the undisclosed broadcast of Bush administration VNRs on Iraq, Afghanistan and airport security, among other issues, while noting that VNR use "also occurred in the Clinton administration."

The nonpartisan investigative arm of Congress, the Government Accountability Office, ruled in 2005 that any government VNR that does not make its source clear to news audiences constitutes illegal covert propaganda. However, the Bush administration's Justice Department and Office of Management and Budget dismissed that ruling, finding that government VNRs are permissible, as long as they are "informational." Temporary measures passed by the US Congress required "a clear notification" for government VNRs, without defining what that means. These measures have since expired, leaving whether, and how, to disclose government VNRs to the discretion of the federal agency and the television stations involved.

Regarding the debate over government VNRs, Federal Communications Commission (FCC) Commissioner Jonathan Adelstein commented, "The surprising thing, though, is nobody bothered to mention that there are separate disclosure requirements enforced by the FCC under the Communications Act." As summarized in an April 2005 Public Notice from the FCC, the Act's sponsorship identification rules require, "whenever broadcast stations and cable operators air VNRs, licensees and operators generally must clearly disclose to members of their audiences the nature, source and sponsorship of the material." The FCC also asserts in the Notice, "Listeners and viewers are entitled to know who seeks to persuade them."

However, as of mid-2007, the way the Communications Act (which was written in 1934) and its sponsorship identification rules (which reflect the radio payola controversies of the 1950s) apply to VNRs remained a controversial question. The FCC has not penalized any TV stations for airing VNRs without disclosure.

The FCC did open its first-ever VNR investigation in August 2006, sending letters of inquiry to the owners of the seventy-seven TV stations named in the first part of the Center for Media and Democracy study. The agency asked the stations for information about the particular VNR broadcasts, for copies of any agreements with the PR firms that provided the VNRs, and whether the stations had received any payment or services in exchange for airing the VNRs. Although the station responses were due by October 2006, as of mid-2007 no further information about the FCC investigation has been released. The agency also has not moved to investigate the thirty-six new TV stations and ten repeat offenders named in the second part of the Center for Media and Democracy study.

While FCC investigators and members of Congress seem to have forgotten about the fake news issue, lawyers and lobbyists for the public relations industry and broadcasters are busily addressing it. They've challenged the application of the Communications Act to most VNRs, claiming that the Act only requires VNRs to be disclosed if the segments deal with controversial or political issues, or if TV stations are paid to air them.

The Center for Media and Democracy and other disclosure advocates make three basic arguments regarding current laws and regulations. One is that the Communications Act's sponsorship identification rules apply when payment is made anywhere up or down the chain of production of broadcast material. Since clients pay PR firms to produce VNRs, the client must be revealed to news audiences when a VNR is aired.

The second argument is that VNRs save TV stations thousands of dollars in production, filming, and editing costs for each minute that VNR footage substitutes for the station's own reporting. Therefore, a VNR represents a substantial in-kind contribution or "consideration" paid to TV stations, which also triggers the Act's sponsorship identification requirements.

The last pro-disclosure argument points to TV stations' obligation to serve the "public interest, convenience, and necessity," as described in the Communications Act. In exchange for their free use of the public airwaves—a limited and valuable resource—stations agree to act as public trustees. Broadcasting promotional segments while denying viewers the information needed to evaluate what's being presented as "news" is clearly not in the public interest. Therefore, airing undisclosed VNRs violates the terms of stations' licenses, as well as the Act.

Whether current laws and regulations mandate VNR disclosure is not an academic question. If the FCC were to begin actively requiring VNR disclosure, all TV stations—broadcast and cable—could be impacted. Moreover, all VNRs—whether funded by public or private entities—would likely be covered. This is important because, as of mid-2007, all of the disclosure measures debated and passed by Congress apply to government VNRs only, though corporations fund the vast majority of VNRs. In 2004, the chair of the Medialink Worldwide firm told a trade magazine that government agencies account for only 5 percent of his business.

It is possible that new rules, legislation, and/or court decisions may be necessary to clarify TV stations' obligations with regard to VNR disclosure. This is not surprising, and may well be the best way for Congress and the FCC to catch up to what's been a common PR and media practice for decades.

DEFENDERS OF THE STATUS QUO

As might be expected, the PR firms that produce VNRs don't want independent oversight of their industry. Broadcasters' groups have taken a similar stance. As controversies about undisclosed VNRs have surfaced periodically over the years, these groups have steadfastly promoted industry self-regulation and opposed any government action.

In 1991, the nonprofit organization Consumers Union released a report titled, "Are Video News Releases Blurring the Line Between News and Advertising?" In 1992, *TV Guide* ran a cover story on VNRs titled "Fake News." In an accompanying editorial, *TV Guide* suggested that "when a TV news organization includes film or tape prepared by an outside source in a broadcast, the label 'VIDEO SUPPLIED BY [COMPANY OR GROUP NAME]' should be visible for as long as the material is on screen."

In response, the Public Relations Society of America (PRSA) promoted a voluntary "Code of Good Practice for Video News Releases." Medialink Worldwide's Larry Moskowitz explained at the time, "When you see a potential problem, whether real or imagined, you respond. We're taking a page right out of the crisis management textbooks."

In 2004, after the Government Accountability Office found some government VNRs to be covert propaganda, PRSA suggested that publicists not use the word "reporting" when narrating VNRs. In June 2005, PRSA called for "vigorous self-regulation by all those involved at every level in the production and dissemination of prepackaged broadcast materials."

On behalf of broadcasters, the Radio-Television News Directors Association (RTNDA) issued new ethical guidelines for VNR use, following the March 2005 *New York Times* exposé on Bush administration VNRs. In June 2005, RTNDA told the FCC that an "informal survey" of its members had confirmed their adherence to voluntary disclosure standards. Shortly afterwards, RTNDA president Barbara Cochran compared VNRs to the Loch Ness Monster, telling the *Washington Times*, "Everyone talks about it, but not many people have actually seen it."

In 2006, following the first part of the Center for Media and

Democracy's study and the FCC's subsequent launch of its VNR investigation, fourteen PR firms announced the formation of a new lobbying group, the National Association of Broadcast Communicators. The group subsequently issued joint statements with PRSA, objecting to the FCC investigation. RTNDA went further, asking the FCC to halt its investigation and claiming that the Center for Media and Democracy was "unrelenting in its hostility to free speech and a free press." The PR industry and broadcasters' groups additionally claimed that any VNR disclosure requirements would abridge broadcasters' First Amendment rights and impede the "free flow of information."

Of course, these groups' main motivations for opposing VNR disclosure are slightly less lofty than their public pronouncements suggest. "Actions that the Federal Communications Commission (FCC) may take with regard to broadcasters could have the effect of reducing the number of broadcasters that air our clients' material," warned Medialink Worldwide's 2006 annual report. "Any actions by the FCC on this matter . . . could reduce the effectiveness of certain of our services and therefore could have a material adverse effect on our business, operating results, and financial condition."

More objective observers, such as Australian academic Peter Simmons, have raised questions about "the quality of the information flowing freely to the public." Simmons wrote, "When information flows as news, the public's interest is best served when it can make decisions about the credibility of the information based on clear identification of the source and balanced discussion of motives." This echoes the FCC's stated principle, that "listeners and viewers are entitled to know who seeks to persuade them."

US public opinion is not only pro-VNR disclosure; it's pro-*mandated* disclosure. In 2005, PRSA commissioned a poll that included the following question: "Television news programs sometimes show stories that are not produced by a news organization, but come from companies, government, or other types of organizations. These stories are created to communicate a particular position or message to the public. Do you think government should require TV news shows to state the sources for these stories, or not?" Seventy-one percent of the members of the general public, 87 percent of Congressional staffers, and a whopping 89 percent of corporate executives surveyed said yes, the government *should* ensure disclosure.

For some reason, PRSA chose not to highlight this finding in its summary or promotion of the poll results.

ALL THE WORLD'S A SCREEN

While the debate over TV stations' VNR disclosure responsibilities continues—mostly in corporate boardrooms and lobbyist suites—PR firms are increasingly exploring online venues for VNRs, including news websites, video blogs, video search engines, video podcasts, and cell phones. "Hurt by public criticism of VNRs, possible Federal Communications Commission oversight, and a shrunken news hole, these companies are looking for ways to survive," the trade publication *PR Week* reported in December 2006. "Making the Internet a bigger part of their offerings could be the answer."

"If Shakespeare were alive today he might have written 'All the World's a Screen,'" quipped Larry Moskowitz. In addition to more traditional VNR packages, Medialink offers "broadcast media tours" that simultaneously target radio and television outlets, websites, cell phones and other media platforms, using webcasts, podcasts, video blogs and video sharing sites like YouTube.

"Podcasting is becoming perhaps a greater-use element of [VNRs] than broadcasting," observed Jack Trammell, the president of the firm VNR-1 Communications. Another PR firm, On the Scene Productions, "created a network of twenty viral video sites dubbed 'Christine, On the Scene,' to which all of its projects are automatically sent," including YouTube, Friendster, and MySpace, reported *PR Week*.

Ironically, newspapers are among the top online targets for VNRs. "Newspaper Web sites are hungry for video content," said Shoba Purushothaman of the NewsMarket firm. The high-tech PR firm Text 100 has gone farther, bragging that it is "the first public relations agency to establish a presence inside Second Life," a virtual world and rapidly growing online community.

PR professionals believe that focusing on online communications will allow them to better target audiences, while limiting potential government oversight. From a public interest perspective, this is a troubling proliferation of fake news. Unlike the VNRs streaming into TV newsrooms, those posted online often don't make clear what they are or who paid for them. Unlike television, Internet news providers are not licensed and therefore cannot be held accountable by government regulators for non-disclosure of sponsored material.

The fake news problem has become so large that it requires a multi-pronged approach to address it. "Old media" disclosure requirements must be clarified and strengthened, so that VNRs aired during newscasts (as well as broadcasts of other sponsored content) are clearly disclosed. The FCC should also require TV stations to keep information about their VNR broadcasts in their public file. Congress should require government agencies to post all VNRs funded with taxpayer money on publicly available websites. At the very least, Congress must make permanent its temporary and expired measures mandating disclosure of government-funded broadcast material.

In addition, more information should be gathered on the intrusion of fake news into "new media," so that effective online disclosure standards can be developed. Lastly, there must be a serious, wide-ranging public discussion of news providers' responsibilities, and what it means in the digital age to have the right to know "who seeks to persuade" you.

It is possible to banish government and corporate propagandists from the public airwaves, and to check their rapid intrusion into online media. Even partial victories are important in the fight against fake news and will create more space for genuine reporting that reflects the realities and priorities of our communities.

Diane Farsetta is a Senior Researcher at the Center for Media and Democracy. www.prwatch.org

Source: Fake TV News: Widespread and Undisclosed: A multimedia report on television newsrooms' use of material provided by PR firms on behalf of paying clients. www.prwatch.org/fakenews/execsummary.

CHAPTER 10

Fear and Favor 2006
Institutionalizing Conflict of Interest

by Janine Jackson

"Fear and favor" describes the various pushes and pulls on journalists to use something other than journalistic values in producing the news.

The intense corporatization of media makes the precise contours of such compromise difficult to trace. Pressure to cut costs and please financially powerful players is, as it were, "in the air" in corporate America; who can say how far into the journalistic process such budgetary concerns intrude?

One practice employed by the Fort Myers, Florida-based *News-Press* is to have ad salespeople, drumming up sponsors for an upcoming story, be accompanied on sales calls by the reporter, as reported in the *Washington Post* (12/4/06): "The logic: The reporter understands the project and can explain it best to potential advertisers." Keeping reporters away from the business side of the paper is "old-school snobbery," says *News-Press* managing editor Mackenzie Warren.

There is, then, the question of how long we can speak of the "encroachment" of non-journalistic values, when journalistic outlets themselves seek out situations they ought to avoid, and relationships that ought to be eschewed are instead institutionalized without apology, such as with Los Angeles Univision station KMEX's "partnership" with healthcare provider Kaiser Permanente Southern California. The deal goes well beyond a single segment: Kaiser physicians are interviewed on a range of topics on KMEX's various news programs, news footage is shot at Kaiser facilities, and news segments feature Kaiser patients and support groups (*Hollywood Reporter*, 3/16/06).

A Univision spokesperson described the Kaiser deal as "a win-win for both of us." The "us," it must be noted, does not include the viewers, since the paid-for plugs, dubbed "integrations," are not disclosed as such. "Typically news isn't for sale because you need to maintain your integrity," the spokesperson continued. "However, you also need to be creative to find ways to include your advertisers without damaging your credibility."

If following up a basic credo of journalism with "however" is a sign of the times, it isn't the whole story. Some journalists seem to find the slope less slippery than others. When Scripps Howard News Service (SHNS) discovered that one of its columnists, Michael Fumento, had received payments from Monsanto—the subject of frequent, glowing praise in Fumento's writings—it severed its relationship with him. In a formal statement printed in *Business Week* (1/13/06), SHNS explained that Fumento "did not tell SHNS editors, and therefore we did not tell our readers, that in 1999, Hudson [Institute, where Fumento was a senior fellow] received a $60,000 grant from Monsanto. Our policy is that he should have disclosed that information. We apologize to our readers." Seems simple enough.

As always, we note that our list is, sadly, far from comprehensive.

IN ADVERTISERS WE TRUST

➤ In 2006, Wal-Mart trumpeted a new policy extending employees a 10 percent discount on a single item during the holidays ("beyond the normal 10 percent employee discount," as the December 4 *New York Times* helpfully explained). The policy struck James Murren, a columnist at the Hanover, Pennsylvannia-based *Evening Sun*, as funny. "Are you kidding me? Next to Exxon-Mobil, Wal-Mart is the biggest profit-making company in the world, and their 1.3 million employees only get 10 percent off that Made in China thingy-ma-bob?" Murren wrote in a December 10 column headlined, "Shaft Your Workers, Gag Your Critics: Wal-Mart's Holiday Cheer." The column was Murren's last for the paper.

"One column critical of Wal-Mart in my 10 years and the editor with no backbone submits to them," Murren told *CounterPunch* (12/19/06). Readers were given no explanation for his disappearance from the paper.

➤ "We essentially let the government of Australia become our news directors." That was the description of one "appalled" staffer, who "declined to be named, fearing retribution," of Bay Area TV station KRON's "Australia Week," a five-day production in which three hours of the station's five-hour morning newscast were converted, essentially, to a travel brochure. With travel, food, and lodging all paid for by Tourism Australia, KRON reporters produced segments promoting the glories of, for example, seeing Sydney by hot-air balloon, or shopping for Australian fish. One segment was simply a sit-down with an Australian tourism official.

The deal may have appalled some reporters, but it was increasingly par for the course at KRON, where so-called integration deals have proliferated since the station was bought by Young Broadcasting six years ago. In that time, a station once known for a "deep bench of reporting talent, in-depth stories and documentaries" (*San Francisco Chronicle,* 4/5/06) has been host to the likes of February 2006's "Spa Spectacular"; spas that were featured all paid a fee, in addition to buying ads, and station anchors hawked spa coupons at the end of each segment.

It's easy to cringe at the rationalizations of KRON general manager Mark Antonitis, who appears to have coined the term "win-win-win" to describe such arrangements. "We bring on people all the time to talk about books, products, and interesting new ideas anyway," Antonitis told Reuters (3/5/06). "So if we can have the added benefit of a new revenue source and give something to our viewers that they wouldn't be able to get otherwise, and advertisers get their products advertised, it's a win-win-win."

Less humorous is his contention that such deals are the lesser of two evils: "I really don't like to lay people off, and there are lots of families that are counting on me to protect them from the ups and downs of the economic cycle."

➤ WTVH news anchor Maureen Green saw no problem with serving as "tour host" on a ten-day Hawaii trip, organized by a Wisconsin company that charges up to $4,499 per person (Syracuse *Post Standard,* 3/13/06): "It's not a sales vehicle as far as I'm concerned." Others disagree, citing the fact that Green's travel costs, and those of her son who accompanied her, were paid by the tour company, which promoted the tour heavily on WTVH. Les Vann, Green's general manager, shares her view that conflict of interest is all a matter of how you feel. "I think it's ridiculous for anyone to think someone would lose their journalistic objectivity for being on a trip for ten days," charged Vann, who acknowledged that the station also received "some financial benefit" from the tour company, while declining to provide details.

➤ What do you call it when a TV news program accepts free "deluxe guest rooms" from a hotel, for its anchors (wine and chocolate included), in exchange for broadcasting its show from the hotel?

"That would be like a trade, I guess," was how Carolyn Aguayo, spokesperson for Los Angeles station KTLA, put it in the *Pasadena Star-News* (2/28/06).

The "trade" meant that viewers of KTLA's *Morning Show* program on February 23 were regaled with details of the amenities to be found at Pasadena's newly renovated Ritz-Carlton Huntington Hotel; they were treated to interviews with the hotel's general manager, and with its chef, who prepared braised short ribs on air. Viewers were not, however, treated to the information that the news program had done the segment in exchange for free accommodation and goodies.

That nondisclosure didn't jibe so well with the statement of *Morning Show* executive producer Rich Goldner in the *Los Angeles Times* (3/1/06): "We're not trying to hide anything here, and the viewer knows that." Goldner told the *Times* (which, like KTLA, is owned by the Tribune Company) that "the important thing to remember here is that we are always in control of the content."

But for those not consoled to learn that a news program needs no inducement for this sort of PR-driven fare, Goldner offered another, seemingly contradictory, explanation: "People often come to us with these things. We don't go to them." Whichever it is, with such a slippery grasp of conflicts of interest, Goldner's most confusing remark may have been this declaration: "If there's something we don't like or feel is inappropriate, we won't put it on the air. . . . We're a news show."

➤ When *San Francisco,* a prize-winning magazine that began forty years ago as *San Francisco Focus,* was bought by Modern Luxury Media, a publisher more devoted to style than substance, there were doubters. "Combining investigative journalism and lifestyles of the rich and famous is an oxymoron," magazine industry analyst Samir

Husni told the *San Francisco Chronicle* (11/20/05). "Sooner or later, they are going to find themselves in conflict."

Make that sooner. In January 2006, the new *San Francisco* killed a story just before publication, apparently out of fear of offending an advertiser (*San Francisco Chronicle*, 1/13/06). Modern Luxury CEO Michael Kong refused comment, but *San Francisco's* editor and executive editor unhappily confirmed the spiking of freelancer Peter Byrne's report on sexual harassment lawsuits against the Sacramento-area Thunder Valley Casino. *San Francisco* president Steven Dinkelspiel explained that "multiple factors come into play" in such decisions, but declined to say whether the full-page ad in the magazine's December issue for Red Rock Resort, owned—like Thunder Valley—by the Station Casinos chain, represented one of those factors.

A former editor of *San Francisco Focus* was unamused. "I don't think of myself as the Lone Ranger," John Burks, now chair of the journalism department at San Francisco State University, told the *Chronicle*. "But if you're going to do that, why do journalism? Why not just put out catalogs?"

POWERFUL PLAYERS & PR

➤ News staffers at Atlanta's WGCL (CBS-46) say that, after a heated exchange between one of their reporters and Georgia Governor Sonny Perdue, a Perdue aide threatened to withhold $500,000 in campaign advertising if footage of the incident aired (*Creative Loafing*, 12/13/06). WGCL reporter Wendy Saltzman had repeatedly confronted the governor about a policy that had removed about 2,200 severely ill children from Georgia's Medicaid program. Responding to her persistent inquiries at a press conference, Perdue told Saltzman, "We've addressed that with you, and I think probably from the way you've approached this subject you might want to think about some other markets like Chattanooga and Columbia and Tallahassee."

After that, WGCL staffers claim, Perdue's office mentioned pulling advertising. Perdue's then–chief of staff, John Watson, denied any threat but confirmed that he spoke to the station's general manager and news director, to "register our disgruntlement about" Saltzman, who had "invaded the governor's space."

In any event, Perdue's testy outburst did not air, nor did

Saltzman's planned follow-up segments on the Medicaid story. "Wendy was told," claimed one staffer, "that we could lose more money than the station spends on investigative reporting."

➤ The *Sacramento Bee* describes Jeff Kagan as "an independent telecommunications analyst in Atlanta" (12/21/06)—as do the *Detroit Free Press* (11/1/06), *Chicago Daily Herald* (7/17/06), *Philadelphia Inquirer* (4/21/06), *Denver Post* (4/17/06), *Rocky Mountain News* (2/15/06), Jackson (Miss.) *Clarion-Ledger* (2/12/06), and *Washington Times* (1/6/06).

Kagan does live in Atlanta and is an analyst, but independent? Not so much. Actually, Kagan receives a fee (reportedly typically $10,000 a month) from companies like Sprint and Bell South to speak to the media about the telecommuniucations companies and their industry. These outlets "rarely if ever mention the financial ties," reported the *New York Post*'s Tim Arango (5/3/06). Arango included his own paper among those that cited Kagan's "expertise" minus the information his own Web site boasts prominently: "Kagan is a 'fee-based' analyst."

For his part, Kagan says reporters sometimes ask whether he has an "investment relationship" with the companies he talks about, but virtually never inquire if he's actually on the payroll.

➤ When your computer crashes, you get it fixed, end of story. But for David Pogue, *New York Times* online tech columnist and CBS News contributor, his hard drive crash was just the start of the story—several stories, in fact, that Pogue wrote for NPR, the *New York Times* and CBS, featuring DriveSavers, the company that retrieved his data. DriveSavers, for its part, waived Pogue's $2,000 bill. Such a deal is, fairly obviously, a no-no, and was labeled as such by *SF Weekly*'s Matt Smith in a widely circulated piece (3/15/06), leading to a rare on-air apology from CBS's Charles Osgood (3/12/06).

Pogue went on to claim (*SF Weekly*, 4/5/06) that CBS knew about the trade in advance. A CBS spokesperson begged to differ, as did the *New York Times* representative asked about Pogue's contention that "the *Times* has no policy on services. I can send you copies of the ethical guidelines, and there's absolutely no reference to what to do about reviewing services." "David Pogue had apparently misunderstood the policy," countered the *Times*' Diane McNulty. "And his editor told him so."

THE BOSS'S BUSINESS

➤ "A poster child for the evils of corporate synergy" is how Mark Jurkowitz of the *Boston Phoenix* (5/3/06) described a *Boston Globe* front-pager hyping a "VIP travel package" offered by *Globe* corporate sibling the Boston Red Sox. Filled with photos and straight-from-the-press-release lines like "the biggest selling point is perhaps the Sox's access to players," the piece merely masqueraded as a news story, Jurkowitz wrote. And, he added, "the story's disclosure of the New York Times Company's 17 percent interest in the ball club in the 15th paragraph on the jump page doesn't cut the mustard as a get-out-of-jail-free card."

➤ Readers of the *Miami Herald* may have wondered why the paper appeared so fascinated by the story of Philip Blumberg, a local businessman and civic leader who fell from grace with a January 2006 arrest for drug possession. The story was newsworthy, certainly, but the *Herald*'s focus—a series of prominent reports culminating in a lengthy profile (4/9/06) replete with embarrassing details about Blumberg's private life—struck some as a bit obsessive (*CJR*, 7–8/06). Among those taking note, evidently, were Blumberg's lawyers; it may have been their efforts that resulted in the paper running a "disclosure" (4/9/06) letting readers in on the fact that Knight Ridder, the *Miami Herald*'s parent, was involved in an ongoing and bitter dispute with Blumberg over a failed business partnership.

➤ "A suggestion for Fox 5: Why not just put Jack Bauer in the anchor's chair?" That was one commentator's exasperated conclusion (*CJR Daily*, 3/29/06) after monitoring the New York City Fox affiliate's incessant promotion of the torture-friendly show *24*—aired, perhaps needless to say, on the Fox network.

One newscast (3/29/06) began with an announcer intoning: "Next. It's *24*'s secret weapon. It's not the dialogue or the surprising plot twists. The one thing you see on *24* that you don't see on most other shows." Minutes into the broadcast, viewers got another tease from the entertainment reporter ("We can't get enough of it because *24* dares to do what no other network show will") before the newscast's anchors asked viewers to "Sound Off" on the pressing question: "What do *you* think is the real secret weapon on 24 that makes the show such a success?"

Another broadcast promised to probe "the real reason 24 is better than ever, next at ten," though viewers were actually forced to endure more teases, as well as some actual news, before reporter Toni Senecal's report, forty-three minutes after the hour, exploring the "lots of reasons the show is such a huge success." Nonstop, unapologetic flackery from network affiliates apparently did not make the list.

➤ *Columbia Journalism Review* (5–6/06) offered a critical "dart" to *Variety*, for leaving something out of their "full-throated" review of the Hollywood remake of the movie *Fun With Dick and Jane*: namely, the fact that Peter Bart, the trade magazine's editor in chief, was a producer of both the new film and the original. Headlined the media review: "Impart Bart's Part in Art, Sez Dart."

➤ Geoff Dougherty says he got into journalism "because it seemed like a good way to raise hell" (*Chi-Town Daily News*, 2/7/06). That goal was evidently not appreciated by Dougherty's bosses at the *Chicago Tribune*, where he worked as a reporter until 2005, or more precisely, until he wrote an article on CEO salaries. "As I crunched the numbers," he recalled, "it became apparent that [*Tribune* CEO Dennis] FitzSimons' pay would figure prominently in the article. It seemed like an article we needed to publish, even if it would reflect negatively on the *Tribune*'s top exec." Seemed to Dougherty, that is. Thirty-six hours before publication, Dougherty's piece was killed without explanation, his follow-up questions gaining him nothing but "months of evasive corporate-speak." Dougherty's definition of journalism didn't change, just his idea of where he could do it. He resigned from the paper and reported the story—of FitzSimons' pay and of how the *Tribune* kept its readers from learning about it—for his own new Web site, the *Chi-Town Daily News*.

FRONTIERS OF FREE ENTERPRISE

By definition, of course, advertisers are always involved in commercial news media. Still, new ways to involve advertisers are continually being invented, and with each new technique, there are those who embrace it (with or without a show of resistance), and those for whom it is simply too much.

What about the idea of selling news stories by the word? A *Wall Street Journal* article (11/27/06) found mixed reactions to the proposal. Forbes.com said no, after finding "our editorial staff was very uncomfortable with the concept." But FoxNews.com said, why not? So those reading a story on the site about, say, former House Speaker Dennis Hastert would find the word "speaker" double-underlined, and clicking on it would bring readers an ad for the Ask.com search service, promising more information on "speakers."

The *Atlanta Journal-Constitution* was on board ("You have to try new things," says the paper's Internet VP, Hyde Post), as was *Popular Mechanics*—no matter that the results can be somewhat jarring, as when a story on "How to Survive a Riot" (5/04) included the sentence "stay away from the windows," with the word "windows" serving double-duty as a plug for the Microsoft operating system.

The fact that the news department doesn't know which words are for sale means there's "definitely a firewall there," claimed a spokesperson for Fox (and Ask.com isn't really an advertiser because they help people "find out more information about a topic").

If in-text advertising has a hint of brave new world, another threat to the integrity of online journalism is more familiar, and potentially more ominous. Google, the ubiquitous search engine, has found a way to satisfy the perennial desire of sponsors to control the context in which their ads appear, and specifically to avoid running ads next to controversial content.

Google's AdSense service, which places ads on thousands of websites and blogs, has become a significant source of revenue for some online outlets. Advertisers appreciate the service's ability to match up ads with related content (airline ads with travel stories, etc.), but, just as in other media, there are some stories they literally don't want to get near. In 2003, in response to advertisers' concerns, Google developed "sensitivity filters" that scan partner sites for "unacceptable" material; ads found near content deemed offensive are replaced with public service announcements, and the site loses the revenue.

According to Chris Thompson of *East Bay Express* ("Publishers vs. the Censorbot," 8/2/06), the effect has been felt at a range of outlets: *Salon* found itself seeking other "partners" after Google pulled ads from stories on British attitudes toward rape victims and a Senate hearing on pornography, while the one-person blog SilflayHraka.com lost all its Google ads the day its host posted a message headlined "Have You Boycotted Sony Products Yet?"

Most serious is the potential effect on smaller news sites. Thompson interviewed a publisher from "a prominent news Web site" who would only speak anonymously. When his site ran a series of stories about a major bombing in Iraq, the source claims, the Google ads disappeared within hours: "They said we had the word 'kill' on our site, and that killed the ads." Complaining that as a news site they could hardly avoid such topics, the publisher says he was told, "Those are the rules." Google accounts for a third of the site's revenue.

Google would not provide a list of "forbidden" words. Spokesperson Shuman Ghosemajumder told Thompson, "We're not trying to create very specific rules so much as we're trying to determine, 'What is the topic of a particular story such that viewers would have a negative reaction?'" In the end, Thompson noted, Ghosemajumder acknowledged that "some stories may be too unpleasant to be paired with paying advertisers."

Janine Jackson is FAIR's program director and a frequent contributor to FAIR's magazine, *Extra!* She coedited *The FAIR Reader: An Extra! Review of Press and Politics in the '90s* (Westview Press). And she cohosts and produces FAIR's syndicated radio show, *CounterSpin*—a weekly program of media criticism airing on more than 130 stations around the country.

CHAPTER II

The Right to Blog
Index on Censorship Annual Report

by Jo Glanville

The prosecution and imprisonment of bloggers is one of the more chilling developments of the past year. The extraordinary freedom offered by the Web that has led to such flowering of comment, information, writing, and activism has inevitably resulted in a clampdown. As bloggers tend to be young, and as the Internet has provided a unique forum for new voices, there is something particularly disturbing about this new branch of censorship. It is, however, the same old game, with the usual charges, but more sinister is the enthusiasm with which authoritarian regimes have embraced the new technology of the Web, wanting all the economic benefits of the boom, while stifling the emergence of a more open society. Their success in having their cake and eating it is deeply depressing for anyone who saw the Internet as boundary-breaking for free speech and as a circumvention of the stranglehold of repressive governments.

Let's focus on Egypt, where bloggers have been making a notable political impact and are now in the grip of a backlash. In the spring of 2006, activist and blogger Mohamed el-Sharqawi, was arrested, raped, and beaten. At the time of writing, no action has been taken to investigate the assault—one lawyer described it as the worst case of police abuse in more than a decade. According to Human Rights Watch, el-Sharqawi has since been accused, along with other bloggers, of "spreading false news" that could harm Egypt's image abroad and of organizing demonstrations.

All of the accused actively use their blogs to campaign against police brutality, causing alarm to the powers that be. They are bringing stories which would otherwise be suppressed to the attention of Egyptian—and international—society. In November 2006, footage was posted on the Internet of an Egyptian bus driver being sodomized by the police, leading to the arrest of two officers. It was also bloggers who broke the 2006 story of the shocking mass assault on women on the streets of Cairo. Bloggers not only report—they bring evidence by taking pictures and filming events.

The crackdown on bloggers forms part of a wider move against the growing campaign for democracy and reform which began in May 2006. Two judges, Hisham el-Bastawisi and Mahmoud Mekki, faced a disciplinary hearing that spring for speaking out against electoral fraud. Demonstrations and confrontations with police followed as President Mubarak extended the Emergency Law, which bans public protest and allows authorities to detain individuals indefinitely without charge. Here, too, bloggers have continued to hold Egypt accountable by filming and reporting police behavior at demonstrations.

Later last year, the twenty-two-year-old Egyptian blogger Abdul Kareem Nabeel Suleiman (who wrote under the name Kareem Amer) was charged with insulting Islam, defaming the president, and "spreading information disruptive of the social order." He has been sentenced to four years—the first blogger to be imprisoned in Egypt. Index on Censorship awarded him a 2006 Freedom of Expression prize.

The next target was journalist and blogger Abdel Moneim Mahmoud, who was arrested and charged with belonging to a banned organization and funding an armed group. He was later released. Mahmoud is a member of the Muslim Brotherhood, and as elections approached in the summer of 2007, the Egyptian government turned up the pressure. Mahmoud has also criticized the government for its human rights record—in particular, torture. Other bloggers have been summoned for questioning during the year by prosecutors, following the launch of a criminal libel suit by a senior Egyptian judge, Abdel Fattah Mourad.

At first, Abdel Fattah Mourad gave the impression of being enlightened. When a young blogger, Amr Gharbeia, saw that the judge had written a book about the Internet, *The Scientific and Legal Foundations of Blogs*, he was initially excited by this discovery— Gharbeia had been active in campaigning for an independent judiciary and felt that he might have found an ally. So he contacted the judge and said that he wanted to write a review. However, when Gharbeia began reading, he was disappointed—and shocked. The 800-page book was far from being blogger-friendly. While some parts of the book appeared to support freedom of expression, others constituted a guide to prosecuting bloggers. He also discovered, as he read more closely, that figures he had himself given to a human rights organization, the Arabic Network for Human Rights Information, for a report on Internet freedom, had been quoted without citing the source. Whole pages from the report had been incorporated without being properly referenced.

Following Gharbeia's discovery, the Arabic Network for Human Rights made a public protest and the judge hit back with all his legal force. He filed a lawsuit calling for the blocking of twenty-one "terrorist" Egyptian Web sites (largely political reform and human rights Web sites and blogs), claiming that they tarnished the reputation of the Egyptian government and insulted the Egyptian president. Protests against the judge developed into a wide campaign, supported by the pillars of Egyptian civil society. The judge then expanded his lawsuit to include fifty Web sites, including our own Index on Censorship Web site.

What appears to be a petty, personal vendetta has very serious implications for freedom of expression and for Egypt's chances of becoming a less repressive society.

The campaign has also taken its toll. Human rights activists pulled together in a show of great solidarity, but as Gharbeia says, "After two years of blogging protests, and now legal problems, I am running out of steam for this kind of Web and street activism."

The Internet has provided Egypt's young activists with a fabulous tool for challenging an authoritarian regime. As blogger Noura Younis commented on her Web site, "To have uncontrollable bloggers in Egypt who shape public opinion and force topics of torture, sexual harassment, corruption, and election falsification on mainstream media is not something a police state would accept. State security in Egypt controls Egypt." The government can block or shut down Web sites considered a threat to "national security." Some bloggers have
given up the fight and abandoned their sites, including Hala Helmy Botros, who closed down her own blog, Copts Without Borders, which monitored persecution of the Christian Coptic minority. Botros was harassed by the authorities, made the subject of a judicial investigation, and banned from leaving the country.

One hopes that this season on bloggers will be short-lived and that the dynamic Web-based movement in Egypt will prove to be a resilient new form of activism and free expression, and a forum for change. Dissenters can no longer be removed quietly in the night—there is an international network not only alerting the world to events, but publicly shaming the methods of repressive governments. Egypt has a relatively benign international image in contrast to Iran or Syria, chiefly because it has not been in America's interests to ostracize President Mubarak. Its recent record shows that it's high time that the rest of the world revised its opinion.

With special thanks to Amr Gharbeia

INDEX INDEX

"Index index" is a regularly updated chronicle of free expression violations worldwide, logged by Index on Censorship and published in the magazine. Here are selections from just some of the entries for the more than ninety countries we tracked in 2006.

AFGHANISTAN

Two German journalists were killed in the northern part of the country by supposed Taliban fighters on October 7. Karen Fischer and Christian Struwe of the Deutsche Welle network were conducting research for a documentary.

AZERBAIJAN

Nijat Huseynov, a journalist for the leading opposition daily Azadlig, was beaten and stabbed by four assailants outside his home on December 25. The attack occurred in broad daylight, and the attackers made no effort to cover their faces. Huseynov's jacket bears the marks of the stabbing and the fingerprints of some of the attackers, but it has still not been registered as evidence by the police.

BELARUS

Thirteen journalists from the independent media were placed under administrative detention for fifteen days following disputed elections in Belarus. The thirteen were Aliaxey Shein, arrested on March 20; Igor Banster, Andrzej Pisalnik, Yuri Chavusau, Alexy Rads, and

Dzmitry Hurnevich, arrested on March 21; Andrey Dynko, Vadim Aleksandrovitch, and Andrij Lukka, arrested on March 22; Ivan Roman, Viktor Yarashuk, Anton Tavas, and Sergey Salash, arrested on March 23. The Belarusian Association of Journalists alleged "very serious attacks on press freedom" during the campaign.

CAMBODIA

On November 27, police in Phnom Penh prevented protestors for freedom of expression from entering a park in front of the national assembly building. The protestors, led by the Alliance for Freedom of Expression in Cambodia, intended to fly one hundred kites bearing an "f" symbolizing freedom of expression. Deputy Governor for the Daun Penh District Pich Socheata claimed AFEC didn't have a permit for the protest and that it was in danger of disturbing public order. During negotiation proceedings, around forty armed police seized the kites.

CHAD

In an attempt to constrain the onslaught of ethnic violence spilling over from Darfur, Chad's government declared a state of emergency on November 13. Heavy media censorship was introduced, including prohibition of radio broadcasts thought to "threaten public order," enforced by newly appointed special officials. Communications Minister Hourmadji Moussa Doumgor accused the media of disseminating false reports. Doumgor also alleged that some newspapers were passing information to Arab militias, who have stirred up conflict between Arab and non-Arab communities in the eastern part of the country.

CHILE

On May 31, six reporters were injured and detained as they covered student protests demanding more state investment in the education system. Among them was Julio Oliva, editor of the weekly *El Siglo*, who was punched and arrested after trying to help a protester who was hit by a car. More than a million young people joined the protests, which were met with clubs and tear gas. The government later condemned police reaction, sacking the head of the police's paramilitary units.

CHINA

Articles produced by foreign media will require the approval of the Xinhua News Agency under new regulations announced on September 10. It will be an offense to publish articles that, among other things, "endanger China's national security."

COLOMBIA

Reporter Olga Cecilia Vega fled her home in Florencia on February 5 after receiving death threats. The threats came in the wake of her interview with a guerrilla leader, published in the Miami-based newspaper *El Nuevo Herald*. She was the third journalist forced to leave the area in 2006. The government said it planned to take steps to prevent attacks and defend press freedom.

COSTA RICA

On May 3, the Supreme Court rejected a call on behalf of the daily *Extra* newspaper to amend criminal defamation provisions in the country's press law. The 104-year-old clause allows courts to jail journalists for up to 120 days in prison for defamation or insult, and the paper insists the law is in breach of the country's constitution.

CYPRUS

Television reporter Adonis Pallikarides and cameraman Nikitas Dalitis of Sigma TV were arrested and detained on August 25 in the northern region of the country. The Turkish Cypriot journalists were accused of videotaping military installations.

DENMARK

Flemming Rose, the editor who commissioned the controversial cartoons of the Prophet Mohammed, was sent "on leave" after he vowed to reprint cartoons commissioned for an Iranian newspaper lampooning Holocaust victims. He later retracted the promise. Rose, cultural editor of Jyllands-Posten, was urged to take a vacation as a result of the "inhuman pressure" he had suffered, newspaper executives said.

EGYPT

Bloggers have come under renewed attack from the government. Leading bloggers Alaa Seif al-Islam, Alaa Abd El-Fatah, Mohamed Sharkawy, and Karim El-Shaer were among scores of bloggers questioned following protests against the extension of the Emergency Law. Blogger Mohamed el-Sharqawi accused Egyptian security services of sexually abusing and torturing him during an eight-hour ordeal after his arrest at a demonstration on May 25. He had only just been freed from detention following his arrest at an earlier protest on April 29.

ERITREA

At least nine media workers have been arrested since November 12 and are being held at an undisclosed location. The latest crackdown comes following the defection of several journalists holding prominent positions in the Ministry of Information. Those detained by the security forces are accused of being friends or in contact with the defecting journalists, who have recently fled the country.

ESTONIA

A new bill before Parliament called for a ban on the display of Nazi and Soviet symbols, arguing that they incite hatred. Lawmakers also hope to end the practice of waving the Soviet flag at memorial services. While bans on displaying the Nazi swastika are not uncommon among European countries, the hammer and sickle has only seen bans in a few other countries, such as Latvia and Hungary.

FRANCE

Muslim youths armed with iron rods forced a café in Paris to censor an exhibition of cartoons satirizing religious hypocrisy. "Censored" signs were placed over some of the cartoons. One showed a barman serving a drunken man who gives the Muslim honorific "God is great" in thanks.

GERMANY

At the Berlin opera house Deutsche Oper, a controversial production of Mozart's *Idomeneo* that was dropped from the schedule in September has been put back on the program after the opera house's general manager, Kirsten Harms, was widely accused of limiting artistic freedom. The production features a scene showing the severed heads of Mohammed, Jesus, and Buddha. The scene caused controversy since the production's premier in 2003.

IRAN

Rioting broke out in the northern Iranian city of Tabriz on May 19 after the local weekly *Friday Supplement* published a cartoon depicting a cockroach speaking Azeri. Despite the arrest of editor Mehrdad Qassemfar and cartoonist Mana Neyestani, discontent among the country's Azeri ethnic minority spread across the northern part of the country, prompting fierce clashes between protesters and security forces. Several deaths were reported. Officials blocked the Azeri ethnic media from covering the events, detaining Vahid Dargahi, editor of the weekly *Avay Ardabil*; Ali Nazari and Reza Kazemi, editor and managing editor of the weekly *Araz*; Amin Movahedi, a known critic of the Tehran government; and journalist Orouj Amiri, between May 25 and 27.

IRAQ

The death toll of media workers in Iraq has exceeded one hundred. On August 7, Mohammad Abbas Mohammad, editor of Shia-owned *Al Bayinnah Al-Jadida*, was shot dead as he left his Baghdad home; the body of kidnapped journalist Ismail Amin Ali was found on the same date. Among journalists killed recently are Adel Naji al-Mansouri of *Al-Alam*, Riyad Muhammad Ali of *Talafar al-Yawm*, Abdul Wahab Abdul Razeq Ahamad Al Qaisie of *Kol al Dounia*, Riya Atto of *Talafar al Youm*, Adel Naji Al Mansouri of Al Alam TV, freelance photographer Safa Isma'il Enad, and freelance journalist Hadi Anawi al-Joubouri.

ISRAEL

Fadel Shana, a freelance cameraman for Reuters, and Sabbah Hmaida, a cameraman for Media Group, were seriously injured on

August 26 when the armored car they were in was hit by a missile fired by Israeli forces. The vehicle was clearly marked "press."

ITALY

On June 13, the trial of journalist Oriana Fallaci, accused of defaming Islam in a 2004 book, began and was quickly adjourned. Seventy-seven-year-old Fallaci, who lives in New York, did not attend the hearing in the northern town of Bergamo. The charge was brought against her by Adel Smith, head of the Italian Muslim Union, who objected, among other things, to the book's view that Muslims were secretly plotting to conquer Europe through immigration.

KENYA

Masked gunmen believed to be police officers raided Nairobi's *East African Standard* newspaper on March 2. Newspapers were burned, and employees searched and beaten with AK-47s. The raids came after three *Standard* journalists were arrested for publishing articles critical of President Moi Kibaki's handling of corruption scandals. The paper's sister organization, Kenya Television Network, was also raided. The *Standard* published articles about the raid.

MEXICO

On August 9, Enrique Perea Quintanilla, editor of monthly crime magazine *Dos Caras, Una Verdad*, was found dead on the outskirts of Chihuahua with gunshot wounds to his head and chest. Ten journalists have now been killed in Mexico over the last two years.

MONTENEGRO

Poet and author Jevrem Brkovic was attacked by gunmen outside his home on October 25. His driver was killed in the attack. Brkovic was well known as a harsh critic of the Serbian government in the 1990s. He is said to believe that his latest novel, *A Duklja Lover*, which focuses on the criminal underworld, is one of the motives for the attack.

NEPAL

Seven of the 114 journalists arrested while participating in pro-democracy demonstrations on January 20 have yet to be released. They are Bheem Rai of Aujaar, JB Ghale Magar from the Federation of Nepalese Journalists (FNJ), Teekaram Ghimire from Udghosh, Sudarshan Aacharya from White Paper, Bhaktadhwaj Bohara from FNJ, Shyam Shrestha from Mulyankan, and Tej Narayan Sapkota from Yojana.

PALESTINE

Seven Palestinian journalists in Gaza reported receiving death threats linked to their reports on Hamas's performance since taking nominal power in March, according to the Palestinian Journalists' Union on May 1. Hamas spokesman Sami Abu Zuhri denied responsibility, saying the calls were an attempt to "damage Hamas's image." He urged security forces to investigate.

PHILIPPINES

A wave of killings renewed demands for the government to take steps to confront attacks on journalists. On May 3, columnist Nicolas Cervantes was shot dead; radio reporter Paul Manaog was seriously wounded three days later; photographer Albert Orsolini of Saksi Ngayon was shot dead ten days after that in Calcooncan City, and radio journalist Fernando Batul was murdered on May 22. Batul was the forty-second media worker to be killed under President Arroyo's rule, and the fifth this year.

RUSSIA

Well-known journalist Anna Politkovskaia was found shot dead in an elevator in Moscow on October 7. World leaders ranging from former Soviet President Mikhail Gorbachev to then–UN Secretary-General Kofi Annan have denounced the killing and are calling for an investigation. Novaya Gazeta, the paper that Politkovskaia worked for, claims that the murder was politically motivated and tied to Politkovskaia's critical reporting on the Russian government's handling of Chechnya.

RWANDA

The editor of Umoco newspaper, *Bonaventure Bizumuremyi*, is in hiding after receiving a police summons over articles criticizing the president and the judicial system. Another Umoco reporter, Jean-Léonard Rugambage, was released on July 28 after an eleven-month sentence but colleagues continue to be concerned for his safety.

SENEGAL

Pape Cheikh Fall, a correspondent for the private radio station RFM, was attacked on May 5 after he spoke critically of local Islamic leader Cheikh Béthio Thioune. Thioune told the daily *L'Observateur* on April 28, "People who insult me should take responsibility for their actions."

SINGAPORE

In April, the government proposed to extend its control over the media by expanding penal codes to cover offenses by electronic media. The proposed amendments would mean that bloggers and other Internet users who cause racial or religious offense or make statements said to lead to "public mischief" might face a prison sentence or fine for defamation. The changes would also mean that the government could prosecute those living abroad, by making it illegal to abet an offense carried out in the country.

SOMALIA

Swedish freelance photographer Martin Adler was shot dead by a hooded gunman in Mogadishu during a June 23rd demonstration in support of the peace accord between the Somali interim government and the Union of Islamic Courts.

SRI LANKA

Since the resumption of conflict between the army and the rebel Tamil Tigers (LTTE) Movement, hordes of Tamil journalists have been killed, forced into hiding, or prevented from reporting. In the latest effort to curtail press freedom, the Commander of the 512th Army division summoned three editors of Tamil dailies to his Jaffna office on November 6. The editors were allegedly warned not to publish any news related to LTTE, including messages about the Tamil "Heroes Day" on November 27. Army officials also criticized their coverage of the humanitarian crisis in the Jaffna Peninsula, which suggested that military embargoes were largely to blame.

SUDAN

On September 6, National Security Service staff entered Rai-Al-Shaab and ordered the removal of all reports about that day's demonstrations in Khartoum. On September 9, police seized all copies of al-Sudani, saying it was necessary for the safety of journalists after the murder of Mohammed Taha. On September 11, security agents ordered al-Sahafa to remove two articles and an editorial. Agents also seized articles from al-Sudani about recent rioting and ordered the removal of other parts of that day's issue.

SWAZILAND

The country's media have been warned against criticizing the king. On August 24, Information Minister Themba Msibi said media should exercise respect, responding to a radio program in which a human rights lawyer criticized the king's sweeping constitutional powers.

SYRIA

Journalist Adel Mahfouz was arrested and charged on February 7 for writing an article advocating peaceful dialogue instead of violent protests as a means of dealing with cartoons of the Prophet Mohammed. Arrested hours after publication of the article on the independent daily news Web site Rezgar, Mahfouz was charged with insulting public religious sentiment.

THAILAND

The new military regime has tightened its grip on power by banning political party meetings and introducing tough new controls on the media. The regime had already dissolved parliament and banned gatherings of more than five people. Among tighter media controls are the closing of 300 community radio stations. A Web site set up to encourage Thais to air their views on the coup, www.19sep.com, was shut down within twenty-four hours of its establishment.

TURKEY

On November 17, a court in Istanbul banned the publication and distribution of the pro-Kurdish newspaper, *Ülkede Özgür Gündem*, for fifteen days pending investigation into the nature of certain articles. Prosecutors claimed that the newspaper had openly praised the outlawed Kurdistan Workers' Party (PKK) and had published statements by its leaders. Delivering its decision, the court claimed that the newspaper had abused its freedom of speech and was promoting terrorist propaganda.

UNITED KINGDOM

On October 27, the Ministry of Defense banned ITV news from all its facilities, including reports from embedded journalists, effectively banning ITV from frontline reporting. The disagreement came following a series of news reports about arrangements to treat injured soldiers alongside civilians through the National Health Service. The reports followed similar claims issued by the new chief of defense staff General Sir Richard Dannatt, in the *Daily Mail*, that military personnel should be treated in dedicated wards.

UNITED STATES

The Supreme Court refused to overturn a lower court's order that the *New York Times* turn over phone records to the government on November 27. The records reveal the source of a leak within the government that provided the paper with information on the government's freeze on the accounts of charities suspected of terrorist connections shortly after 9/11.

ZIMBABWE

On May 26, the government officially announced its proposed Interception of Communication Bill 2006. If passed by parliament, the bill will make it legal for state agencies to spy upon and intercept telephone conversations, post, and e-mail messages of private citizens.

Jo Glanville is the editor for Index on Censorship in London.

SOURCES

Africa Free Media Foundation, Agence France-Presse, Amnesty International, ARTICLE 19, Associated Press, the *Baltic Times*, BBC, Center for Media Reform and Responsibility, Committee to Protect

Journalists, EurasiaNet.org, the *Guardian*, International Federaton of Journalists, International Relations and Security Network, Media Institute of Southern Africa, Press Gazette, Radio Free Europe, Reuters, Reporters Sans Frontieres, Southeast Asian Press Alliance, *Sudan Tribune*, Turan, Voice of America, Writers in Prison Committee/International PEN, Xinhua News Agency

CHAPTER 12

Promising Practices to Protect Children from the Increasing Power of Big Media

by Jacques Brodeur

Civil society in North America has developed strategies to oppose child-abusing techniques used by the marketing industry. The struggle to reduce the influence of advertising and violent entertainment on children and teens has led to victories that have obtained little or no coverage by the press.

INTRODUCTION

Over the last half century, while some industries polluted air, water, and food, the marketing industry increasingly poisoned children's cultural environment. After decades of efforts by civil society, governments have been forced to regulate our physical environment. But few governments have shown the capacity to regulate the use of marketing that targets children. The increasing power of the media on public opinion has instilled such fear on decision makers that very few have dared to take action. This has left the industry free to decide what children will watch on television, what products will be offered to entertain them, what strategies will be used to manipulate their wishes, desires, values, and understanding of life. With concentration of ownership, a handful of conglomerates now control 85 percent of all media.[1] These conglomerates have become the "hidden departments of global culture."[2] They control information, which gives them the privilege to decide what will be marketed to children. After witnessing the increasing amount of insidious and sophisticated advertising carried by television, more citizens have searched for and experienced ways to protect children from these media. The increasing power of the media over children has inspired resistance from parents, teachers, child rights advocates, and citizens in all regions of North America.[3] Some underreported promising practices have been experienced in Canada and in the US.

THE PURPOSE OF TELEVISION

Television does not exist primarily to inform and entertain. Television is basically a commercial industry that sells viewers to advertisers. Patrick Le Lay, President and Director of French TV network TF1, declared in 2004 that the role of television is essentially to sell brain time to Coca-Cola.[4] To maximize benefits, broadcasters constantly search for various ways to attract and sell more viewers to advertisers who will then agree to pay more to reach them. This type of business is frightening when those for sale are children.[5] Television sells young audiences to advertisers, and advertisers hire psychologists[6] to advise on how to attract children, how to keep them glued and addicted to the tube, how to transform their desires into needs, how to influence their preferences, and how to teach them how to nag their parents. To understand the importance of advertising for marketers, citizens need to know that commercial messages often cost up to ten times more to produce than the program we watch despite the fact that they fill only 20 percent of airtime. In North America today, advertisers spend more than $20 billion per year to reach children, which represents an increase of 2000 percent in less than twenty years.[7]

Advertisers use many techniques to influence youth, to manipulate their needs during the stages of growth into adulthood. Some of the more common vulnerabilities that advertisers take advantage of to sell products include young peoples' need for peer acceptance, love, safety, and identity; their desire to feel powerful or independent; and their aspirations to be and to act older than they actually are. Much of the child-targeted advertising is painstakingly researched and prepared, at times by some of the most talented and creative minds on the planet. Advertisers battle over what they chillingly call "mind share" and some openly discuss "owning" children's minds.[8] Every year, an increasing number of sophisticated ads are used to reach children through television programs, movies, video games, and the Internet.9 As a result, parents and teachers have searched for effective ways to protect children from marketing. Many have lobbied, petitioned, and requested, but very few have obtained support from decision makers in the form of legislation. While some have abandoned efforts, others have created their own means of protecting children from mental manipulation and emotional desensitization. Fortunately, some of these efforts have helped reduce the impact of commercial pollution on the cultural environment and protect the mental health of young citizens. But most victories have gone underreported.

LEGISLATION MOST EFFECTIVE WAY TO PROTECT CHILDREN

As in all areas of human production and commerce, the most effective way to protect children from child abuse by professional marketers is through legislation. Whenever pollution of food, water, or air increases risks to human health and safety, decision makers are often asked to take action to protect the most vulnerable citizens. In the United States and Canada, as in most countries all over the world, a vast majority of citizens supports the regulation of advertising to children.[10] History has shown that other industries have tried to oppose legislation that is conceived to protect citizens. The automobile, tobacco, food, and oil industries have all expended tremendous amounts of money and energy to deprive citizens of protection, while the companies have developed tight commercial links with the industry that controls public information—the media. Therefore, informing the public about child abuse by marketers has become very difficult. Few countries or states have succeeded in regulating the targeting of children in the marketing industry: Greece, Sweden, and Quebec are among them.

LEGISLATION TO BAN ADVERTISING TO CHILDREN

A North American success story was realized in the province of Quebec. A law that deemed advertising to children illegal in the province received unanimous bipartisan approval in 1976, legislation that required not only vision and courage from political decision makers, but also strong support from civil society. Otherwise, it would have been crushed by the media soon after its adoption. By 1980, the rules to enforce the legislation and make it clearly understood by the marketing industry and media were ready. The company Irwin Toys challenged the law in the Supreme Court of Canada, arguing that it restricted the company's freedom of speech, protected by the Quebec Charter of Rights and the Canadian Charter of Rights. In April 1989, after spending hundreds of thousands of dollars on lawyers, the industry received the verdict stating that the Quebec legislation to protect children was fully constitutional. The judges, wording their decision quite clearly, considered the means chosen by the government of Quebec proportional to the objective.

1) There is no doubt that a ban on advertising directed to children is rationally connected to the objective of protecting children from advertising. There is no general ban on the advertising of children's products, but simply a prohibition against directing advertisements to those unaware of their persuasive intent.

2) The ban on commercial advertising directed to children was the minimal impairment of free expression consistent with the pressing and substantial goal of protecting children against manipulation through such advertising.

3) Advertisers are always free to direct their message at parents and other adults. They are also free to participate in educational advertising. The real concern animating Irwin Toys is that revenues are in some degree affected.[11]

The Supreme Court decision includes eighty-three pages which accurately describe how children are vulnerable to sophisticated manipulation techniques used by the marketing industry, why any provincial jurisdiction in Canada has constitutional legitimacy to protect children, why children need such protection until the age of thirteen, and how marketers and broadcasters are not restricted from advertising to adults. The legislation made Quebec the first, and to this day—thirty years after its adoption—the only jurisdiction in North America to protect children from advertising. This raises a few questions. Why do other state jurisdictions in the US refuse to take action against child abuse by the marketing industry?[12] Are Quebecers the only people who care enough for their children to use legislation to protect them from lucrative and powerful industries? The Canadian Supreme Court decision offers a rich lesson in the workings of the media,[13] and analysis of the Irwin Toys decision provides important strategic insights to decision makers all over the world who prepare legislation, and to lawyers who defend the legitimacy of similar legislation in court. Further research is needed to evaluate how the ban has affected childhood obesity[14] and other marketing-related diseases (MRDs) in Quebec. Statistics Canada data shows that young Quebecers are less obese than other young Canadians and that Quebecers commit fewer violent crimes than the rest of Canada.[15]

Recently, the American Psychological Association, along with a coalition of organizations advocating for children's rights, requested similar legislation to protect children in the US.[16] According to the *Washington Post*,[17] a survey conducted in 2006 showed that more than 80 percent of US citizens agreed that advertising to children under the age of nine should be prohibited.[18] Commercial Alert campaigned for similar legislation to ban advertising targeting children under the age of twelve.[19]

IMPACT OF LEGISLATION ON QUALITY PROGRAMS FOR CHILDREN

During the years following its adoption, while the legislation was challenged in the courts, intensive lobbying by advertisers argued that children in Quebec would be punished by this legislation since TV networks were prevented from selling time to advertisers. Lack of income would force broadcasters to reduce the quality and the quantity of programs for kids, therefore prohibition would punish children instead of protecting them. Fifteen years after the law was enacted, the Government of Quebec decided to evaluate the actual impact of the law. Researchers from the University of Montreal investigated the arguments of the industry: Were young viewers rushing for US networks? Have young Quebecers been deprived of the "educational opportunity" to become savvy consumers? Has it been healthy to isolate Quebec's children from other young North Americans, and have they suffered rather than enjoyed protection from commercial harassment?

Research compared programs offered to children in two Canadian cities: Montreal, where advertising was illegal, and Toronto, where "freedom" existed. The study revealed that programming for children was richer, more diverse, of better quality, and more educational in Montreal compared to Toronto. The percentage of young Quebec viewers watching programs from the US never reached more than 10 percent. The study revealed that *ruling out advertising to kids had undeniably proven to be a very efficient and promising practice to protect children.* Protection from advertising did not have a negative impact on the quality of children's programming.[20]

CHILD ABUSERS PORTRAY THEMSELVES AS VICTIMS OF CENSORSHIP

When requests to regulate marketing to children are made public, the industry is prompt to report about it as if freedom of expression has come under attack. Rivalry between media conglomerates suddenly disappears and they rapidly join forces to make government regulation look futile or suspicious, and to make the public forget that airwaves belong to the public. They quote "experts" who belittle damages to children and advocate in favor of free speech for marketers. The fact that more media outlets now belong to fewer owners allows them to reach considerable numbers of viewers, listeners, and readers. Accusing child rights advocates of being pro-censorship is flagrant misrepresentation of the facts because the use of marketing by big media has nothing to do with freedom of speech.

TELEVISION FEEDS OTHER MARKETING-RELATED DISEASES

The marketing industry has scrutinized children's needs, hopes, fears, dreams, and desires.[21] In order to sell more young audiences to advertisers, television has looked for more attractive programs. Increasing young audiences has meant enormous monetary profits in the short term for these industries, but media exposure also has enormous short-, mid-, and long-term effects on children and society. According to the Canadian and American Academies of

Pediatrics, studies have linked television with numerous MRDs. Links were found between television and obesity, body image, self esteem, violent crime, physical and verbal abuse, anorexia and other eating disorders, smoking, alcohol, attention deficit disorder and hyperactivity, compulsive consumerism, perilous car driving, and more.[22] What other industry can afford to generate so much damages to society without any consequences? When the bacteria E. coli is found in water, meat or spinach, the public is quickly informed about the risks. Why would research about MRDs be deprived of similar coverage?

Let us consider the use of violence as a marketing tool. Violence is actually one of the most powerful marketing devices used to lure children and teens. Exposure to violent entertainment not only teaches children how to act violently; in the child's inexperienced brain, it links inflicting pain with pleasure. Since being informed that the use of violence in entertainment helps increase pain for millions of children around the world, has the industry tried to prevent damages? The answer from marketers is simple: raising children is parents' job, not theirs. The only other group of individuals who would say that are child abusers: "I know that little girl was eight, but it's the parent's job to keep me away from her."[23] The media and marketing industries are functioning with child abuser logic. In September 2005, the United Nations Secretary General ordered UNICEF Canada to prepare a consultation document for analyzing violence against children in North America. The document states clearly that additional legislation is certainly among promising practices.[24] But legislation alone will be ineffective without mobilization by civil society to counter the enormous power of the media, including the video game industry.

CENSORSHIP BY COMMERCE

Citizens usually view censorship as government action that prevents public access to real information. Sometimes censorship is perceived as an old-fashioned attempt to block sex scenes in movies. But consider this: what if censorship is also an instrument of the media, employed to give preference to entertainment products that will hurt children, teens, and society?

Censorship by commerce is on such form of censorship, resulting in contemporary phenomena like gratuitous violence. The first, if not only, rule that big media agrees to respect is the market's rule. In North America, most cultural messages are strained through a commercial filter which uses gratuitous violence as an industrial ingredient to keep viewers tuned in, ratings high, and profits up.[25] Their argument is simple: if people want to watch violent programs, broadcasters have the right to air them and no government should interfere. If the transportation industry acted in a similar way, there would be no speed regulation in school areas, no traffic lights for pedestrians, and no prohibition against carrying dangerous chemicals in tunnels.

The broadcast of unhealthy programs for children is the opposite of freedom. It represents the power of the media to abuse vulnerable children. Between freedom of speech and children's safety, all civilized societies should give consideration to the most vulnerable.

Parents, teachers, and child rights advocates requesting regulation of TV programs for children—and the sale of video games to children—do not promote censorship; they oppose censorship by commerce. By 1997, the Dean Emeritus of the Annenberg School for Communication at the University of Pennsylvania had monitored television for over thirty years. After finding Saturday morning children's programs filled by four times more scenes of violence per hour than prime time television, he described censorship by the media. "When you can dump a *Power Rangers* on 300 million children in eighty countries, shutting down domestic artists and cultural products, you don't have to care who wants it and who gets hurt in the process. Mindless TV violence is (. . .) the product of de facto censorship: a global *marketing formula imposed on program creators* and foisted on the children of the world."[26]

In the early 1980s, in addition to advertising through commercials, companies produced their own TV programs and paid to have them broadcast on weekdays and Saturday mornings. In 1984 *GI Joe* carried eighty-four acts of violence per hour and *Transformers* eighty-one.[27] This marketing strategy was so profitable that toy manufacturers reused it in 1989 with the *Teenage Mutant Ninja Turtles*, in 1993 with the *Mighty Morphin Power Rangers*, and in 1999 with *Pokémon*. The primary purpose was to manipulate children so they would nag their parents and Santa Claus to give them Hasbro toys. Product placement in television programs for children included fantasies and stereotypes that support an aggressive culture of violence, sexism, and war.

Citizens have the right to legislate child abuse out of public airwaves, just as they have the right to regulate street traffic. Big media do not defend freedom of speech, *they systematically impose silence on child abusers' opponents.* Violent programs are aired because content is controlled by the industry, and the decision to show violence is made by somebody who's elected by nobody, unknown to the public, and hired and paid to give priority to cruelty, aggressiveness, and hatred wherever it sells. Broadcasters receive money for making the decisions to allow the Ninja Turtles, the Terminator, Fifty Cent, and South Park to come into our living rooms and promote antisocial values instead of other, healthier programs that carry a different message. Profits increase after airing violent programs. The industry's censorship exists and millions of children pay the price every day.

FAILURE OF SELF-REGULATION

Growing public awareness of the dangers of media violence aimed at young people has put pressure on governments to regulate it. In 1995, to prevent government regulation, Canadian broadcasters agreed to regulate themselves and promised that gratuitous violence would be aired only after nine p.m. Seven years later, two researchers found that self-regulation not only had failed to reduce violence but also helped private broadcasters increase the number of violent acts by 432 percent. Violence aired before nine p.m. had gone up from 53 percent in 1995 up to 88 percent in 2002.[28]

During those seven years, two developments helped to neutralize public concern. First, broadcasters provided funding for media literacy programs. Such funding proved to be a smokescreen to help broadcasters project an ethical image of their industry while increasing toxic doses bombarded at children. A second development was the V-Chip offered to working parents, supposedly to help them block violent programs. The V-Chip has helped shift responsibility for regulating TV violence away from polluters onto parents. Thus, governments gave control of pollution to polluters.

PURPOSE OF VIOLENT ENTERTAINMENT

Media violence is used by the entertainment industry to attract more viewers. Considering that age is a contributing factor to vulnerability, the use of violence is certainly one of the cruelest forms of child abuse. Pokémons, Terminators, Doom, Quake, Basketball Diaries, Grand Theft Auto, Howard Stern, South Parks, and Jackass, like hundreds of other cultural products, have been proven to damage children and teens across the continent.[29] They promote values that help guide children's attitudes, behaviors, clothing, language and also, unfortunately, the way they relate with each other. Eminem, Fifty Cent, Marilyn Manson, and Snoop Dog are used by the music industry to circulate hate propaganda against women and gain profit from it. These "artists," often portrayed as rebels, are rich and famous slaves, but slaves nonetheless, dependent on the industry that gave them a microphone, printed their lyrics, sold their albums, promoted them on MTV, and honored them with Grammies.[30]

It takes experience, knowledge, critical viewing skills, and empathy to understand that these role models actually teach submission, frustration, humiliation, and anger. Misogyny, violence, fear, sexism, racism, and consumerism have nothing in common with freedom and justice; they are the opposite. They have been enemies of humanity for millennia. How could a child know that?

SIZE OF THE EFFECT HIDDEN FROM THE PUBLIC

Research has allowed scientists to measure the correlation between what children watch and how they behave. Research has revealed that the effect of media violence is greater than the effect of exposure to lead on children's brain activity, greater than the effect of calcium intake on bone mass, greater than the effect of homework on academic achievement, greater than the effect of condoms as protection against HIV, greater than the effects of asbestos exposure and second-hand smoke on cancer.[31] Some of these correlations were presented by Professor Craig Anderson in his testimony before the US Senate Commerce Committee hearing in 2001. More recent comparisons were presented by Dr. Doug Gentile in October 2006. Research confirmed short- and long-term effects.[32]

FPS VIDEO GAMES ARE MURDER SIMULATORS

Video game revenues now reach $10 billion a year, which is more than that of television and movies combined, and is increasing. Half of fourth graders play "first-person shooter" (FPS) video games. After playing video games, young people exhibit measurable decreases in social behaviors, a 43 percent increase in aggressive thoughts, and a 17 percent increase in violent retaliation to provocation. *Playing violent video games accounts for 13–22 percent of the variance in teenagers' violent behavior. By comparison, smoking tobacco accounts for 14 percent of the variance in lung cancer.*[33]

Video games have been used by the US army to condition young recruits to kill without thinking. Video games give kids and teens the skill, the will, and the thrill to kill.[34] Apart from the tendency of video games to arouse aggression, these games provide little mental stimulation to the brain's frontal lobe, an area that plays an important role in the repression of antisocial impulses.[35] A lack of stimulation prior to the age of twenty prevents the neurons from thickening and connecting, thereby impairing the brain's ability to control impulses such as violence and aggression.

MEDIA VIOLENCE LINKED WITH BULLYING AND CRIME

Time exposure to television is actually linked with bullying. Youngsters who spent a typical amount of time—about 3 hours daily—in front of the tube had a 25 percent increased risk of becoming bullies between the ages of six and eleven. This shows a very clear effect of television on children's bullying.[36]

Since 1985, school authorities in the US have noticed that violence has crept into lower grade levels. In California, from 1995 to 2001, *assaults nearly doubled.* In Philadelphia, the first part of the 2003–2004 school year brought the suspensions of twenty-two kindergartners. In Minneapolis, more than 500 kindergartners over the past two school years were suspended for fighting, indecent exposure, and persistent lack of cooperation. Minnesota schools have suspended nearly 4,000 kindergartners, first, and second graders for fighting and disorderly conduct. In Massachusetts, the percentage of suspended students in pre-kindergarten through third grade more than doubled between 1995 and 2000. In 2001–2002, schools in Greenville, SC, suspended 132 first graders, seventy-five kindergart-ners, and two preschoolers.37 In Quebec, the number of elementary school students with troubled behaviors has increased by 300 per-cent between 1985 and 2000.38

Media violence has also been linked to later criminal activity, as revealed by a seventeen-year study in which 700 young people were tracked into their adult lives. Hours of viewing were correlated with acts of aggression. Young viewers watching more TV committed more crimes as adults.39 In Canada, the violent crime rate of youth is growing more quickly than that of adults, and in Quebec, though the violent crime rate is lower than in other provinces, the violent crime rate of youth is twice that of adults.40

INFLUENCE OF TOXIC CULTURE CENSORED BY THE MEDIA

In 1977, the (Canadian) LaMarsh Commission Report made the analogy of violence to environmental contamination.41 During the thirty years fol-lowing the report, thousands of studies confirmed that violent entertain-ment influences children. In 1995, a University of Winnipeg researcher found more than 650 studies linking real-life violence to media vio-lence.42 In 2001, only 4 percent of violent programs had a strong antivi-olence theme, and only 13 percent of reality programs presented any alternatives to violence or showed how it could be avoided.43 Epidemiologist Brandon Centerwall estimated that TV violence influ-enced half of real-life violence in the US.44 With increasing exposure to violent entertainment, children become mentally altered and physically inclined to commit, accept, or enjoy watching real-life violence. Exposure to violent entertainment has shown to reduce empathy.

HIJACKING MEDIA EDUCATION A FORM OF CENSORSHIP

Researchers investigated the funding sources of major public health groups, and the studies revealed that after big corporations dump money into their budgets, the groups start promoting the agendas of the corporations.45 In 2006, when MacDonald's launched its own exercise program to prevent obesity, the PR strategy obscured the negative impact of junk food on children's health. North Americans face a similar problem with media education. Organizations funded by media conglomerates have promoted a kind of media literacy that deflects blame from the media to parents. North American schools receive free kits, including "educational tools," which hides the impact of media violence on youth and society.46

VARIOUS EMPOWERING PRACTICES BY CIVIL SOCIETY

If society wants to reduce the manipulation of children by marketers and ban violence from TV programs for children, increased legislation is necessary. The entertainment industry markets products to children that are not appropriate for them, based on the industry's own ratings. For instance, children under seventeen can purchase tickets for movies, music recordings, and video games labeled as suitable for adults only. Self-regulation has clearly proven to be nothing but a smokescreen for the industry to continue marketing violence to children.47 The marketing of violence targeting children contravenes Article 17e of the Child Rights Convention, which obliges all states to recognize the importance of the media and protect children from material dangerous to their well-being.48 Attempts to legislate will require wide mobilization, and coalitions of parents, health professionals, education professionals, grassroots organizations, and activists can succeed where legislators alone have failed.

PRACTICES TO IMPROVE PARENTAL AWARENESS

In 2002, researchers surveyed parents on the supervision of their children's consumption of media, concluding that parental guidance was either very weak or absent. Most parents have little to no knowledge of the harmful effects of media violence on their children, nor are they aware of the amount of violence their children are exposed to through television, the Internet, and video games. Thus, media education is needed for parents as well. Families are important factors in reducing the harmful effects of media violence. Children themselves believe they should be protected.49 Parents need to know why using TV as a babysitter is perilous.

Promising practices to protect North American children from media violence have emerged as a result of powerful lobby groups opposing current regulations. A report sent to the UN Secretary General as a contribution to the *Study on Violence against Children* highlights twenty such promising practices by civil society.50 Among these innovative practices, the SMART Program and the 10-Day Challenge have proven to be empowering. They have helped parents, teachers, and students come together to oppose the increasing power of commercial media.

STUDENT MEDIA AWARENESS TO REDUCE TELEVISION (SMART)

The SMART Program was tested in 1996–1997 by Dr. Thomas N. Robinson in San Jose, California. It consisted of eighteen lesson plans for teachers, to prepare third and fourth graders to turn off the television and stop playing video games for ten days. The students also had to cut TV viewing to less than seven hours per week during the following months. A 2001 study in the *Journal of the American Medical Association* revealed that SMART helped reduce verbal violence by 50 percent, and physical violence by 40 percent.51 The study also proved that reducing television and video games helped reduce another damaging MRD: obesity.52

The SMART Program was widely disseminated in 2004 by the Stanford Health Promotion Resource Center (SHPRC), affiliated with the Stanford University School of Medicine,53 and proved to be effective in a controlled experiment, conducted by the university, in Michigan. In 2004–2005, the program was successfully implemented in one school in Michigan, with other schools joining in over the next year.54 Administrators and teachers found short-term results striking: less aggressive behavior and, in some cases, better standardized test scores.55 In 2006–2007, the school district was granted $2.3 million for sharing the program, and the Delta–Schoolcraft school district in Escanaba, Michigan, became the first to use the SMART curriculum across the entire district. It resulted in an 80 percent reduction in violence, a 15 percent increase in math scores, and an 18 percent increase in writing scores when compared to seven non-participating schools.[56]

The SMART Program is among the most promising programs in North America intended to protect children from media violence, but that information has not been made available in the mass media. Why was the public so quickly informed about E. coli bacteria in spinach from California, but given so little information about the damage created by television and effective ways to protect children?

THE 10-DAY CHALLENGE: TV- AND VIDEO GAME-FREE

The 10-Day Challenge was used for the first time in April 2003, in partnership with a parents' association in the Quebec City region. The Challenge reached all students from kindergarten to sixth grade, in eleven participating schools. In its first year, it received funding from the Public Safety Departments of Quebec and Canada, and was covered by the Canadian Press (CP) in St. Malachie, where one hundred students participated,[57] and in *Green Teacher* magazine.[58] In April 2004, the challenge's second year, the parents' association launched a twenty-minute video (in French), which was further publicized by the Canadian Observatory on School Violence Prevention (COSVP).[59] In fact, the Challenge received extensive coverage by the press in all regions or cities where it was held. Since its inception, the Challenge has been used in more than fifty schools in the provinces of Quebec and Ontario, and has been deemed successful through evaluations by parents, students, and teachers from six elementary schools.[60] In 2005, the Quebec Consumers Protection Office added the Challenge to its list of recommended consumer practices.[61]

In April 2005, on the sixth anniversary of the Columbine High School shooting in Littleton, Colorado, factors around this dramatic event were scrutinized. Analysis presented in Michael Moore's movie *Bowling For Columbine* was considered incomplete, having minimized the role violent entertainment played in the shooting.[62] When teen students in Louis-Jacques-Casault High School in Montmagny, Quebec, prepared for the 10-Day Challenge, media education actually helped reduce verbal and physical violence. One thousand teenagers attending the high school were encouraged to turn off TV and video games for ten days and half of them actually did. Teachers, parents, and students evaluated the outcome,[63] and interviews with teenagers who participated in the Challenge were aired by CBC Radio. Further evaluation confirmed the value of the 10-Day Challenge as a "promising practice" with teenagers, having shown to be a motivational tool and an efficient way to mobilize the entire community and develop awareness.

IMPACT ON THE COMMUNITY AS A WHOLE

In the 2003–2004 school year, twenty elementary schools in Quebec and Ontario offered media education workshops to prepare students and parents to turn off the TV. Tabulation of participation revealed that 1,354 students succeeded in reclaiming 19,377 hours of their lives by not watching TV or playing video games.[64] Elementary school students turned TV off for an average of seven days. In April 2004, teens turned TV off for an average of five days. In 2005–2006, ten more schools participated and evaluated their experiences, and the results showed an increase in participants' levels of exercise, reading, time with parents and friends, and less fighting and name-calling at school and at home. In some communities, the reduction of verbal violence at home was more important than at school. Teachers noticed that homework performance was better and that participating students were more attentive in class. All participants said that they wanted to do it again, including parents, students, and teachers.

The fact that the Challenge was accepted by parents was very important; it was an adults' mobilization to support children's motivation and decision-making, and it generated a precious opportunity to value the family unit.

Preparation for the 10-Day Challenge seemed to be more important than the act of turning off the TV. Workshops for students, professional development training for teachers, conferences for parents, follow-up activities by teachers, and promotional activities in the community were all ingredients that helped make the Challenge a success. Community involvement in the 10-Day Challenge increased the reputation of the schools, the importance of education, and the children's sense of belonging. Since the challenge was billed as the equivalent of an Olympic performance, communities expressed admiration and support for students, thus reinforcing youth's self-esteem and pride.

Surprisingly, during and after the 10-Day Challenge, students found themselves in the middle of intense media coverage. Newspapers, magazines, and broadcasters reported on their performance in an appreciative way, and in areas where poverty is common, media reported on crimes and fights. When students organized to stand up against small screens, they attracted attention and admiration for their neighborhoods.

The successes of the SMART Program in Michigan and California, and of the 10-Day Challenge in Quebec and Ontario, are great news for all North American parents, and their triumphs would ideally be known across the continent.

Teachers appreciate this innovative approach to violence prevention; the reduction of exposure to TV and video game violence, along with lessons to increase awareness against media violence, have proven efficient in preventing violence and bullying in school. The next step is to endure that all health professionals and education professionals in North America are informed. By spreading information about these successes, the media can actually contribute to youth violence prevention in the global village.

P.S. Readers can access a more complete version of this chapter at this address: http://www.edupax.org/Assets/divers/documentation/1_articles/1_082_Project_Censor ed_2008.pdf. An addendum to this chapter is also available and gives information about the evaluation by parents, teachers, children, and teens attending participating schools: http://www.edupax.org/Assets/divers/documentation/1_articles/1_083_Evaluation_10D _Challenge_2003_2004.pdf.

Jacques Brodeur has thirty years of experience as a physical education teacher. In 1986, and again in 1988, he coordinated the collection of war toys in schools across the Province of Quebec. The toys were reused in 1990, to build two monuments symbolizing peace in Montreal and Quebec City. In 1987, he helped create PACIJOU and participated in the writing of Cessez-le-feu (Cease-Fire), a teachers' guide to opposing violent entertainment and promoting peace education. He coordinated peace education activities for seven teachers' unions in the Quebec City area from 1988 to 1999. In 1990, he helped founding PEACE (Positive Entertainment for Children Everywhere) and created the "Youth Vote," an empowering approach to media literacy.

The Roy C. Hill Foundation honored him twice for his pedagogical innovations—the war toys collection in 1987 and the Youth Vote in 1997—both relating to the culture of peace. In 1996, the Physical Education Teachers Federation of Quebec awarded him its Health Education Award. In January 1997, he cochaired the Canadian Coalition for Responsible Television. In March of 1999, he coordinated a collection of 35,000 shoes from thousands of schools across the Province of Quebec, to challenge the US administration's refusal to sign the Ottawa Treaty banning landmines. In January 2001, he became consultant, speaker, and trainer for schools in Quebec and Ontario. Since August 2002, he has coordinated a community mobilization program called EDUPAX to help prevent youth violence and promote peace education through media education. In April 2003, he created the 10-Day Challenge (television and video game-free) and participated in it along with the Parents Association of Quebec. By September 2006, the 10-Day Challenge had participation in over fifty schools in Quebec and Ontario.

JBrodeur@edupax.org
www.edupax.org

Citations

1. Less than ten conglomerates control 85 percent of all media in the US and all over the world. http://www.thenation.com/special/bigten.html.
2. George Gerbner, Dean of the Annenberg School of Communication, used to call the big media conglomerates the hidden Ministers of Global Culture. http://www.mediachannel.org/ownership/moguls-printable-150dpi.pdf.
3. Promising Practices Experienced by North American Civil Society to Protect Children from Media Violence, Child Rights International Network, EDUPAX, 2006. http://www.crin.org/docs/CRIN%20Promising%20Practices%20Media%20Violence%203.doc
4. Patrick Le Lay, President and Director of French TV network TF1. "The business of television is essentially to sell brain time to Coca-Cola." http://www.ledevoir.com/cgi-bin/imprimer?path=/2005/04/25/80175.html.
5. Susan Linn, *Consuming Kids: The Hostile Takeover of Childhood* (New York: The New Press, 2004).
6. "Psychologists and Psychiatrists Call for Limits on the Use of Psychology to Influence or Exploit Children for Commercial Purposes," September 30, 1999. http://www.commercialalert.org/issues/culture/psychology/commercial-alert-psychologists-psychiatrists-call-for-limits-on-the-use-of-psychology-to-influence-or-exploit-children-for-commercial-purposes.
7. P. W. Lauro, "Coaxing the Smile that Sells: Baby Wranglers in Demand in Marketing for Children," *The New York Times* (1999). J. Schor, *Born to Buy* (New York: Scribner 2004), 21. http://www.commercialfreechildhood.org/factsheets/ccfc-facts%20overview.pdf.
8. Gary Ruskin, World Health Organization, Conference on Health Marketing and Youth, April 2002, Treviso, Italy, http://www.commercialalert.org/issues/health/international-public-health/presentation-to-who-conference-on-health-marketing-and-youth.
9. "Six Strategies Marketers Use to Get Kids to Want Stuff Bad," *USA Today* (November 2006). http://www.commercialexploitation.org/articles/sixstrategies.htm.
10. "Survey Supports Limits on Kid-Targeted Ads." Report on Public Attitudes Toward the Youth Marketing Industry and Its Impact on Children, 2004. http://www.knox.edu/x7232.xml.
11. Decision by the Supreme Court of Canada, Irwin Toys Limited versus the Attorney General of the Province of Quebec, 1989. http://www.edupax.org/Assets/divers/documentation/7b5_publicite/irwin_en.html.
12. Ibid. Four other provinces of Canada were represented by their Attorney Generals: Ontario, New Brunswick, British Columbia, and Saskatchewan.
13. Supreme Court of Canada, Irwin Toys Decision, Quebec has constitutional legitimacy to protect children from advertising because they are vulnerable until the age of thirteen. http://www.lexum.umontreal.ca/csc-scc/en/pub/1989/vol1/html/1989scr1_0927.html.

14. Young Quebecers Less Obese than Other Young Canadians, Statistics Canada, August 2006. http://www.statcan.ca/english/freepub/82-003-XIE/82-003-XIE2005003.pdf.

15. Statistics Canada, The Daily, July 2006, Quebec has the lowest crime rate in Canada. http://www.statcan.ca/Daily/English/060720/d060720b.htm.

16. Television Advertising Leads to Unhealthy Habits in Children, American Psychological Association (APA), 2004. http://www.apa.org/releases/childrenads.html.

17. "Information or Manipulation? Regulators Urged to Further Limit Ads Aimed at Children," *Washington Post* (2004). http://www.edupax.org/Assets/divers/documentation/7b5_publicite/PUB_Information_or_Manipulation.html.

18. Survey Supports Limits on Kid-Targeted Ads. Report on Public Attitudes Toward the Youth Marketing Industry and Its Impact on Children, 2004. http://www.knox.edu/x7232.xml.

19. The *Leave Children Alone Act* would ban television advertising aimed at children under the age of 12, Parents Bill of Rights (2004). http://www.commercialalert.org/pbor.pdf.

20. André H. Caron, University of Montreal, "Les émissions pour enfants, Rentabilité économique ou rentabilité sociale, un choix de société," (Television Programs for Children, Financial Profitability or Social Profitability), A Social Choice, Conference on Marketing in Schools, CSQ (2000). www.csq.qc.net/sites/1676/options/opt-20/andrecar.pdf.

21. Enola G. Aird, Who Owns Our Children's Minds, 2000. http://www.dlc.org/ndol_ci.cfm?kaid=114&subid=144&contentid=2147.

22. Dr. Aric Sigman, *Remotely Controlled: How Television is Damaging Our Lives and What We Can Do About It* (London: Vermilion, 2005) http://www.amazon.co.uk/Remotely-Controlled-television-damaging-about/dp/0091902606.

23. Lt. Col. Dave Grossman, Update about SMART (September 2006). http://www.edupax.org/Assets/divers/documentation/4_defi/Update%20About%20Smart.html.

24. Katherine Covell, "Violence Against Children in North America," UNICEF Canada, June 2005, North American Consultation Document for the UN Secretary General's Study on Violence Against Children. ibid. http://www.violencestudy.org/IMG/pdf/Desk_Review.pdf.

25. Mary Megee, "Is Gratuitous Violence in the Media A Form of Censorship By Commerce?" International Conference on Violence in the Media (St. John's University, NY, October 1994).

26. George Gerbner, press release (1994).

27. ICAVE, International Coalition Against Violent Entertainment, quoted by PACIJOU in *Cessez-le-Feu*, Fides, 1987. http://www.modern-psychiatry.com/tv_violence.htm.

28. Jacques DeGuise and Guy Paquette, Centre d'études sur les médias, Laval University, "Principaux indicateurs de la violence sur les réseaux de télévision au Canada (Most Important Violence Indicators on Canadian Television Networks)," (April 19, 2002). http://www.cem.ulaval.ca/decembre2004.pdf.

29. Ralph Nader, Introduction. *Corporate predators: The Hunt for Mega-Profits and the Attack on Democracy* by Russell Mokhiber and and Robert Weissman (Monroe, ME: Common Courage Press,1999). http://www.corporatepredators.org/nader.html.

30. Valerie Smith, "Hip Hop Goes on Trial: Human Rights Body Weighs Charge that Rap Pushes Violence Against Women," *NOW Magazine* (November 2005) http://www.fradical.com/HMV_selling_hate.htm.

31. Impact of Entertainment Violence on Children, Joint Statement to the Congressional Public Health Summit by four organizations: the American Academy of Pediatrics, the American Academy of Child & Adolescent Psychiatry, the American Psychological Association, the American Medical Association (July 2000). http://www.aap.org/advocacy/releases/jstmtevc.htm.

32. Dr. Doug Gentile, correlations presented at 3rd ACME Summit, Burlington, VT, October 2006. Correlations also confirmed by the Media Resource Team of the American Association of Pediatrics, "Media Violence," *Archives of Pediatric Adolescent Medicine* 108:5 (2001). http://www.aap.org/policy/re0109.html.

33. Michael Rich, "Protecting Children in the Information Age, Center on Media and Child Health," Harvard School of Public Health, presentation at 3rd ACME Summit, Burlington, VT. http://www.aap.org/advocacy/rich-mediaviolence.pdf.

34. Dave Grossman and Gloria DeGaetano, *Stop Teaching Our Kids To Kill, A Call To Action Against TV, Movie, & Video Game Violence* (New York: Crown Publishing, 1999). http://www.killology.com/reviewbaehr.htm.

35. "Computer Games Can Stunt Kids Brains," *Daily Telegraph* (August 20, 2001). http://www.edupax.org/Assets/divers/documentation/7b4_jeux_video/Video%20Game%20Use.html.

36. Jill Mahoney, "Study Ties TV Time to School Bullying," *Globe and Mail* (April 5, 2005). http://www.edupax.org/Assets/divers/documentation/7b8_television/Study%20ties%20TV%20time%20to%20school%20bullying.html.

37. "School violence hits lower grades," *USA Today* (January 13, 2003). http://www.edupax.org/Assets/divers/documentation/17_violence/School_violence_hits_lower_grades.html.

38. The number of students with troubled behaviors in Quebec elementary schools increased by 300 percent in fifteen years. Three factors have been cited: changes in family structure, lack of parental supervision, and repeated exposure to media violence. http://www.cse.gouv.qc.ca/EN/Article/index.html?id=2001-05-003&cat=2001-05-01_EN.

39. Violent crime rate of youth twice higher than adults', Public Safety Department of the Province of Quebec (2001), 24. http://www.edupax.org/Assets/divers/documentation/3_criminalite/violent_youth_crime_rising.html.

40. Brad Bushman, "Long Term Study (17 Years) Ties Television Viewing to Aggression, Adults Affected as well as Children," *Washington Post* (2002). http://www.edupax.org/Assets/divers/documentation/11_recherches/3%20Articles%20on%20Influence%20of%20Tv.html.

41. Report of the Ontario Royal Commission on Violence in the Communications Industry, LaMarsh Commission, 1977. "If the amount of depicted violence that exists in the North American intellectual environment could be expressed in terms of a potentially dangerous food or drug additive, an air or water pollutant, such as lead or asbestos or mercury, or other hazards to humans, there is little doubt that society long since would have demanded a stop to it." http://www.peacemagazine.org/archive/v08n5p16.htm.

42. Wendy Josephson, "Television Violence: A Review of the Effects on Children of Different Ages," Department of Canadian Heritage, 1995. Data confirmed by the Kaiser Family Foundation: "How TV Violence Affects Children," Television Violence Fact Sheet http://www.kff.org/content/2003/3335 Canadian Teachers poll (June 2001) revealed that 80 percent of Canadians expect governments to take steps to limit media violence exposed to children. http://www.ctf-fce.ca/en/default.htm?press.htm.

43. Media Awareness Network (September 30, 2001). http://www.media-awareness.ca/. Also: "Malaises dans l'éducation," *Le Monde diplomatique*, (November 2001). www.monde-diplomatique.fr/2001/11/DUFOUR/15871?var_recherche=t%E9l%E9+violence.

44. Brandon Centerwall, "Exposure to Television as a Risk Factor for Violence," *American Journal of Epidemiology*, 129:4 (1989). "TV and other Forms of Violent Entertainment, A Cause of 50 Percent of Real Life Violence." http://www.modern-psychiatry.com/the_evidence.htm Also quoted in Action Agenda, A Strategic Blueprint for Reducing Exposure To Media Violence in Canada. http://www.fradical.com/Action_Agenda_November_2004.pdf.

45. Robert Weissman and Russell Mokhiber, "On the Rampage: Corporate Predators and the Destruction of Democracy." The American Diabetes Association (ADA) currently has a $1.5 million sponsorship deal with Cadbury Schweppes. Pharmaceutical companies sponsor the ADA's primary convention. Six out of seven members of the ADA's pre-diabetes panel have financial relationships with Big Pharma. The American Heart Association (AHA) has been brokering agreements with the American Beverage Association and snack food companies that keep brand names and vending machines operating in US schools. The AHA accepted millions of dollars from food makers. http://www.nytimes.com/2006/11/25/health/25ada.html.

46. Dr. Sut Jhally, Media Education Foundation, 2003, founding member of ACME. "Media literacy is so dangerous to media corporations that they have moved to hijack the movement as it builds momentum." Quoted in Taking Lessons from Columbine, ibid.

47. Katherine Cobell, ibid. http://www.violencestudy.org/IMG/pdf/Desk_Review.pdf.

48. Child Rights Convention, Article 17E. http://www.ohchr.org/english/law/pdf/crc.pdf.

49. Katherine Covell, ibid.

50. Promising Practices to Protect Children from Media Violence Experienced by North American Civil Society, Child Rights International Network, CRIN, 2006. http://www.crin.org/docs/CRIN%20Promising%20Practices%20Media%20Violence%203.doc.

51. "Effects of Reducing Children's Television and Video Game Use on Aggressive Behavior," *Journal of the American Medial Association* (January 2001). http://www.edupax.org/Assets/divers/documentation/4_defi/SMARTAggressivity.pdf.

52. "Reducing Children's Television Viewing to Prevent Obesity," *Journal of the American Medical Association* (October 1999). http://www.edupax.org/Assets/divers/documentation/4_defi/SMARTObesity.pdf.

53. Student Media Awareness to Reduce Television, SMART, Stanford Health Promotion Resource Center (SHPRC) affiliated to Stanford University School of Medicine, CA, 2004. http://hprc.stanford.edu/pages/store/itemDetail.asp?169.

54. "Michigan Kids Urged to Kick TV Habit," Associated Press (February 2006). http://www.fradical.com/Michigan_kids_urged_to_kick_tv_habit.htm. Also: "Kicking TV Habit in a Rural Michigan Town," Associated Press (February 2006). http://www.msnbc.msn.com/id/11602458/.

55. Lt. Col. Dave Grossman, Update About the SMART Curriculum in Michigan (July 2006). http://www.edupax.org/Assets/divers/documentation/4_defi/Update%20About%20Smart.html.

56. Ibid.

57. "The 10-Day Challenge in St. Malachie, QC," Canadian Press (May 2003). http://www.edupax.org/Assets/divers/documentation/4_defi/article_cyberpresse_030520.html

58. Jacques Brodeur, "Confronting Violence in Entertainment," *Green Teacher* (December 2003). http://www.edupax.org/Assets/divers/documentation/1_articles/Confronting_Violence.pdf

59. Canadian Observatory on School Violence Prevention, press release for the launching the 10-Day Challenge Video by the Parents Association of Quebec and Chaudière-Appalaches (March 2004). http://www.preventionviolence.ca/html/Avideo.html.

60. Each participating school is the organizational basis for the 10-Day Challenge. http://www.edupax.org/Assets/divers/documentation/4_defi/10_days_challenge.html.

61. Consumers Protection Office, "Développement durable, Consommation responsable, De quoi parle-t-on? (Sustainable Development, Sustainable Consumption, What Does It Mean ?)" (2004). http://www.opc.gouv.qc.ca/dossier/dossier_themtq_dev_dur.asp#top.

62. Jacques Brodeur, "Preventing Youth Violence with Media Education, Taking Lessons From Columbine" (2005). http://www.edupax.org/Assets/divers/documentation/1_articles/OCPVE%20Media%20Education%20For%20Violence%20Prevention.htm.

63. Evaluation of the 10-Day Challenge in a High School, April 2004, Montmagny, QC. http://www.edupax.org/Assets/divers/documentation/1_articles/Teens%2010Day%20Strike.htm.

64. The 10-Day Challenge in Six Elementary Schools and One High School in 2003–2004, Report to the Public Safety Departments of Quebec and Canada (May 2004. http://www.edupax.org/Assets/divers/documentation/4_defi/defi_acp0312/bilan_2003/Le_rapport.htm.

CHAPTER 13

The Media Spectacle of Alienated Youth

by Benjamin Frymer

> At the point of virtually every measure of social crisis—
> race relations, drugs, censorship, pornography, gender,
> sexuality, families, poverty, waning tradition—sits the
> loosely defined, yet rhetorically forceful, youth. . . .
> The politics of youth has to do with the
> politics of spectacle. . . .
> Charles Acland, *Youth, Murder, Spectacle* (1995)

The recent rampage shootings at Virginia Tech brought back to the surface the youth alienation, rage, and violence that have changed the landscape of American schooling and public discourse about youth since the Columbine shootings. Yet for the most part, media coverage of the rampage did not focus on the troubles of youth. Instead, as the media revealed the details of the horror and proceeded to desperately outline an array of possible causes, they generated numerous discussions about gun control, the mental health system, the experience of immigrants, and school safety. However, the most contentious and lasting discussion centered on the media's own role in covering the rampage.

The decision by NBC news producers to air Seung-Hui Cho's video created a firestorm of discussion about journalistic ethics, the role of the media in informing the public of "news," and the media's impact on the psychological motivations of school shooters. However, there was very little discussion about how prime-time broadcasts of Cho's video actually became part of the phenomenon itself—a media spectacle that altered the meaning, significance, and consequences of the rampage; socially constructed a vivid representation of youth rage and violence; and turned Cho into a celebrity killer. As such, the spectacle of Virginia Tech very much mirrored that of Columbine.

On April 20, 1999, two high school seniors just months away from their graduation ceremony drove to their suburban Colorado high school with the stunning intent to blow up the entire school and kill everyone inside. Although their plans went awry and the bombs they had planted failed to go off, Eric Harris and Dylan Klebold still managed to kill thirteen people at Columbine High School before shooting themselves to death. The magnitude of the killing and the suburban Colorado location of the crime generated immediate and enormous attention from media outlets worldwide. From the continuous live local and national television coverage to the sustained barrage of print headlines, articles, and editorials, Columbine was from the beginning a full-blown media spectacle.

The spectacle of Columbine generated numerous accounts to explain this watershed moment in American education, yet one of the most prominent discourses from beginning to end focused upon the problem of alienated youth. Although youth alienation has frequently generated "moral panics" in American life, especially since the 1950s (Goodman, 1960; Keniston, 1965), media coverage of Columbine reconstructed and reconfigured the phenomenon in novel ways, generating a new fear of "alien" youth. Eric Harris and Dylan Klebold soon came to represent an entire constellation of threats coming from formerly harmless suburban and rural white middle-class youth. These troubles were typically framed in terms of alienation, as new forms of adolescent estrangement from parents, schools, and the major institutions and dominant culture of American life. Although media accounts captured some of the historical shifts that have altered the lifeworlds of youth in postmodernity, the real novelty is the media discourse itself and its construction of what may be termed a postmodern spectacle of youth alienation.

According to French theorist Guy Debord (1994), media spectacles are symptomatic of the development of an entire capitalist "society of the spectacle." Publishing his explosive book by this same title in the year just preceding the revolutionary May 1968 uprisings in Paris, Debord sought to renew the relevance of Marx's analysis of commodity fetishism and Lukacs's theory of reification for a later stage of capitalist development. For Debord, building upon Henri Lefebvre's analysis of estrangement in everyday life, capitalism had to be analyzed anew since the alienation produced through the dialectic of capital and labor had been matched by a parallel realm of alienation in the cultural sphere and in everyday experience. Just as, for Marx, workers were transformed into exploited objects under the conditions of alienated labor, for Debord, entire populations of capitalist spectators were estranged from their human powers in the constellation of images that came to control daily social life. In fact, for Debord and the revolutionary Situationist movement he helped found,[1] alienation, in the form of new separations of the subject from everyday social life, was the hallmark of late capitalist "non-life." The society of the spectacle transformed potentially communal human relations and active subjects into one based upon objects and images passively consumed by a stupefied population.

Following Debord, early twenty-first-century capitalist societies, particularly that of the United States, can be seen to be substantially organized through the integrative work of the spectacle. The September 11 terrorist attacks, broadcast live to the world on television, represented only the most spectacular set of media images to capture the imagination of the public. Although, according to Debord, these and other less dramatic media spectacles are a central part of late capitalist social life, societies have become saturated with all sorts of spectacular events, processes, and institutions (Kellner, 1995). Politics has become a spectacle, with the low voter turnouts in US presidential elections an extraordinary example of the population's political estrangement in a formally democratic society. Sports and celebrity spectacles, from the Super Bowl to the saga of Paris Hilton's imprisonment, continue to saturate everyday social life, positioning large segments of the population as consumers of vivid entertainment. Print and television news, as this chapter argues, has also been thoroughly integrated into the society of the spectacle. One doesn't need to witness the nightly car chases on the Los Angeles evening news to see the remarkable blurring of the lines between news and entertainment in a new age of infotainment.

The spectacle of alienated youth, generated within the historical and cultural milieus of media simulacra, anxiety over crime and terrorism, and the "fear of falling" on the part of the middle class (Ehrenreich, 1988), works to construct youth as the Other of late capitalist society. After Columbine, disaffected suburban and rural white youth came to stand for youth as a troubled, disturbed, and thoroughly estranged *class* of alien Americans. Genuine differences expressed by young people, as a badge of authentic identity and forced marginalization from more popular peer groups, became converted into troubling signs of degeneration, social and cultural isolation, and the demonic potential for impulsive violence. The media panic of alienated youth reified young people as fundamentally different in essence and substance: a new historical breed of teenager that could no longer be understood by their parents or other adults.

The media coverage following the Columbine shootings constitutes a discursive, spectacular construction of "new" youth alienation. Mainstream television, newspapers, and magazines attempted to account for the killings at Columbine in terms of sinister, mysterious forms of contemporary youth estrangement haunting the American landscape, and this coverage reflects a substantial portion of the larger media coverage of school shootings, including that of Virginia Tech. Whether presented in terms of new demons in our midst or "alien" beings with mysterious secret lives, youth were constructed as fundamentally estranged from American life and thus unknowable strangers. Suburban and rural youth following Columbine became the ultimate Other to be examined and watched carefully, yet ultimately to be feared and controlled.

An extensive part of the media discourse following the shootings reified youth difference through the psychological spectacle of age-old youth conflict. The archetypal school bully as king of the jungle became yet another demon or beast to excite and be feared by anxious middle-class parents. In spectacle discourse, bullying became a narrative that mirrored the essentialist social hierarchies in schools. Both emanated from a logic positing difference in terms of fixed essential categories of being, thereby transforming difference into a problem outside of *social* processes of struggle and change. Focused on individual psychopathology, or biomedical causes, media discourses on bullying all too often neglected the sociocultural and political bases of school cliques—specifically the politics of exclusion, difference, and recognition. Or, as in the case of Columbine's own principal, who persistently denied there was a problem at his school, the problem of hierarchical violence in schools was simply made invisible.

Gender, one of the major social and political forces at work at Columbine and in other recent school shootings, was another major component of the politics of difference that became reified by the media spectacle. As Klein and Chancer (in Spina, 2000) argue, "masculinity matters" in understanding the high-profile school shootings that culminated in Columbine. Klein and Chancer point out that media coverage of these shootings has almost completely neglected the significance of gender besides the seemingly obvious point that all the perpetrators were boys, despite some striking gendered commonalities in the motivations for the shootings (e.g. anger at being feminized through homophobic insults of "faggot"), and despite the fact that they were *shootings* instead of some other type of less violent response. They make the crucial point that the media, in covering the series of rural and suburban school shootings, naturalized male violence by obscuring the social and historical connections between hegemonic conceptions of masculinity and violence. When media reports did address gender, it was typically reduced to psychological and biological explanations of what had gone wrong for a generation of "lost boys" (Garbarino, 1999). In this way, gender as a constitutive principle of recent youth violence became perhaps the main casualty of the reification of difference in the media spectacle.

From the beginning, Columbine, and now Virginia Tech, were products of a late capitalist society of the spectacle. Even before the shootings took place in Colorado, spectacular life had given rise to the fantasies upon which the architecture of destruction was built. Then, following the killing spree itself, the mass media turned Columbine into a series of signs for a whole host of American social ills, particularly the phenomenon of youth alienation. The meaning of Columbine gradually arose from its multifaceted spectacular construction as the master signifier of alien youth for Americans. The media spectacle of Columbine turned youth into commodified objects of consumption. As "aliens" in the spectacle, their disturbing proclivities were produced and displayed for an audience of consumers who, like other audiences, became attracted to the emotional symbols and narratives of the ongoing show. In the process, the mass media constructed and defined the problems of youth alienation and violence to both ease and stimulate the anxiety provoked by the unknown social and historical conditions that mark our age.

YOUTH ALIENATION

To a large extent, then, the meanings and understandings that were constructed once more through media coverage of Columbine center on the dilemma of youth alienation. At many points in American history, youth have been deemed a problem, an issue, or a question.[2] And, from immigrant youth at the turn of the twentieth century to the black and Latino gangs of the last few decades, the demonization of youth is typically framed in terms of the inherent or essential pathology of some subclass of kids themselves. For example, an extensive set of social science and popular discourses since the 1960s has represented African American youth in terms of some nebulous but debilitating "culture of poverty" (Moynihan, 1965; Ryan, 1971).

In the postwar period, however, a new discourse of youth emerged when suburban white and economically privileged youth began to turn away from the vision of life that had been provided for them (or at least promised). At this point, the problem of youth could no longer be understood in terms of the inherent pathology of an impoverished subculture, or solely in terms of some essence of class or race. Instead, the whiteness and middle-class status of these new troubled youth demanded a more abstract, general examination of American society as a whole. All of a sudden, youth and their troubles (particularly those of boys and young men) came to signify a crisis of American society *itself*. As white middle-class boys began to rebel yet again, their cultures of refusal signified not inherent estrangement and pathology, but that of the larger social system. It was not until the 1950s and '60s that the presumed disconnection and aimlessness of millions of youth came to represent the possibility of some deep-seated social pathology in the American landscape. White, middle-class youth were more than just some deviant subclass marked by race or poverty (Keniston, 1965; Goodman, 1960); they *were* "America" itself.

The series of school shootings in white rural and suburban areas, beginning in the 1997–98 school year and culminating at Columbine, reawakened the specter of youth alienation, this time in the more frightening form of deadly violence. Although school shootings in urban black and Latino areas had been taking place for decades, particularly during the volatile period of the 1980s crack epidemic, the magnitude of the urban killing failed to jolt the popular imagination or lead the media to declare a national emergency of disaffected youth. Instead, judging by the lack of national media attention, youth violence in the inner cities was almost to be expected, perceived to be a kind of local adaptive feature of the new "culture of poverty" that was said to form under conditions of deprivation (Moynihan, 1965; Lewis, 1959). Though in culture of poverty discourses youth violence among the poor and youth of color was treated as almost natural, a seemingly unavoidable result of cultural pathology, the late 1990s violence among rural and suburban white youth was, by contrast, constructed as something completely inexplicable. Like the widespread youth estrangement of the 1950s and '60s amid the supposedly fulfilling conditions of the affluent society, white youth violence in 1990s America was an alarming novel problem in search of a desperate explanation. Furthermore, it quickly became a widespread signal that something was possibly wrong at the core of "American life" (as defined by the privileged classes), or even with modernity itself.

Therefore, the Columbine incident on the one hand provoked the necessity to revisit the question of youth alienation for a new generation (of both alienated youth and their parents), yet quickly became one the media answered itself, before the opportunity for public dialogue arose. I believe it's important to reopen the conversation and pose youth alienation as a question again; or rather, a set of questions:

➤ In what ways could the Columbine killers Eric Harris and Dylan Klebold, and now Seung-Hui Cho, be understood to be alienated youth?

➤ Should their symbolic status as the new face of American youth alienation stand for a more general and serious crisis in American society?

➤ Is there some essential connection to be drawn between youth alienation and recent youth violence?

➤ Have the media accounts of Columbine and Virginia Tech adequately represented such a connection and the larger phenomenon of estrangement?

➤ And, do Columbine and Virginia Tech reveal a new form of youth alienation in comparison to that of the 1950s and '60s?

Alienation in a Spectacle Society

Part of what distinguishes Columbine and Virginia Tech—both the events and their respective media coverage—from previous school or youth violence, and from successive historical waves of moral panic regarding youth, is the extent to which they capture the culture of late capitalist mediated society. The media coverage of both rampages does not simply represent bias or evidence of the media's increasing role in the lives of youth. Rather, the lives of youth are thoroughly mediated and caught up in a spectacle society. Eric Harris, Dylan Klebold, and Seung-Hui Cho all created dramatic, elaborate videos to publicize their rage and violence, correctly believing the media would turn them into celebrity killers. The form and extent of the violence they inflicted were inextricably part of a mediated culture marked by social actors caught in webs of images, discourses, myths, and fantasies.

A capitalist culture driven by media simulacra raises important questions about the problem of identity and estrangement for contemporary youth. Alienation as a category of modern social and critical theory has typically been defined and generated through reference to an essential human nature, universal human capacities, or a transhistorical human condition. For example, Marx's early theory of estrangement in the capitalist labor process posits a unique human species that becomes separated from the laborer in the process of capitalist production. Although Lukacs and the Frankfurt school shifted Marx's emphasis on alienated labor to the cultural and ideological realm, the present conditions of postmodernity require new perspectives on the problem of estrangement. In contrast to earlier Western Marxist approaches that confined the treatment of alienation to the spread of reification and instrumental rationality, and tended to investigate identity in terms of class, the present social landscape calls for more multiperspectival approaches (Best and Kellner, 1997; Kellner, 1995) taking into account multiple forms of social identification and self-formation.

In terms of youth, contemporary alienation must be understood within the context of dramatic new material and cultural conditions generating, on the one hand, different forms of estrangement by race, class, gender, and sexuality, and on the other, common dilemmas of forging identity, meaning, and connection for youth as a whole. Unquestionably, contemporary postindustrial capitalism creates profoundly different material opportunities and deprivations for entire groups of youth according to their class and race location. An entire generation of black, Latino, and Native American, as well as white and Asian working-class youth, have witnessed new forms of economic dislocation and marginality under postindustrial urban conditions (MacLeod, 1995; Wacquant, 1994, 1996; Wilson, 1987, 1996). The estrangement of youth in these categories is inextricably connected to the real material marginality of blocked economic, educational, and social opportunities.

Yet, the cultural developments of the digital age, its corresponding malaise, and the fragmentation of identity transcend class and race location. Although kids continue today to "grow up absurd" in Paul Goodman's sense, concrete and meaningful bases for youth identity are even more difficult for kids to find. Under the reign of media hyperreality, what is real identity anymore? The conditions of absurdity have deepened and become more widespread. Youth estrangement emanates from the evisceration of the formerly stable grounds of everyday life.

Thus if Columbine and Virginia Tech introduce the possibility of new youth alienation, they do so within the realm of even larger questions about the meaning and consequences of a whole constellation of changes in postmodern capitalist societies. Its analysis engenders an examination of the concrete historical conditions that have given rise to substantial shifts in economy and society, and in culture and consciousness, in the last several decades. Has the digital age—the age of "teletechnology" (Clough, 2000) and infotainment, of virtual reality and simulacra, of media spectacle and surveillance, and of the network society (Castells, 2000)—brought about equivalent shifts in identity and processes of self-formation, and thus novel forms of self and social estrangement? Is some strange unknowable postmodernity wrought with an ever intensifying confusion over the nature of identity in an age of multiple, virtual selves? If the self has imploded in hyperreality, can one even speak of alienation anymore?[3]

The Dialectics of Youth Alienation

Youth today are simultaneously integrated into and alienated from the society of the spectacle. On one hand, kids regardless of class, race, gender, and sexuality confront an integrated lifeworld of consumer objects and corporate dreamworlds made concrete by major social institutions and in the sphere of media culture. Bombarded by advertising, television, the Internet, film, and shopping malls, as well as their peers, friends, and family, youth can hardly escape the uniform voice of the consumer society. For adolescents, who are in these years undergoing the formative process of deciding who they are and what they want to be, the society of the spectacle constitutes the ground, or more accurately the lack of ground, that makes growing up "absurd." As Goodman and Friedenberg argued decades ago, youth struggle, often in determined and purposeful ways, to find themselves and form stable, meaningful identities in societies dominated by modes of abstraction. Meaningful identity, let alone dignity and freedom, depends upon the young being able to root themselves in interpersonal relationships, community life, place, and social institutions such as school and work, which provide ties to some sense of transcendent purpose beyond anomic desire. Yet the society of the spectacle tends toward uprootedness, as life is made wholly abstract by the endless proliferation and circulation of commodity images. Although the lifeworlds of youth are not completely colonized by spectacular life, and genuine agency is a constant, the pervasive landscape of abstraction undermines the grounding of the self and its projects.

Moreover, for youth, even the process of schooling has become integrated into the spectacle, predicated upon various divisions of unified populations. Competition to get into the right school (beginning in some areas with preschool), as well as for test scores, grades, and ever loftier credentials, inserts students into the commodification process whether they happen to be "competitive" by inclination or not. *Institutionalized* competition in capitalist schooling generates the material separation of student from student, and class from class. With an increase in deskilled teachers (Apple, 1993), constrained in their lessons to prepare students for No Child Left Behind and standardized state examinations, the everyday life of schools becomes abstract and detached—organized around a logic that has progressively removed schooling from the process of education. Thus, the ends of education are lost. Although youth as a class are substantially integrated into this new commodity culture, whole segments of contemporary youth have also been pushed to its margins and designated the Other. They have been rendered alien to and by the society of the spectacle. To be sure, youth were viewed as "a tribe apart" (Hersch, 1999) long before capitalism developed into its present advanced, digital, mass-mediated form. As a historically constructed and socially imagined group of people, youth as a class have been at times exoticized as foreigners, or demonized as threats (Lesko, 2001). In fact, the historical construction of "adolescence" as a distinct phase of social-psychological and moral development, affirmed by scientific psychology, psychiatry, and popular discourse, marked teenagers as a categorically separate population with uniquely troubling developmental qualities and characteristics (Lesko, 2001).

Yet this process of imagining has been characterized by a kind of collective cultural splitting, with the adult society at large identifying youth as both a source of attraction and repulsion. Although on the one hand, the imagined beauty, energy, sensuality, and spirit of youth have historically seduced the collective imagination of American society, the constructed category of youth has also been subject to profound fear and loathing. As an object of fantasy during recurrent historical periods, American youth have become a spectacle themselves. The American adult population simultaneously experiences fear, anger, excitement, and anxiety as they watch, listen, or read about the latest incident of youth crime integrated into spectacular form. Many young people have become alien to and within America, and, in this way, alienated from themselves as well. Youth easily become the Other, the enemy—the specter of evil in anxious times.

The Columbine shootings and their aftermath represent both dialectical poles of the spectacle's incorporation of contemporary youth. More than any other incident in recent American history, the Columbine shootings and media coverage of the crime generated a pervasive moral panic about youth as an imagined category. Following on the heels of several other suburban and rural school shootings, Columbine *catalyzed* middle-class anxiety over their changing fortunes in new times and set off a full-blown fear of alienated youth. As the antithesis of reason, progress, maturity, and self-control, youth in this alien form represent an entity incorporated into the spectacle as the repressed Other of middle-class adulthood. "Alienation," as the essence of adolescent subjectivity, came to signify youth as an object of fear.

Yet the construction of youth as Other did not just generate hatred and fear of the uncontrollable. The spectacle's representations of youth also became a highly attractive commodity themselves: a pleasurable transgression of the stifling boundaries of rationalized, estranged life and existential passivity. Through Columbine and other school shootings, the violent transgressions of middle-class kids served as a perverse collective media representation of the seductions of crime (Katz, 1988). Thus the set of mass-mediated representations of angry, alien, out-of-control youth, coming to stand for a whole population of American kids, constitutes one pole of Columbine as spectacle.

Although Columbine as a social phenomenon is subject to multiple interpretive lenses, particularly through the workings of social class, race, and gender in the shootings, its complex, mysterious, and disturbing character as an event with a particular trajectory only begins to make sense when viewed in terms of the spectacle's structuring of the horizon of everyday life (Lefebvre, 2002). Even before the Columbine killers were made to stand for everything alien to white middle-class America, in many ways their lives took the form of typical suburban American teens searching for identity amid the consumer abstractions of mass-mediated capitalism.

Youth themselves can't help but be pulled into the "society of the spectacle" that attempts to empty the particular lifeworlds of youth and youth cultures and turn them into abstract commodified media categories. The media categories in turn feed back into the lifeworlds of American youth, perpetuating a dynamic that exposes the internal relationship between rationality and irrationality in constructions of youth alienation. In turn, the public comes to believe in the reality of this alienation, ignoring the concrete social conditions that give rise to the everyday lives of youth, generate violence and other pathologies, and foster very different, meaningful forms of resistance. As a result, media constructions of youth alienation generate a social dynamic of demonization that moves between the poles of abstraction and emotionality, transforming reified objectification of youth into irrationality (fear and anger), and irrationality back into objectification.

In a related sense, Columbine and its aftermath also signify another dialectical process—one of domination and resistance for marginalized youth. Eric Harris and Dylan Klebold represent millions of economically and racially privileged youth who, despite material and cultural advantages, find themselves subjected to forms of interpersonal and symbolic violence in American high schools and suburban communities. Their lives, colonized by spectacular life, are turned into living nightmares as they confront school and capitalist cultures that are hostile to expressions of difference that threaten abstract, hierarchical norms and values. Historically, adolescents like these, who suffer from the isolation of a marginal existence in America's suburban and rural schools, have turned to suicide as the way out of a situation perceived to have no other exit (Gaines, 1991). But the recent series of high-profile school shootings indicates that white kids who find themselves on the outside looking in have seized upon a new, very limited form of resistance to their plight, one that ends up having even more tragic consequences. This essential, internal relationship between domination and the tragic nature of their resistance is precisely what the media spectacle of Columbine obscured.

Analyzing the processes involved in the social construction of reality, exemplified here by the media discourse about Columbine and youth alienation, is of central importance because they provide the basis for public understanding and strategies of control. If teenagers purportedly kill because they belong to inherently nihilistic youth subcultures, then schools and the larger structures in which they are immersed are not rendered problematic or responsible in any way. It is dangerous youth who must be controlled. If confusion, detachment, and anger are deemed to be natural byproducts of being an adolescent, little or no attention is paid to the conditions of modern suburban life that systematically disengage significant groups of American youth.

By comparing media accounts to alternative social analyses, it is possible to trace the ideological content in the process of social construction. Media spectacles become ideological, in one sense, to the extent that they legitimize particular social interests and forms of power to the exclusion of others. Although rarely studied,4 of central importance is the media construction of youth alienation, and the extent to which the narratives that are developed converge or diverge from the actual living conditions and experiences of American youth. For today's generation of youth, the discussion about alienation has been generated, and the framework defined, almost entirely by the mass media itself through such incidents as the Columbine shootings. Yet, alienation is not simply a media fiction.

The violence at Columbine and other American schools is indeed symptomatic of widespread youth alienation in contemporary American society. Although still a minority, alienated youth comprise a significant proportion of America's young people, and this minority is often thoroughly and deeply estranged from established

American institutions, especially suburban schools such as Columbine. In fact, they may reject much of the dominant capitalist culture, the identities it requires, and the institutional channels for success it mandates. In simple terms, the educational opportunities that beget a mainstream American life and future career don't matter to them. Educational researchers and sociologists in the past thirty years have begun to document different strands of this alienation, particularly that of working-class youth (Willis, 1977; McLaren, 1986; MacLeod, 1995) and youth of color (Fine, 1991; Wexler, 1992; MacLeod, 1995; Fordham, 1996). Yet, since the popular sociology of the 1950s and '60s, there have been few explorations of the more puzzling problem of disaffected suburban youth who, in their own circumstances, find themselves on the outside looking in.[5]

To conclude, a major part of Columbine's significance therefore lies in the dramatic mediated narratives of youth alienation that followed the shootings, whether presented in terms of the psychological disturbance of the shooters or the nihilistic culture of gothic outsiders. These narratives worked to produce a series of naturalizing myths that covered up the roots of most school shootings in the closed worlds of many present-day kids. The series of rural and suburban school shootings that so dramatically seized the collective imagination of the American public was presented as if it took place on an island untouched by history and social forces. As a result, the ideological lenses of commercialized media shaped the public imagination through sensational portraits of individual demons or psychopaths. The media transformed youth into objects of fear out of a complex mixture of attractive and repulsive displays. They thereby severely limited the possibilities for reflection, discussion, and understanding of the contingent historical and social conditions giving rise to so many disaffected, angry, and ultimately violent boys in what constitutes one aspect of a contemporary youth crisis.

To say that relatively privileged suburban and rural white boys are in crisis may appear to be a striking overstatement given the millions of American kids who grow up in poverty, subject to concrete forms of material deprivation and physical violence. Nevertheless, the current despair, isolation, and resistance of many suburban and rural "outsiders" speaks to more than just individual psychological estrangement and rage, but to a social condition of mediated capitalist life and the breakdown of modern cultural bonds. In the late nineteenth century, Emile Durkheim used the term anomie to describe uniquely modern social pathologies of aimlessness, lack of meaning, moral fragmentation, and loss of self-direction as Western life dissolved into an unchecked, relentless pursuit of individual gratification. In clear terms that apply to the lives of youth, Gaines states that "To be anomic is to feel disengaged, adrift, alienated. Like you don't fit in anywhere" (in Spina, 2000, 124). This anomic condition of modernity has intensified in postmodern spectacle societies, to the extent that the inward violence of teenage suicide that could be traced to these modern conditions has been joined by the parallel phenomenon of violence directed outward. Alienated youth outsiders in our spectacle society no longer just kill themselves, they lash out at the real and symbolic sources of their pain. With so few real sources of meaning and transcendent purpose to strive toward, those kids on the outside of suburbia looking in see no escape from their anguish and the larger absurdity of it all.

In a world where non-commodified identity is continually elusive and dangerous, the anger of those boys who don't fit into the packaged personas of capitalist culture may serve as the only anchor that keeps them afloat. Out of the mediated void of nihilistic spectacles, the anomic desire for violent revenge and celebrity infamy become the only hollow bases for self-worth and identity these despised kids possess. At risk of being adrift in a sea of spiritual violence, youth pushed to the margins now become engulfed by its physical forms. It is their last desperate hope of escaping a situation that appears to have no escape (Aronowitz in Spina, 2000). In this sense, suburban school shooters represent only the latest, most destructive form of student opposition to oppressive circumstances. However, their attempt to transcend their own alienated despair through a masculine, spectacular fantasy of violent revenge provides no escape for anyone. Tragically, to an even greater extent than the working-class "lads" of Willis's study (1981), their resistance occurs in a form that ends in defeat and the reproduction of the very structure of life they oppose.

Ben Frymer is a sociologist and assistant professor at the Hutchins School of Liberal Studies at Sonoma State University.

References

Acland, Charles R. 1995. *Youth, Murder, Spectacle: The Cultural Politics of "Youth in Crisis."* Boulder, CO: Westview Press.

Apple, Michael W. 1993. *Official Knowledge: Democratic Education in a Conservative Age.* New York: Routledge.

Best, Steven, and Douglas Kellner. 1997. *The Postmodern Turn.* New York: Guilford Press.

Castells, Manuel. 2000. *The Rise of the Network Society.* Oxford, UK: Blackwell Publishers.

Clough, Patricia Ticineto. 2000. *Autoaffection: Unconscious Thought in the Age of Teletechnology.* Minneapolis: University of Minnesota Press.

Debord, Guy. 1994. *The Society of the Spectacle.* New York: Zone Books.

Ehrenreich, Barbara. 1989. *Fear of Falling: The Inner Life of the Middle Class.* New York: Pantheon Books.

Fine, Michelle. 1991. *Framing Dropouts: Notes on the Politics of an Urban Public High School.* Albany, NY: State University of New York Press.

Fordham, Signithia. 1996. *Blacked Out: Dilemmas of Race, Identity, and Success at Capital High.* Chicago: University of Chicago Press.

Friedenberg, Edgar Zodiag. 1959. *The Vanishing Adolescent.* Boston: Beacon Press.

Gaines, Donna. 1991. *Teenage Wasteland: Suburbia's Dead End Kids.* New York: Pantheon Books.

Garbarino, James. 1999. *Lost Boys: Why Our Sons Turn Violent and How We Can Save Them.* New York: Free Press.

Goodman, Paul. 1960. *Growing Up Absurd: Problems of Youth in the Organized Society.* New York: Random House.

Hersch, Patricia. 1998. *A Tribe Apart: A Journey into the Heart of American Adolescence.* New York: Fawcett Columbine.

Katz, Jack. 1988. *Seductions of Crime: Moral and Sensual Attractions in Doing Evil.* New York: Basic Books.

Kellner, Douglas. 1995. *Media Culture: Cultural Studies, Identity, and Politics Between the Modern and the Postmodern.* New York: Routledge.

Keniston, Kenneth. 1965. *The Uncommitted: Alienated Youth in American Society.* New York: Harcourt Brace & World.

Larkin, Ralph W. 1979. *Suburban Youth in Cultural Crisis.* New York: Oxford.

———. 2007. *Comprehending Columbine.* Philadelphia: Temple.

Lefebvre, Henri. 2002. *Critique of Everyday Life, Vol. II.* New York: Verso.

Lemert, Charles C. 1997. *Postmodernism is Not What You Think.* Malden, MA: Blackwell Publishers.

Lesko, Nancy. 2001. *Act Your Age!: A Cultural Construction of Adolescence.* New York: Routledge/Falmer.

Lewis, Oscar. 1959. *Five Families: Mexican Case Studies in the Culture of Poverty.* New York: Basic Books.

MacLeod, Jay. 1995. *Ain't No Makin' It: Aspirations and Attainment in a Low-income Neighborhood.* Boulder: Westview Press.

Males, Mike A. 1996. *The Scapegoat Generation: America's War on Adolescents.* Monroe, ME: Common Courage Press.

———. 1999. *Framing Youth: Ten Myths about the Next Generation.* Monroe, ME: Common Courage Press.

McLaren, Peter. 1986. *Schooling as a Ritual Performance: Towards a Political Economy of Educational Symbols and Gestures.* Boston: Routledge & Kegan Paul.

Moynihan, Daniel P. 1965. *The Negro American.* Cambridge, MA: American Academy of Arts and Sciences.

Ryan, William. 1971. *Blaming the Victim.* New York: Pantheon Books.

Schwendinger, Herman and Schwendinger, Julia. *Adolescent Subcultures and Delinquency.* New York: Praeger, 1985.

Spina, Stephanie Urso. 2000. *Smoke and Mirrors: The Hidden Context of Violence in Schools and Society.* Lanham, MD: Rowman & Littlefield.

Wacquant, Loïc J. D. 1994. "The New Urban Color Line: The State and Fate of the Ghetto in PostFordist America." *Social Theory and the Politics of Identity.* Edited by Craig J. Calhoun. Cambridge: Basil Blackwell.

———. 1996. "The Rise of Advanced Marginality: Notes on its Nature and Implications." *Acta Sociologica* 39: 121–143.

Wexler, Philip. 1992. *Becoming Somebody: Toward a Social Psychology of School.* Washington, DC: Falmer Press.

Willis, Paul E. 1981. *Learning to Labor: How Working Class Kids Get Working Class Jobs.* New York: Columbia University Press.

Wilson, William J. 1987. *The Truly Disadvantaged: The Inner City, the Underclass, and Public Policy.* Chicago: University of Chicago Press.

———. 1996. *When Work Disappears: The World of the New Urban Poor.* New York: Knopf.

Citations

1. A merger of different radical artistic groups, the Situationist International formed in 1957, continuing the utopian strand of Dada and Surrealism but engaging in more concrete political acts for which they created "situations" to disrupt the status quo.
2. See Lesko (2001) for a detailed analysis of historical representations of youth.
3. Although this work analyzes part of a cultural and social development which I contend is "postmodern," it does not thereby assume there is no such thing as identity or an essential self which can be alienated by social conditions. On the contrary, I work within the modernist tradition of critical theory that bases its very analysis and critique of modern societies on this assumption, thus holding out the possibility and hope for the transcendence of alienation.
4. See Males (1996,1999), and Acland (1995) for different analyses of the media construction of "youth alienation."
5. For a prominent exception, see the work of Schwendinger and Schwendinger (1985) on the connection between capitalist development and middle-class youth delinquency. Also see Larkin (1979, 2007).

CHAPTER 14

Perception Management
Media & Mass Consciousness in an Age of Misinformation

by Greg Guma

Debates over press responsibility and information policy date back to the 1890s, particularly after the impact of media propaganda was dramatically demonstrated during the Spanish-American War. In 1922, the president of General Electric warned Europe about the downside of radio, urging nations to stop hurling insults at each other "in furious language." Five years later, the League of Nations passed a resolution opposing "obviously inaccurate, highly exaggerated, or deliberately distorted" news, urging the press not to undermine international peace. By the early '30s, an International Federation of Journalists had established a tribunal to deal with information that promoted hate and violence.

From the start, the US government opposed or remained aloof from proposals designed to impose sanctions or promote balance, even though its leaders recognized the danger of a European news cartel and, later, the power of fascist and Nazi propaganda. The prevailing US stance, then as now, was that only private-sector ownership can ensure the so-called free marketplace of ideas. The fact that commercially-based media are subject to abuses and distortions was ruled irrelevant, while arguments for a "new international information and communication order," one that would be democratic, support economic development, enhance the exchange of ideas, share knowledge among all the world's people, and improve the quality of life, was called demagoguery, the leading edge of a plan to impose a global socialist state.

In the early 1980s, this battle came to a head in the US effort to discredit the United Nations Educational, Scientific, and Cultural Organization (UNESCO), established in 1945 to promote the worldwide exchange of thought and ideas in hopes of promoting peace and prosperity. Although never completely comfortable with this agenda, the US went along until the late '70s, when calls for a New International Information Order (NIIO) directly challenged the West's "cultural imperialism." Information flows shouldn't be one-directional, all nations should have equal access to information and international transmission channels, the power of existing transnational media monopolies should be reduced, and additional media voices should be heard—these were some of the NIIO's lofty goals.

Not surprisingly, the response from the US government and media conglomerates was negative and sometimes savage, using all the power at their disposal to derail this challenge to the "free marketplace" gospel. During a 1980 interview, for example, Associated Press (AP) President Keith Fuller told me flatly that NIIO was nothing more than an attempt by authoritarian regimes to censor "straight reportage," while promoting "open advocacy." He did admit, however, that most commercial media coverage of international matters lacked "coherence," that it focused mainly on conflicts and presented life in isolated pieces.

Once Ronald Reagan became president, the Heritage Foundation, a conservative think tank that developed many of his policies, accelerated the attacks. The new goal was not only to squelch talk about media reform, but also to discredit UNESCO and the entire UN system. Mainstream media pitched in, casting the issue as a power play by Third World dictators out to destroy the "free press"—a widely accepted euphemism for media in private hands, largely financed by advertising, and not subject to government controls or demands for social responsibility.

The attack on UNESCO climaxed with the US withdrawal in 1985. With that, hopes for a "new world information and communication order" evaporated. Some critics have suggested that the approach was doomed anyway, since it was promoted by political and intellectual elites, and focused on the role of states rather than individuals and civil society. Basically, they argue that such a campaign for "democratization from above" would empower only governments, and likely produce new forms of censorship and control.

DEADLY OMISSIONS

The US imports so little data and entertainment from other parts of the world, despite being such a massive exporter, that its citizens have become cross-culturally handicapped. Meanwhile, other nations, even most of those resisting "Americanization," are bombarded with the western flavor and bias of imported arts and news, undermining their efforts to sustain indigenous traditions through the use of locally sensitive mass media. The premium placed on timeliness also carries a price tag, as speed has not enhanced the ability to understand situations. The resulting lack of reflection has contributed greatly to a persistent jingoism in the handling of fast-breaking foreign political stories, along with unchallenged misinformation and glaringly cynical blackouts.

To make the latter point, one need only cite the case of East Timor in the late 1970s. While Hodding Carter was Assistant Secretary of State for Public Affairs under President Carter, thousands of people were being slaughtered there by Indonesian invaders. Yet even Hodding Carter and his wife, who were deeply concerned about rumors of atrocities and repression, couldn't get the government to act or the media to pay any attention. He concluded afterward, "What is news is defined by what the government decides is news."

And why was East Timor ignored? Henry Kissinger had seen to it earlier that Indonesian aggression was played down and, as Hodding Carter admitted, the administration he served did nothing to change that situation. In fact, he encountered considerable resistance. Both the Ford and Carter administrations agreed that the need to cultivate an alliance with strategically located Indonesia was too important to shine the light of news on East Timor. And so, no light was seen at all. Reports of mass murder were systematically excluded from the US press, and the rare reports that did get through consisted mainly of handouts from Indonesian propagandists. In 1976, according to an exhaustive study by linguist and social critic Noam Chomsky, when the Indonesian army was starting to annihilate simple mountain people, coverage in the *New York Times* for the whole year was half a column of news. The next year, 1977, while this massacre was reaching awesome proportions, *Times* coverage dropped to five lines.

This horrific omission suggested, at the very least, the tacit acceptance by major media of a cynical government policy. When we spoke, Hodding Carter went a step further. "The real definers of news are not the boys on the bus but the boys in the press bullpen." He meant the editors back home. Their propensity to go for the lowest common denominator often drives out the best and the challenging. For many information consumers, the consequence is enforced ignorance.

"The more independent a news entity can be, the better off you are as a reader." That's the Associated Press gospel, as summarized for me by Keith Fuller. To the extent that he would admit to any problems in foreign coverage by his or other major news services, the solution was "competition" and freedom from government intrusion. But he had absolutely no use for "developmental journalism," an approach marked by background research, more attention to the context, and perhaps even some sympathy. "Developmental journalism" is mere camouflage to corporate media, Fuller charged. "Nine times out of ten you have a hostile government, and they just want their propaganda reported."

Perhaps better than statistics, that "informed opinion" suggests the barrier faced by underdeveloped nations. Fuller's attitude, still common among media managers, is reinforced constantly through a daily barrage of superficial and often ethnocentric coverage. A report about land reclamation is still considered propaganda, while stories about atrocities in countries that are not among our "vital interests" don't rate as news at all.

CULTURAL CONVERSATION

The information superhighway, like many systems of production and distribution before it, is mainly driven by the market, which defines what services consumers can get and how much they will pay. Those lacking sufficient bucks—a group that still includes the vast majority of the world's population—are simply shut out. The companies investing in this highway want control of access to consumers to recoup their investments. The Internet—currently both a commercial marketplace and a public meeting place where people exchange information, search databases, play games, organize, share images and ideas, and chat—has clearly attracted the attention of the international business community. Once its effectiveness as a vehicle for advertising and sales is further refined, this public, relatively unregulated, uncensored, pluralistic network could yet devolve into a global electronic shopping mall.

A century after the power of global communications was first acknowledged, we are still being fed the same old line: the market best protects the free exchange of information, and is certainly preferable to any form of state or global intervention. There is, however, another point of view, though not one our corporate gatekeepers have deigned to mention. It is embodied in the People's Communication Charter (PCC), a global initiative developed by Third World Network in Malaysia, the Center for Communication and Human Rights in Amsterdam, the US-based Cultural Environment Movement, and the World Association of Community Radio Broadcasters.

The PCC articulates essential rights and responsibilities that ordinary people should have in relation to their cultural environment. "All people are entitled to participate in communication, and in making decisions about communication within and between societies," it asserts in a preamble. "The majority of the world's peoples lack minimal technological resources for survival and communication. More than half of them have not yet made a single telephone call. Commercialization of media and concentration of media ownership erode the public sphere and fail to provide for cultural and information needs, including the plurality of opinions and the diversity of cultural expressions and languages necessary for democracy. Massive and pervasive media violence polarizes societies, exacerbates conflict, and cultivates fear and mistrust, making people vulnerable and dependent."

In eighteen articles, the charter outlines a set of principles that provide the basis for a campaign to transform global communications. Building on existing treaties and the Universal Declaration of Human Rights, it calls for broad rights to access and literacy, international protection of journalists, and argues that "All people have the right of reply and to demand penalties for damage from media misinformation." It addresses the issues of cultural identity, language diversity, and protecting children from harmful media products. In addition, it deals with privacy rights, equitable use of cyberspace, protection of consumers from promotion disguised as news or entertainment, and accountability through self-regulatory bodies, based on the standards outlined in the charter.

Finally, reflecting its focus on "democracy from below," the PCC deals with the vital question of independence. The right to participate in and benefit from self-reliant communication structures, it explains, "requires international assistance to the development of independent media; training programs for professional media workers; the establishment of independent, representative associations, syndicates or trade unions of journalists and associations of editors and publishers; and the adoption of international standards."

To date, corporate media's response has been to ignore that there is anything to discuss, aside from some self-indulgent hand wringing about whether the press focuses too much on polls and conflicts and not enough on content. But many people understand what they are really focused on—ratings—which, in the end, means money. Still, the charter's agenda does go straight to the heart of what worries many people about our brave new media world. The questions are whether enough of them will see through the "free marketplace" spin, and whether civil society will seize the initiative before it's too late.

When people think and act according to the prescriptions they receive from media, consciousness of self and one's relationship with the world can easily be lost. In other words, the victims of "news imperialism" aren't only the people of underdeveloped nations, inundated with western news and mental popcorn at low prices, and ultimately presented to US consumers as either hapless peasants or ideological fanatics. Cultural colonialism also reaches into the homes of Middle America, coloring the awareness of domestic consumers and even press workers themselves.

That is mass media at its worst. The same vehicles, on the other hand, can help people to speak to one another, creating what could one day be a conversation of our culture on the global level. There is still the potential, through new technologies, as well as through more skillful and constructive uses of old forms, to promote through our media not nationalism and misunderstanding, but instead global dialogue.

THE POWER TO MISINFORM

Once upon a time, Walter Cronkite was "the most trusted man in America"—that is, if you believed *Reader's Digest*, which offered a glimpse of life behind the scenes at CBS in the late 1970s. With typical *Digest* brevity, Cronkite provided his basic philosophy. "We have to set ourselves up as judges of the news," he explained. "A good journalist doesn't just know the public, he is the public."

It wasn't likely, however, that the people who trusted Cronkite did so because he felt the same things as they did. His pretense of identification with the millions masked his role as the ultimate insider, projecting the agenda of the electronic status quo. In 1979, for example, when he noted each night how many days US hostages had been held in Tehran, it wasn't just because he and the viewing public felt so strongly. It was corporate policy.

Early in that hostage crisis, the networks realized the power of a real-life drama to draw in a vast new audience for news. ABC soon launched a nightly wrap-up report, featuring satellite hookups between Washington, Moscow, Tehran, and ABC studios. Ted Koppel conducted business as if he expected to resolve the crisis on the air. Not to be left behind, CBS opted for symbolism. Every major news broadcast began and ended with the hostage coda. When US news people were banned from Iran, CBS radio devoted an entire broadcast to a monotonous repetition of the phrase, "There are fifty American hostages being held . . ."

With the world appearing ever more strife-ridden, the TV networks took the opportunity to develop a surreal version of the domino theory in living color. At first, NBC wasn't as keen about the crisis as the other two major commercial networks. But after Soviets troops marched into Afghanistan (months after the launching of covert US operations designed to spark just such a response), and any chance that the network would handle exclusive coverage of the upcoming Summer Olympics in Moscow was gone, it launched a series of specials: "US vs. USSR: Cold War or Nuclear War?" Analysts offered Pentagon statistics while footage implied that the US would be hopelessly outclassed in a Middle East conflict.

ABC gradually modified its own international coverage. Late night broadcasts on "The Iranian Crisis" continued, but the content shifted; shows were often devoted to Afghanistan or Yugoslavia. When this began to look foolish, the program's name was changed to *Nightline*, which went on to become the Gold Standard of late night talk TV. The network also developed its own specials, including "US: Arsenal of Democracy," which delved into the "problem" US industry faced in producing enough weapons and equipment to handle a possible hot war.

The assumptions of crisis coverage were taking hold. First the Iranian Crisis, then the Afghanistan Crisis, rippling out into mini-crises in Pakistan, Western Europe, Latin America, and in the US military itself. Expert speculation became commonplace, bandied about with no doubt concerning the "objectivity" of these well-placed sources. The "New Cold War" had become the nation's hottest story. The scenarios were unlimited, and the nightly reinforcement made them sound reasonable and imminent.

And what, meanwhile, was Walter Cronkite up to? On the day *Reader's Digest* visited CBS, the top national story at midday was about an oil tanker in Galveston, Texas, that had been burning for a month. But Cronkite cut the story short so that Marvin Kalb could present the State Department's daily spin on the "Iranian Crisis."

Sandy Socolow, the executive producer, came to Cronkite minutes before airtime to suggest, "We can drop Marvin." The program was just too long. But the most trusted man in America said, "No, we have to have Marvin." As he explained later, Cronkite wanted his viewers to get not just what they wanted, but "what they needed as well."

What this had to do with balance and objectivity is anyone's guess. Yet Cronkite and his network colleagues insist that their credibility rests not only on their judgments but also on a dispassionate viewpoint. "A successful journalist," Cronkite once noted on the air, "owes his credibility to the fact that he has served as an objective witness, an observer who has earned a reputation for shedding or controlling his own biases and telling it as it is." But sometimes they tell the same story too often, mainly because it's the kind of reportage that wins ratings or panders to popular prejudices. And some stories don't get told at all.

Today, if a crisis isn't available almost every week, the networks simply invent them. Almost any pretext will do. And once the feeding frenzy begins, the credibility of the latest Cronkite clone soon convinces millions that the new disaster is the most important event affecting their lives. As Voltaire put it, reality is the lie agreed upon. Assuming that is true, then crisis coverage by the major TV networks is one of the most effective ways to engineer such deceptive consent.

CENSORSHIP 101: A GUIDE TO PERCEPTION MANAGEMENT

Corporate media's handling of the news has become increasingly unreliable since the late 1970s, that crucial moment when wall-to-wall crisis coverage was institutionalized. In fact, mainstream journalists find it difficult, if not dangerous, to cover stories that do not fit neatly into what is known as the "Washington Consensus." Meanwhile, corporations have developed sophisticated strategies to promote the stories they want to see, and to prevent others from being aired or published. The result is perception management, a highly effective form of social engineering. Here is a brief review of some common tactics, drawn mainly from the cusp of the last millennium.

Embracing the Basic Assumption

Corporate control of the news isn't mainly about censoring specific stories. Rather, it involves the general acceptance of some basic assumptions. One of the most pervasive of these is the sanctity of the "free enterprise" system—otherwise known as capitalism. That's why we are more likely to hear about the peccadilloes of sleazy politicians than the atrocities of callous corporations. Working mainly in competitive businesses—and being competitive about their own work—most journalists find it easy to accept the tenets of free enterprise. And why not? They mesh well with the basic conceit of mainstream journalism; that the job of the press is simply to inform in a "free marketplace of ideas."

But this marketplace is only open to those few who own the means of communication, their employees, and those they choose to admit. As Noam Chomsky puts it, "The point is not that the journalists or commentators are dishonest; rather, unless they happen to conform to the institutional requirements, they will find no place in the corporate media." As a result, they rarely voice anything that suggests basic doubts about the essential nature of the capitalist system.

Chomsky and Ed Herman call the fact that the interests of owners shape what is defined as news one of the main structural "filters" underlying news gathering in corporate media. That goes a long way toward explaining most mainstream coverage of protests against corporate globalization. Consider, for example, the basic assumptions underlying reports on the Free Trade Area of the Americas (FTAA) Summit in April 2001. Its goal was to "tear down barriers to goods and services, trade and investment from the Arctic to Tierra del Fuego," trumpeted Bloomberg News on April 3. "The agreement would facilitate free trade among the hemisphere's 783 million people and could represent 40 percent of the world's gross product," Reuters explained two days later. Such formulations were not presented as the viewpoint of a specific source, but as statements of fact.

When confronted, journalists frequently object that such a critique is merely "conspiracy" thinking. Translation: it's paranoid, extreme, and therefore irrelevant. Unlike any other employee, they claim to be totally independent of supervisory control or outside influences, free to pursue any story, wherever it leads, as long as they adhere to the first commandment—objectivity. But as anyone who has worked in a newsroom knows, each story involves a series of subjective judgments about what is important, relevant, or permissible. And almost every source brings to a story an agenda of his or her own.

Promoting Spin

Journalists get squirrelly at the suggestion that their jobs involve anything but gathering the facts and revealing the truth. Yet, most also know from experience that the truth isn't always obvious or simple, and that some facts or stories are more acceptable than others.

In March 1998, for example, the three biggest commercial TV networks got the same bright idea at precisely the same time: let's air special reports on the progress being made in the war on cancer! Stranger still, their special coverage was scheduled for launch on the same day. But it wasn't just a coincidence. News on cancer "breakthroughs" often received prominent coverage at this time of year. Why? Because it was just a few weeks before the American Cancer Society (ACS) began its annual fundraising drive.

Like other major institutions that know how to mobilize the media, the ACS primes reporters and editors to provide "good" news at the most opportune moment. Following up on that March 1998 coverage, it held an annual Science Writers Seminar for influential mainstream journalists. After hearing the inside scoop on research and treatment, they eagerly disseminated it to the general public. On the surface, this sounded like a benign public service. But let's dig a little.

At the time, the Clinton administration was contemplating a major infusion of funds for cancer research, so positive coverage helped set the stage. But another angle wasn't covered. According to economics professor James Bennett, coauthor of *CancerScam: Diversion of Federal Cancer Funds to Politics*, the proposed increase in funding was merely a replay of the usual money grab. "The problem is not so much a lack of federal cancer funds," he noted, "but how it is spent. Through the 'peer review' process and by funding 'seed grants,' the American Cancer Society is able to give those who support its approaches to cancer research a massive edge in competing for federal research grants." According to Bennett's book, the National Cancer Institute has squandered millions at the behest of the ACS. But we certainly didn't hear much about that during the Society's media blitz.

Another example: While international news crews were in Iraq, anticipating a US attack in 1998, some filmed horrid conditions inside hospital wards, a grim testament to the effects of UN sanctions. But their heartbreaking footage, broadcast in the Netherlands, Britain, Spain, and France, never made it onto the air in the US. It simply didn't fit in with the hype of the moment.

When a cameraman from one major US news network was asked why he wouldn't enter a hospital, he bluntly explained, "We've already done hospitals." It was a disingenuous excuse, since fear of repetition didn't stop the daily barrage of footage on F-16's lifting off of runways, UN vehicles inspecting possible chemical weapon sites, and infomercials—disguised as news—for US firepower.

The same technique was used in covering the actions of anti-globalization activists: at first general silence (except occasionally in the business press), followed by favorable spin from trade delegations, official spokesmen, and financial institutions. In 2000, the World Bank set a major press offensive in motion just before the protests in DC, sending out letters to the media and spokespersons who provided "background" for weekend features stories. The objective was to create the appropriate "context" for covering the protests. The next step, once people were in the streets, was to marginalize the opposition as naïve, confused, and pointlessly (or even criminally) disruptive. At times, this has been fairly easy, given the visuals some protesters have chosen to provide.

Protecting Relationships

Issues of journalistic ethics and judgment often revolve around two basic questions: What's the right thing to do? And then, will I do it? But even when the first question is easy to answer—and it often isn't—acting on principles can be complicated by institutional constraints, commercial imperatives, or a tendency toward self-censorship.

Ask almost any journalist whether the owner of a media outlet influences coverage and no doubt you'll be told, "Not mine." Sometimes this is actually true. But in many cases, a relationship between the medium and an object of scrutiny may be at stake. One journalist who found this out the hard way was Roberta Baskin, who brought the story of Nike's labor practices in Vietnam to national prominence on *48 Hours*. When Baskin attempted to do a follow-up, however, at first she didn't understand why CBS News President Andrew Heyward vetoed it. Then she watched the 1998 Winter Olympics. There were CBS News reporters, wearing the network logo on one side of their parkas and Nike's on the other.

"When I saw CBS correspondents adorned with the Nike 'swoosh'," Baskin wrote in an angry memo to the network brass, "it became clear to me why Heyward had spiked all follow-up reports on my Nike investigation and blocked my reply to the criticisms printed in the *Wall Street Journal*."

Predictably, Heyward denied her charges. "There is no connection whatsoever—NONE—between Nike's sponsorship of the Olympic Games or any other CBS program it might sponsor and CBS News coverage of the Nike story," he proclaimed. He also instructed news correspondents to stop displaying Nike logos during the Games. But reporters for CBS Sports continued to wear the "swoosh" on their parkas, and CBS Sports spokesperson Dana McClintock admitted, "There is a deal. We can't disclose the terms of the contract, but Nike is paying CBS and we're wearing the logo."

Self-interest can also produce distorted coverage. A prominent, although vastly underexposed, example came from Detroit in the late 1990s, where 2,500 newspaper workers were on strike for more than two years against the Gannett and Knight-Ridder chains. Relying on press statements from management, reporters for those dailies did eventually cover the story, especially when a settlement was reached with five unions. This played as a breakthrough. But what the accounts failed to mention was that the "tentative agreement" covered only 115 people, while nearly 1,400 workers were still locked out of their jobs.

Confusing Rumor with Fact

Let's start with the influential journalists who have a habit of presenting spurious claims from government or corporate sources as credible information. Then add the others who make hay by straight-out deception or picking easy targets. Although this happens in all media, it is especially easy on radio and TV, where a rumor can spread without real accountability or the traditional standard for sources. During globalization protests in 1999 and 2000, for example, unsubstantiated rumors circulated about bombs being brought to demonstration sites. This had the added benefit of providing a pretext for raids and other invasive actions.

In some cases, sources succeed in using their access to skew coverage or disseminate spurious accusations; occasionally they almost write the story. The feeding frenzy over Bill Clinton's sex life provided more than ample evidence. For both sides in this media mega-series (as opposed to a miniseries, which ends at a predetermined point), the line between conjecture and fact was often blurred, obscuring the "whole truth" while deepening public cynicism. Ultimately, the journalist who started it all, David Brock, admitted that his *American Spectator* piece on "Troopergate" was actually part of a conservative plot to discredit the President. His sources probably lied, he acknowledged, and he was all too willing to believe them.

He certainly wasn't the first reporter to shade the facts in order to advance him/herself or a political agenda. Joe Klein, who initially lied about his authorship of the political satire *Primary Colors*, built his reporting career largely by accusing inner-city blacks of "pathology," often stereotyping them as dishonest. When asked by media watchdog Norman Solomon whether his own ethical lapse led him to reassess his stern judgments about the morals of poor African Americans, he replied, "Are you out of your mind?"

For several years, George Will, who publicly praised Ronald Reagan's "thoroughbred performance" in a crucial 1980 debate with incumbent President Jimmy Carter, concealed his role as Reagan's coach for that event. According to ABC's Jeff Greenfield, rather than hurting Will's credibility, the secret liaison gave him "insider magic." In both cases, a career soared.

But at least Will, Klein, and Brock make no pretense of being objective. Ultimately, this may make them less dangerous than journalists who try to con the public—and sometimes themselves—that judgments, sources, and employer pressure don't influence their work.

Ethically speaking, the "right thing" for any journalists to do is to try for fairness and accuracy. It would also help to admit more often that the "bare facts" are only part of most stories—and that what they write is just one, perhaps well-informed, point of view. Such candor probably won't prevent a convenient war or a corporate PR juggernaut. But it would arm their readers better for media assaults and perhaps even prevent more people from becoming casualties.

Blurring Reality

In July 1998, CNN retracted a story alleging US military use of nerve gas on defectors during the Vietnam War. That retraction followed closely the *Cincinnati Enquirer* front-page apology to Chiquita Brands for the use of stolen voice mail in a story questioning the company's business practices. In a sense, both the *Enquirer* and CNN were admitting what many people long suspected, that the mainstream media have a shaky grip on reality and ethics.

And let's not forget the outright fabrications. Patricia Smith, a Pulitzer Prize finalist, was forced to resign from the *Boston Globe* after making up people and quotations for four columns. *New Republic* associate editor Stephen Glass was fired after confessing he had "embellished" a story about computer hackers. Apparently, he had already invented news in dozens of articles. Glass even used bogus quotes in a profile of Vernon Jordan published in *George Magazine*. Considerably more reprehensible, during the 1999

Yugoslavia War, most of the press corps helped promote the bombings by distorting and speculating about both the negotiations and the body count. Afterward, claims of genocide were quietly dropped. But the early impression remained.

Even after issuing a correction or apology, however, the truth often remains hazy. For Floyd Abrams, the attorney hired to check the accuracy of the CNN nerve gas report, the mea culpa didn't "necessarily mean that the story isn't true." It just meant, "We simply do not have enough evidence." Almost four years later, the Defense Department finally admitted to spraying live nerve and biological agents on ships and sailors in Cold War-era experiments to test the Navy's vulnerability to toxic warfare. It remained unclear whether any servicemen gave their permission to become human guinea pigs in medical experiments.

CNN producer April Oliver also stood by the Vietnam nerve gas story. "We have several deep off-the-record sources," she noted. "But, of course, the 'deniability' voices are very loud right now, and they are getting a lot of attention. Many of my fellow journalists over at the Pentagon are portraying me as a gullible female believing fattened up war stories from old men." As a result, she and the other producer involved, Jack Smith, were fired. "These shadow warriors don't like us looking into their business and their dark spaces," Oliver said afterward, referring to the military's Special Forces. "They're doing their best to make sure that no one else does."

Similarly, the *Enquirer*'s apology didn't prove the charges against Chiquita were false. Despite his questionable newsgathering technique, reporter Michael Gallagher did present a strong case that the company used life-threatening pesticides on Latin American banana farms, urged the Honduran military to raze a village, and bribed Colombian officials. Although the newspaper made a $10 million settlement with the corporation, a Security and Exchange Commission investigation followed, and the European Union took note.

So, what does such hand-wringing reveal? That just because something—a story, or even a retraction—gets into the papers or onto TV doesn't make it completely true. Unfortunately, this leaves the public confused and cynical, caught between accepting questionable stories and rejecting information that they ought to be taking seriously.

Rationalizing Mistakes and Omissions

More often than not, when mistakes are made, the media doesn't apologize. Instead, it covers up with slippery qualifications. At the other end of the spectrum are solid stories by hard-working journalists that end up distorted or censored by their bosses, sometimes in collusion with powerful interests.

A troubling example, which ought to worry anyone who consumes dairy products, was Fox TV's handling of a series on Monsanto's controversial bovine growth hormone (BGH). In this case, two Florida reporters were fired by Fox affiliate WTVT for "refusing to broadcast what we knew to be lies and distorted information about BGH." Legal in the US, but banned in Europe and elsewhere, BGH has found its way into much of the US milk supply, despite unresolved health concerns.

After Monsanto's lawyer sent a letter to Roger Ailes, Fox Network president (and a former GOP heavy hitter), reporters Jane Akre and Steve Wilson were ordered to make script changes that downplayed criticisms and presented Monsanto's views without qualifications. When the journalists threatened to go to the Federal Communications Commission (FCC), the station offered them $200,000 to shut up. When they said no to that, they ended up rewriting the story seventy-three times over the remaining months of their contracts. Six airdates were canceled, and in December 1997, the reporters were fired.

In May 1998, after hiring a new investigative reporter, WTVT finally did air a series on the subject. It did precisely what Wilson and Akre had resisted—toned down evidence of unethical practices by Monsanto and the dairy industry. What did not air, among other things, was information on Monsanto's lawsuits to keep ecologically-conscious companies from labeling its milk, attempts by grocery chains to mislead customers, and Monsanto's history of manufacturing government-approved products that later proved harmful, including Agent Orange. In their lawsuit, the original reporters claimed that the station violated Florida's whistle-blower law by firing them after they threatened to report wrongdoing to federal authorities.

Omission, of course, is usually the first and easiest option. During a financial summit, for example, you will seldom find stories about frustrated negotiators or divisions with the ruling elite, not to mention polling data on attitudes toward trade or corporate responsibility. They're out there, but far too threatening. During the 2001 FTAA Summit in Canada, for example, one of the remarkable stories completely ignored by the US mainstream press concerned unionized prison guards in Quebec City. Linking their own wage issues to the global topics under discussion, the guards decided to join the protesters. A week before the event, realizing that the authorities wanted to empty a local prison to make room for activists they expected to arrest, they decided to slow down the transfer of inmates. They even made barricades to block access to the prison, forcing the police to arrest thirteen corrections workers. This was only one of the dramatic and highly newsworthy stories that didn't make the cut.

Misplacing the Blame

A story's impact can also be strongly influenced by its placement, or how any responsibility for misdeeds is defined. If an enemy like Saddam Hussein is being called to account, the placement is normally prominent and the wording unequivocal. But when the culprit is an ally—at least at the moment, the story is frequently buried and the phrasing gets fuzzy, disconnecting who's done what to whom.

In June 1998, for example, two stories connected to the slaughter of an estimated 250,000 people by the Guatemalan army ran in the *New York Times* on the same day. Yet eleven pages separated them. The page one article was a grisly account of Guatemalans excavating hundreds of mass graves. The second story, buried inside, was a dry admission about how Arthur Hays Sulzberger, *Times* publisher from 1935 to 1961, had helped the CIA to black out coverage of a covert operation there in 1954.

Remarkably, the front-page story managed to avoid mentioning the CIA, despite its role in putting the army in power back in 1954. President Reagan's renewed support for the Guatemalan army in the 1980s, just as counterinsurgency terror was devastating rural Indian communities and creating more mass graves, was also omitted. The article on page eleven meanwhile left out the butchery that followed the coup Sulzberger helped cover up. There was also no condemnation of Sulzberger's journalistic violations, a far cry from the *Times'* strong criticism of the *San Jose Mercury News* during the same period for its stories on cocaine trafficking by CIA-backed Nicaraguan contra rebels. When *Mercury News* editor Jerry Ceppos finally distanced himself from that series, as you might guess, the *Times* played it on page one.

Finding Convenient Targets

Having a designated villain apparently means never having to say you're sorry. Parroting the State Department line in 1997, for example, the national press screamed that Saddam Hussein was hiding weapons of mass destruction in eighty-three palaces. No proof was needed; it just seemed self-evident. But when Iraq agreed to inspections, the number was quickly revised down to eight. Still later, seven of those sites were redefined as guest residences. No weapons or evidence of programs was found. Was there a clarification? Hardly.

The follow-up was a charge that VX gas traces on a Scud missile fragment were discovered at a destroyed Iraqi site. The source was a US Army lab, whose findings were leaked to the *Washington Post*. Coming shortly after statements that progress had been made, the timing was extremely convenient. UN chief weapons inspector Richard Butler, who said he regretted the disclosure, agreed that it had not been corroborated. A French UN official was more blunt. "I'm suspicious," he said. "This smells of manipulation." The scare faded away, but no correction was issued.

Enemies rarely receive apologies from the media, or even sympathy. Take a *Dateline* report by John Hockenberry on the effects of Iraq sanctions. Dismissing statistics about a fivefold increase in levels of child mortality, Hockenberry preferred to express surprise that the situation was not worse. Problems like the lack of medicine, sanitation devices, and food apparently failed to impress him. The point, after all, was to debunk evidence about the devastating effects of the embargo. No need to worry. After all, Saddam was to blame.

Concealing Hidden Agendas

The best way to deal with news that doesn't fit, of course, is to make believe it doesn't exist. As a result, potential US links to terrorist attacks on Cuba have been ignored for many years. That kind of thing doesn't happen, does it? Well, the evidence, including bombings at Cuban hotels and restaurants, apparently in hopes of scaring away tourists, plus assassination attempts on Castro himself, suggests otherwise. Cuban cops eventually traced the conspiracy to a CIA-trained Cuban exile, Luis Posada Carriles, with financing from Miami and New Jersey. A US investigation ensued. But until Castro is dead, don't hold your breath until such an exposure makes the evening news.

Reporters generally don't like such "conspiracy" stories. Even less so when they raise questions about media coverage. But what is a conspiracy? In the dictionary, it is an agreement by two or more people to do something evil or unlawful. Using that definition, Fox TV and Monsanto conspired to kill that Florida dairy story. Right-wingers conspired to get something—anything—on Bill Clinton. In fact, there are enough conspiracies out there to keep the media busy for decades.

For most reporters, though, the words "conspiracy" and "wackos" go together nicely, an easy way to dispose of anything they choose not to pursue. On 60 Minutes, Leslie Stahl equated the two in a 1997 piece on rumors then circulating over the Internet. The implication was that more control would help, lest cyberspace weirdos muddle reality with their groundless theories. The real message: perception management should be left to the professionals.

But what if the professional has a hidden agenda? After all, Stahl did attend the 1997 meeting of the Bilderbergers, a shadowy fraternity of CEOs, politicians, and journalists from Western Europe and the US that has met annually since the 1950s. This elite group has worked long and hard, with considerable success, to strengthen the Atlantic alliance and develop a political/business consensus beyond the power of nation-states. And if any journalist knew what they were up to in the late '90s, it was certainly Stahl. Yet, for some reason, she decided that the Bilderbergers weren't news, but instead just another Internet rumor.

PROPAGANDA CREEP

In the Reagan Era, it was known as public diplomacy. The Bush administration has called it strategic influence. What both terms describe is the US government's ability to influence mass perceptions around the world and, when necessary, at home.

If you don't think it's been going on for years and continues to this very moment, well, then, it's working.

As the Iraq war began, we did get a peek behind the curtain. Word leaked out that a new Pentagon Office of Strategic Influence was gearing up to sway leaders and public sentiment by disseminating sometimes-false stories. Facing censure, Defense Secretary Donald Rumsfeld publicly denounced and disbanded it. A few months later, however, he quietly funded a private consultant to develop another version. The apparent goal was to go beyond traditional information warfare with a new perception management campaign designed to "win the war of ideas"—in this case, against those classified as terrorists.

It's actually nothing new. Beginning in the 1950s, more than 800 news and public information organizations and individuals carried out assignments for the CIA, according to the *New York Times.* By the mid-'80s, CIA Director Bill Casey had taken the practice to the next level: an organized, covert public diplomacy apparatus designed to sell a new product—Central America—while stoking fear of communism, the Sandinistas, Gadhafi, and others.

Sometimes this involved so-called white propaganda—stories and editorials secretly financed by the government. But they also went black, pushing false story lines.

The US Department of Defense officially defines perception management as a type of psychological operation. Traditionally, it's supposed to be directed at foreign audiences and basically involves conveying (or denying) information to influence their emotions, motives, and objective reasoning. The goal is to influence enemies and friends alike, to provoke desired behavior.

During George Herbert Walker Bush's administration, the scope officially expanded to include domestic disinformation, using the CIA's public affairs office. This operation was charged with turning intelligence failures into successes by persuading reporters to postpone, change, hold, or even scrap stories that could have adversely affected national security interests.

The Clinton-era approach, outlined in Directive 68, was known as the International Public Information System (IPI). Again, no distinction was made between what could be done abroad and at home. To defeat enemies and influence minds, information for US audiences would be "deconflicted" through IPI's work. One strategy turned out to be inserting "psyop"—the term of art meaning psychological operations—specialists into newsrooms. In February 2000, a Dutch journalist revealed that CNN and the Army had agreed to do precisely that in Atlanta.

Once you realize that managing perceptions is standard procedure, some news stories take on a different meaning. In 2003, for example, a popular storyline about postwar resistance in Iraq was that only a few Saddam loyalists and dead-enders were involved. Meanwhile, the opposition was sending videotaped messages, saying things like, "We are not followers of Saddam Hussein. We are sons of Iraq." More recently, a central assumption has been that, whatever problems we now face, leaving without "winning" would be worse.

Another approach, described already, is warping the facts to promote spin. Thus, in January 2004, *USA Today* could headline a story, "Attacks down 22 percent since Saddam's capture." Actually, the number of troops killed went up 40 percent during that period, but the US military sources making the news preferred to focus on the number of incidents.

Or just fabricate the news—from the Al Qaeda–Saddam link to those illusive weapons of mass destruction. And when something goes wrong? It's simple: just misplace the blame. Thus, when photos of soldiers humiliating Iraqi prisoners came to light in May 2004, the first line of defense was to call it an aberration—people somehow operating outside the chain of command—and ignore reality.

During the first Gulf War, military intelligence officers didn't even need to ask: GIs routinely forced surrendering Iraqis to strip and pose for photos in groups. The new element was sexual humiliation, persuasive evidence that it was a psyop.

According to journalist Seymour Hersh, the abuse was part of a Pentagon operation called Copper Green, which used physical coercion and the sexual humiliation of Iraqis to generate intelligence about growing insurgency. The theory was that some prisoners would do anything—including spying on their associates—to avoid dissemination of shameful photos to family and friends. Not exactly the work of a few out-of-control grunts.

To most of the world, the photos from Abu Ghraib prison were evidence of potential war crimes, or at least punctured US pretensions about moral superiority. For those who orchestrated them, however, it was merely a psyop warfare tactic, a more violent form of perception management.

In terms of generating information that could reduce violence,

Copper Green didn't work: the insurgency continued to grow. And the unintended consequences were enormous. But in the psyop world, this happens so often that there's even a term for it—"blowback"—meaning an operation that has turned on its creators. Put another way, you reap what you sow.

PARADOXES OF THE INFORMATION AGE

It's no accident that George Orwell made the "telescreen" one of the primary symbols of a totalitarian society in his prescient novel, *1984*. Even when he wrote the book in 1948, the importance and dangers of telecommunications were already clear. Half a century later, information technologies are bringing rapid and fundamental change to almost every aspect of society. In his book, *What Are People For?*, Wendell Berry rejects the notion that computers are liberatory tools, pointing to their cost, reliance on resource exploitation, and use of electrical energy. And in *Four Arguments for the Elimination of Television*, Jerry Mander makes an even more devastating critique. He writes: "Television produces such a diverse collection of dangerous effects—mental, physiological, ecological, economic, political; effects that are dangerous to the person and also to society and the planet— that it seems to me only logical to propose that it should never have been introduced, or once introduced, be permitted to continue."

Yet, television, computers, and related information technologies also offer opportunities for global democratization and empowerment. During the late 1980s and early 1990s, for instance, VCRs served as revolutionary tools in Poland, fax machines helped open up politics and economics in the Soviet Union, and audio cassettes kept the hope of freedom alive in South Africa. Beginning in 1994, laptop computers helped secure international support for the Zapatista movement. More recently, activists resisting globalization and war across borders have used the Internet and a new network of independent radio, electronic, and print outlets to start building a movement for global justice and democracy. In short, small, accessible, and affordable technologies can help people to challenge the "knowledge" monopoly of elites.

Perhaps the best guarantee that information will be used on behalf of humanity is to work for its free flow. That isn't to say "more" is always "better." But repressive regimes and secretive institutions are normally the first to oppose broad access to information. After all, information is power, and open societies are usually characterized by high per capita availability of televisions, telephones, and computer terminals.

Instant communication clearly opens up possibilities for social change. Like Gutenberg's invention of moveable type, modern information processing creates at least the possibility of widespread information literacy. Moveable type took the printed word beyond the privileged few; telecommunications and computers could make information accessible to all. They might even help spur a shift in values from uniformity to diversity, from centralization to local democracy, and from organizational hierarchy to cooperative problem-solving units.

But this will depend largely on the growth of a social movement that promotes self-management of information, along with the cultivation of new skills. One of the main skills needed is the knack of making connections between disparate bits of information. Effective media organizers are often techno-generalists able to create knowledge out of large information flows, and also pattern-finders who work easily in a team environment. We have only begun to experience the Information Age. The personal computer revolution is little more than thirty years old. Even bigger changes lie ahead, some dangerous, others with liberating potential, and some with both. Those who become and remain "literate" can help harness new technologies to extend freedom and meet the needs of the planet and humanity.

Concentration of information and the emergence of high-tech sweatshop conditions would be tragic outcomes of this potentially revolutionary time. After all, these new technologies at the very least permit cooperation, group action, global consciousness, and decentralized, small-scale production. They can increase our productivity and reduce our travel time. Perhaps they can even reduce the gap between the "in-the-knows" and "know-nots."

Marshall McLuhan, prophet of the Information Age, once provided a relevant prediction. "Our new environment compels commitment and participation," he wrote. "We have become irrevocably involved with, and responsible for, each other." Humanity will shortly find out whether he was correct.

AFFIRMING FREEDOM

Speech is usually considered a negative right; that is, a restriction on government's ability to restrain communication by the people or the press. Yet a fair analysis of contemporary problems reveals that the greatest threat is not mainly government, but instead the manipulation and abuse of media by private institutions with enormous economic and information power at their disposal. Protecting free speech therefore requires affirmative action to reopen the marketplace of ideas. Failure to fulfill this responsibility leaves the power to inform and, ultimately, to censor, self-censor, and control mass consciousness in the hands of economic elites and private interests.

Although institutional media claim special rights due to their important public function, they normally deny that they have a responsibility to keep their doors open. In the face of such hypocrisy, intervention is sorely needed if the right of self-expression is to have any real meaning in the years ahead.

The survival of a free society depends ultimately on the actions of self-governing people. But people cannot manage their society, or their own lives, if they lack the sense of dignity that comes from exercising the right of self-expression. No government can guarantee democracy. No business can manufacture it. And the media cannot sell it. The best any of them can do is to keep the door open. If they simply do that, the vast potential of humanity will assert itself, and the promise of a self-governing society may yet be kept.

Cynics often complain that government cannot be trusted, or suggest that humanity simply isn't capable of self-rule. Sectarian ideologues often argue that all reforms are futile and the only way to transform society is through a disruptive (and inevitably destructive) break with the past. But both responses carry the burden of despair, a loss of faith in the possibility of moving, day-by-day, toward a new and freer world. What cynics and ideologues often lack is that richness of spirit essential for lasting change. Hope offers the prospect that communities can cocreate a benign social order. It fills us with the sound belief that people can discover their better selves. It fuels our most inspiring visions, and illuminates the path from here to there.

Greg Guma is the Executive Director of Pacifica Foundation, the radio network based in Berkeley. He is a cofounder and former editor of the *Vermont Guardian*, a statewide weekly newspaper and daily Web site. Prior to that he edited *Toward Freedom*, an international newsletter, and an alternative weekly, the *Vermont Vanguard Press*. He is the author of books such as *Uneasy Empire: Repression, Globalization, and What We Can Do*, and *The People's Republic: Vermont and the Sanders Revolution*, and a play about the threats to civil liberties, *Inquisitions (and Other Un-American Activities)*.

Consulted Books

Most of this chapter was developed through my ongoing work as a journalist and editor, covering various stories and media issues over the past three decades. Personal interviews were conducted with a number of the sources. In addition, the following books provided specific inspiration and insights for various sections.

Berry, Wendell. *What Are People For?* San Francisco: North Point Press, 1990.

Chomsky, Noam and Edward Herman. *The Washington Connection and Third World Fascism, Vol. 1.* Boston: South End Press, 1979.

Lasch, Christopher. *The Culture of Narcissism.* New York: W.W. Norton, 1979.

Mander, Jerry. *Four Arguments for the Elimination of Television.* New York: Quill, 1978.

Mazzocco, Dennis W. *Networks of Power: Corporate TV's Threat to Democracy.* Boston: South End Press, 1994.

Neuman, Johanna. *Lights, Camera, War: Is Media Technology Driving International Politics.* New York: St. Martin's Press, 1996.

Index

About the Editors

Peter Phillips is a professor of sociology at Sonoma State University and director of Project Censored. He teaches classes in media censorship, sociology of power, political sociology, and sociology of media. He has published ten editions of *Censored: Media Democracy in Action* from Seven Stories Press. Also from Seven Stories Press is *Impeach the President: The Case Against Bush and Cheney* (2006) and *Project Censored Guide to Independent Media and Activism* (2003).

Phillips writes op-ed pieces for independent media nationwide having published in dozens of publications newspapers and Web sites including *Truthout, Z Magazine, Counterpunch, Common Dreams, Buzzflash,* and *Social Policy.* He frequently speaks on media censorship and various socio-political issues on radio and TV talks shows including *Talk of the Nation,* Air America, Talk America, World Radio Network, *Flashpoints,* and the *Jim Hightower Show.*

Phillips earned a B.A. degree in Social Science in 1970 from Santa Clara University, and an M.A. degree in Social Science from California State University at Sacramento in 1974. He earned a second M.A. in Sociology in 1991 and a Ph.D. in Sociology in 1994. His doctoral dissertation was entitled *A Relative Advantage: Sociology of the San Francisco Bohemian Club:* http://libweb.sonoma.edu/regional/faculty/Phillips/bohemianindex.htm.

Phillips is a fifth-generation Californian, who grew up on a family-owned farm west of the Central Valley town of Lodi. Phillips lives today in rural Sonoma County with his wife Mary Lia.

Andrew L. Roth is an assistant professor of sociology at Sonoma State University and associate director of Project Censored. He teaches classes in sociological theory, environmental sociology, language and society, the sociology of religion, and documentary film.

Roth has published research articles on communities organizing for urban parklands (in the journal *City and Community*), journalists' questioning of electoral candidates (*Harvard International Journal of Press/Politics*), public commentary on federal tobacco control legislation (*Social Studies of Science*), and social interaction in broadcast news interviews (*Language in Society* and *Media, Culture & Society*).

He earned a B.A. in Sociology & Anthropology at Haverford College (1990). He earned his M.A. (1992) and Ph.D. (1998) in Sociology at UCLA, where he studied social interaction and news media. His dissertation, *Who Makes the News: Social Identity and the Explanation of Action in the Broadcast News Interview*, undertook comparative analysis of interviewing techniques in the UK and US.

Roth is a third-generation Californian who grew up in Claremont, where his mother and father both served as teachers. In his spare time he enjoys distance running, preferably on wilderness trails.

How To Support Project Censored

NOMINATE A STORY

To nominate a *Censored* story send us a copy of the article and include the name of the source publication, the date that the article appeared, and page number. For Internet-published news stories of which we should be aware, please forward the URL to Censored@sonoma.edu. The final deadline period for nominating a *Censored* story is March of each year.

Criteria for project censored news stories nominations

1. A censored news story is one which contains information that the general United States population has a right and need to know, but to which it has had limited access.

2. The news story is timely, ongoing, and has implications for a significant number of residents in the United States.

3. The story has clearly defined concepts and is backed up with solid, verifiable documentation.

4. The news story has been publicly published, either electronically or in print, in a circulated newspaper, journal, magazine, newsletter, or similar publication from either a foreign or domestic source.

5. The news story has direct connections to and implications for people in the United States, which can include activities that US citizens are engaged in abroad.

SUPPORT PROJECT CENSORED BY MAKING A FINANCIAL GIFT

Project Censored is a self-supported 501-C-3 non-profit organization. We depend on tax deductible donations and foundation grants to continue our work. To support our efforts for freedom of information send checks to the address below or call 707-664-2500. Visa and Mastercard accepted. Donations can be made through our website at: www.projectcensored.org.

Project Censored
Media Freedom Foundation
P.O. Box 571
Cotati, CA 94931
e-mail: censored@sonoma.edu